THE PLAYERS

Actors in
Movies On
Television and
Videocassette

Peter Chapman

WINDSOR PRESS

NEW YORK

The Players
Actors in Movies on Television and Videocassette

Published by:
 Windsor Press
 P.O. Box 82
 Planetarium Station
 New York, New York 10024
 U.S.A.

Manufactured in the United States of America

Library of Congress Catalog Card Number: 93-60509
ISBN 0-9637047-3-7

INTRODUCTION

Welcome to the first edition of *The Players: Actors in Movies on Television and Videocassette*. As the title suggests, the book is a guide to actors who appear in movies that air on television or that we rent from the video store. While there are other actors' reference books available, *The Players* is focused only on those performers you are likely to see when you watch a feature film on the small screen. The purpose of this book is to help you identify all of the principal actors in the movie.

The 1,000 actors in this book are the supporting and less well-known leading actors in the movies of the last thirty years. It is assumed that you are familiar with the major stars of recent years and have no difficulty identifying the Meryl Streeps and the Paul Newmans of the film world. *The Players* will enhance your viewing pleasure by allowing you to identify the many hundreds of other actors who aren't super-stars or big celebrities.

The Players is a guide. It is meant to be a companion to the small screen movie-watcher. To use it, simply look up the movie you are watching in the index and then use the page numbers to locate the actors. A large photograph will enable you to spot the actor on the screen while his film credits and the names of his characters will provide an association with other movies you may have seen him in.

Each of the 1,000 actors in this book has had four or more feature roles in a select group of about 4,000 films. Since, in the majority of movies, there are no more than five or six principal players, only those actors that received billing in the top six spots were eligible for inclusion. Approximately 80% are supporting players while the remaining are the less familiar leading actors. Some of the older actors were stars during the thirties, forties and fifties, but have taken character parts in recent years.

To select the actors, I concentrated on a core list of over 4,000 movies, those most likely to be seen on television, from the approximately 6,000 domestic films released since 1960. Another 2,000 foreign films, mostly British, were largely excluded. Only feature films released to theaters were considered, although some direct-to-video pictures inevitably slipped in. TV-movies were not included.

You are most likely to watch a US-made movie released in the last 30 years. Most movies airing on television or available for rental are contemporary, defined here as meaning they have been released since 1960. Foreign-language films and English-language foreign films are not seen with great frequency although certain British, Canadian and Australian movies are popular in the American market.

The decision to include a particular movie in the core group rested on whether it has a distributor in the television syndication market, whether it actually aired in certain East Coast television markets in 1992 and 1993 during prime viewing hours, and whether the subject matter is suitable for network television, independent broadcasters and mainstream cable TV. The likelihood of its being stocked by local video dealers was also a factor.

Therefore, screen credits are not listed for each and every movie in which an actor has appeared. Only those contemporary films popular with broadcasters and video dealers were considered. Brief biographies were written for all actors.

In closing, I would like to thank Howard Mandlebaum, Ron Mandlebaum and Ed Maguire of Photofest for their beautiful photographs, the staff of the New York Public Library's Performing Arts Research Collection for their outstanding collection and assistance and my parents, William and Christine Chapman, for their informative and well-written biographical sketches.

Peter Chapman
December, 1993

JOSS ACKLAND

(1928 -   )

The British character actor started in films in 1950, but did not become a cinema mainstay until the early 1970s. He has often played types who masked an underlying evil with outward appearances of goodwill. Ackland spent time as a tea planter in Central Africa and has been employed for narrations, commercials and voice-overs. He played the Soviet Ambassador to the U.S. in Sean Connery's *The Hunt for Red October*.

Year	Movie	Character
1974	S*P*Y*S	Martinson
1976	Operation Daybreak	Janak
1978	Who is Killing the Great Chefs of Europe?	Cantrell
1979	Saint Jack	Yardley
1987	The Sicilian	Don Masino Croce
1988	To Kill a Priest	Colonel
1989	Lethal Weapon 2	Arjen Rudd
1990	The Hunt for Red October	Andrei Lysenko
1991	Bill & Ted's Bogus Journey	De Nomolos
1991	The Object of Beauty	Mr. Mercer
1992	The Mighty Ducks	Hans
1992	Once Upon a Crime	xxx
1993	Nowhere to Run	Franklin Hale

EDIE ADAMS

(1929 -   )

Although most people consider her a nightclub singer, Adams has appeared in many films. Born in Kingston, PA, the singer/actress studied at the Juilliard School of Music and the Columbia School of Drama. She spent 19 years as the Muriel Cigar spokeswoman and was married to Ernie Kovacs until his death.

Year	Movie	Character
1960	The Apartment	Miss Olsen
1961	Lover Come Back	Rebel Davis
1963	It's a Mad Mad Mad Mad World	Monica Crump
1963	Love With the Proper Stranger	Barbie
1963	Call Me Bwana	Frederica Larsen
1963	Under The Yum Yum Tree	Irene
1964	The Best Man	Mabel Cantwell
1966	Made in Paris	Irene Chase
1966	The Oscar	Trina Yale
1967	The Honey Pot	Merle McGill
1978	Up in Smoke	Tempest Stoner

LUTHER ADLER

(1903 - 1984)

Adler was born into a leading Yiddish theater family in New York City and was acting on stage from the age of 5. The son of a founder of the Adler Yiddish Theater Company, he was often on stage with as many as eight members of his family. He became a regular screen performer after World War II.

Year	Movie	Character
1966	Cast a Giant Shadow	Jacob Zion
1968	The Brotherhood	Bertolo
1974	Crazy Joe	Falco
1976	Voyage of the Damned	Professor Weiler
1981	Absence of Malice	Malderone

MATT ADLER

(19?? -   )

Adler spent the second half of the 1980s in several teen movies and is best known for his lead roles in *North Shore* with Nia Peeples and *Diving In* with Kristy Swanson. Critics described his *North Shore* performance as "fresh and spontaneous." Adler is an L.A. native who has devoted time to counseling teenagers around the country with a group called Young Artists United about the dangers of drugs and alcohol.

Year	Movie	Character
1985	Teen Wolf	Lewis Erikson
1986	Flight of the Navigator	Jeff (16 years)
1987	North Shore	Rick
1987	White Water Summer	Chris
1988	Doin' Time on Planet Earth	Dan Forrester

JENNY AGUTTER

FRANKLIN AJAYE

(1952 -   )

The British actress made her film debut as a child in *East of Sudan*, but her Hollywood breakthrough came with the 1976 sci-fi thriller *Logan's Run*. On being an uprooted Londoner living in L.A., a then 24-year-old Agutter commented: "Los Angeles is like a desert. The only thing that exists is the work you do. You have that sense of living a precarious existence." Agutter spent her childhood travelling through the Middle and Near East, where her father was an army officer.

Year	Movie	Character
1968	Star!	Pamela
1976	Logan's Run	Jessica
1976	The Eagle Has Landed	Molly Prior
1978	China 9, Liberty 37	Catherine
1981	Amy	Amy
1981	An American Werewolf in London	Alex
1990	Child's Play 2	Joanne Simpson
1990	Darkman	Doctor

(1949 -   )

After dropping out of Columbia's law school to work as a comedian, Ajaye rose from the stand-up circuit to become a fixture on the late-night TV comedy scene. The Brooklyn-born, but California-raised actor brought an intellectual, low-key focus to comedy. In recent years he has drawn attention to himself for disparaging rap music because, as he feels, it glorifies the ghetto.

Year	Movie	Character
1976	Car Wash	T.C.
1978	Convoy	Spider Mike
1980	The Jazz Singer	Bubba
1983	Get Crazy	xxx
1988	The Wrong Guys	Franklyn

CLAUDE AKINS

(1918 -   )

The burly actor began his screen career in 1953's *From Here to Eternity* and, because of his looks and size (6' 2" and 200 lbs. at one point), spent most of the next two decades playing bad guys. "Between the war movies I've been in and the heavies I've played, I have about 1,000 dead behind me," Akins once said. "I've been killed a good many times, but I took a lot of guys with me." He got to play the good guy on such television shows as *Movin' On* (1974-76) and *Lobo* (1979-81).

Year	Movie	Character
1960	Comanche Station	Ben Lane
1960	Inherit the Wind	Rev. Brown
1962	Merrill's Marauders	Sgt. Kolowicz
1964	A Distant Trumpet	Seely Jones
1964	The Killers	Earl Sylvester
1966	Return of the Seven	Frank
1966	Ride Beyond Vengeance	Elwood Coates
1967	Waterhole #3	Sgt. Henry Foggers
1968	The Devil's Brigade	Rocky Rockman
1969	The Great Bank Robbery	Slade
1972	Skyjacked	Sgt. Ben Puzo
1973	Battle for the Planet of the Apes	Aldo
1977	Tentacles	Capt. Robards

EDWARD ALBERT

(1951 -   )

The multitalented son of Eddie Albert attended UCLA and got his start in films while working as a production assistant on *Patton* in Spain. Music is his first love: he plays 14 instruments, sings and composes his own tunes and has worked as a studio musician in L.A. and London. He is also a photographer who has exhibited his work in L.A.

Year	Movie	Character
1972	Butterflies are Free	Don
1973	Forty Carats	Peter Latham
1976	Midway	Lt. Tom Garth
1977	The Domino Principle	Ross Pine
1978	The Greek Tycoon	Nico Tomasis
1980	When Time Ran Out...	Brian
1981	Galaxy of Terror	Cabren
1986	Getting Even	'Tag' Taggar
1987	Distortions	xxx
1988	The Rescue	Commander Merrill

JACK ALBERTSON

LOLA ALBRIGHT

(1910 - 1981)

Born in Malder, MA, Albertson spent 50 years entertaining as a comic and dramatic actor, singer, dancer, comedian and vaudevillian. He was one of only three men in show biz to win all of the Big Three: the Oscar, the Tony, and Emmy awards, the latter for his role as the crusty old garage owner who played opposite Freddie Prinze in NBC's *Chico and the Man.* He died of cancer.

(1925 -   )

Born in Akron, OH, Albright's career progressed from radio to modeling to the movies. She studied piano for 12 years and also worked as a switchboard operator and a stenographer. Her screen debut came in 1948 in *The Pirate.*

Year	Movie	Character
1961	Lover Come Back	Fred
1962	Days of Wine and Roses	Trayner
1962	Period of Adjustment	Desk Sergeant
1962	Who's Got the Action?	Officer Hodges
1964	A Tiger Walks	Sam Grotz
1964	Kissin' Cousins	Capt. Robert Salb
1965	How to Murder Your Wife	Dr. Bentley
1967	The Flim Flam Man	Mr. Packard
1968	How to Save a Marriage (And Ruin Your Life)	Mr. Slotkin
1968	The Subject Was Roses	John Cleary
1969	Justine	Cohen
1971	Willy Wonka and the Chocolate Factory	Grandpa Joe
1972	The Poseidon Adventure	Manny Rosen

Year	Movie	Character
1962	Kid Galahad	Dolly Fletcher
1966	Lord Love a Duck	Marie Greene
1967	The Way West	Rebecca Evans
1968	The Impossible Years	Alice Kingsley
1968	Where Were You When the Lights Went Out?	Roberta Lane

9

RUTANYA ALDA

(1945 -   )

Born in Riga, Latvia, Alda, along with her mother and brother, was separated from her father when the Russians overran Latvia during World War II. They spent nine years in displaced persons camps in the U.S. sector of Germany before moving to Arizona in 1955. After college, she went to New York City and became a member of the emerging group of New York filmmakers there that included Robert De Niro and Brian De Palma.

Year	Movie	Character
1973	Pat Garrett and Billy the Kid	Ruthie
1973	Scarecrow	Woman in camper
1976	Next Stop, Greenwich Village	Party Guest
1978	The Fury	Kristen
1981	Mommie Dearest	Carol Ann
1982	Amityville II: The Possession	Deloris Montelli
1982	Vigilante	Vickie
1984	Racing With the Moon	Mrs. Nash
1986	Black Widow	Irene
1988	Apprentice to Murder	Elma Kelly
1989	Gross Anatomy	Mama Slovak
1989	Prancer	Aunt Sarah
1992	Article 99	xxx

TOM ALDREDGE

(1928 -   )

Primarily a stage actor, Aldredge believes that listening is the key to a good performance. The Dayton, OH native once told an interviewer: "You must absolutely listen and watch for what everybody does. Listening is a great tool in all acting. Listening is what it all comes from. When you stop listening, you're not acting. You're just reciting from memory. The whole secret to successful acting to me is just listening and responding to what is said in as genuine a way as you can."

Year	Movie	Character
1964	The Troublemaker	Jack Armstrong
1969	The Rain People	Mr. Alfred
1987	*batteries not included	Sid
1991	Other People's Money	Ozzie
1991	What About Bob?	Mr. Guttman

JANE ALEXANDER

(1939 -   )

Alexander made her screen debut in a reprisal of her Tony award-winning role as James Earl Jones' mistress, in *The Great White Hope*. Oscar-nominated for that part, she went on to receive three more nominations, including one for her portrayal of a bookkeeper in the Nixon re-election committee in *All the Presidents Men*. The Boston native was appointed by President Bill Clinton to head the National Endowment of the Arts in 1993.

Year	Movie	Character
1970	The Great White Hope	Eleanor Bachman
1971	A Gunfight	Nora Tenneray
1972	The New Centurions	Dorothy
1976	All the President's Men	Bookkeeper
1978	The Betsy	Alicia Hardeman
1979	Kramer vs. Kramer	Margaret Phelps
1980	Brubaker	Lillian
1981	Night Crossing	Doris Strelzyk
1983	Testament	Carol Wetherly
1984	City Heat	Addy
1987	Square Dance	Juanelle

JOAN ALLEN

(1956 -   )

Allen got her professional start as a founding member of Chicago's Steppenwolf Theater Co., where she has performed in over 20 shows. A native of Rochelle, IL, she began acting in high school plays, after she failed to make the cheerleading squad.

Year	Movie	Character
1986	Manhunter	Reba
1986	Peggy Sue Got Married	Maddy Nagle
1988	Tucker: The Man and His Dream	Vera
1989	In Country	Irene
1993	Ethan Frome	Zeena Frome
1993	Josh and S.A.M.	Caroline
1993	Searching for Bobby Fischer	Bonnie Waitzkin

NANCY ALLEN

MARIA CONCHITA ALONSO

(1955 -   )

(1957 -   )

Allen is best known as the menaced victim in the films directed by her former husband Brian De Palma: *Carrie*, *Dressed to Kill* and *Blow Out*. Growing up the daughter of a New York City policeman may have prepared her for violence in the movies. "Our dinner conversation was always about someone being raped or a woman chopping up her husband or someone freaking out on acid," she once recalled. The former model played a cop herself in the *Robocop* pictures.

Singer/actress Alonso was born in Cuba and raised in Venezuela. In 1971, she was named "Miss Teenager of the World" and, in 1975, became Miss Venezuela. She had acted in four features and ten soaps before moving to the U.S. She has also recorded several albums; four went gold and one platinum.

Year	Movie	Character
1973	The Last Detail	Nancy
1976	Carrie	Chris Hargenson
1978	I Wanna Hold Your Hand	Pam Mitchell
1979	1941	Donna
1980	Dressed to Kill	Liz Blake
1981	Blow Out	Sally
1983	Strange Invaders	Betty
1984	Philadelphia Experiment	Allison
1984	The Buddy System	Carrie
1987	Robocop	Lewis
1988	Poltergeist III	Patricia Gardner
1989	Limit Up	Casey Falls
1990	Robocop 2	Anne Lewis
1993	Robocop 3	Anne Lewis

Year	Movie	Character
1984	Fear City	xxx
1984	Moscow on the Hudson	Lucia Lombardo
1986	A Fine Mess	Claudia Pazzo
1986	Touch and Go	Denise DeLeon
1987	Extreme Prejudice	Sarita Cisneros
1987	The Running Man	Amber Mendez
1988	Colors	Louisa Gomez
1990	Predator 2	Leona
1991	McBain	Christina

TRINI ALVARADO

JOHN AMOS

(1967 -   )

(1940 -   )

A native of New York, Alvarado's father is from Spain while her mother is from Puerto Rico. After appearing on Broadway in *Runaways* she attended the Professional Children's School in New York. She has appeared in NBC's Movie of the Week, After School Specials for PBS, and has performed at the Kennedy Center in Washington. She later attended Fordham University on an on-and-off basis.

Born in Newark, NJ, and educated at Colorado State, Amos worked as a professional football player, a social worker (heading New York's Vera Institute of Justice) and an advertising copywriter before turning his attention to the entertainment world. In addition to his film appearances, he has written TV comedy material and performed stand-up comedy in New York City's Greenwich Village.

Year	Movie	Character
1979	Rich Kids	Franny Philips
1980	Times Square	Pamela
1984	Mrs. Soffel	Irene Soffel
1987	Sweet Lorraine	Molly
1988	Satisfaction	May "Mooch" Stark
1990	Stella	Jenny Claire
1992	The Babe	Helen Ruth
1993	American Friends	Elinor

Year	Movie	Character
1975	Let's Do It Again	Kansas City Mack
1980	Touched by Love	Tony
1982	The Beastmaster	Seth
1985	American Flyers	Dr. Conrad
1988	Coming to America	Cleo McDowell
1989	Lock Up	Meissner
1990	Die Hard 2	Capt. Grant
1991	Ricochet	xxx
1993	Mac	Nat

JOHN ANDERSON

(1922 - 1992)

The tall character actor who caught our attention playing the used car salesman in Alfred Hitchcock's *Psycho* was known best for his TV work in more than 500 roles, including *The Twilight Zone* and *MacGyver*. Anderson began acting on a Mississippi River showboat, went to the Cleveland Playhouse, and on to Broadway and Off-Broadway. He died at 69 of a heart attack at his Sherman Oaks, CA home.

Year	Movie	Character
1960	Psycho	Used car salesman
1962	Ride the High Country	Elder Hammond
1965	The Hallelujah Trail	Sgt. Buell
1965	The Satan Bug	Reagan
1966	Namu, the Killer Whale	Joe Clausen
1967	Welcome to Hard Times	Ezra and Isaac Maple
1968	Day of the Evil Gun	Capt. Addis
1968	Five Card Stud	Marshal Dana
1969	Heaven with a Gun	Asa Beck
1969	The Great Bank Robbery	Kincaid
1974	The Dove	Mike Turk
1980	In Search of Historic Jesus	Caiaphas
1980	Smokey and the Bandit II	Govenor
1981	Zoot Suit	Judge
1983	Lone Wolf McQuade	Burnside
1988	Eight Men Out	xxx

KEVIN ANDERSON

(1960 -   )

Anderson found fame early on the stages of Chicago, New York and London as a hyperactive shut-in in the critically acclaimed dark comedy *Orphans*. He later brought his role to the screen in Alan Pakula's 1987 movie. He was cast opposite Julia Roberts in *Sleeping With the Enemy*, because, as the film's director, Joseph Ruben, explained at the time: "He's the real thing. He's from the Midwest, a small town. He's got that kind of warmth to him. He's also got an edge." Anderson is from Gurnee, IL.

Year	Movie	Character
1983	Risky Business	Chuck
1987	Orphans	Phillip
1988	Miles From Home	Terry Roberts
1989	In Country	Lonnie
1991	Liebestraum	Nick Kaminsky
1991	Sleeping With the Enemy	Ben
1992	Hoffa	Robert Kennedy
1993	Rising Sun	Bob Richmond
1993	The Night We Never Met	Brian McVeigh

BIBI ANDERSSON

(1935 -   )

Closely associated with the films of Ingmar Bergman, the Swedish actress appeared in such classics as *The Seventh Seal* (1956) and *Wild Strawberries* (1957). An extra on film sets as early as 14, Andersson studied at the Royal Dramatic Theatre School in Stockholm, which boasts such alumnae as Greta Garbo and Ingrid Bergman. On Bergman she once commented, "As a young actress I was very lucky to work with the best, which I didn't always do later. But at least I knew the difference when I made the compromises."

Year	Movie	Character
1966	Duel at Diablo	Ellen Grange
1977	I Never Promised You a Rose Garden	Dr. Fried
1979	Concorde-Airport '79	Francine
1979	Quintet	Ambrosia
1983	Exposed	Margaret

DANA ANDREWS

(1909 - 1992)

A leading man of the 40's and 50's, Andrews was once described by the New York Times as a "sturdy, square-jawed archetypal American hero." His star faded by the end of the 1950s as producers felt he was too old and not a big enough draw for the blockbusters they were planning. As president of the S.A.G. in the early 1960s, he worked to protect actors' wage scales and publicly criticized actresses who appeared nude in movies, warning of exploitation. He died in Orange County, CA, after being hospitalized with pneumonia.

Year	Movie	Character
1960	The Crowded Sky	Dick Barnett
1965	Battle of the Bulge	Col. Pritchar
1965	In Harm's Way	Adm."Blackjack" Broderick
1965	The Loved One	Gen. Brinkman
1965	The Satan Bug	The General
1968	The Devil's Brigade	Brig. Gen. Walter Naylor
1974	Airport 1975	Scott Freeman
1976	The Last Tycoon	Red Ridinghood
1979	Good Guys Wear Black	Government Man
1979	The Pilot	xxx
1984	Prince Jack	The Cardinal

EDWARD ANDREWS

(1914 - 1985)

Andrews was born in Griffin, GA, the son of parents who were avid theater-goers. He attended the University of Virginia for three years before heading for New York. His major career break was a role in *Of Mice and Men*. He made his movie debut in 1955 as a back slapping heavy in *The Phenix City Story*. Andrews died of a heart attack.

Year	Movie	Character
1960	Elmer Gantry	George Babbitt
1961	The Young Doctors	Bannister
1961	The Young Savages	Dan Cole
1962	Advise and Consent	Senator Knox
1963	Forty Pounds of Trouble	Herman
1963	The Thrill of It All	Gardiner Fraleigh
1964	A Tiger Walks	The Govenor
1964	Kisses for My President	Senator Walsh
1964	Send Me No Flowers	Dr. Morrissey
1965	Fluffy	Griswald
1966	The Glass Bottom Boat	Gen. Wallace Bleecker
1969	The Trouble With Girls	Johnny
1971	How to Frame a Figg	Mayor
1972	Avanti!	J.J. Blodgett
1984	Sixteen Candles	Howard

HARRY ANDREWS

(1911 - 1989)

This strong-featured British actor first appeared at the Liverpool Playhouse in 1933 and for the next 56 years enjoyed an international career that took him from playing the classics on stage in London and on Broadway to making movies in Hollywood after his 1952 film debut. Andrews played no-nonsense characters with gruff exteriors. He died of a viral infection complicated by asthma.

Year	Movie	Character
1962	Barabbas	Peter
1963	Nine Hours to Rama	General Singh
1964	633 Squadron	Air Marshal Davis
1965	Sands of the Kalahari	Grimmelman
1965	The Hill	Sgt/Major Wilson
1965	The Agony & the Ecstasy	Bramante
1968	The Night They Raided Minsky's	Jacob Schpitendavel
1969	Battle of Britain	Senior Civil Servant
1971	Nicholas and Alexandra	Grand Duke Nicholas
1972	Man of La Mancha	Innkeeper/Govenor
1973	The Mackintosh Man	Mackintosh
1976	Sky Riders	Carl Auerbach
1976	The Blue Bird	Oak
1978	Death on the Nile	Barnstaple
1978	Superman	Second Elder
1978	The Big Sleep	Butler Norris
1986	Mesmerized	Old Thompson

MICHAEL ANSARA

(1922 -   )

Ansara found fame as an Apache Indian Chief named Cochise who became a blood brother to a white man in television's *Broken Arrow* (1956-58). He was married to TV star Barbara Eden for 15 years and appeared frequently as a guest on her hit sereis *I Dream of Jeannie*. Ansara was born in Syria, but immigrated to the U.S. as a child and grew up in New England and L.A. He studied drama at UCLA and the Pasadena Playhouse and made his movie debut in 1944's *Action in Arabia*.

Year	Movie	Character
1961	Voyage to the Bottom of the Sea	Alvarez
1965	Harum Scarum	Prince Draga
1965	The Greatest Story Ever Told	Herod's Commander
1966	Texas Across the River	Iron Jacket
1968	Daring Game	Pres. Eduardo Delgado
1968	Sol Madrid	Captain Ortega
1969	Guns of the Magnificent Seven	Col. Diego
1978	The Manitou	Singing Roc
1987	Assassination	Senator Bunsen

SUSAN ANSPACH

(1945 -   )

A native New Yorker, Anspach discovered acting at Washington, D.C.'s Catholic University after majoring briefly in pre-law and then pre-med. Upon returning to New York, she became involved with the Actors Lab, working with then unknowns Jon Voight, Dustin Hoffman and Robert Duvall. She broke into film after 11 Off-Broadway and Broadway plays as well as a stint as a country/folk singer.

Year	Movie	Character
1970	Five Easy Pieces	Catherine Van Ost
1972	Play It Again, Sam	Nancy
1973	Blume in Love	Nina
1978	The Big Fix	Lila
1979	Running	Janet Andropolis
1981	The Devil and Max Devlin	Penny
1981	Montenegro	Marilyn Jordan
1984	Misunderstood	Lily
1987	Into the Fire	Rosalind Winfield

ANNE ARCHER

(1947 -   )

After 15 years as a movie actress, Archer finally struck gold (and an Oscar nomination) as Michael Douglas' supportive wife in *Fatal Attraction* and as Harrison Ford's wife in *Patriot Games*. She is pleased with her success, but knows it can be fleeting as she grew up in a Hollywood family: "Seeing my mother's success on TV [Marjorie Lord in *Make Room for Daddy*], then seeing her dropped like a hot potato after the show went off the air. It made me leery of ever thinking that you're sitting on top of the world."

Year	Movie	Character
1972	Cancel My Reservations	Crazy
1972	The Honkers	Deborah Moon
1976	Lifeguard	Cathy
1976	Trackdown	Barbara
1978	Paradise Alley	Annie
1979	Good Guys Wear Black	Margaret
1980	Hero at Large	J. Marsh
1980	Raise the Titanic!	Dana
1985	The Naked Face	Ann Blake
1985	Too Scared to Scream	Kate
1986	The Check is in the Mail	xxx
1987	Fatal Attraction	Beth Gallagher
1990	Love at Large	Miss Dolan
1990	Narrow Margin	Carol Hunnicut
1991	Eminent Domain	Mira Burski
1992	Patriot Games	Cathy Ryan
1993	Body of Evidence	Joanne Braslow
1993	Family Prayers	Rita Jacobs
1993	Short Cuts	Claire Kane

BESS ARMSTRONG

(1953 -   )

Armstrong grew up in the suburbs of Baltimore, MD, the daughter of two teachers who were, as she has recalled, "always involved in the theater, either acting, directing, doing makeup, or all three together." Before hitting Broadway, she had been in over 100 plays at the Bryn Mawr School for Girls and Brown University.

Year	Movie	Character
1979	The House of God	Dr. Worthington
1981	The Four Seasons	Ginny Newley
1983	High Road to China	Eve
1983	Jaws 3-D	Kathryn
1986	Nothing in Common	Donna Mildred Martin
1989	Second Sight	Sister Elizabeth

CURTIS ARMSTRONG

(19?? -   )

Prior to Armstrong's move to film, he had gathered extensive stage experience working in Off-Broadway and regional theater. He performed at the Pittsburgh Regional Theater, the New Jersey Shakespeare Festival and the Attic Theater.

Year	Movie	Character
1983	Risky Business	Miles
1984	Revenge of the Nerds	Booger
1985	Bad Medicine	Dennis Gladstone
1985	Better Off Dead	Charles
1986	One Crazy Summer	Ack Ack Raymond
1986	The Clan of the Cave Bear	Goov
1987	Revenge of the Nerds II: Nerds in Paradise	Booger

R.G. ARMSTRONG

(1917 -   )

Director Sam Peckinpah has often cast Armstrong as a bad guy in his films because, as he once said, he played "righteous villainy better than anybody I've ever seen." The veteran character actor originally wanted to be a writer. He obtained a master's degree in English from the University of North Carolina and taught briefly at Chapel Hill. After having written several plays, he moved to New York in hopes of having them produced, but ended up acting in a play produced by the Actors Studio.

Year	Movie	Character
1960	The Fugitive Kind	Sheriff Talbott
1962	Ride the High Country	Joshua Knudsen
1965	Major Dundee	Rev. Dahlstrom
1967	El Dorado	Kevin MacDonald
1970	The Ballad of Cable Hogue	Quittner
1970	The Great White Hope	Cap'n Dan
1973	Pat Garrett and Billy the Kid	Ollinger
1973	Running Wild	xxx
1973	White Lightning	Big Bear
1975	Race With The Devil	Sheriff
1975	White Line Fever	Prosecutor
1976	Stay Hungry	Thor Erickson
1977	Mr. Billion	Sheriff
1977	The Car	Amos
1978	Heaven Can Wait	General Manager

(continued on page 505)

PATRICIA ARQUETTE

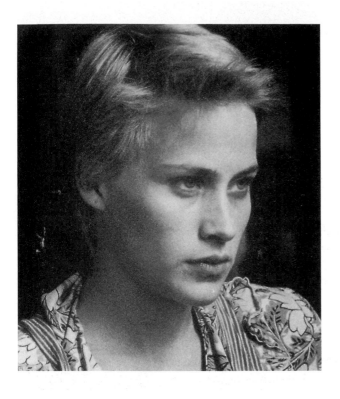

(1966 -   )

The younger sister of actress Rosanna Arquette, Patricia grew up in California and the Midwest and spent time on an artists' commune in Virginia. Of that time, she once reminisced: "there wasn't a day when all five members of my family weren't improvising, creating our own little sketches or tie-dying." Early fame came with her role in *A Nightmare on Elm Street 3*.

Year	Movie	Character
1987	A Nightmare on Elm Street 3: Dream Warriors	Kristen Parker
1988	Far North	Jilly
1991	Prayer of the Rollerboys	Casey
1991	The Indian Runner	Dorothy
1993	Ethan Frome	Mattie Silver
1993	True Romance	Alabama Whitman

ELIZABETH ASHLEY

(1939 -   )

Born into Southern gentry in Ocala, FL, Ashley got her acting career off to a start in television commercials in New York. A year long run in Broadway's *Take Her, She's Mine* in 1961 catapulted her into the big time.

Year	Movie	Character
1964	The Carpetbaggers	Monica Winthrop
1965	Ship of Fools	Jenny
1971	The Marriage of a Young Stockbroker	Nan
1973	Paperback Hero	Loretta
1975	92 in the Shade	Jeannie Carter
1976	Great Scout and Cathouse Thursday	Nancy
1978	Coma	Mrs. Emerson
1981	Paternity	Sophia
1982	Split Image	Diana
1987	Dragnet	Jane Kirkpatrick

JOHN ASHTON

(19?? -   )

Often portraying policemen and other law enforcement types, Ashton began his screen career in the early 1970s in such B-movies as *Psychopath* (1973) and *The Private Afternoons of Pamela Mann* (1974). He landed the role of Willie Joe Garr for a year on television's *Dallas* (1978-79) and proceeded to become very active in movies and television. His best known cop role is that of John Taggart in the *Beverly Hills Cop* movies.

Year	Movie	Character
1979	Breaking Away	Mike's Brother
1980	Borderline	Charlie Monroe
1984	Beverly Hills Cop	Sgt. Taggart
1986	King Kong Lives	Colonel Nevitt
1987	Beverly Hills Cop II	John Taggart
1987	Some Kind of Wonderful	Cliff Nelson
1988	Midnight Run	Marvin Dorfler
1988	She's Having a Baby	Ken

LUKE ASKEW

(1937 -   )

Active in film and television during the 1960s and 1970s, Askew went to Hollywood after working as a television announcer and the manager of a waste-paper plant. His early acting experience was gained Off-Broadway and he is usually cast as a villain, often in westerns.

Year	Movie	Character
1967	Cool Hand Luke	Boss Paul
1967	Hurry, Sundown	Dolph Higginson
1967	The Happening	Motorcycle Officer
1968	The Devil's Brigade	Hubert Hixon
1968	The Green Berets	Sgt. Provo
1968	Will Penny	Foxy
1969	Flareup	Alan
1972	Culpepper Cattle Company	Luke
1972	The Magnificent Seven Ride!	Skinner
1973	Pat Garrett and Billy the Kid	Eno
1975	Part 2, Walking Tall	Pinky
1977	Rolling Thunder	Slim
1979	Wanda Nevada	Muldoon

ARMAND ASSANTE

(1949 -   )

Born in New York to an Irish mother and an Italian father, Assante grew up in the city and its exurbs. After graduation from high school, he entered the American Academy of Dramatic Arts and then began his career on the New York stage. He is the third graduate of the leather jacket B-movie *The Lords of Flatbush* to achieve prominence in film and television. The other two to come from the 1974 film were Henry Winkler and Sylvester Stallone.

Year	Movie	Character
1974	The Lords of Flatbush	Wedding Guest
1978	Paradise Alley	Lenny
1979	Prophecy	Hawks
1980	Little Darlings	Gary
1980	Private Benjamin	Henri Tremont
1982	I, the Jury	Mark Hammer
1982	Love and Money	Lorenzo Prado
1984	Unfaithfully Yours	Maxmillian Stein
1986	Belizaire the Cajun	Belizaire Breaux
1988	The Penitent	Juan Mateo
1989	Animal Behavior	Mark Mathias
1990	Q & A	Bobby Texador
1991	The Marrying Man	Bugsy Siegal
1992	1492: Conquest of Paradise	Sanchez
1992	Hoffa	Carol D'Allesandro
1992	The Mambo Kings	Cesar Castillo
1993	Fatal Instinct	Ned Ravine

SEAN ASTIN

(1971 -   )

Born in Santa Monica, CA, Astin is the son of John Astin and Patty Duke. He made his television debut at age 7 opposite his mother on an ABC After School Special. He once said that his biggest fear in life was that: "I'm gonna waste time."

Year	Movie	Character
1985	The Goonies	Mickey
1987	Like Father, Like Son	Trigger
1987	White Water Summer	Alan Block
1989	Staying Together	Duncan McDermott
1989	The War of the Roses	Josh at 17
1991	Toy Soldiers	Billy Tepper
1992	Encino Man	Dave Morgan
1990	Memphis Belle	Richard "Rascal" Moore
1993	Rudy	Rudy Ruettiger

WILLIAM ATHERTON

(1947 -   )

Atherton grew up in New Haven, CT, and, as a high school student, became the youngest member ever of the Connecticut-based Long Wharf Theater Company. He studied drama at the Pasadena Playhouse and the Carnegie Tech. School of Drama. He also studied "Aesthetic Realism" with Eli Siegel, the founder of the discipline Atherton says is not religious, but educational and has helped him to realize "self."

Year	Movie	Character
1972	The New Centurions	Johnson
1973	Class of '44	Fraternity President
1974	The Sugarland Express	Clovis
1975	The Day of the Locust	Tod
1975	The Hindenburg	Boerth
1977	Looking for Mr. Goodbar	James Morrissey
1984	Ghostbusters	Walter Peck (EPA)
1985	Real Genius	Prof. Hathaway
1986	No Mercy	Allan Deveneux
1988	Die Hard	Thornburg
1990	Die Hard 2	Dick Thornberg
1991	Oscar	Overton

TOM ATKINS

(19?? -   )

A veteran character actor, Atkins first fell in love with film while watching horror movies in his hometown of Pittsburgh. The original version of *The Thing* (1951) left an especially strong impression on him. He has appeared in many of the films of the well-known action/horror director John Carpenter and at one time he had hoped to become the "next Vincent Price."

Year	Movie	Character
1980	The Fog	Nick Castle
1980	The Ninth Configuration	Sgt. Krebs
1981	Escape from New York	Rehme
1982	Halloween III: Season of the Witch	Dr. Challis
1986	Night of the Creeps	Ray
1987	Lethal Weapon	Michael Hunsaker

RENE AUBERJONOIS

(1940 -   )

Auberjonois was born in New York City; his father came from an aristocratic Swiss family and his mother was a descendant of Napoleon's sister. He is a founding member of the American Conservatory Theater in San Francisco and spent six years on TV's *Benson* as Governor Gatling's prissy chief of staff.

Year	Movie	Character
1968	Petulia	xxx
1970	M*A*S*H	Dago Red
1971	McCabe and Mrs. Miller	Sheehan
1972	Pete 'n' Tillie	Jimmy Twitchell
1975	The Hindenburg	Major Napier
1976	King Kong	Bagley
1976	The Big Bus	Father Kudos
1978	Eyes of Laura Mars	Donald Phelps
1980	Where the Buffalo Roam	Harris
1986	3:15	Horner
1988	My Best Friend Is a Vampire	Modoc
1988	Walker	Maj. Siegfried Henningson
1989	The Feud	Reverton
1993	The Ballad of Little Jo	Streight Hollander

VAL AVERY

(1924 -   )

Born in Philadelphia, Avery is the son of Mgerdich der Abrahamian, a revolutionary Armenian and a founder of the Republic of Armenia. His mother was a former dramatic actress in Turkey whose career was cut short when she was sold into slavery in Syria. Avery is a graduate of the University of Pennsylvania and is a superb chef, excelling in Armenian and Chinese cookery.

Year	Movie	Character
1963	Hud	Jose
1965	Sylvia	xxx
1965	The Hallelujah Trail	xxx
1966	Assault on a Queen	Trench
1966	Nevada Smith	Buck Mason
1967	Hombre	Delgado
1968	The Brotherhood	Jake Rotherman
1971	Minnie and Moskowitz	Zelmo Swift
1971	The Anderson Tapes	Parelli
1971	Who Says I Can't Ride a Rainbow?	The Marshal
1973	The Laughing Policeman	Pappas
1975	Let's Do It Again	Lt. Bottomley
1975	Lucky Lady	Dolph

(continued on page 505)

24

HOYT AXTON

(1938 -   )

One of America's top folk recording stars, Axton's first foray into acting came in 1963 when he was cast in an episode of *Bonanza*. He began writing songs at age 15 and was performing around San Francisco's coffee-house circuit in 1958. In 1964, he composed the song, *The Pusher* which was recorded by the rock group Steppenwolf and heard in the film *Easy Rider*.

Year	Movie	Character
1979	The Black Stallion	Alex's Father
1982	Endangered Species	Ben
1983	Heart Like a Wheel	Tex Roque
1984	Gremlins	Rand
1989	Disorganized Crime	Sheriff Henault
1989	We're No Angels	Father Levesque

LEW AYRES

(1908 -   )

A leading man of the thirties and forties, Ayres found fame as the star of MGM's *Dr. Kildare* series which ran from 1938 to 1947. His decision to be a conscientious objector during World War II put a damper on his film career, although he continued to work in movies and television into the 1980s. Ayres is a native of Minneapolis.

Year	Movie	Character
1962	Advise and Consent	Vice-President
1964	The Carpetbaggers	McAllister
1972	The Biscuit Eater	Mr. Ames
1979	Battlestar: Galactica	Adar

CANDY AZZARA

(1947 -   )

The Brooklyn-born Azzara began her acting career in regional theaters in the East after acting studies with Gene Frankel, Hugh Whitfield and Lee Strasberg, voice studies with David Craig, Neyneen Pives and Nora Dunfee and dance with Delores Bagley. She was in the public eye on television and in film during the late 1970s and early 1980s.

Year	Movie	Character
1971	Who is Harry Kellerman and Why is He Saying Those Terrible Things About Me?	Sally
1975	Hearts of the West	Waitress
1978	House Calls	Ellen Grady
1980	Fatso	Lydia
1982	Pandemonium	Bambi
1983	Easy Money	Rose
1988	Doin' Time on Planet Earth	Edna Pinsky

BARBARA BABCOCK

(1937 -   )

A TV veteran, Babcock's small screen career got moving during the latter half of the 1960s with voice characterizations on episodes of *Star Trek*. She also acted in that series, but may be best remembered by fans of *Dallas* where she played Liz Craig (1978-82) and *Hill Street Blues* for her Emmy-award winning portrayal of Grace Gardner (1981-85). She grew up in Tokyo speaking Japanese, and received her B.A. from Wellesley and language certificates from the University of Lausanne and the University of Milan.

Year	Movie	Character
1969	Heaven with a Gun	Mrs. Andrews
1973	Bang the Drum Slowly	Team Owners
1980	The Black Marble	Madeline Whitfield
1983	The Lords of Discipline	Abigail
1985	That Was Then, This is Now	Mrs. Douglas
1989	Happy Together	Ruth Carpenter
1989	Heart of Dixie	Coralee Claibourne
1992	Far and Away	Nora Christie

HERMIONE BADDELEY

(1906 - 1986)

Born in Brosely, England, Baddeley went on stage at six and later became known as London's Musical Revue Queen. She was an exuberant, bawdy, comic character who gave in and finally went to Hollywood. For three years she was Mrs. Naugatuck on TV's *Maude*. Among her celebrity friends was playwright Tennessee Williams who considered her one of the great actresses. She died of complications from a stroke.

Year	Movie	Character
1960	Midnight Lace	Dora
1964	Mary Poppins	Ellen
1964	The Unsinkable Molly Brown	Mrs. Grogan
1965	Do Not Disturb	Vanessa Courtwright
1965	Marriage on the Rocks	Jeannie MacPherson
1979	C.H.O.M.P.S.	Mrs. Fowler

G.W. BAILEY

(1945 -   )

Considered one of the most dependable and easily identifiable character/comedy actors in the business, Bailey is a native of Port Arthur, TX. He studied law at Texas Technical University, but decided that the world of the lawyer was not for him, and kicked off a theatrical career as the artistic director of the Lubbock Theater Center.

Year	Movie	Character
1984	Police Academy	Lt. Harris
1984	Runaway	Chief
1985	Rustlers' Rhapsody	Peter
1985	Warning Sign	Tom Schmidt
1986	Short Circuit	Skroeder
1987	Burglar	Ray Kirschman
1987	Mannequin	Felix
1987	Police Academy 4: Citizens on Patrol	Captain Harris
1988	Police Academy 5: Assignment Miami Beach	Harris
1989	Police Academy 6: City Under Siege	Harris

DIANE BAKER

(1938 -   )

Baker was born in a Hollywood hospital, educated in schools in and around Hollywood, and before becoming an active part of the Hollywood scene, She attended USC. Her early work as a model enabled her to tour the U.S. at a young age and her film career began when she was barely out of her teens.

Year	Movie	Character
1963	Nine Hours to Rama	Sheila
1963	The Prize	Emily Stratman
1963	The Stolen Hours	Ellen Pember
1964	Marnie	Lil Mainwaring
1964	Strait-Jacket	Carol
1965	Mirage	Shela
1969	Krakatoa—East of Java	Laura
1976	Baker's Hawk	Jenny
1979	The Pilot	xxx
1990	The Closer	Beatrice Grant
1991	The Silence of the Lambs	Sen. Ruth Martin
1993	The Joy Luck Club	Mrs. Jordan

JOE DON BAKER

(1936 -   )

Texas-born and raised, Baker has made a career for himself by maintaining the image of a two-fisted, hard-hitting hero, a role which earned him wide recognition as Sheriff Buford Pusser in the original *Walking Tall*. He switched his studies from business administration to drama at North Texas University and, following a stint in the army, he moved to New York City, where he studied at the Actors Studio.

Year	Movie	Character
1967	Cool Hand Luke	xxx
1969	Guns of the Magnificent Seven	Slater
1971	The Wild Rovers	Paul Buckman
1972	Junior Bonner	Curly Bonner
1972	Welcome Home, Soldier Boys	Danny
1973	Charley Varrick	Molly
1973	Walking Tall	Buford Pusser
1974	The Outfit	Cody
1975	Framed	Ron
1984	The Natural	The Whammer
1985	Fletch	Chief Karlin
1986	Getting Even	King R. Kenderson
1987	Leonard Part 6	Snyderburn
1987	The Killing Time	Carl Cunningham
1987	The Living Daylights	Brad Whitaker
1989	Criminal Law	Detective Mesel
1991	Cape Fear	Claude Kersek
1992	The Distinguished Gentleman	Olaf Andersen

KATHY BAKER

(1950 -   )

Born in Midland, TX, and raised in Albuquerque, NM, Baker decided to become an actress at age 10. However, after acting in grade school and high school she abruptly stopped. Following her graduation from the University of California at Berkeley with a degree in French, she moved to Paris. There she studied at the Cordon Bleu and ran a small catering business before returning to the U.S. and commencing a theatrical career.

Year	Movie	Character
1983	The Right Stuff	Louise Shepard
1987	Street Smart	Punchy
1988	Clean and Sober	Charlie Standers
1988	Permanent Record	Martha Sinclair
1989	Dad	Annie
1989	Jacknife	Martha
1990	Edward Scissorhands	Joyce Monroe
1992	Article 99	Dr. Diana Walton
1992	Jennifer Eight	Margie Ross
1993	Mad Dog and Glory	Lee

BOB BALABAN

(1945 -   )

A native of Chicago, Balaban was born into a family of showmen. His father was the youngest of seven brothers who owned the Balaban & Katz chain of 175 theaters in Chicago. His uncle was a long time president of Paramount Pictures and his grandfather was once head of production at MGM. He studied with the famed Second City troupe while still in high school and later attended NYU's film school.

Year	Movie	Character
1969	Midnight Cowboy	Young Student
1970	Catch-22	Capt. Orr
1974	Bank Shot	Victor Karp
1975	Report to the Commissioner	Joey Egan
1977	Close Encounters of the Third Kind	Interpreter Laughlin
1978	Girlfriends	Martin
1980	Altered States	Arthur Rosenberg
1981	Absence of Malice	Rosen
1981	Prince of the City	Santimassino
1981	Whose Life Is It Anyway?	Carter Hill
1984	2010	R. Chandra
1987	End of the Line	Gerber
1989	Dead-Bang	Elliot Webly
1990	Alice	Sid Moscowitz
1993	Amos & Andrew	Hostage Negotiator
1993	For Love or Money	Mr. Drinkwater

ADAM BALDWIN

(1962 -   )

Raised on Chicago's North Shore, in the wealthy suburb of Winnetka, Baldwin attended the exclusive New Trier high school. Alumni from that school include Rock Hudson, Charlton Heston, Ann-Margret, Ralph Bellamy and Bruce Dern. The actor was discovered by agents touring the country on a casting call for the 1980 film *My Bodyguard*.

Year	Movie	Character
1980	My Bodyguard	Linderman
1983	D.C. Cab	Albert
1984	Reckless	Randy
1986	3:15	Jeff Hanna
1987	Full Metal Jacket	Animal Mother
1988	The Chocolate War	Carter
1989	Cohen and Tate	Tate
1989	Next of Kin	Joey Rosselini
1990	Predator 2	Garber
1992	Radio Flyer	The King

ALEC BALDWIN

(1958 -   )

Baldwin started out in television, spending 2 1/2 years with the New York soap opera *The Doctors* in the early 80's and then moving to L.A. to join the cast of *Knots Landing* in 1984. He built his film career with secondary roles in movies with directors he respected, eschewing leads until he took the chance of playing a screen hero in *The Hunt for Red October*. Predicted to join the ranks of such "A" list stars as Kevin Costner and Harrison Ford, a public spat with Disney over *The Marrying Man* may have delayed such a move.

Year	Movie	Character
1987	Forever, Lulu	Buck
1988	Beetlejuice	Adam
1988	Married to the Mob	"Cucumber" Frank De Marco
1988	She's Having a Baby	Davis McDonald
1988	Talk Radio	Dan
1988	Working Girl	Mick Dugan
1989	Great Balls of Fire!	Jimmy Swaggart
1990	Alice	Ed
1990	Miami Blues	Frederick J. Frenger, Jr.
1990	The Hunt for Red October	Jack Ryan
1991	The Marrying Man	Charley Pearl
1992	Glengarry Glen Ross	Blake
1992	Prelude to a Kiss	Peter Hoskins
1993	Malice	Dr. Jed Hill

INA BALIN

(1937 - 1990)

A Brooklyn native who was a model before her 1957 Broadway debut, Balin was a rising star in the 1960s. She became better known as an activist who helped Reverend Martin Luther King in his Civil Rights campaign and later as the actress who rescued 217 Vietnamese orphans during the fall of Saigon. She died of pulmonary hypertension.

Year	Movie	Character
1960	From the Terrace	Natalie
1961	The Comancheros	Pilar
1961	The Young Doctors	Cathy Hunt
1964	The Patsy	Ellen Betz
1965	The Greatest Story Ever Told	Martha of Bethany
1967	Run Like a Thief	Mona Shannon
1969	Charro!	Tracy

IAN BANNEN

(1928 -   )

The Scottish character actor has been a fixture on the stage and in film on both sides of the Atlantic for more than four decades. He debuted on the Dublin stage and then spent four seasons at Stratford-on-Avon. He made his first London appearance in 1955 in *Prisoners of War* and launched his film career the following year. Bannen played William Hurt's immediate superior, a smiley Soviet chief prosecutor, who urges Hurt to continue his murder investigation in *Gorky Park*.

Year	Movie	Character
1965	Mister Moses	Robert
1965	The Hill	Sgt. Harris
1966	Flight of the Phoenix	Crow
1966	Penelope	James B. Elcott
1973	The Mackintosh Man	Slade
1973	The Offense	Baxter
1975	Bite the Bullet	Norfolk
1980	The Watcher in the Woods	John Keller
1981	Eye of the Needle	Godliman
1981	Night Crossing	Josef Keller
1983	Gorky Park	Iamskoy
1985	Defence of the Realm	Dennis Markham
1987	Hope and Glory	Grandfather George
1990	Ghost Dad	Sir Edith Moser

SANDY BARON

(1938 -   )

Baron started out as a comedian in the early 1960s with an act that has been described as "neo-Lenny Bruce" and "post-Catskills." In movies, he had a memorable role as an Italian-American who has a disastrous meeting with his cousins in Venice in the 1969 comedy, *If It's Tuesday, This Must Be Belgium*. Baron grew up in the impoverished Brownsville section of Brooklyn in New York City.

Year	Movie	Character
1969	If It's Tuesday, This Must Be Belgium	John Marino
1970	The Out of Towners	TV Man
1978	Straight Time	Manny
1984	Birdy	Mr. Columbato
1984	Broadway Danny Rose	Himself
1986	Vamp	Vic
1990	The Grifters	Doctor

BARBARA BARRIE

(1931 -   )

Barrie grew up in Corpus Christi, TX, and graduated from the University of Texas before attempting New York for a dramatic career. She made her stage debut in 1955 after studying at the Herbert Berghof studio. Memorable screen roles include bike-racer Dennis Christopher's mom in *Breaking Away* and Goldie Hawn's upper-middle class Jewish mom in P*rivate Benjamin*.

Year	Movie	Character
1963	The Caretakers	Edna
1979	Breaking Away	Mrs. Stohler
1979	The Bell Jar	Jay Cee
1980	Private Benjamin	Harriet Benjamin
1987	End of the Line	Jean
1987	Real Men	Mom

BILLY BARTY

BELINDA BAUER

(1924 -   )

(19?? -   )

Barty's career in film began at age three, shortly after his family moved to L.A. While walking with his father past the old Goldwyn Studios, where a Mickey Rooney featurette was being shot, Barty turned a cartwheel for the director and was hired on the spot. He is 48 inches tall and has performed in vaudeville, night clubs, legitimate theater, television and motion pictures.

Bauer began her acting career in her native Australia when she became connected with the Sydney Arts Council. As a child she studied classical ballet. She later spent three years travelling through Southeast Asia, Northern India, England, Europe and the Middle East before settling in New York. There she resumed her acting classes and ballet training.

Year	Movie	Character
1965	Harum Scarum	Baba
1975	The Day of the Locust	Abe
1976	The Amazing Dobermans	Clown
1978	Foul Play	MacKuen
1979	Skatetown, U.S.A.	Jimmy
1981	Under The Rainbow	Otto
1985	Night Patrol	Captain Lewis
1985	Legend	Screwball
1986	Tough Guys	Philly
1987	Body Slam	Tim McClusky
1987	Masters of the Universe	Gwildor
1988	Willow	High Aldwin
1989	UHF	Noodles
1991	Life Stinks	Willy

Year	Movie	Character
1979	The American Success Company	Sara
1979	Winter Kills	Yvette
1983	Flashdance	Katie Hurley
1983	Timerider	Claire Cygne
1987	The Rosary Murders	Pat Lennon
1990	Robocop 2	Dr. Juliette Faxx

STEVEN BAUER

(1956 -   )

Born in Havana, Cuba, Bauer moved with his family to Miami at age three and later studied acting at Miami's Dade Junior College. His breakthrough came with a part on Public Television's *Que Pasa U.S.A.?* after which he was signed by Columbia Television and moved to California.

Year	Movie	Character
1983	Scarface	Manny Ray
1984	Thief of Hearts	Scott Muller
1986	Running Scared	Frank
1988	The Beast	Taj
1989	Gleaming the Cube	Al Lucero
1990	A Climate for Killing	xxx
1992	Raising Cain	Jack

BARBARA BAXLEY

(1925 - 1990)

Baxley started out as a struggling actress in New York during the 1940s after moving there from California. She grew up in Stockton, CA, in a family of pioneer stock—they came west from Maine—and graduated from the College of the Pacific. She made her Broadway debut in 1948 and spent most of her career on the stage or in television. Memorable film roles include the hardened saloon operator in *Nashville*. She died of a heart attack in New York.

Year	Movie	Character
1968	Countdown	Jean
1968	No Way to Treat a Lady	Belle Poppie
1975	Nashville	Lady Pearl
1979	Norma Rae	Leona
1982	A Stranger is Watching	Lally
1989	Sea of Love	Miss Allen
1990	A Shock to the System	Lillian
1990	The Exorcist III	Shirley

JENNIFER BEALS

NED BEATTY

(1963 -   )

Beals was an overnight success at only 17 playing an arc welder by day and disco dancer by night in *Flashdance*. She beat out 4,000 girls for that part, but her next picture, *The Bride*, did poorly at the box office and she has since largely vanished into a series of foreign and low-budget pics. "It was a great thing in terms of making myself known," she once said of *Flashdance*. "But in a way it would have been wise to go through the back door in this business and work my way in, rather than come through the front door all at once."

(1937 -   )

A professional performer since age 10, when he earned spending change by singing in barbershops and gospel quartets in and around his hometown of St. Matthews, KY, Beatty originally planned to become a preacher. Later, he joined Virginia's famed Barter Theater, so named because during the Depression it swapped hams or fruit for theater tickets. He honed his skills there through 70 performances in seven years.

Year	Movie	Character
1983	Flashdance	Alex Owens
1985	The Bride	Eva
1988	Split Decisions	Barbara Uribe
1991	Blood and Concrete	Mona

Year	Movie	Character
1972	Cancel My Reservations	xxx
1972	Deliverance	Bobby
1972	The Life and Times of Judge Roy Bean	Tector Crites
1973	Hard Driver	Hackel
1973	The Thief Who Came to Dinner	Deams
1973	White Lightning	Sheriff Connors
1975	Nashville	Delbert Reese
1975	W.W.and the Dixie Dancekings	xxx
1976	All the President's Men	Dardis
1976	Network	Arthur Jensen
1976	Silver Streak	Sweet
1976	The Big Bus	Shorty Scotty
1977	Exorcist II: The Heretic	Edwards

(continued on page 505)

JOHN BECK

(1943 -   )

Born and raised outside Chicago, Beck dropped out of Joliet Junior College to act in plays in towns outside the city. After moving to California, he spent two years doing TV commercials before getting parts in television shows such as *FBI*, *Gunsmoke* and *Mission Impossible*. He prefers to live in the more rural areas of Los Angeles County, raising his own rabbits, ducks and chickens and growing organically most of the vegetables and fruits served to his family.

Year	Movie	Character
1971	Lawman	Jason Bronson
1971	Mrs. Pollifax—Spy	Lulash
1973	Paperback Hero	Pov
1973	Sleeper	Erno
1975	Rollerball	Moonpie
1976	Sky Riders	Ben Miller
1976	The Big Bus	Shoulders O'Brien
1977	The Other Side of Midnight	Larry Douglas
1987	Deadly Illusion	Alex Burton
1990	A Climate for Killing	xxx

MICHAEL BECK

(1949 -   )

Beck has said that his best roles came from television. In addition to numerous TV guest spots, he co-starred as police officer Sgt. Levon Lundy in CBS' *Houston Knights* for one year. His feature film career has been spotty even though it got off to a good start in *The Warriors*. "That picture created an awareness of me in the industry," he once said. "It opened a lot of doors that *Xanadu* then shut." He gravitated into a few B-pictures after that critical and financial letdown, before landing the role in *Houston Knights*.

Year	Movie	Character
1979	The Warriors	Swan
1980	Xanadu	Sonny Malone
1982	Megaforce	Dallas
1982	Warlords of the 21st Century	Hunter

GRAHAM BECKEL

(1949 -   )

Beckel made a strong impression in 1973's well-received *The Paper Chase* with Timothy Bottoms and John Houseman, but then disappeared from the Hollywood scene until the late 1980s. In that memorable movie he played a supremely confident Harvard man, the leader of Bottoms' notorious study group.

Year	Movie	Character
1973	The Paper Chase	Ford
1989	Lost Angels	Richard Doolan
1990	Welcome Home, Roxy Carmichael	Les Bossetti
1991	Liebestraum	Sheriff Ricker
1992	Jennifer Eight	John Taylor

BONNIE BEDELIA

(1946 -   )

Perhaps best known for her portrayal of a race-car driver in the critically-acclaimed film, *Heart Like a Wheel*, Bedelia's performing career started when she was three. She was accepted into the legendary George Balanchine's School of American Ballet and by age 13 had already danced in four New York ballet productions. She had also sung in three opera productions and had been a featured actress in many live TV programs emanating from New York City by the same age.

Year	Movie	Character
1969	The Gypsy Moths	Annie Burke
1970	Lovers and Other Strangers	Susan
1972	The Strange Vengeance of Rosalie	Rosalie
1978	The Big Fix	Suzanne
1983	Heart Like a Wheel	Shirley Muldowney
1985	Death of an Angel	Grace
1986	The Boy Who Could Fly	Charlene
1986	Violets Are Blue...	Ruth Squires
1987	The Stranger	Alice Kildee
1988	Die Hard	Holly Gennaro McClane
1988	The Prince of Pennsylvania	Pam Marshetta
1989	Fat Man and Little Boy	Kitty Oppenheimer
1990	Die Hard 2	Holly McClane
1990	Presumed Innocent	Barbara Sabich
1993	Needful Things	Polly Chalmers

ED BEGLEY

(1901 - 1970)

The much-admired character actor, overweight and jowly-faced, moved from radio to stage to films and television with ease and authority. As a boy, Begley ran away from his Hartford, CT, home often, gave up school at 13, served in the U.S. Navy in World War I, became a radio announcer in Hartford, and went to New York where he got his first stage role in 1943. He won a best-supporting Oscar for his role in the 1963 *Sweet Bird of Youth* based on the Tennessee Williams play. He died of a heart attack in L.A.

Year	Movie	Character
1962	Sweet Bird of Youth	"Boss" Finley
1964	The Unsinkable Molly Brown	Shamus Tobin
1966	The Oscar	Grobard
1967	Warning Shot	Capt. Roy Klodin
1967	Billion Dollar Brain	Gen. Midwinter
1968	Firecreek	Preacher Broyles
1968	Hang 'Em High	Cap'n Wilson
1968	Wild in the Streets	Sen. Allbright
1970	The Dunwich Horror	Dr. Armitage

ED BEGLEY, JR.

(1949 -   )

The son of character actor Ed Begley, Begley, Jr. made his acting debut in 1967 on CBS's series *My Three Sons*. He spent eight years working as a stand-up comic and also worked as an assistant camera-man on commercials. He is probably best known as Dr. Victor Erlich on the television series *St. Elsewhere* and received four Emmy nominations during the show's six year run.

Year	Movie	Character
1973	Showdown	Pook
1978	Blue Collar	Bobby Joe
1978	Goin' South	Mr. Haber
1979	Battlestar: Galactica	Ensign Greenbean
1979	The Concorde—Airport '79	xxx
1979	The In-Laws	Barry Lutz
1981	Private Lessons	Jack
1982	Cat People	Joe
1982	Eating Raoul	Bit
1983	Get Crazy	Colin
1984	Protocol	Hassler
1984	Streets of Fire	Ben
1985	Transylvania 6-5000	Gil Turner
1987	Amazon Women on the Moon	Griffin
1988	The Accidental Tourist	Charles
1989	She-Devil	Bob Patchett
1991	Meet the Applegates	Dick Applegate

KATHLEEN BELLER

(1957 -   )

Beller launched her career as an actress with TV commercials and a role in the daytime soap, *Search for Tomorrow*. She was born in New York City, where her father taught high school math and her mother was a psychiatric social worker. As a youngster, Beller studied French, German and Russian, judo, art, classical ballet, guitar, flute and piano. Drama lessons came at age 13 in Bristol, England.

Year	Movie	Character
1978	Movie, Movie	Angie Popchik
1978	The Betsy	Betsy Hardeman
1979	Promises in the Dark	Buffy Koenig
1981	Fort Apache, The Bronx	Theresa
1982	The Sword and the Sorcerer	Alana
1983	Touched	Jennifer
1989	Time Trackers	R.J.

ROBERT BELTRAN

(1957 -   )

Beltran became interested in theater while in high school in California and has admitted that his original incentive was to meet girls. At Bakersfield College, however, he became more serious about acting and appeared in many productions. His movies include the cult hit *Eating Raoul*, where he played Raoul, a Mexican locksmith who tries to cut himself in on the outrageous money-making scheme of his new friends the Blands.

Year	Movie	Character
1982	Eating Raoul	Raoul
1983	Lone Wolf McQuade	Kayo
1984	Night of the Comet	Hector
1987	Gaby—A True Story	Luis
1991	Bugsy	xxx

ANNETTE BENING

(1959 -   )

Bening gained most of her early experience with theatrical schooling and extensive stage work at the American Institute of Theater Arts and the American Conservatory Theater, both in San Francisco. After more hard work in regional theaters and the New York stage, she landed the role of the cunning sex-kitten, Myra, in the film, *The Grifters* and received an Oscar nomination for her efforts. Bening has co-starred with husband Warren Beatty in *Bugsy* and Harrison Ford in *Regarding Henry*.

Year	Movie	Character
1988	The Great Outdoors	Kate
1990	The Grifters	Myra Langtry
1990	Postcards From the Edge	Evelyn Ames
1991	Bugsy	Virginia Hill
1991	Guilty by Suspicion	Ruth Merrill
1991	Regarding Henry	Sarah

POLLY BERGEN

(1930 -   )

Born in Knoxville, TN, this self-described workaholic started in show business as a country singer, moved to pop music and film, and then finally, to television. Bergen was a professional singer by age 13. In recent years she has been involved in such business ventures as marketing cosmetics and designing shoes.

Year	Movie	Character
1962	Cape Fear	Peggy Bowden
1963	Move Over, Darling	Bianca Steele Arden
1963	The Caretakers	Lorna Melford
1964	Kisses for My President	Leslie McCloud
1987	Making Mr. Right	Estelle Stone
1990	Cry-Baby	Mrs. Vernon-Williams

SENTA BERGER

(1941 -   )

Growing up in Vienna, Austria, during World War II, Berger watched her mother steal eggs to feed the family, saw her father go off to prison camp and fled into musty cellars to avoid the bombing. She was signed to a multiple picture contract by Columbia in 1964 because, according to studio executives, of her "beauty, sex appeal, and solid acting ability."

Year	Movie	Character
1963	The Victors	Trudi
1965	Major Dundee	Teresa Santiago
1965	The Glory Guys	Lou Woodward
1966	Cast a Giant Shadow	Magda Simon
1966	The Quiller Memorandum	Inge
1967	The Ambushers	Francesca
1975	The Swiss Conspiracy	Denise
1977	Cross of Iron	Eva

HERBERT BERGHOF

(1909 - 1990)

Berghof began directing for the stage in his hometown of Vienna, Austria, but fled the Nazis in 1939 to begin his own acting studio in New York. It became a training ground for actors like Anne Bancroft, Matthew Broderick, Robert De Niro, Al Pacino and hundreds of others. Berghof also acted in and directed many New York stage productions during his 50-year teaching career. He died of heart failure.

Year	Movie	Character
1974	Harry and Tonto	Rivetowski
1979	Voices	Nathan Rothman
1980	Those Lips, Those Eyes	Dr. Julius Fuldauer
1980	Times Square	Dr. Huber
1985	Target	Schroeder

STEVEN BERKOFF

(1937 -   )

Actor, playwright and director, Berkoff was born in London of Russian-Rumanian heritage. After acting for many years in repertory, he formed his own company: the London Theater Group. He has staged and starred in his own productions all over the world. Perhaps best known for his off-center theater work, Berkoff once described himself as "a mixture of Muhammed Ali and Franz Kafka—somewhere between Laurence Olivier and Marcel Marceau, Picasso and Salvador Dali."

Year	Movie	Character
1967	Prehistoric Women	John
1971	A Clockwork Orange	Constable
1975	Barry Lyndon	Lord Ludd
1983	Octopussy	Orlov
1984	Beverly Hills Cop	Victor Maitland
1985	Rambo: First Blood Part II	Podovsky
1985	Revolution	Sgt. Jones
1986	Under the Cherry Moon	Mr. Sharon
1986	Absolute Beginners	The Fanatic

WARREN BERLINGER

(1937 -   )

Berlinger's acting career began when a talent scout happened to see him playing in the streets of his native Brooklyn. He was eight years old at the time and the chance encounter resulted in a stage role with Ethel Merman in *Annie Get Your Gun* that lasted three years. His career has included both stage and film roles, as well as hundreds of television appearances.

Year	Movie	Character
1960	The Wackiest Ship in the Army	Sparks
1961	All Hands on Deck	Ensign Rush
1964	Billie	Mike Benson
1966	Spinout	Philip Short
1975	The Four Deuces	Chico
1982	The World According to Garp	Stew Percy
1989	Ten Little Indians	Blore

CORBIN BERNSEN

JAMES BEST

(1953 -   )

(1926 -   )

Bernsen is best known for his role as the male-chauvinist divorce attorney Arnie Becker in the long-running TV series *L.A. Law*. He is the son of the popular daytime-television actress Jeanne Cooper and has spent time himself on a soap opera: *Ryan's Hope*. He has a master's degree in playwrighting from UCLA and has formed a theater company around a theater he built.

The veteran TV and movie actor was recruited for Hollywood while doing summer stock in Monticello, NJ. A coal miner's son, he holds a black belt in karate and is a former B-17 gunner. Best is also a respected drama coach who discovered Gary Busey and Lindsay Wagner. He found fame as Sheriff Rosco on the TV series *The Dukes of Hazzard* (1979-85).

Year	Movie	Character
1974	Three the Hard Way	Boy
1976	Eat My Dust	xxx
1981	S.O.B.	xxx
1987	Hello Again	Jason Chadman
1989	Bert Rigby, You're a Fool	Jim Shirley
1989	Disorganized Crime	Frank Salazar
1989	Major League	Roger Dorn
1991	Shattered	Jeb Scott
1992	Frozen Assets	Zach Shepard

Year	Movie	Character
1960	The Mountain Road	Niergaard
1964	The Quick Gun	Scotty Grant
1965	Shenandoah	Carter
1966	Three on a Couch	Dr. Ben Mizer
1968	Firecreek	Drew
1972	Sounder	Sheriff Young
1976	Nickelodeon	Jim
1976	Ode to Billy Joe	Dewey Barksdale
1977	Rolling Thunder	Texan
1978	Hooper	Cully

RICHARD BEYMER

(1939 -   )

Born in Avoca, IA, Beymer moved with his family to Los Angeles at age 10. He broke into show business as a dancer on a children's show on pioneer TV station KTLA. From there he got a role as the nephew in Vittorio De Sica's 1953 film *Indiscretion of an American Wife*. At age 25, he left Hollywood and spent time teaching in Mississippi and working with SNCC to help with the black voter registration drive. He did not return to film until the 1980s.

Year	Movie	Character
1960	High Time	Bob Bannerman
1961	West Side Story	Tony
1962	Bachelor Flat	Mike
1962	The Longest Day	Pvt. Dutch Schultz
1963	The Stripper	Kenny

MICHAEL BIEHN

(1957 -   )

Biehn grew up in Lincoln, NE, where he started performing at an early age in community theater. He attended the University of Arizona on a drama scholarship and then moved to L.A. to pursue an acting career. He recalls being typecasted in his initial roles as a "blond 18-year-old surfer, the kid on the football team, or the kid in high school who gets his girlfriend pregnant."

Year	Movie	Character
1981	The Fan	Douglas Breen
1983	The Lords of Discipline	Alexander
1984	The Terminator	Kyle Reese
1986	Aliens	Corporal Hicks
1988	The Seventh Sign	Russell Quinn
1989	The Abyss	Lt. Coffey
1990	Navy SEALS	Lt. James Curran
1991	Timebomb	Eddy Kay
1992	K-2	Taylor Brooks
1993	Deadfall	Joe Donan

RAMON BIERI

(1929 -   )

Bieri has a substantial stage background as well as several roles in film and television. He has appeared on television in *Gunsmoke*, *Mannix* and *Bonanza* and has acted Off-Broadway in the Circle in the Square, at the New York Shakespeare Festival and the Old Globe Theater in San Francisco. He is a native of Windsor, CT, and was educated at Boston's Emerson College.

Year	Movie	Character
1970	The Grasshopper	Roosevelt
1972	The Honkers	Jack Ferguson
1974	Badlands	Cato
1977	Sorcerer	Corlette
1979	The Frisco Kid	Mr. Jones
1984	Grandview USA	Pearson
1987	The Sicilian	Quintana
1988	Vibes	Eli Diamond

TONY BILL

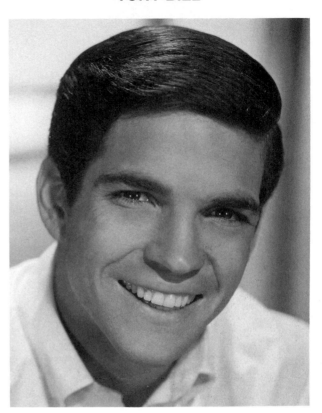

(1940 -   )

Bill is a film director as well as an actor and feels "the difference...is 1000 percent. As a director you have total responsibility for everything that happens. But as an actor, you only need to know your lines...I think directing can be a tremendous ego trip. You're in total control, you have the power." Born and raised in San Diego, he has a master's degree in English from the University of Notre Dame.

Year	Movie	Character
1963	Come Blow Your Horn	Buddy
1965	Marriage on the Rocks	Jim Blake
1965	None But the Brave	Keller
1966	You're a Big Boy Now	Raef
1968	Ice Station Zebra	Lt. Russell Walker
1969	Castle Keep	Lt. Adam Amberjack
1975	Shampoo	Johnny Pope
1979	Heart Beat	Dick
1985	Pee-wee's Big Adventure	xxx
1987	Less Than Zero	Bradford Easton

JENNIFER BILLINGSLEY

(1942 -   )

An army brat who grew up all over the globe, Billingsley's original claim to fame was her striking resemblance to Brigitte Bardot. An honors graduate from Fort Smith Senior High School in Arkansas, her energetic performance in the Broadway musical, *Carnival* caused one observer to claim, "she has an animal vitality. You cannot take your eyes off this girl." Her film debut came as a hopped-up teenage moll in *Lady in a Cage.*

Year	Movie	Character
1964	Lady in a Cage	Elaine
1970	C.C. and Company	Pom Pom
1972	Welcome Home, Soldier Boys	Broad
1973	White Lightning	Lou

PETER BILLINGSLEY

(1972 -   )

Child actor Billingsley had starred in two feature films, two TV-movies, three TV series and over 120 commercials by age 11. As a teenager, he was a science and computer buff and was the national spokesman for U.S. President Ronald Reagan's Young Astronaut Council, an educational program aimed at kids. Kids know him best as "Messy Marvin" of the Hershey's syrup commercials.

Year	Movie	Character
1982	Death Valley	Billy
1983	A Christmas Story	Ralphie
1986	The Dirt Bike Kid	Jack Simmons
1987	Russkies	Adam
1989	Beverly Hills Brats	Scooter

EDWARD BINNS

(1916 - 1990)

The veteran character actor made his Broadway debut in the 1949 production of *Command Decision* after training at the Cleveland Playhouse. During the 1950s, Binns appeared in hundreds of live plays on television and starred in the cop show *Brenner* which ran from 1959 to 1964. The Philadelphia native died of a heart attack.

Year	Movie	Character
1961	Judgment at Nuremberg	Senator Burkette
1964	The Americanization of Emily	Adm. Thomas Healy
1975	Night Moves	Joey Ziegler
1978	Oliver's Story	Phil Cavilleri
1979	The Pilot	xxx
1982	The Verdict	Bishop Brophy

THORA BIRCH

(1982 -   )

The child actress had her first brush with show business in a commercial with the California Raisins. She now has over 30 commercials to her credit. Birch has said that she "always want[s] to be in the acting business...maybe behind the scenes as a director or a producer." Hobbies include karate and playing the keyboard.

Year	Movie	Character
1988	Purple People Eater	Molly Johnson
1991	All I Want for Christmas	Hallie O'Fallon
1991	Paradise	Billie Pike
1992	Patriot Games	Sally Ryan
1993	Hocus Pocus	Dani

JOAN BLACKMAN

(1938 -   )

Born in San Francisco, Blackman left high school with intentions of becoming a model, but signed with the Hecht-Hill-Lancaster company while in Hollywood and made her TV debut. This company provided many newcomers with their introduction to Hollywood including the actor Robert Vaughn.

Year	Movie	Character
1960	Visit to a Small Planet	Ellen Spelding
1961	Blue Hawaii	Maile Duval
1961	The Great Imposter	Catherine Lacey
1962	Kid Galahad	Rose Grogan
1968	Daring Game	Kathryn Carlyle
1974	Macon County Line	Carol Morgan
1974	The Moonrunners	Reba

RUBEN BLADES

(1948 -   )

A Panamanian, Blades studied law and political science at the University of Panama and graduated from Harvard with an L.L.M. He then worked as an attorney for the Banco Nacional de Panama. The actor is a composer, singer and writer as well and has recorded award-winning albums for the Elektra/Asylum label. He has toured the U.S., Central America and Europe with his band Seis de Solar.

Year	Movie	Character
1987	Critical Condition	Louis
1987	Fatal Beauty	Carl Jiminez
1988	Homeboy	xxx
1988	The Milagro Beanfield War	Sheriff Bernabe Montoya
1989	Disorganized Crime	Carlos Barrios
1990	Mo' Better Blues	Petey
1990	Predator 2	Danny
1990	The Lemon Sisters	C.W.
1990	Two Jakes	Mickey Nice
1991	The Super	Marlon

ROBERT BLAKE

(1933 -   )

A child actor, Blake was a regular member of the cast of MGM's popular *Our Gang* comedies during the early 1940s. He hated it. "I acted only because I was told to," he once told an interviewer. "Forcing a kid to become a performer is one of the worst things that can happen to a child. It's turning them into adults while they're still youngsters." Blake spent three years (1975-78) in the title role of the police series *Baretta* for which he won an Emmy.

Year	Movie	Character
1963	PT 109	"Bucky" Harris
1966	This Property is Condemned	Sidney
1967	In Cold Blood	Perry Smith
1969	Tell Them Willie Boy Is Here	Willie Boy
1973	Electra Glide in Blue	John Wintergreen
1974	Busting	Patrick Farrel
1980	Coast to Coast	Charlie
1981	Second-Hand Hearts	Loyal

RONEE BLAKELY

(1946 -   )

Blakely made her film debut in Robert Altman's *Nashville* as a country-and-western singer on the verge of a nervous breakdown and recieved a best supporting Oscar nomination for her efforts. She is also a singer and a composer. She composed music for Fox's 1971 *Welcome Home, Soldier Boys* and did the same, in addition to scripting, producing and directing, for a 1985 film called *I Played It for You*. The native of Stanley, ID, has made appearances on the New York stage and the TV series *Vega$*.

Year	Movie	Character
1975	Nashville	Barbara Jean
1977	The Private Files of J. Edgar Hoover	Carrie DeWitt
1978	The Driver	The Connection
1980	The Baltimore Bullet	Carolina Red
1984	A Nightmare on Elm Street	Marge Thompson
1987	A Return to Salem's Lot	Sally
1987	Student Confidential	Jenny Selden

SUSAN BLAKELY

(1950 -   )

The daughter of a career soldier in the U.S. Army, Blakely was born in Germany and grew up on Army bases in many far-off places, including Hawaii and Korea. After spending a year at the University of Texas, she moved to New York City and became one of the country's top fashion models, represented by the prestigious Ford Agency. Between modeling assignments and TV commercials, she studied acting at the famous Actors Studio.

Year	Movie	Character
1974	The Lords of Flatbush	Jane
1974	The Towering Inferno	Patty Simmons
1975	Capone	Iris
1975	Report to the Commissioner	Patty Butler
1979	Dreamer	Karen
1979	The Concorde—Airport '79	Maggie
1987	Over the Top	Christina Hawk

CLAIRE BLOOM

(1931 -   )

She's starred with Charlie Chaplin, Richard Burton, Laurence Olivier, John Gielgud and George C. Scott, but ultimately Bloom proved too British for Hollywood and was never positioned for major stardom. Her film career got a good boost opposite Charlie Chaplin in his 1952 film *Limelight* following a few featured roles in London plays. She was on the cover of *Time* that year. Her autobiography makes it clear that she prefers the stage over films and her U.K. films over her U.S. ones.

Year	Movie	Character
1962	The Chapman Report	Naomi
1962	The Wonderful World of the Brothers Grimm	Dorothea Grimm
1964	The Outrage	Wife
1965	The Spy Who Came in From the Cold	Nan Perry
1968	Charly	Alice Kinian
1970	Red Sky at Morning	Ann Arnold
1977	Islands in the Stream	Audrey
1981	Clash of the Titans	Hera
1985	Deja Vu	Eleanor Harvey
1989	Crimes and Misdemeanors	Miriam Rosenthal

VERNA BLOOM

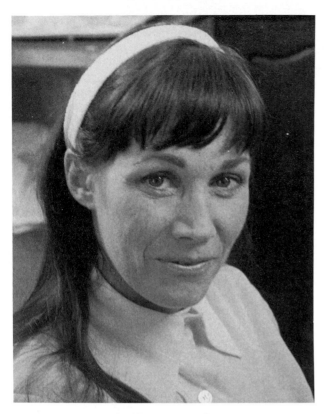

(1939 -   )

Bloom once said that she preferred films to stage because acting in theater seemed phony. However, much of her experience has come in a theater in Denver located in an old church that she also managed with her husband. She has had memorable roles in big pictures including the Dean of Faber College's swinging wife in *National Lampoon's Animal House* and the wife of the local hotelier in Clint Eastwood's *High Plains Drifter*. A native of Lynn, MA, Bloom studied drama in New York.

Year	Movie	Character
1973	Badge 373	Maureen
1973	High Plains Drifter	Sarah Belding
1978	National Lampoon's Animal House	Marion Wormer
1982	Honkytonk Man	Emmy
1985	After Hours	June
1985	The Journey of Natty Gann	Farm Woman

ROBERTS BLOSSOM

(1924 -   )

Blossom is a playwright and a poet as well as an actor. He did not plan to become an actor, but started out as a therapist. In the 1950s and 1960s he was involved with the "filmstage" concept: the simultaneous presentation of live actors with film and/or slides. He was born in New Haven, CT, and attended Harvard. He has won four Obies and a Show Business Award. Blossom recently put out some of his dramatic poems on video.

Year	Movie	Character
1971	The Hospital	Hospital Victim
1972	Slaughterhouse Five	Wild Bob Cody
1977	Close Encounters of the Third Kind	Farmer
1979	Escape from Alcatraz	Doc
1980	Resurrection	John Harper
1983	Christine	George LeBay
1983	Reuben, Reuben	Frank Spofford
1984	Flashpoint	xxx
1985	Vision Quest	Grandpa
1989	Always	Dave
1990	Home Alone	Marley
1991	Doc Hollywood	Judge Evans

LISA BLOUNT

MARK BLUM

(1955 -   )

(1950 -   )

Blount is an Arkansas native who quit high school at sixteen and enrolled at the University of Arkansas without a high school diploma. After appearing in several college and repertory theater productions, she auditioned as an extra, but instead landed a leading role in James Bridges' *9-30-55*, a film about the death of James Dean. A memorable performance opposite Richard Gere in *An Officer and a Gentleman* thrust her into the limelight.

After fashioning a theater major at the University of Pennsylvania, Blum moved on to a joint program with the University of Minneapolis and the Guthrie Theater in Minneapolis. There he received intensive training in various theater skills and a master's degree. In addition to film roles, he has had regular parts on television's *Ryan's Hope* and *One Life to Live*, but has done most of his work on the stage.

Year	Movie	Character
1977	9/30/55	Billie Jean
1982	An Officer and a Gentleman	Lynette Pomeroy
1985	Cease Fire	Paula Murphy
1985	What Waits Below	Leslie Peterson
1986	Radioactive Dreams	xxx
1987	Prince of Darkness	Catherine
1987	South of Reno	Anette
1989	Blind Fury	Annie Winchester
1989	Great Balls of Fire!	Lois Brown

Year	Movie	Character
1985	Desperately Seeking Susan	Gary
1986	"Crocodile" Dundee	Richard Mason
1987	Blind Date	Denny Gordon
1988	The Presidio	Arthur Peale
1989	Worth Winning	Ned Braudy

LLOYD BOCHNER

(1924 -   )

Bochner began acting lessons in his hometown of Toronto when he was 10 years old. The following year he earned his first money as an actor on a Toronto radio station; in fact, radio wages paid his way through high school and college. Bochner entered the Royal Canadian Navy as an ordinary seaman and was discharged as a lieutenant after three years of duty in the North Atlantic. His start in Hollywood began in numerous well-known television programs.

Year	Movie	Character
1965	Sylvia	Bruce Stamford III
1967	Point Blank	Frederick Carter
1967	Tony Rome	Rood
1968	The Detective	Dr. Roberts
1968	The Young Runaways	Raymond Marquis Allen
1970	The Dunwich Horror	Dr. Cary
1972	Ulzana's Raid	Captain Gates
1987	Crystal Heart	Frank Newley
1989	Millennium	Walters
1991	The Naked Gun 2 1/2: The Smell of Fear	Baggett
1993	Morning Glory	Bob Collins

JOSEPH BOLOGNA

(1938 -   )

Bologna is primarily a playwright and screenwriter who usually collaborates on comedies with his wife and partner Renee Taylor. His first brush with acting occurred while he was a student at Princeton. Cast as Willy Loman in *Death of a Salesman*, the complexity of the role gave him second thoughts. He gave up on acting temporarily and later turned to writing ad copy and material for nightclub comics. He has likened writing to "putting your head in a vise and vomiting your brains out."

Year	Movie	Character
1971	Made for Each Other	Giggy
1976	The Big Bus	Dan Torrance
1979	Chapter Two	Leo Schneider
1982	My Favorite Year	King Kaiser
1984	The Woman in Red	Joe
1985	Transylvania 6-5000	Dr. Malavaqua
1990	Coupe de Ville	Uncle Phil

SORRELL BOOKE

(1930 -   )

Booke is best known to fans of TV's *The Dukes of Hazzard* (1979-85) as Davis Hogg, the local politico, an overweight, cigar-chomping corrupt buffoon who got his comeuppance every week from the Dukes. He began in radio dramas as a kid in Buffalo, NY, and spent several years as a stage actor before going to Hollywood. He has degrees from Columbia and Yale and has made a specialty of languages and dialects. "I've always been good at voices and I think the most important part of acting is voice," he once said.

Year	Movie	Character
1966	A Fine Madness	Leonard Tupperman
1967	Up the Down Staircase	Dr. Bester
1968	Bye Bye Braverman	Holly Levine
1972	What's Up, Doc?	Harry
1972	Slaughterhouse Five	Lionel Merble
1974	Bank Shot	Al. G. Karp
1974	The Take	Oscar
1977	The Other Side of Midnight	Lanchon
1977	Freaky Friday	Mr. Dilk

RICHARD BOONE

(1916 - 1981)

Boone was a popular choice for perennial villain in films until he made it big as Paladin in the long-running TV series *Have Gun, Will Travel* (1957-63). Voted best actor three times by National TV critics, he later played the tough guy in action films. An aerial gunner in the Navy during World War II, he gave up the art major of his college days to study acting at the New York Neighborhood Playhouse and the Actors Studio. He died of throat cancer.

Year	Movie	Character
1960	The Alamo	Gen. Sam Houston
1961	A Thunder of Drums	Capt. Stephen Maddocks
1964	Rio Conchos	Lassiter
1965	The War Lord	Bors
1967	Hombre	Grimes
1969	The Arrangement	Sam Anderson
1970	Madron	Madron
1971	Big Jake	John Fain
1975	Against a Crooked Sky	Russian
1976	The Shootist	Sweeney
1978	The Big Sleep	Lash Canino
1979	Winter Kills	xxx

JAMES BOOTH

(1933 -   )

Raised in Yorkshire, England, Booth was originally typecast for cock-ney-boy parts until he worked at the Theatre Royal, Stratford East and won recognition in Shakespearean theater at Stratford-on-Avon. He once described himself as "a sort of eccentric actor. Sometimes I think I'm out of my time—either old-fashioned or too advanced."

Year	Movie	Character
1970	Macho Callahan	"King Harry" Wheeler
1970	Adam's Woman	Dyson
1981	Zorro, the Gay Blade	Velasquez
1985	Pray for Death	Limehouse
1986	Avenging Force	Adm. Brown
1991	American Ninja 4: The Annihilation	Mulgrew

POWERS BOOTHE

(1949 -   )

A relative newcomer, Boothe burst onto television screens as the "rev-erend" who led his followers to mass suicide in *Guyana Tragedy: The Story of Jim Jones* in 1980. The role won him an Emmy. Born and raised on a farm near Snyder, TX, he first studied drama during high school, then earned a bachelor's degree in theater from Southwestern Texas State University and a master's from SMU.

Year	Movie	Character
1981	Southern Comfort	Hardin
1984	A Breed Apart	Michael Walker
1984	Red Dawn	Lt. Col. Andrew Tanner
1985	The Emerald Forest	Bill Markham
1987	Extreme Prejudice	Cash Bailey
1992	Rapid Fire	Mace Ryan

PHILIP BOSCO

(1930 -   )

A native of Jersey City, NJ, Bosco attended the famed theater department of Catholic University before finding his way to the New York stage. He did not receive much formal training in his early years, preferring to rely on, according to him, "performance by experience—I'm a great stickler for that. Act in anything you can in front of an audience; that's the best teacher of all."

Year	Movie	Character
1983	Trading Places	Doctor
1984	The Pope of Greenwich Village	Paulie's Father
1985	Heaven Help Us	xxx
1986	The Money Pit	Curly
1986	Children of a Lesser God	Dr. Curtis Franklin
1987	3 Men and a Baby	Det. Melkowitz
1987	Suspect	Paul Gray
1988	Working Girl	Oren Trask
1988	Another Woman	Sam
1989	The Dream Team	O'Malley
1989	The Luckiest Man in the World	Sam Posner
1990	Quick Change	Bus Driver
1990	Blue Steel	Frank Turner
1991	F/X 2	Ray Silak
1991	True Colors	Sen. Steubens
1992	Straight Talk	Gene Perlman
1992	Shadows and Fog	Mr. Paulsen

JOSEPH BOTTOMS

(1954 -   )

The younger brother of actor Timothy Bottoms, Joseph was born in Santa Barbara, CA, the son of school teacher parents. After acquiring an interest in acting while in junior high school, he went on to appear in so-called 'fringe theater' and from there moved on to television.

Year	Movie	Character
1974	The Dove	Robin Lee Graham
1979	The Black Hole	Lt. Charles Pizer
1981	King of the Mountain	Buddy
1984	Blind Date	Jonathon Ratcliffe
1988	Born to Race	Al Pagura

TIMOTHY BOTTOMS

(1950 -   )

A native Californian, Bottoms credits his father, an ex-art teacher turned ecologist and part-time urban planner, for the way he's turned out. "When he was a teacher, he gave everyone an 'A'—everyone who tried, that is," Bottoms has said. "And, as far as I'm concerned now, everyone starts with an 'A'. You hold it or confirm it or you lose it." The actor, who has been described as "moody" and "sensitive," jumped right into feature films, bypassing theater and television.

Year	Movie	Character
1971	The Last Picture Show	Sonny Crawford
1972	Love and Pain (and the Whole Damn Thing)	Walter Elbertson
1973	The Paper Chase	Hart
1976	Operation Daybreak	Jan
1976	A Small Town in Texas	Poke
1977	Rollercoaster	Young Man
1978	The Other Side of the Mountain Part 2	John Boothe
1979	Hurricane	Jack Sanford
1985	What Waits Below	Major Stevens
1986	Invaders From Mars	George
1988	The Drifter	Arthur
1990	Texasville	Sonny Crawford

TOM BOWER

(19?? -   )

Bower's nomadic childhood was spent attending 14 different schools and living with his parents in the city and his grandparents in the country. "Without a sense of permanence and established relationships I withdrew from people and developed an active internal fantasy life," relates Bower, whose childhood of "pretending and observing" targetted him to an acting career. In recent years, he has been involved in all aspects of filmmaking—from the business end to the artistic interpretation.

Year	Movie	Character
1983	The Ballad of Gregorio Cortez	Boone Choate
1984	Wildrose	Rick Ogaard
1986	River's Edge	Bennett
1988	Distant Thunder	Louis
1989	True Believer	Cecil Skell
1992	Raising Cain	Sergeant Cally

BRUCE BOXLEITNER

(1950 -   )

This native of Elgin, IL, is recognized as a diligent, reliable performer in TV series, miniseries and made-for-television movies. Boxleitner got his theatrical start after high school, when he studied acting, set design and lighting at the Goodman Theater in Chicago. The Old West is a major study of his life with a minor in the history of the Civil War. He collects western antiques and American Indian Art.

Year	Movie	Character
1980	The Baltimore Bullet	Billie Joe Robbins
1982	Tron	Alan Bradley/Tron
1992	The Babe	Jumpin' Joe Dugan
1992	Kuffs	Brad Kuffs

STEPHEN BOYD

(1928 - 1977)

In spite of his dark Irish good looks, Boyd was a character actor who wowed audiences with his role of Messala in the 1950 *Ben Hur*. A native of Belfast, Northern Ireland, he made films world-wide, started his own production company, and was a regular on television. He died at 48 after a heart attack while playing golf.

Year	Movie	Character
1962	Billy Rose's Jumbo	Sam Rawlins
1964	The Fall of the Roman Empire	Livius
1965	Genghis Khan	Jamuga
1966	The Oscar	Frank Fane
1966	Fantastic Voyage	Grant
1968	Shalako	Bosky Fulton

LARA FLYNN BOYLE

(1971 -   )

Active in films and television only since 1988, Boyle has already won an ACE Award nomination from the National Cable Television Association for the best actress in a dramatic series for her 1991 performance in *The Hidden Room* on Lifetime. She was born in Davenport, IA, and studied acting at the Chicago Academy for the Arts.

Year	Movie	Character
1988	Poltergeist III	Donna Gardner
1989	How I Got into College	Jessica Kailo
1990	The Rookie	Sarah
1991	Mobsters	Mara Motes
1992	Wayne's World	Stacy
1993	The Temp	Kris Bolin
1993	Red Rock West	Suzanne

LORRAINE BRACCO

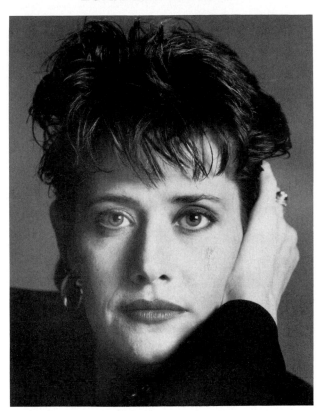

(1955 -   )

The daughter of a Brooklyn fishmonger, Bracco was voted the ugliest girl in the sixth grade, but grew up to be a Paris fashion model. She has been described as a "tough New Yorker," "cocky and determined" and "the new Debra Winger." A veteran of many Hollywood movies, she lives in Manhattan with her husband and children.

Year	Movie	Character
1987	The Pick-up Artist	Carla
1987	Someone to Watch Over Me	Ellie Keegan
1989	Sing	Miss Lombardo
1989	The Dream Team	Riley
1990	Goodfellas	Karen Hill
1991	Talent for the Game	Bobbie
1991	Switch	Sheila
1992	Medicine Man	Dr. Rae Crane
1992	Traces of Red	Ellen Schofield
1992	Radio Flyer	Mary

SCOTT BRADY

(1924 - 1985)

Usually appearing in action roles, the rugged Brooklyn-born Brady was once a lumberjack and later served in World War II. On his base he won the light-heavyweight boxing championship. In the movies, he began as a good-looking leading man and as he aged became a valuable character actor. He died of respiratory failure.

Year	Movie	Character
1964	Stage to Thunder Rock	Sam Swope
1965	John Goldfarb, Please Come Home	Sakalakis
1969	They Ran for Their Lives	xxx
1972	Dollars	Sarge
1979	The China Syndrome	Herman DeYoung
1984	Gremlins	Sheriff

NEVILLE BRAND

(1920 - 1992)

A decorated war hero, Brand joined the peacetime army when he was 16, and served through World War II. He took part in the Dieppe raid and was among the 99 men (out of 3,000) who returned to England from that ill-fated Allied venture. After the war, he began attending acting classes at the American Theater Wing under the G.I. Bill. Hollywood followed several Broadway plays. He may be best remembered as the sympathetic guard in *Birdman of Alcatraz*. Brand died of emphysema in Sacramento.

Year	Movie	Character
1960	The Adventures of Huckleberry Finn	Pap
1961	The Last Sunset	Frank Hobbs
1962	Birdman of Alcatraz	Bull Ransom
1969	The Desperados	Sheriff
1973	Scalawag	Brimstone/Mudhook
1973	Cahill—U.S. Marshal	Lightfoot
1980	The Ninth Configuration	Groper

ROSSANO BRAZZI

(1916 -   )

An international film star of the 1950s and 1960s, the Italian actor was raised in a poor neighborhood of Rome. As a teenager, Brazzi was an amateur featherweight champion and, at 19, earned a law degree. He began an acting career shortly thereafter as the legal business was slow. During World War II, he was a leader in the anti-fascist movement in Rome. Although he found it difficult to break into Hollywood, he finally established himself during the 1950s playing a series of Latin lovers.

Year	Movie	Character
1962	Light in the Piazza	Signor Naccarelli
1967	Woman Times Seven	Giorgio
1967	The Bobo	Matabosch
1969	Krakatoa—East of Java	Giovanni Borghese
1970	The Adventurers	Baron de Coyne
1981	The Final Conflict	DeCarlo
1984	Fear City	Carmine

EILEEN BRENNAN

(1935 -   )

One of the entertainment industry's preeminent comediennes and dramatic actresses, Brennan has won Emmys, the Golden Globe, most of Broadway's highest honors and an Oscar nomination for her part in *Private Benjamin*. Her career was interrupted in 1982 by a near-fatal accident in which she was hit by a car while crossing the street. Her courageous battle to overcome her injuries and the resultant dependency on pain-killers has served as an inspiration to others suffering similar misfortune.

Year	Movie	Character
1967	Divorce American Style	Eunice
1971	The Last Picture Show	Genevieve
1973	The Sting	Billie
1973	Scarecrow	Darlene
1975	At Long Last Love	Elizabeth
1975	Hustle	Paula Hollinger
1976	The Great Smokey Roadblock	Penelope
1976	Murder by Death	Tess Skeffington
1978	The Cheap Detective	Betty DeBoop
1978	FM	Mother
1980	Private Benjamin	Capt. Doreen Lewis
1982	Pandemonium	Special Appearance
1985	Clue	Mrs. Peacock
1988	The New Adventures of Pippi Longstocking	Miss Bannister
1988	Sticky Fingers	Stella
1990	Texasville	Genevieve
1990	White Palace	Judy
1990	Stella	Mrs. Wilkerson

WILFORD BRIMLEY

(1934 -   )

Widely regarded as one of the best character actors in the business, Brimley came to acting in his thirties after he lost his ranch in Idaho and needed money. Born in Salt Lake City, UT, he moved to Santa Monica, CA, at age six where his father worked in real estate. At the outbreak of the Korean Conflict, he left high school and enlisted in the U.S. Marine Corps where he spent a three year hitch in the Aleutian Islands. Brimley's horse-riding ability got him his start in countless film and TV westerns.

Year	Movie	Character
1979	The Electric Horseman	Farmer
1979	The China Syndrome	Ted Spindler
1980	Borderline	Scooter Jackson
1980	Brubaker	Rogers
1981	Absence of Malice	Wells
1982	The Thing	Blair
1982	Death Valley	Sheriff
1983	Tough Enough	Bill
1983	High Road to China	Bradley Tozer
1983	Ten to Midnight	Capt. Malone
1983	Tender Mercies	Harry
1984	The Stone Boy	George Jansen
1984	Hotel New Hampshire	Iowa Bob
1984	Country	Otis

(continued on page 505)

RICHARD BROOKS

(19?? -   )

Brooks, pictured above in a scene from *84 Charlie Mopic*, has appeared in a slew of movies since 1986. His most memorable performances have come in *To Sleep With Anger* where he played a frustrated L.A. buppie impatient with his Southern-bred parents' old-country thinking and in *Shakedown*. In that film, *Variety* stated that he made "a particularly strong impression" as the drug-dealing murder defendant.

Year	Movie	Character
1986	Good to Go	Chemist
1987	The Hidden	Sanchez
1988	Off Limits	xxx
1988	Shakedown	Michael Jones
1989	84 Charlie Mopic	OD
1989	Shocker	Rhino
1990	To Sleep With Anger	Babe Brother

BLAIR BROWN

(1948 -   )

Raised as an only child in Washington, D.C., and Virginia, acting was not always Brown's primary interest; at one point she wanted to be a doctor. Her formal training began after two years of college at the National Theatre School of Canada in Montreal. She once described herself as "very much a Taurus in a world of illusion. I've always stubbornly pursued the realities in life and my career—and searching for that truth is what acting is really all about."

Year	Movie	Character
1977	The Choirboys	Mrs. Lyles
1980	Altered States	Emily Jessup
1980	One Trick Pony	Marion
1981	Continental Divide	Nell
1988	Stealing Home	Ginny Wyatt
1992	Passed Away	Amy Scanlan

BRYAN BROWN

(1947 -   )

Born and raised in Australia, Brown never thought of becoming an actor until he became bored with his insurance job. Bright and athletic, he had turned down a university scholarship to get on with his life, only to end up studying actuarial tables. After quitting his job, he spent five years acting, writing and directing for the community play-house The Genesian Theatre. His professional career took off upon his move to England in 1972.

Year	Movie	Character
1979	Breaker Morant	Lt. Peter Handcock
1986	F/X	Rollie Tyler
1986	Tai-Pan	Tai-Pan
1988	Gorillas in the Mist	Bob Campbell
1988	Cocktail	Doug Coughlin
1991	F/X 2	Rollie Tyler

CLANCY BROWN

(1959 -   )

Born in the small town of Urbana, OH, where his father was a newspaper publisher and his mother was a concert pianist, Brown began acting at age 6 when he debuted in summer stock. A solid athlete, he attended Northwestern University on a track scholarship as a talented discus-thrower. After two seasons, his track coach saw him in a Northwestern production of *The Merchant of Venice* and told him that he was "a better actor than a discus-thrower."

Year	Movie	Character
1983	Bad Boys	Viking Lofgren
1985	The Bride	Viktor
1986	Highlander	Kurgen
1987	Extreme Prejudice	Sgt. Larry McRose
1988	Shoot to Kill	Steve
1990	Waiting for the Light	Joe
1990	Blue Steel	Nick Mann

REB BROWN

(1948 -   )

Brown debuted as a muscular basketball player in 1979's popular *Fast Break* and went on to play tough guys in a series of actioners. He was a Vietnam vet accompanying Gene Hackman into Laos on an M.I.A. search in *Uncommon Valor* and also as a friend of John Lithgow in *Distant Thunder*. Brown played the lead in the 1987 Italian muscleman film, *Yor, Hunter from the Future* and sparred with ex-Hulk, Lou Ferrigno in 1989's *Cage*.

Year	Movie	Character
1979	Fast Break	Bull
1983	Uncommon Valor	Blaster
1985	Howling II: Your Sister is a Werewolf	Ben White
1988	Distant Thunder	Harvey Nitz

ROSCOE LEE BROWNE

(1925 -   )

Actor, poet, writer, teacher and track star, Browne was born in Woodbury, NJ. He progressed through public schools to Lincoln University in Pennsylvania and then did post-graduate work in comparative literature and French at Vermont's Middlebury College and Columbia University. Browne returned to teach these subjects at Lincoln University, which conferred upon him the honorary degree of Doctor of Humane Letters. An international track star between 1946-56, his acting career began on the New York stage.

Year	Movie	Character
1967	The Comedians	Petit Pierre
1969	Topaz	Philippe Dubois
1970	The Liberation of L.B. Jones	Lord Byron Jones
1972	The Cowboys	Jebediah Nightlinger
1973	Superfly T.N.T.	Dr. Lamine Sonko
1974	Uptown Saturday Night	Congressman Lincoln
1976	Logan's Run	Box
1977	Twilight's Last Gleaming	James Forrest
1980	Nothing Personal	Paxton
1986	Jumpin' Jack Flash	Archer Lincoln
1986	Legal Eagles	Judge Dawkins
1992	The Mambo Kings	xxx

HORST BUCHHOLZ

(1933 -   )

Born in Berlin and, as a child, evacuated to Czechoslovakia during the war years, Buchholz gained his first fame in European films that were popular with American audiences. Following his success in Europe, he went to New York to co-star with Kim Stanley in the Broadway production of *Cheri*, which in turn brought him to the attention of American film producers.

Year	Movie	Character
1960	The Magnificent Seven	Chico
1961	Fanny	Marius
1961	One, Two, Three	Otto
1963	Nine Hours to Rama	Naturam Godse
1966	Marco, The Magnificent	Marco Polo
1966	That Man in Istanbul	Tony
1979	Avalanche Express	Scholten
1984	Sahara	von Glessing
1985	Code Name: Emerald	Walter Hoffman

BETTY BUCKLEY

ELLEN BURSTYN

(1947 -   )

Born in Big Spring, TX, Buckley graduated from Texas Christian University and worked for one year on a local newspaper before heading to New York to try her luck as an actress. On her first day there, she was cast as one of two women in the Broadway musical *1776*. She is a singer and composer, and spent four years portraying Abby on the hit television series *Eight is Enough* (1977-81).

Year	Movie	Character
1976	Carrie	Miss Collins
1983	Tender Mercies	Dixie
1987	Wild Thing	Leah
1988	Another Woman	Kathy
1988	Frantic	Sondra Walker
1993	Rain Without Thunder	Beverly Goldring

(1932 -   )

Born Edna Rae Gillooly in Detroit, Burstyn was in love with movies at an early age. A high school dropout, she eventually found her way to New York and the stage and then to Hollywood. In 1975, she won both a Tony (*Same Time, Next Year*) and an Oscar (*Alice Doesn't Live Here Anymore*). In 1982, she became the first female president of Actor's Equity in its 69-year history and was named co-artistic director with Al Pacino of the Actors Studio, succeeding the late Lee Strasberg.

Year	Movie	Character
1964	For Those Who Think Young	Dr. Pauline Thayer
1964	Goodbye Charlie	Franny
1971	The Last Picture Show	Lois Farrow
1973	The Exorcist	Mrs. MacNeil
1974	Harry and Tonto	Shirley
1975	Alice Doesn't Live Here Anymore	Alice Hyatt
1978	Same Time, Next Year	Doris
1980	Resurrection	Edna
1981	Silence of the North	Olive Fredrickson
1984	The Ambassador	Alex
1985	Twice in a Lifetime	Kate
1988	Hanna's War	Katalin
1991	Dying Young	Mrs. O'Neil
1993	The Cemetery Club	Esther Moskowitz

TONY BURTON

(19?? -)

Burton is best remembered as Apollo Creed's (actor Carl Weathers) trainer in the first four *Rocky* films. Apollo Creed was Stallone's rival-turned-friend who beat Rocky in the first movie, but lost to him in the second. They were friends by the third.

Year	Movie	Character
1976	Assault on Precinct 13	Wells
1980	Inside Moves	Lucius Porter
1985	Rocky IV	Duke
1991	House Party 2	Mr. Lee

STEVE BUSCEMI

(1958 -)

Growing up in suburban Long Island, Buscemi's heroes in high school were the comedians George Carlin and the late Freddie Prinze. Planning to become a stand-up comic and, then, an actor, he moved into Manhattan. He studied at the Actors Studio and worked at the Improv and Comedy Strip. Buscemi is a devotee of the films of the late directorJohn Cassavetes because they are actor-intensive and spontaneous-yet-controlled.

Year	Movie	Character
1987	Heart	Nicky
1988	Call Me	Switchblade
1989	Mystery Train	Charlie
1989	New York Stories	Gregory Stark
1990	Tales From the Darkside	Bellingham ("Lot 249")
1990	King of New York	Moses
1991	Barton Fink	Chet
1991	Billy Bathgate	Irving
1992	CrissCross	Louis
1993	Rising Sun	Willy "the Weasal" Wilhelm
1993	Trusting Beatrice	Danny

BILLY GREEN BUSH

(1935 -   )

Bush has been a Hollywood mainstay for over 20 years, but garnered his highest praise in his early 1970s pictures. In *Five Easy Pieces*, he was considered by critics to be "brilliantly accurate as the oil rigger on the lam" and "excellent as the lazy headed representative of grassroots America." His performance as the leader of a cattle drive in *Culpepper Cattle Company*, prompted *Time* to say, "Bush, so good as Jack Nicholson's hillbilly buddy in *Five Easy Pieces*, is even better here—prickly and sardonic."

Year	Movie	Character
1970	Five Easy Pieces	Elton
1970	Monte Walsh	Powder Kent
1972	Culpepper Cattle Company	Frank Culpepper
1972	Welcome Home, Soldier Boys	Sheriff
1973	Forty Carats	J.D. Rogers
1973	Electra Glide in Blue	Zipper Davis
1975	Alice Doesn't Live Here Anymore	Donald
1980	Tom Horn	Joe Belle
1984	The River	Harve Stanley
1986	Critters	Jay Brown
1986	The Hitcher	Trooper Donner
1993	Jason Goes to Hell: The Final Friday	Sheriff Landis

RED BUTTONS

(1919 -   )

Buttons grew up in a four-story walkup apartment building in the Bronx where four families shared one bathroom. The comedian and actor began singing on street corners at age 5 to earn a few pennies. Later he worked the nightclub circuit in the Catskills and went on to join Minsky's burlesque shows. He was famous during the 1950's for his television shows and appearances.

Year	Movie	Character
1961	One, Two, Three	M.P. Sergeant
1962	Five Weeks in a Balloon	Donald O'Shay
1962	Hatari!	Pockets
1962	The Longest Day	Pvt. John Steele
1964	Your Cheatin' Heart	Shorty Younger
1965	Harlow	Arthur Landau
1966	Stagecoach	Mr. Peacock
1972	The Poseidon Adventure	Martin
1976	Gable and Lombard	Cooper
1977	Viva Knieval!	Ben Andrews
1977	Pete's Dragon	Hoagy
1978	Movie, Movie	Jinks Murphy
1979	C.H.O.M.P.S.	Bracken
1980	When Time Ran Out...	Francis Fendly
1988	18 Again!	Charlie
1990	The Ambulance	Elias

GABRIEL BYRNE

(1950 -   )

Born in Dublin, Ireland, Byrne received a degree from Ireland's University College and worked as an archaeologist for a time. He then became a Spanish professor at a school for girls, where he required his students to improvise dramatic scenes using Spanish as their primary language. After work in both theater and television in England, he moved to America and found success in TV miniseries.

Year	Movie	Character
1981	Excalibur	Uther
1985	Defence of the Realm	Nick Mullen
1987	Siesta	Augustine
1987	Hello Again	Kevin Scanlon
1987	Lionheart	The Black Prince
1990	Miller's Crossing	Tom Reagan
1992	Cool World	Jack Deebs
1993	Point of No Return	Bob
1993	A Dangerous Woman	Mackey
1993	Into the West	Papa Riley

MICHAEL CALLAN

(1935 -   )

Born Martin Harris Calinoff, of Polish-Jewish stock in North Philadelphia, Callan was originally a dancer whose boyhood idol was Gene Kelly. After creating the role of Riff in the original Broadway hit production of *West Side Story*, Callan left the show to sign a seven-year contract with Columbia Pictures.

Year	Movie	Character
1961	Gidget Goes Hawaiian	Eddie Horner
1962	13 West Street	Chuck
1962	The Interns	Dr. Considine
1964	The New Interns	Alec
1965	Cat Ballou	Clay Boone
1972	The Magnificent Seven Ride!	Noah Forbes
1988	Freeway	Lt. Boyle

DEAN CAMERON

(1962 -   )

Cameron's screen career began in television in the early 1980s with such programs as *Things are Looking Up* (1983) and *Facts of Life* (1984). The native of Morrison, IL, studied acting in L.A. with Ron Burrus and with William Traylor and Peggy Feury at the Loft Studio. He is a founding member of L.A.'s Young Artists United and a member of that city's Christic Institute.

Year	Movie	Character
1987	Summer School	Chainsaw
1988	Bad Dreams	Ralph
1990	Men at Work	Pizza Man
1990	Rockula	Ralph

COLLEEN CAMP

(1953 -   )

Once known as "The Bird Girl of Hollywood" for her work with birds at Busch Gardens in Los Angeles, Camp was born in San Francisco and raised in the San Fernando Valley of California. Her work with the birds paid for drama lessons which enabled her to find work on such television programs as *Marcus Welby, M.D.* and *Love, American Style*.

Year	Movie	Character
1975	Smile	Connie Thompson
1979	Game of Death	Ann
1979	Apocalypse Now	Playmate
1981	They All Laughed	Christy Miller
1982	The Seduction	Robin
1983	Smokey and the Bandit 3	Dusty Trails
1983	Valley Girl	Sarah
1984	Joy of Sex	Liz
1985	Doin' Time	Catlett
1985	D.A.R.Y.L.	Elaine
1985	Police Academy 2: Their First Assignment	Kirkland
1985	Clue	Yvette
1987	Walk Like a Man	Rhonda Shand
1988	Illegally Yours	Molly Gilbert
1989	Wicked Stepmother	Jenny
1990	My Blue Heaven	Margaret Snow
1992	Wayne's World	xxx
1993	Sliver	Judy

J.D. CANNON

(1922 -)

He may be best remembered for his role as Chief of Detectives Peter Clifford on NBC's *McCloud* which lasted from 1970-77. Jack Cannon is a native of Salmon, ID, who moved to New York immediately after high school to study acting. Although he found artistic success with Joseph Papp's New York Shakespeare Festival, he eventually moved west to Hollywood for a steady paycheck.

Year	Movie	Character
1966	An American Dream	Lt. Leznicki
1967	Cool Hand Luke	Society Red
1969	Heaven with a Gun	Mace
1970	Cotton Comes to Harlem	Calhoun
1971	Lawman	Hurd Price
1973	Scorpio	Filchock
1980	Raise the Titanic!	Capt. Burke
1982	Death Wish II	New York D.A.
1989	Street Justice	xxx

KATE CAPSHAW

(1953 -)

After earning degrees in the History of Education and Learning Disabilities, Capshaw worked as a teacher in her hometown of St. Louis. Unhappy in her chosen profession, she fled to New York City with husband and child and became a model. She soon divorced, began acting in soap operas, did her first movie (*A Little Sex*) and finally packed her bags for Hollywood.

Year	Movie	Character
1982	A Little Sex	Katherine
1984	Windy City	Emily
1984	Dreamscape	Jane
1984	Best Defense	Laura
1984	Indiana Jones and the Temple of Doom	Willie Scott
1986	SpaceCamp	Andie
1986	Power	Sydney Betterman
1989	Black Rain	Joyce Kingsley
1990	Love at Large	Ellen McGraw
1991	My Heroes Have Always Been Cowboys	Jolie Meadows

HARRY CAREY, JR.

(1921 -   )

Active as a film actor for over 40 years, Carey is the son of the actor Harry Carey, Sr. (1878-1947). His career began after a five year stint in the navy during World War II. He was in semi-leading roles as cowboys or soldiers in films directed by his father's friend, John Ford, but moved to character parts fairly quickly. The native of Saugus, CA, gained some early acting experience with summer stock in Maine.

Year	Movie	Character
1961	Two Rode Together	Jackson Clay
1965	Shenandoah	Jenkins
1966	Alvarez Kelly	Cpl. Peterson
1967	The Way West	McBee
1969	The Undefeated	Webster
1970	Dirty Dingus Magee	Stuart
1971	Big Jake	Pop Dawson
1973	Cahill—U.S. Marshal	Hank
1976	Nickelodeon	Dobie
1980	UFOria	xxx
1980	The Long Riders	George Arthur
1982	Endangered Species	Dr. Emmer
1984	Gremlins	Anderson
1985	Mask	Red

(continued on page 505)

MICHELE CAREY

(1943 -   )

Formerly a child prodigy at the piano and a model, Carey moved to Hollywood from Denver. Queried after making her first movie, *El Dorado*, she stated, "I just tried to get the job done and go home."

Year	Movie	Character
1967	El Dorado	Joey MacDonald
1968	Live a Little, Love a Little	Bernice
1968	The Sweet Ride	Thumper
1970	Dirty Dingus Magee	Anna Hotwater

TIMOTHY CAREY

(1924 -   )

Carey has entertained movie audiences in a variety of movie genres, often in oddball roles. He was seen in westerns and beach movies in the 1960s. He played Lord High 'n' Low in the Monkees' vehicle *Head* and was a nut in an all-night restaurant in John Cassavetes *Minnie and Moskowitz*. 1976 found him in a mild sexploitation pic, *Chesty Anderson, USN*.

Year	Movie	Character
1961	One-Eyed Jacks	Howard Tetley
1964	Bikini Beach	South Dakota Slim
1965	Beach Blanket Bingo	South Dakota Slim
1967	The Long Ride Home	Billy Cat
1967	Waterhole #3	Hilb
1971	Minnie and Moskowitz	Morgan Morgan
1974	The Outfit	Menner
1982	Fast Walking	Bullet
1986	Echo Park	xxx

JULIE CARMEN

(1954 -   )

Carmen got her start in experimental Off-Broadway plays, some of which she has described as "off-off-awful." The native of Millburn, NJ, was an instant success in her screen debut, however, as the doomed mother of a small boy in John Cassavetes' *Gloria* and won a best supporting actress prize at the Venice Film Festival. A ballerina for seven years, Carmen fell in love with plays and acting at age 4 when her father took her to see a production of *Hansel and Gretel* at New York's Metropolitan Opera House.

Year	Movie	Character
1980	Gloria	Jeri Dawn
1980	Night of the Juggler	Marie
1983	Last Plane Out	Maria
1988	The Milagro Beanfield War	Nancy Mondragon
1988	The Penitent	Corina
1989	Paint It Black	Gina
1989	Fright Night Part II	Regine Dandridge

JOHN CARRADINE

(1906 - 1988)

Carradine was a famous character actor whose work spanned Hollywood's golden years and whose sons, David, Keith and Robert, carry on the family name and talent. He made more than 220 films in 60 years beginning in 1930 with Cecil B. De Mille's extravaganzas. He became typecast in horror and fantasy films because of his lean, gaunt looks, but was also welcome in Shirley Temple pictures. His acting career began after a stint as a sketch artist in New Orleans. Carradine died at 82 in Milan, Italy.

Year	Movie	Character
1962	The Man Who Shot Liberty Valance	Maj. Cassius Starbuckle
1964	The Patsy	Bruce Alden
1964	Cheyenne Autumn	Jeff Blair
1966	Munster, Go Home	Cruikshank
1969	They Ran for Their Lives	Laslow
1969	The Trouble With Girls	Drewcott
1972	Everything You Always Wanted to Know About Sex (But Were Afraid to Ask)	Dr. Bernardo
1972	Boxcar Bertha	H. Buckram Sartoris
1973	Terror in the Wax Museum	Dupree
1975	Shock Waves	Ben
1976	The Shootist	Beckum

(continued on page 505)

KEITH CARRADINE

(1951 -   )

When not acting in a film, music is the most important part of Carradine's life. He often has a film script in his lap and a guitar at his side when he travels. Memorable movie roles include that of the rock star in Robert Altman's *Nashville* and the photographer in *Pretty Baby* who befriends and sets up house with 12-year-old whore Brooke Shields. Born in San Mateo, CA, Carradine attended the exclusive Ojai Valley School, but left college after only three months.

Year	Movie	Character
1971	A Gunfight	Cowboy
1971	McCabe and Mrs. Miller	Cowboy
1973	Emperor of the North	Cigaret
1974	Thieves Like Us	Bowie
1975	Nashville	Tom Frank
1978	Pretty Baby	Bellocq
1979	An Almost Perfect Affair	Hal
1980	The Long Riders	Jim Younger
1981	Southern Comfort	Spencer
1984	Choose Me	Mickey
1987	Backfire	Reed
1988	The Moderns	Nick Hart
1989	Cold Feet	Monte Latham
1990	Daddy's Dyin'...Who's Got the Will?	Clarence
1991	The Ballad of the Sad Cafe	Marin Macy
1992	CrissCross	John Cross

ROBERT CARRADINE

(1954 -   )

The youngest of seven brothers and the third (along with David and Keith) to embrace the acting profession, Carradine originally wanted to be a race car driver. But this was not to be. As an understudy to Keith on a production of *Tobacco Road*, he took over the part after his brother was unable to complete it. Pleased with the remuneration he continued with acting full time.

Year	Movie	Character
1972	The Cowboys	Slim Honeycutt
1973	Mean Streets	Boy with gun
1975	Aloha, Bobby and Rose	Moxey
1976	Jackson County Jail	Bobby
1976	Cannonball	Jim
1977	Orca	Ken
1978	Coming Home	Bill Munson
1980	The Long Riders	Bob Younger
1980	The Big Red One	Zab
1981	Heartaches	Stanley
1984	Revenge of the Nerds	Lewis
1984	Just the Way You Are	Sam
1987	Number One With a Bullet	Berzak
1987	Revenge of the Nerds II: Nerds in Paradise	Lewis
1989	Buy & Cell	Herbie Altman
1989	Rude Awakening	Sammy

BARBARA CARRERA

(1945 -   )

Carrera switched from modeling to acting because, as she once said, "I got bored and I knew I wanted to do something else. I had a lot of creative energy and no outlet." A Nicaraguan, she grew up inside the U.S. Embassy compound in Nicaragua where her American-born father worked as a ArialBold. She believes that "the secret to modeling is to develop character before the camera. In addition to looking beautiful, you need to develop a personality, to add intrigue. I think that also applies to acting."

Year	Movie	Character
1977	The Island of Doctor Moreau	Maria
1980	When Time Ran Out...	Iolani
1981	Condorman	Natalia
1982	I, the Jury	Dr. Charlotte Bennett
1983	Never Say Never Again	Fatima
1983	Lone Wolf McQuade	Lola
1985	Wild Geese II	Kathy Lukas
1987	Love at Stake	Faith Stewart
1989	Loverboy	Alex Barnett
1989	Wicked Stepmother	Priscilla

ELPIDIA CARRILLO

T.K. CARTER

(1961 -)

Born in the small Mexican village of Pavacuara, Michoacan, Carrillo left home at 12 for the larger village of Uruapan to live with an older sister and find work. While waitressing and attending high school, she was spotted by a photographer who snapped her picture and sent it to the director Rafael Corkik. Carrillo's movie career began shortly thereafter with a small role in *Pafnucio Santo*.

(1957 -)

Actor and comedian, Carter was born and raised in Southern California. Show biz came early to him after winning a talent show contest in his hometown by mimicking Bill Cosby's famous Lone Ranger skit. His stand-up career followed and soon he was opening for acts like James Brown and Luther Vandross.

Year	Movie	Character
1982	The Border	Maria
1983	Beyond the Limit	Clara
1986	Salvador	Maria
1986	Let's Get Harry	Veronica
1987	Predator	Anna
1990	Predator 2	Anna

Year	Movie	Character
1980	Seems Like Old Times	Chester
1981	Southern Comfort	Cribbs
1982	The Thing	Nauls
1983	Doctor Detroit	Diavolo
1985	Runaway Train	Dave Prince
1987	He's My Girl	Reggie/Regina
1990	Ski Patrol	Iceman
1991	A Rage in Harlem	Smitty

VERONICA CARTWRIGHT

(1949 -   )

Known for giving Beaver Cleaver his first screen kiss in TV's *Leave It to Beaver* at age 10, Cartwright made the transition from child actress to adult actress. Born in England, but raised in California, she won an Emmy at age 14 for her role in *Tell Me Not in Numbers*, where she played a girl who "spoke" in numbers, not in words. Cartwright played Jessica Tandy's daughter in *The Birds*.

Year	Movie	Character
1962	The Children's Hour	Rosalie
1963	The Birds	Cathy Brenner
1963	Spencer's Mountain	Becky Spencer
1978	Goin' South	Hermine
1978	Invasion of the Body Snatchers	Nancy Bellicec
1979	Alien	Lambert
1983	The Right Stuff	Betty Grissom
1983	Nightmares	Claire
1986	Flight of the Navigator	Helen Freeman
1986	Wisdom	Samantha Wisdom
1987	The Witches of Eastwick	Felicia Alden
1987	Valentino Returns	Pat Gibbs
1992	Man Trouble	Helen Dextra

DAVID CARUSO

(1956 -   )

He has been a Hollywood player since the early 1980s, but Caruso has only recently garnered attention because of his nude scenes in *NYPD Blue*, television's first prime-time show with flashes of nudity. At first his bright red hair gave many in Hollywood doubts about his prospects. One agent even told him, "Your look is wrong, you've got red hair, nobody's going to know what to do with you." The New Yorker proved them wrong, however, after receiving much acclaim as the high-strung carhop in *Thief of Hearts*.

Year	Movie	Character
1982	First Blood	Mitch
1984	Thief of Hearts	Buddy Calamara
1986	Blue City	Joey Rayford
1987	China Girl	Johnny Mercury
1988	Twins	Al Greco
1990	King of New York	Dennis Gilley
1991	Hudson Hawk	Kit Kat
1993	Mad Dog and Glory	Mike

BERNIE CASEY

(1939 -   )

Casey spent eight years as a pro-football player with the L.A. Rams and the San Francisco 49ers before he switched his sights to acting. He is an accomplished painter whose work has been exhibited widely, and a poet with several books published. The actor grew up in a Columbus, OH, ghetto and was an outstanding student in high school, receiving several awards in scholarship and athletics. He has a B.A. and a M.A. in Fine Arts from Bowling Green State University.

Year	Movie	Character
1969	Guns of the Magnificent Seven	Cassie
1972	Hit Man	Tyrone
1972	Boxcar Bertha	Von Morton
1976	The Man Who Fell to Earth	Peters
1977	Brothers	David Thomas
1981	Sharky's Machine	Arch
1983	Never Say Never Again	Leiter
1984	Revenge of the Nerds	U.N. Jefferson
1985	Spies Like Us	Col. Rhombus
1987	Backfire	Clint
1987	Steele Justice	Reese
1988	I'm Gonna Git You Sucka	John Spade
1988	Rent-a-Cop	Lemar
1989	Bill & Ted's Excellent Adventure	Mr. Ryan
1990	Another 48 Hours	Kirkland Smith
1993	The Cemetery Club	John

ROSALIND CASH

(1938 -   )

A native of Atlantic City, NJ, Cash moved to New York City immediately after graduating from high school where she was an honor student. In New York, she took English literature classes at City College and entered an acting workshop at the Harlem YMCA. Broadway, summer stock, road tours and a season of children's theater at Washington's Arena Stage followed. Her career took off after her forming and working with the Negro Ensemble Company.

Year	Movie	Character
1971	The Omega Man	Lisa
1972	The New Centurions	Lorrie
1972	Hickey & Boggs	Nyona
1972	Melinda	Terry Davis
1974	Uptown Saturday Night	Sarah Jackson
1982	Wrong is Right	Mrs. Ford

SEYMOUR CASSEL

(1935 -   )

Cassel, known for his long association with John Cassavetes, has been in four of the actor/director's films. His role in *Faces* (1968) won him an Oscar nomination and the New York Film Critic's Circle Award as best supporting actor. He is an accomplished stage director as well, having received the Los Angeles Critics' Award for his production of *Jesse and the Bandit* at the L.A. Stage Theater

Year	Movie	Character
1968	Coogan's Bluff	Young Hood
1971	Minnie and Moskowitz	Moskowitz
1977	Valentino	George Ullman
1977	Black Oak Conspiracy	Homer
1978	Convoy	Gov. Haskins
1979	The Ravagers	Blindman
1979	Sunburn	Dobbs
1979	California Dreaming	Duke
1980	The Mountain Men	LaBont
1981	King of the Mountain	Barry Tanner
1986	Eye of the Tiger	Sheriff
1987	Tin Men	Cheese
1988	Johnny Be Good	Wallace Gibson
1989	Wicked Stepmother	Feldshine
1990	Dick Tracy	Sam Catchem
1991	White Fang	Skunker
1993	Boiling Point	Leach
1993	Indecent Proposal	Mr. Shackleford

JOANNA CASSIDY

(1944 -   )

Born and raised in New Jersey, Cassidy studied art for one year at Syracuse University before dropping out to marry a young doctor. Her professional career began in California as a model struggling to raise two children by herself after her marriage dissolved. Television and film roles soon followed.

Year	Movie	Character
1973	The Laughing Policeman	Monica
1974	Bank Shot	El
1974	The Outfit	Rita
1976	Stay Hungry	Joe Mason
1977	The Late Show	Laura Birdwell
1982	Blade Runner	Zhora
1983	Under Fire	Claire
1986	Club Paradise	Terry Hamlin
1988	Who Framed Roger Rabbit	Dolores
1988	1969	Ev
1989	The Package	Eileen Gallagher
1990	Where the Heart Is	Jean McBain
1991	Don't Tell Mom the Babysitter's Dead	Rose Lindsey

PHOEBE CATES

(1963 -   )

After a serious knee injury ended her hopes of becoming a ballerina, Cates turned to modeling. She quickly rose to become a top international cover girl, travelling to all corners of the world on different assignments. Her acting career began after she was discovered while dancing at Studio 54 in New York.

Year	Movie	Character
1982	Fast Times at Ridgemont High	Linda Barrett
1982	Paradise	Sarah
1983	Private School	Christine
1984	Gremlins	Kate
1987	Date With an Angel	Patty Winston
1988	Bright Lights, Big City	Amanda
1989	Heart of Dixie	Aiken
1989	Shag	Carson
1990	I Love You to Death	Girl at Disco
1990	Gremlins 2 The New Batch	Kate Beringer
1991	Drop Dead Fred	Elizabeth
1993	Bodies, Rest & Motion	Carol

KIM CATTRALL

(1956 -   )

The Canadian actress has been acting since she was eleven when she studied and performed with the London Academy of Music and Dramatic Arts. Her screen debut came after graduating from New York's American Academy of Dramatic Arts when Otto Preminger cast her in his 1975 picture *Rosebud*. Cattrall co-starred with Kurt Russell as a local attorney with green eyes in *Big Trouble in Little China* and played an Ivy-League type in *Police Academy*.

Year	Movie	Character
1980	Tribute	Sally Haines
1981	Porky's	Honeywell
1981	Ticket to Heaven	Ruthie
1984	Police Academy	Karen
1985	Turk 182!	Danny Boudreau
1986	Big Trouble in Little China	Gracie Law
1987	Mannequin	Emmy
1988	Masquerade	Brooke Morrison
1988	Midnight Crossing	Lexa Shubb
1990	Honeymoon Academy	Chris Nelson
1990	The Bonfire of the Vanities	Judy McCoy
1991	Star Trek VI: The Undiscovered Country	Lt. Valeris
1992	Split Second	Michelle

JOHN CAZALE

(1936 - 1978)

The intense actor was Al Pacino's brother in *The Godfather, I and II*, and did a good job of scene-stealing. A Boston native, Cazale graduated from B.U., performed in regional theater and won a couple of Obies. He was a partner to Gene Hackman in Francis Ford Coppola's electronic bugging picture, *The Conversation*, and to Al Pacino again in *Dog Day Afternoon*. He died at 42 of cancer in New York.

Year	Movie	Character
1972	The Godfather	Fredo Corleone
1974	The Godfather, Part II	Fredo Corleone
1974	The Conversation	Stan
1975	Dog Day Afternoon	Sal
1978	The Deerhunter	Stan

GEORGE CHAKIRIS

(1933 -   )

Born to parents of Greek extraction in Norwood, OH, Chakiris had wanted to be an actor and a dancer ever since his high school days in Arizona and California. After high school he held down a day job in L.A. while studying nights at the American School of Dance. His dancing abilities landed him small roles in screen musicals. But real success came with his Oscar-winning portrayal of a young Puerto Rican gang leader in the film version of *West Side Story*.

Year	Movie	Character
1961	West Side Story	Bernardo
1962	Diamond Head	Dr. Dean Kahana
1963	Kings of the Sun	Balam
1964	Flight from Ashiya	Lt. John Gregg
1964	633 Squadron	Lt. Erik Bergman
1969	The Big Cube	Johnny

STOCKARD CHANNING

(1944 -   )

A native of New York City, Channing graduated cum laude from Radcliffe and overcame parental opposition to pursue her acting career. Theatrical training came with various repertory companies in New York, Boston and Washington. She achieved success on the New York stage and remains known primarily for her work in theater.

Year	Movie	Character
1971	The Hospital	xxx
1972	Up the Sandbox	Judy Stanley
1975	The Fortune	Freddie
1976	The Big Bus	Kitty Baxter
1978	The Cheap Detective	Bess
1978	Grease	Rizzo
1979	The Fish that Saved Pittsburgh	Mona Mondieu
1982	Safari 3000	J.J.
1983	Without a Trace	Jocelyn Norris
1986	Heartburn	Julie
1988	A Time of Destiny	Margaret
1989	Staying Together	Nancy Trainer
1991	Meet the Applegates	Jane Applegate
1993	Married to It	Iris Morden

MILES CHAPIN

(1954 -   )

According to Chapin, he was born and raised in Manhattan "amidst the worlds of music, opera, theater and film." His father managed the Metropolitan Opera while his mother served on several arts boards including the New York State Council on the Arts. He was spotted by a talent scout while singing in the Children's Chorus of the New York City Opera. His film debut came at age 8 in *Ladybug Ladybug*.

Year	Movie	Character
1971	Bless the Beasts and Children	Shecker
1979	French Postcards	Joel
1979	Hair	Steve
1981	Buddy, Buddy	Eddie the Bellhop
1981	The Funhouse	Richie
1982	Pandemonium	xxx
1983	Get Crazy	Sammy

GERALDINE CHAPLIN

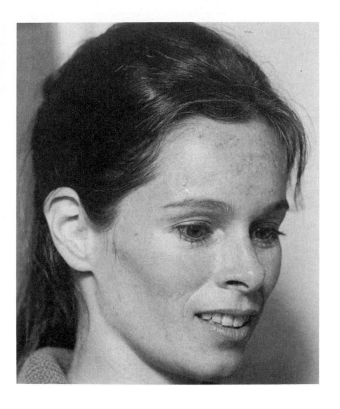

MAURY CHAYKIN

(1944 -   )

The eldest of Charlie Chaplin's eight children by his second wife Oona O'Neill, Chaplin is American by birth, British by extraction and European by adoption. She grew up in Switzerland from the age of eight, and eventually moved to London to attend the Royal Ballet School. Her trademark was a crazy, funny eccentric in the films of Robert Altman in the mid-1970s such as *Nashville*, *Buffalo Bill and the Indians* and *A Wedding*.

(1949 -   )

During his college days at the University of Buffalo, Chaykin and friends formed the "Swamp Fox Group", an acting troupe that toured the world performing original material. After college, he spent a few years of show business unemployment in New York before his career got a needed boost via a play in Canada. Since then, he has performed on both sides of the border in film, theater and television.

Year	Movie	Character
1965	Doctor Zhivago	Tonya
1970	The Hawaiians	Purity
1974	The Three Musketeers	Anne of Austria
1975	The Four Musketeers	Anne of Austria
1975	Nashville	Opal
1976	Buffalo Bill and the Indians,or Sitting Bull's History Lesson	Annie Oakley
1980	The Mirror Crack'd	Ella Zielinsky
1988	The Moderns	Nathalie de Ville
1992	Chaplin	Hannah Chaplin

Year	Movie	Character
1980	Nothing Personal	Kanook
1984	Mrs. Soffel	Guard Reynolds
1984	Harry and Son	Lawrence
1985	Turk 182!	Man in wheelchair
1986	The Vindicator	Burt
1987	The Bedroom Window	Pool Player
1987	Wild Thing	Trask
1988	Twins	Burt Klane
1988	Caribe	Capt. Burdoch
1988	Iron Eagle II	Downs
1988	Stars and Bars	Freeborn
1989	Millennium	Roger Keane
1989	Breaking In	Tucci
1990	Mr. Destiny	Guzelman
1990	Where the Heart Is	Harry
1990	Dances With Wolves	Major Fambrough
1993	Josh and S.A.M.	Pizza Man
1993	Money for Nothing	Vincente Goldoni

LOIS CHILES

(1950 -   )

A Texan, Chiles moved to New York to attend Finch College after a brief stay at the University of Texas. There, she fell into modeling and was soon represented by the prestigious Wilhelmina agency. To break into films, she ditched her modeling career, moved to L.A. and studied acting full time. Perhaps her best known film role has been that of James Bond's girl in outer space in *Moonraker* where she played a CIA agent working undercover as a NASA scientist.

Year	Movie	Character
1973	The Way We Were	Carol Ann
1974	The Great Gatsby	Jordan Baker
1978	Death on the Nile	Linnet Ridgeway
1978	Coma	Nancy Greenly
1979	Moonraker	Holly Goodhead
1986	Sweet Liberty	Leslie
1987	Creepshow 2	Annie Lansing
1987	Broadcast News	Jennifer Mack
1988	Twister	Virginia
1989	Say Anything...	Mrs. Court

DENNIS CHRISTOPHER

(1955 -   )

Born Dennis Correlli in Philadelphia, Christopher credits a high school English teacher for steering him towards acting. "I was well on my way to becoming just another South Philadelphia creep," he has recalled. "I was into being tough, one of the gang, hanging out. That teacher taught me everything—art, beauty, creativity, communication. And I went with it." Christopher has garnered most of his attention with his role as the bicycle-racing Italophile in the film, *Breaking Away*.

Year	Movie	Character
1977	9/30/55	Eugene
1979	Breaking Away	Dave Stohler
1979	California Dreaming	T.T.
1981	Chariots of Fire	Charles Paddock
1982	Don't Cry, It's Only Thunder	Brian
1986	Jake Speed	Desmond Floyd
1990	Circuitry Man	Leech

CHARLES CIOFFI

(1935 -   )

Cioffi was, according to him, "coralled into playing character parts" while a student in high school because of his size and deep voice. He has B.A. and M.A. degrees from Michigan State and has taught classes at the University of Minnesota on the history of live television. He is also a charter member of the Tyrone Guthrie Theater in Minneapolis. Cioffi played a family friend and business associate of a man missing in New York in *Klute* and an ominous U.S. military attaché in *Missing*.

Year	Movie	Character
1971	Klute	Peter Cable
1971	Shaft	Vic Androzzi
1973	Lucky Luciano	Vito Genovese
1973	The Thief Who Came to Dinner	Henderling
1974	Crazy Joe	Coletti
1976	The Next Man	Fouad
1979	Time After Time	Lt. Mitchell
1982	Missing	Capt. Ray Tower
1983	All the Right Moves	Pop
1985	Remo Williams: The Adventure Begins	George Grove
1992	Newsies	xxx

CANDY CLARK

(1947 -   )

After a childhood spent in Oklahoma and Texas, Clark went to New York with plans to stay only two weeks. It was soon clear that she wouldn't be returning to Texas. A modeling career led to Hollywood where she was Oscar-nominated for her role in *American Graffiti* as the young girl who agrees to go cruising with Charles Martin Smith after he tells her she looks like Connie Stevens. Clark was Roy Scheider's helpful girlfriend in *Blue Thunder* and David Bowie's mate in *The Man Who Fell to Earth*.

Year	Movie	Character
1972	Fat City	Faye
1973	American Graffiti	Debbie
1976	The Man Who Fell to Earth	Mary-Lou
1978	The Big Sleep	Camilla Sternwood
1979	More American Graffiti	Debbie Dunham
1983	Blue Thunder	Kate
1983	Amityville 3-D	Melanie
1985	Cat's Eye	Sally Ann
1986	At Close Range	Mary Sue
1988	The Blob	Fran Hewitt
1991	Cool as Ice	Grace Winslow
1992	Buffy, the Vampire Slayer	Buffy's Mom

FRED CLARK

(1914 - 1968)

Comic actor Clark, with his bald pate and slow-burn style played the neighbor in the *Burns and Allen Show* for 74 episodes, appeared in 12 Milton Berle shows, did commercials for a dog food company, also starred on Broadway and in London, and played the heavy in movies. He took a pre-med course at Stanford, but decided to become an actor and, on a scholarship, studied at the American Academy of Dramatic Arts in New York. He died of a liver problem in Santa Monica, CA.

Year	Movie	Character
1960	Bells are Ringing	Larry Hastings
1960	Visit to a Small Planet	Roger Putnam Spelding
1963	Move Over, Darling	Mr. Codd
1965	Dr. Goldfoot and the Bikini Machine	D.J. Pevney
1965	John Goldfarb, Please Come Home	Heinous Overreach

MATT CLARK

(1936 -   )

A native of Arlington, VA, Clark attended George Washington University in D.C. after a two-year stint in the U.S. Army. He left school to go to New York where he studied with the renowned drama coach Herbert Berghof, and became a member of Julian Beck and Judith Malina's famous Living Theater. Notable performances on the New York stage led to film and television roles. Clark played an undercover man working with Burt Reynolds to infiltrate a gang of bootleggers in *White Lightning*.

Year	Movie	Character
1968	Will Penny	Romulus
1969	The Bridge at Remagen	Col. Jellicoe
1970	Monte Walsh	Rufus Brady
1972	The Life and Times of Judge Roy Bean	Nick the Grub
1972	Culpepper Cattle Company	Pete
1972	Jeremiah Johnson	Qualen
1973	The Laughing Policeman	Coroner
1973	White Lightning	Dude Watson
1973	Emperor of the North	Yardlet
1974	The Terminal Man	Gerhard
1975	Hearts of the West	Jackson
1977	Outlaw Blues	Billy Bob
1978	The Driver	Red Plainsclothesman

(continued on page 505)

SUSAN CLARK

(1940 -   )

The Canadian actress began her career in 1960 with studies at London's Royal Academy of Dramatic Arts and appearances in repertory productions in England. Upon her return to Canada she established a solid TV career and soon thereafter signed a 10-year contract with Universal Studios. She played detective Gene Hackman's wife in *Night Moves* and a New York City probation officer who falls for Clint Eastwood in *Coogan's Bluff.*

Year	Movie	Character
1967	Banning	Cynthia
1968	Coogan's Bluff	Julie
1968	Madigan	Tricia Bentley
1969	Tell Them Willie Boy Is Here	Liz Arnold
1971	Valdez is Coming	Gay
1971	Skin Game	Ginger
1973	Showdown	Kate
1974	The Midnight Man	Linda
1974	Airport 1975	Mrs. Patroni
1975	Night Moves	Ellen
1979	Murder by Decree	Mary Kelly
1979	The North Avenue Irregulars	Anne
1979	Promises in the Dark	Fran Koenig
1981	Nobody's Perfekt	Carol
1981	Porky's	Cherry Forever
1986	Double Negative	xxx

DAVID CLENNON

(1943 -   )

A veteran of stage, film and television, Clennon studied at the Yale Drama School for three years and spent an additional year in the school's professional acting company. He's done Off-Broadway and regional theater and has been a regular performer at New Haven's famous Long Wharf Theater. He spent two seasons on TV's *thirtysomething* as Miles Drentell, the cold, cunning head of a large advertising firm. The actor hails from Waukegan, IL.

Year	Movie	Character
1973	The Paper Chase	Toombs
1978	Coming Home	Tim
1979	Being There	Thomas Franklin
1981	Ladies and Gentlemen, The Fabulous Stains	Dave
1982	Missing	Consul Phil Putnam
1982	The Escape Artist	Newspaper Editor
1982	The Thing	Palmer
1983	Star 80	Geb
1983	The Right Stuff	Liaison Man
1984	Falling In Love	Brian Gilmore
1985	Sweet Dreams	Randy Hughes
1986	Legal Eagles	Blanchard
1987	He's My Girl	Mason Morgan
1988	Betrayed	Jack Carpenter
1988	The Couch Trip	Lawrence Baird
1990	Downtown	Jerome Sweet
1992	Man Trouble	Lewie Duart

87

RANDALL "TEX" COBB

(19?? -   )

Cobb was a professional boxer before becoming an actor. He competed in the WBC Heavyweight Championship in 1982 and the PKA Heavyweight Championship in 1984. In fact, his film debut was in MGM/UA's boxing movie, *The Champ* in 1979. One of his most memorable roles is that of the motorcycle-riding baby hunter in *Raising Arizona*. He has done television as well, appearing in such action series as *Miami Vice*, *MacGyve*r and *Hardcastle and McCormick*.

Year	Movie	Character
1983	Uncommon Valor	Sailor
1986	The Golden Child	Til
1987	Critical Condition	Box
1987	Raising Arizona	Leonard Smalls
1989	Fletch Lives	Ben Dover
1989	Blind Fury	Slag
1989	Buy & Cell	Wolf
1990	Ernest Goes to Jail	Lyle
1992	Diggstown	Wolf Forrester

IMOGENE COCA

(1908 -   )

Together with her partner, Sid Caesar, actress/comedienne Imogene Coca entertained America weekly between 1950 and 1954 on the legendary TV program, *Your Show of Shows*. The comedy/variety show was broadcast live for 90 minutes and included sketches by the two hosts, song and dance numbers, and top-name guest stars. Coca was born in Philadelphia and made her Broadway debut in *New Faces* in 1934.

Year	Movie	Character
1963	Under The Yum Yum Tree	Dorkus
1978	Rabbit Test	Madam Marie
1983	National Lampoon's Vacation	Aunt Edna
1984	Nothing Lasts Forever	Daisy

GEORGE COE

(19?? -   )

Coe's career began on the stage and in the early television shows emanating from New York, notably the *Armstrong Circle Theater* and the *U.S. Steel Hour*. Theater work includes Broadway, numerous stock productions and several national tours. Coe attended New York's Hofstra University and the American Academy of Dramatic Arts. He played ad exec Dustin Hoffman's boss in *Kramer vs. Kramer*.

Year	Movie	Character
1979	The House of God	xxx
1979	Kramer vs. Kramer	Jim O'Connor
1984	Micki + Maude	Govenor Lanford
1985	Remo Williams:	
	The Adventure Begins	Gen. Scott Watson
1986	Head Office	Sen. Issel
1987	Best Seller	Graham
1987	Blind Date	Harry Gruen
1989	Cousins	Phil
1991	The End of Innocence	Dad

DABNEY COLEMAN

(1932 -   )

Often portraying villains, Coleman once said, "I've played good guys and nice guys, but the truth is that I'd rather be nasty than nice. The bad guys are always better written and more fun to play." A native of Texas, Coleman attended Virginia Military Institute and served in the U.S. Army. He dropped out of the University of Texas Law School to study acting at New York's Neighborhood Playhouse.

Year	Movie	Character
1965	The Slender Thread	Charlie
1966	This Property is Condemned	Salesman
1968	The Scalphunters	Jed
1969	The Trouble With Girls	Harrison
1969	Downhill Racer	Mayo
1973	Cinderella Liberty	Executive Officer
1974	The Dove	Charles Huntley
1974	The Towering Inferno	Asst. Fire Chief
1975	The Other Side of the Mountain	Dave McCoy
1975	Bite the Bullet	Jack Parker
1976	Midway	Capt. Murray Arnold
1977	Rolling Thunder	Maxwell
1977	Viva Knieval!	Ralph Thompson
1979	North Dallas Forty	Emmett

(continued on page 506)

JOHN COLICOS

(1928 -)

Colicos started out as a stage actor in 1946 in his native Canada and went on to perform in hundreds of plays on three continents for more than two decades before appearing in front of a camera. He went to Hollywood in the early-1970s and spent twelve years there. He moved back to Canada in 1986 because, as he once explained, "I was homesick, typecast and bored doing the same role over and over again." One of the reasons he remained so long in California was his passion for horseback riding.

Year	Movie	Character
1969	Anne of the Thousand Days	Cromwell
1970	Red Sky at Morning	Jimbob Buel
1971	Raid on Rommel	Mackenzie
1971	Doctors' Wives	Mort
1972	The Wrath of God	Colonel Santilla
1973	Scorpio	McLeod
1976	Drum	Bernard
1976	Breaking Point	Vincent Karbone
1979	Battlestar: Galactica	Count Baltar
1979	The Changeling	Capt. DeWitt
1981	The Postman Always Rings Twice	Nick Papadakis
1987	Nowhere to Hide	Gen. Howard

MARGARET COLIN

(1957 -)

Colin began her career in soap operas. She was Paige Madison in *The Edge of Night* and the flamboyant Margo Montgomery in *As the World Turns*. She stayed with that popular daytime drama until she took a starring role as a young Boston assistant D.A. in the prime-time series *Foley Square* in 1985. The actress grew up on Long Island's south shore and attended Hofstra University.

Year	Movie	Character
1986	Pretty in Pink	English Teacher
1986	Something Wild	Irene
1987	Like Father, Like Son	Ginnie Armbruster
1987	3 Men and a Baby	Rebecca
1989	True Believer	Kitty Greer
1990	Martians Go Home	Sara Brody
1991	The Butcher's Wife	Robyn
1993	Amos & Andrew	Judy Gillman

STEPHEN COLLINS

(1947 -   )

Often cast as the clean-cut, all-American boy type, the actor has been a fixture in film, television and theater since his 1972 Broadway debut in *Moonchildren*. Born in Iowa, but raised in New York, Collins is a graduate of Amherst College.

Year	Movie	Character
1976	All the President's Men	Hugh Sloan, Jr.
1979	Star Trek—The Motion Picture	Decker
1979	The Promise	Michael
1980	Loving Couples	Gregg
1985	Brewster's Millions	Warren Cox
1986	Jumpin' Jack Flash	Marty Phillips
1986	Choke Canyon	David Lowell
1990	Stella	Stephen Dallas

ANJANETTE COMER

(1942 -   )

Television and movie roles came in a rush for Comer. A Texas native, she was determined not to be just another Hollywood starlet. She honed her craft at the renowned Pasadena Playhouse for two years before taking feature roles in such successful 1960s TV series as *Gunsmoke*, *Dr. Kildare*, *Ben Casey*, *Combat* and *Bonanza*. Leading roles in films came next.

Year	Movie	Character
1965	The Loved One	Aimee Thanatogenos
1966	The Appaloosa	Trini
1967	Banning	Carol
1967	Guns for San Sebastian	Kinita
1973	The Manchu Eagle Murder Caper Mystery	Arlevia

DIDI CONN

(1951 -)

Conn's fling with Hollywood movies was, according to her, not very satisfying. She has recalled her debut in *You Light Up My Life* as "a very nasty experience" and that her next role, in *Almost Summer*, had very little relevance for her: "I was 26, playing a 17-year-old. In my real life, I was going through a divorce, and in that movie, I had to have a pimple problem." The Brooklyn-born actress played Robert Guillaume's secretary on the TV sitcom *Benson* for four seasons (1981-85). She broke in with TV commercials in 1973.

Year	Movie	Character
1977	You Light Up My Life	Laurie
1978	Almost Summer	Donna
1978	Grease	Frenchy
1982	Grease 2	Frenchy

JENNIFER CONNELLY

(1970 -)

Born in the Catskill Mountains of New York State, Connelly was modeling from age 10 and made her first acting appearances in TV commercials and a music video for the rock band Duran Duran. She began making movies during her vacations from school.

Year	Movie	Character
1984	Once Upon a Time in America	xxx
1986	Labyrinth	Sarah
1989	Some Girls	Gabriella
1990	The Hot Spot	Gloria Harper
1991	The Rocketeer	Jenny
1991	Career Opportunities	Josie McClellan

MICHAEL CONSTANTINE

(1927 -   )

The New York-trained actor went to Hollywood in the early 1950s and once recalled, "In those days there was a combination of respect and contempt. Respect came out of the fact that they knew you were a real actor and not some pretty boy trying to be a movie star. Contempt came from the fact they thought you might be one of these Method people and you were going to show up late and you were going to hold up production with your preparation." Constantine was principal Kaufman in TV's *Room 222* (1969-74).

Year	Movie	Character
1961	The Hustler	Big John
1966	Hawaii	Mason
1969	Justine	Memlik Pasha
1969	If It's Tuesday, This Must Be Belgium	Jack Harmon
1969	The Reivers	Mr. Binford
1979	The North Avenue Irregulars	Marv
1985	Pray for Death	Newman
1987	In the Mood	Mr. Wisecarver
1989	Prancer	Mr. Stewart/Santa
1993	My Life	Bill Ivanovich

RICHARD CONTE

(1914 - 1975)

Often cast as a Mafioso in movies, the talented character actor appeared in 75 Hollywood films after his Broadway career and guest-starred in several TV series. Born in Jersey City, NJ, Conte was a rebellious kid whose acting technique grew from his roots. His father was a barber and his friend and co-star was Frank Sinatra. His first two notable films were war dramas and he was outstanding. Conte died at 65 of a massive heart attack at the UCLA Medical Center.

Year	Movie	Character
1960	Ocean's Eleven	Anthony Bergdorf
1964	Circus World	Aldo Alfredo
1965	The Greatest Story Ever Told	Barabbas
1965	Synanon	Reid
1966	Assault on a Queen	Tony Moreno
1967	Hotel	Dupere
1967	Tony Rome	Lt. Santini
1972	The Godfather	Barzini

| **TOM CONTI** | **KEVIN CONWAY** |

| **(1941 -   )** | **(1942 -   )** |

Often likened to a British Al Pacino, Conti was born in Glasgow, Scotland, the son of a Scottish mother and Italian father. He originally wanted to be a musician, but became hooked on drama at Glasgow University. He has performed with the Royal Shakespeare Company, one of the world's greatest theater companies, and first achieved fame on BBC-TV. Film roles did not come until later in his life.

The New York native was 24 before he even had an inkling that he might be an actor. An IBM sales analyst at the time, Conway went to see a play at the insistence of a girl he was dating. The girlfriend further insisted that he take acting lessons, and, to his surprise, while studying at the Dramatic Workshop at Carnegie Hall, he enjoyed them. Although he has made Hollywood movies, his base is New York and the theater.

Year	Movie	Character
1983	Merry Christmas,	
	Mr. Lawrence	Colonel John Lawrence
1983	Reuben, Reuben	Gowan McGland
1984	American Dreamer	Alan
1986	Miracles	Dr. Roger Briggs
1986	Saving Grace	Pope Leo XIV
1989	Shirley Valentine	Costas

Year	Movie	Character
1978	Paradise Alley	Stitch
1978	F.I.S.T.	Vince Doyle
1981	The Funhouse	Barker
1984	Flashpoint	Brook
1988	Homeboy	Graziano
1991	Rambling Rose	Dr. Martinson
1991	One Good Cop	Lt. Danny Quinn
1992	Jennifer Eight	Citrine

KEITH COOGAN

(1970 -)

The grandson of Jackie Coogan, Hollywood's first child star, this Coogan began his acting career at age 5 with TV commercials and kiddie parts in such 1970s TV shows as *CHiPs*, *The Love Boat* and *Fantasy Island*.

Year	Movie	Character
1987	Adventures in Babysitting	Brad
1987	Hiding Out	Patrick Morenski
1989	Under the Boardwalk	Andy
1989	Cousins	Mitch Kozinski
1990	Book of Love	Crutch Krane
1991	Don't Tell Mom the Babysitter's Dead	Kenny Crandell
1991	Toy Soldiers	Snuffy Bradberry

JACKIE COOPER

(1922 -)

Cooper was a popular child star in the 1930s and won an Oscar nomination for best actor, at age 8, in *Skippy*. He has been seen sporadically in films as an adult and is more likely to be behind the camera as a director or a producer in the television business. His 1981 autobiography makes clear that success at an early age had its downside.

Year	Movie	Character
1971	The Love Machine	Danton Miller
1978	Superman	Perry White
1980	Superman II	Perry White
1983	Superman III	Perry White
1987	Surrender	Ace
1987	Superman IV: The Quest for Peace	Perry White

GLENN CORBETT

(1934 - 1993)

Corbett divided his time equally between television and feature films. Memorable movie roles include the part of Pat Garrett, the sheriff who guns down Billy the Kid in John Wayne's *Chisum*. He replaced George Maharis as the co-star in television's *Route 66* and had a recurring role in *Dallas*. After his character was eliminated from that series he stayed with the production company as a dialogue director for three years. The L.A. native died at 59 of lung cancer in San Antonio, TX.

Year	Movie	Character
1960	The Mountain Road	Collins
1960	Man on a String	Frank Sanford
1960	All the Young Men	Wade
1961	Homicidal	Karl
1965	Shenandoah	Jacob
1970	Chisum	Pat Garrett
1971	Big Jake	O'Brien
1976	Midway	Lt.Cmdr. John Waldron

BARRY CORBIN

(1940 -   )

Known for his portrayals of good ol' boys, lawmen and jowly generals, Corbin has said: "I've always wanted to be a character actor. One of the first Hollywood actors I admired was Walter Brennan." Very active during the 1980s in films, the Texas native attributes his success partly to luck saying "I'd prefer to downplay the luck part and say it's all because of my pluck and ability—why I'm working. But it's not. It's because I happened to be somewhere at a time when they needed somebody like me."

Year	Movie	Character
1980	Urban Cowboy	Uncle Bob
1980	Stir Crazy	Warden Walter Sampson
1982	Honkytonk Man	Arnspriger
1982	The Best Little Whorehouse in Texas	C.J.
1982	Six Pack	Sheriff
1983	WarGames	General Beringer
1983	The Man Who Loved Women	Roy
1983	The Ballad of Gregorio Cortez	Abernathy
1985	My Science Project	Lew Harlan
1986	Nothing in Common	Andrew Woolridge
1987	Under Cover	Sgt. Irwin Lee
1988	It Takes Two	George Lawrence
1988	Critters 2: The Main Course	Harv
1988	Permanent Record	Jim Sinclair
1989	Who's Harry Crumb?	P.J. Downing
1990	Short Time	Captain
1990	Ghost Dad	Mr. Collins
1990	The Hot Spot	Sheriff
1991	Career Opportunities	Officer Don

ALEX CORD

(1931 -   )

Cord overcame childhood polio to become a star rodeo rider, Shakespearean actor and star of the London stage. His theater training also included the study of Method acting with Lee Strasberg in New York. He did a number of TV shows, including several segments of *Route 66* before signing a seven-year, multiple picture contract with Columbia. He was born Alex Viespi on Long Island, NY.

Year	Movie	Character
1965	Synanon	Zankie Albo
1966	Stagecoach	Ringo
1968	A Minute to Pray, a Second to Die	Clay McCord
1968	The Brotherhood	Vince
1978	Grayeagle	Grayeagle

JEFF COREY

(1914 -   )

Corey became an actor because, as he has said: "I just didn't want to relinquish the fun of being young and imaginative and making believe." A combat photographer in World War II, he was blacklisted during the Red Scare of the 1950s and unable to find work. During this period he began private acting classes in Hollywood for which he became extremely well known and respected.

Year	Movie	Character
1964	Lady in a Cage	The Wino
1966	Seconds	Mr. Ruby
1967	In Cold Blood	Hickock's Father
1968	The Boston Strangler	John Asgeirsson
1969	Butch Cassdy and the Sundance Kid	Sheriff Bledsoe
1969	True Grit	Tom Chaney
1970	They Call Me MISTER Tibbs	Captain Marden
1970	Beneath the Planet of the Apes	Caspay
1970	Getting Straight	Dr. Willhunt
1970	Little Big Man	Wild Bill Hickok
1971	Shootout	Trooper
1977	Moonshine County Express	Preacher Hagen
1977	Oh, God!	Rabbi

(continued on page 506)

BUD CORT

(1950 -   )

Cort remains best known as the bizarre 20-year-old in love with Ruth Gordon in the cult hit *Harold and Maude*. Warned beforehand that he would be typecasted if he took the role, he took it anyway and, afterwards, took five years off because all parts offered to him were for weirdos or the psychotic. Cort went through the windshield of his Honda in an accident on L.A.'s freeway in 1979 that kept him in and out of hospitals for reconstructive facial surgery for several years. Film offers virtually disappeared.

Year	Movie	Character
1970	M*A*S*H	Pvt. Boone
1971	Harold and Maude	Harold
1977	Why Shoot the Teacher?	Max Brown
1980	Die Laughing	Mueller
1983	Love Letters	Danny
1986	Invaders From Mars	NASA Scientist
1987	Love at Stake	Parson Babcock
1988	The Chocolate War	Brother Jacques
1988	Out of the Dark	Stringer

NICOLAS COSTER

(1934 -   )

The son of a film critic, Coster was born in London. At the outbreak of World War II, his father enlisted in the Royal Marines, and in 1940 his mother brought him to the U.S. A veteran of daytime soap operas, he learned to act at the Royal Academy of Dramatic Arts in London. He has studied with Lee Strasberg in New York and performed at the Barter Theater in Virginia and the Arena Stage in Washington, D.C.

Year	Movie	Character
1978	The Big Fix	Spitzler
1979	Goldengirl	Dr. Dalton
1979	The Concorde—Airport '79	Dr. Stone
1979	The Electric Horseman	Fitzgerald
1979	Just You and Me Kid	Harris
1980	Little Darlings	Whitney
1981	The Pursuit of D.B. Cooper	Avery
1981	Reds	Paul Trullinger
1990	Betsy's Wedding	Henry Lovell

RICHARD COX

(1948 -   )

Cox gained his early acting experience in Shakespearean and other classics productions while a student at Yale. He received a B.A. in anthropology from Yale and was awarded fellowships to go to Japan, Bali, Samoa and Poland—sometimes as a guest actor. The New York native also performed in summer theater at The Peterborough Players in New Hampshire.

Year	Movie	Character
1980	Cruising	Stuart Richards
1981	King of the Mountain	Roger
1986	The Vindicator	Alex Whyte
1989	Street Justice	xxx

RONNY COX

(1938 -   )

Cox has said that his starring role in *Deliverance* "was my most important film becaused it opened so many doors for me." In that movie, he was one of the four city slickers on the backwaters canoe trip. He met his death in the rapids. The actor is from Cloudcroft, NM, and majored in drama at Eastern New Mexico University. He made his professional bow with the prestigious Arena Stage Company in Washington, D.C., and debuted on Broadway six years later.

Year	Movie	Character
1972	Deliverance	Drew
1976	Bound for Glory	Ozark Bule
1977	The Car	Luke
1978	Gray Lady Down	Cmdr. Samuelson
1979	The Onion Field	Pierce Brooks
1981	Taps	Colonel Kerby
1982	Some Kind of Hero	Col. Powers
1982	The Beast Within	Eli
1984	Beverly Hills Cop	Lt. Bogomil
1985	Vision Quest	Louden's Dad
1987	Beverly Hills Cop II	Andrew Bogomil
1987	Steele Justice	Bennett
1987	Robocop	Jones
1989	One Man Force	Lt. McCoy
1990	Loose Cannons	Bob Smiley
1990	Total Recall	Cohaagen
1990	Martians Go Home	The President

PETER COYOTE

(1942 -   )

Active in films only since 1980, Coyote was a part of San Francisco's counter culture during the 1960s, hanging out with the Diggers and acting with the San Francisco Mime Troupe. He spent 10 years travelling the country, living in communes and dining on robins. Upon his return to California he became involved in theater and worked for the state's Council for the Arts. He began his screen career with auditions for Steven Spielberg.

Year	Movie	Character
1980	Die Laughing	Davis
1981	Southern Comfort	Poole
1982	E.T. The Extra-Terrestrial	Keys
1982	Endangered Species	Steele
1983	Cross Creek	Norton Baskin
1983	Timerider	Porter Reese
1984	Heartbreakers	Arthur
1985	The Legend of Billie Jean	Ringwald
1985	Jagged Edge	Thomas Krasny
1987	Outrageous Fortune	Michael
1991	Exposure	Peter Mandrake

RICHARD CRENNA

(1926 -   )

A fixture in television, film and radio since his graduation from UCLA in 1952, Crenna spent three years as Walter Denton on the TV series *Our Miss Brooks* (1952-55) and six more on *The Real McCoys* (1957-63). He is also a highly-regarded television director having helmed more than 100 shows. The actor won an Emmy for his role as a tough cop who is sodomized by a gang of thugs in the television-movie *The Rape of Richard Beck*.

Year	Movie	Character
1965	John Goldfarb, Please Come Home	John Goldfarb
1966	The Sand Pebbles	Collins
1966	Made in Paris	Herb Stone
1967	Wait Until Dark	Mike Talman
1968	Star!	Richard Aldrich
1969	Marooned	Jim Pruett
1969	Midas Run	Warden
1970	Red Sky at Morning	Frank Arnold
1971	Doctors' Wives	Pete
1976	Breakheart Pass	Richard Fairchild
1980	Stone Cold Dead	Sgt. Boy
1981	Body Heat	Edmund Walker
1982	First Blood	Trautman
1983	Table for Five	Mitchell
1984	The Flamingo Kid	Phil Brody
1985	Summer Rental	Al Pellet
1985	Rambo: First Blood Part II	Trautman
1988	Rambo III	Col. Trautman
1989	Leviathan	Doc

HUME CRONYN

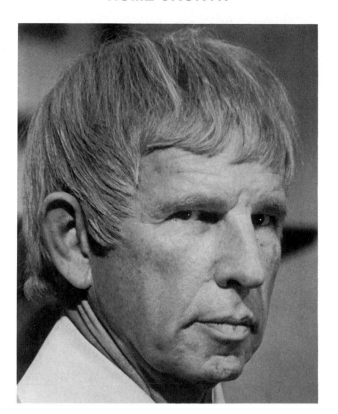

(1911 -   )

Once a boxer who was nominated for the Canadian Olympic boxing team, Cronyn was born in London, Ontario. After a lifelong career devoted to the stage, he was inducted into the Theater Hall of Fame in 1974. He has also worked as a screenwriter, a director and a producer. Cronyn has been married to Jessica Tandy since 1942.

Year	Movie	Character
1963	Cleopatra	Sosigenes
1969	The Arrangement	Arthur
1970	There Was a Crooked Man...	Dudley Whinner
1974	The Parallax View	Rintels
1974	Conrack	Skeffington
1981	Rollover	Maxwell Emery
1981	Honky Tonk Freeway	Sherm
1982	The World According to Garp	Mr. Fields
1984	Impulse	Dr. Carr
1985	Cocoon	Joe Finley
1985	Brewster's Millions	Rupert Horn
1987	*batteries not included	Frank
1988	Cocoon: The Return	Joe Finley

MARY CROSBY

(1959 -   )

Crosby is the daughter of entertainer Bing Crosby and is primarily a television actress. She got her first experience in front of the camera as a child on her father's TV specials during the early 1970s. In recent years she has been seen on *Dallas* (1979-81), episodes of *The Fall Guy* and *Loveboat*, and many other series and TV-movies. She attended the University of Texas at Austin and studied acting at the American Conservatory Theater.

Year	Movie	Character
1983	Last Plane Out	Liz
1988	Tapeheads	Samantha Gregory
1990	Eating	Kate
1990	Body Chemstry	Marlee Redding

HARLEY CROSS

(1979 -   )

Born in New York, Cross was only four when, after being selected from an audience to participate in a children's play, he decided to become an actor. In addition to his film appearances, he has appeared in several TV commercials and a movie-of-the-week titled *Hobo's Christmas*. He is fluent in French and is an avid sports enthusiast who enjoys scuba diving, horseback riding and ice-skating.

Year	Movie	Character
1984	Mrs. Soffel	Clarence Soffel
1986	Where Are the Children?	Michael Eldridge
1987	The Believers	Chris Jamison
1989	The Fly II	10-year-old Martin
1989	Cohen and Tate	Travis
1990	Stanley & Iris	Richard

LINDSAY CROUSE

(1948 -   )

Crouse is the daughter of the playwright Russell Crouse, who co-produced such critically and artistically praised stage productions as *The Sound of Music* and *Life with Father*. The native New Yorker graduated from Radcliffe in 1970 with the first class to receive Harvard diplomas. A longtime fixture on the New York theater scene, choosing a role is a very personal affair for Crouse. "I treat a character as an extension of myself," she once explained. "I look for integrity in the person and a redeeming value in the story."

Year	Movie	Character
1976	All the President's Men	Kay Eddy
1977	Slap Shot	Lily Braden
1981	Prince of the City	Carla Ciello
1982	The Verdict	Kaitlin Costello Price
1983	Daniel	Rochelle
1984	Iceman	Dr. Diane Brady
1984	Places in the Heart	Margaret Lomax
1987	House of Games	Margaret Ford
1989	Communion	Anne Strieber
1990	Desperate Hours	Brenda Chandler

JON CRYER

(1965 -   )

Sometimes likened to Matthew Broderick, Cryer has developed his craft under the often contrasting demands of the stage and filmmaking. "On the stage you develop a character that's different from yourself," he once explained. "In a film, they're always saying, 'Walk over here. Say this line. Be you.' " Cryer grew up in New York City, the son of actors.

Year	Movie	Character
1984	No Small Affair	Charles Cummings
1986	Pretty in Pink	Duckie
1987	Hiding Out	Andrew Morenski
1987	Superman IV: The Quest for Peace	Lenny
1987	O.C. & Stiggs	Randall Schwab, Jr.
1989	Penn & Teller Get Killed	xxx
1991	Hot Shots!	Jim Pfaffenbach

BOB CUMMINGS

(1908 - 1990)

The youthful-looking leading man starred in Hollywood comedies and dramas, then became one of the first to go to television in 1955 playing a swinging bachelor. *The Bob Cummings Show* had two different runs and its popular host also appeared in TV plays and on talk shows. He went into movies to earn money during the Depression after studying engineering and business. Author of a book on nutrition, *How to Stay Young and Virile*, he died of kidney failure.

Year	Movie	Character
1962	My Geisha	Bob Moore
1963	Beach Party	Professor Sutwell
1964	The Carpetbaggers	Dan Pierce
1964	What a Way to Go!	Dr. Steffanson
1966	Stagecoach	Mr. Gatewood

JOAN CUSACK

(1962 -   )

Oscar-nominated for best supporting actress in *Working Girl*, Cusack is a first-class scene stealer who built her career as a comic foil or best friend to the lead. She got her start with a few movies set in Chicago (she's from the suburbs) and, after college, a dismal year on TV's *Saturday Night Live*. She is best known for being funny, but her forte is not the "hard comedy" of *Saturday Night Live*. "Joan's comedy is very warm. It's fused with emotion," that show's producer, Lorne Michaels, once explained.

Year	Movie	Character
1980	My Bodyguard	Shelley
1983	Class	Roscoe
1984	Sixteen Candles	Geek Girl
1987	Broadcast News	Blair Litton
1987	The Allnighter	Gina
1988	Working Girl	Cyn
1988	Stars and Bars	Irene
1988	Married to the Mob	Rose
1989	Say Anything...	Constance
1990	My Blue Heaven	Hannah Stubbs
1990	Men Don't Leave	Jody
1992	Toys	Alsatia Zevo
1992	Hero	Evelyn
1993	Addams Family Values	Debbie Jellinsky

WILLEM DAFOE

(1955 -   )

Dafoe considers himself a very physical actor and has said that he would have pursued a career as a dancer had he not found success as an actor. "I never act," he once explained. "I simply bring out the real animal that's in me." Dafoe achieved a degree of notoriety after portraying Jesus Christ in Martin Scorsese's controversial *The Last Temptation of Christ* in 1988. Born in Appleton, WI, he started acting in high school.

Year	Movie	Character
1983	The Hunger	Phone Booth Youth
1984	Roadhouse 66	Johnny
1984	Streets of Fire	Raven
1985	To Live and Die in L.A.	Eric Masters
1986	Platoon	Sgt. Elias
1988	Off Limits	Buck McGriff
1988	Mississippi Burning	Ward
1989	Born on the Fourth of July	Charlie
1989	Triumph of the Spirit	Salamo Arouch
1990	Wild at Heart	Bobby Peru
1990	Cry-Baby	Hateful Guard
1991	Flight of the Intruder	Lt. Cmdr. Virgil Cole
1992	White Sands	Ray Dolezal
1993	Body of Evidence	Frank Dulaney

CHARLES DANCE

(1946 -   )

Dance was dubbed "The Thinking Woman's Sex Symbol" for his role in the joint BBC/PBS miniseries *The Jewel in the Crown*. The British actor started out as a West End theater stagehand and made his professional stage debut in 1970. He spent the latter half of the 1970s with the Royal Shakespeare Company.

Year	Movie	Character
1985	Plenty	Raymond Brock
1986	The Golden Child	Sardo Numspa
1987	Good Morning, Babylon	D.W. Griffith
1992	Alien 3	Clemens
1993	Last Action Hero	Benedict

BEVERLY D'ANGELO

(1953 -   )

After leaving home (Columbus, OH) at age 16, D'Angelo studied art in Italy, painted cartoons for Hanna-Barbera in Hollywood, sung with a jazz band in New York, wrote commercials in Toronto and studied opera, also in Canada. She believes acting should bring "personal as well as professional growth." "As a matter of fact, I see them tied together," she once explained. "I think personal growth has much to do with acting ability."

Year	Movie	Character
1977	The Sentinel	Sandra
1977	First Love	Shelley
1977	Annie Hall	xxx
1978	Every Which Way But Loose	Echo
1979	Hair	Sheila
1980	Coal Miner's Daughter	Patsy Cline
1981	Honky Tonk Freeway	Carmen Shelby
1981	Paternity	Maggie
1983	National Lampoon's Vacation	Ellen Griswold
1984	Finders Keepers	Standish
1985	Big Trouble	Blanche Rickey
1985	National Lampoon's European Vacation	Ellen Griswold
1987	In the Mood	Francine Glatt

(continued on page 506)

JEFF DANIELS

(1955 -   )

It was Al Pacino's performance in *Dog Day Afternoon* that convinced Daniels to become an actor. So taken with it, he saw the movie six times. He feels fortunate to have worked with good people early on, including Meryl Streep in *Heartburn*, but feels the pressure was that much greater "because everybody else is at a certain level—everybody is either a major star or a major director—and you have to really concentrate, really be serious, really hit it on every take because the take they're going to use is the take where *she's* great."

Year	Movie	Character
1981	Ragtime	O'Donnell
1983	Terms of Endearment	Flap Horton
1985	Marie	Eddie Sisk
1985	The Purple Rose of Cairo	Tom Baxter/Gil Shepherd
1986	Something Wild	Charles Driggs
1986	Heartburn	Richard
1987	Radio Days	Biff Baxter
1988	The House on Carroll Street	Cochran
1988	Sweet Hearts Dance	Sam Manners
1989	Checking Out	Ray Macklin
1990	Welcome Home, Roxy Carmichael	Denton Webb
1990	Arachnophobia	Ross Jennings
1991	The Butcher's Wife	Dr. Alex Tremor
1993	Rain Without Thunder	Jonathan Garson
1993	Gettysburg	Col. Joshua Chamberlain

WILLIAM DANIELS

(1927 -   )

A two-time Emmy winner, for his role as Dr. Mark Craig in NBC's *St. Elsewhere*, Daniels began his professional life as a New York stage actor. His film career got a big boost early on when he played Dustin Hoffman's father in *The Graduate*. Other big pictures include Warren Beatty's *Parallax View*. In it, he was a murdered politician's former aide who fears for his own life. Daniels grew up in New York City where he studied at the High School of Music and Art. He received a B.A. in theater from Northwestern University.

Year	Movie	Character
1965	A Thousand Clowns	Albert
1967	The Graduate	Mr. Braddock
1967	The President's Analyst	Wynn Quantrill
1967	Two for the Road	Howard Maxwell Manchester
1969	Marlowe	Mr. Crowell
1972	1776	John Adams
1974	The Parallax View	Austin
1977	Oh, God!	George Summers
1977	Black Sunday	Pugh
1979	Sunburn	Crawford
1980	The Blue Lagoon	Arthur LeStrange
1981	Reds	Julius Gerber
1981	All Night Long	Richard H. Copleston
1987	Blind Date	Judge Harold Bedford
1989	Her Alibi	Sam

BLYTHE DANNER

(1943 -   )

Critic John Simon once described Danner as "the most underrated and underused major leading lady of our screen and stage." Born and raised on Philadelphia's Main Line, she earned a B.A. in drama at upstate New York's Bard College. She gained her initial stage experience playing repertory in New England and New York.

Year	Movie	Character
1972	1776	Martha Jefferson
1975	Hearts of the West	Miss Trout
1976	Futureworld	Tracy Ballard
1979	The Great Santini	Lillian Meechum
1983	Man, Woman and Child	Sheila Beckwith
1986	Brighton Beach Memoirs	Kate
1988	Another Woman	Lydia
1990	Alice	Dorothy
1990	Mr. & Mrs. Bridge	Grace Barron
1991	The Prince of Tides	Sallie Wingo
1992	Husbands and Wives	Rain's Mother

SYBIL DANNING

(1951 -   )

A self-described "army brat," Danning is the daughter of an Austrian mother and a German father, and was raised in the U.S. and Europe. Often in very physically demanding roles, the former model would engage in weight training, aerobics, jogging, swimming and fencing to keep in shape for her parts.

Year	Movie	Character
1977	Operation Thunderbolt	Halima
1979	The Concorde—Airport '79	Amy
1980	The Man with Bogart's Face	Cynthia
1980	Battle Beyond the Stars	St. Exmin
1981	The Salamander	Lili
1983	Hercules	Arianna
1984	Seven Magnificent Gladiators	Julia
1985	Howling II: Your Sister is a Werewolf	Stirba
1987	Amazon Women on the Moon	Queen Lara

ROYAL DANO

(1922 -   )

Nominated by the New York Critic's Circle as one of the Promising Actors of 1949, Dano began his performing career as a part of the 44th Special Service Provisional Company during World War II. The veteran character actor once told an interviewer, "A supporting actor only has to work that much harder, carefully planning his or her performance to enhance the entire storyline and star players."

Year	Movie	Character
1960	Cimarron	Ike Howes
1961	King of Kings	Peter
1964	7 Faces of Dr. Lao	Carey
1967	Welcome to Hard Times	John Bear
1968	Day of the Evil Gun	Dr. Prather
1969	The Undefeated	Major Sanders
1973	Electra Glide in Blue	Coroner
1973	Cahill—U.S. Marshal	MacDonald
1975	Capone	Cermak
1976	The Killer Inside Me	Father
1976	Drum	Zeke
1980	In Search of Historic Jesus	Prophet
1983	The Right Stuff	Minister
1983	Hammett	Pops

(continued on page 506)

CESARE DANOVA

(1926 - 1992)

Born in Rome, Danova was already known as a leading man in Italy when he signed on with MGM in 1956. His life's work included over 350 film and television productions. Prominent among his television work was the lead in the 1967 series *Garrison's Gorillas*. Danova died of a heart attack at 66.

Year	Movie	Character
1961	Valley of the Dragons	Hector Servadac
1962	Tender is the Night	Tommy Barban
1963	Cleopatra	Apollodorus
1963	Gidget Goes to Rome	Paolo Cellini
1964	Viva Las Vegas	Count Elmo Mancini
1966	Boy, Did I Get a Wrong Number!	Pepe
1973	Mean Streets	Giovanni
1976	Scorchy	Philip
1977	Tentacles	Corey
1978	National Lampoon's Animal House	Mayor Carmine DePasto

MICHAEL DANTE

PATTI D'ARBANVILLE

(1935 -   )

Born Ralph Vitti in Stamford, CT, the actor left home at 17 to play professional baseball. He was signed by the Boston Braves and, later, moved on to play shortstop for the Washington Senators. In the off-season, he attended the University of Miami and majored in drama. He left baseball to sign a contract with MGM and has been in Hollywood ever since.

(1952 -   )

By the time she was 20, D'Arbanville had been a baby model, a disc jockey, an international fashion model and avante-garde film actress. A native of New York's Greenwich Village, her acting studies began with Herbert Berghof at his New York studio. Before turning to Hollywood, she achieved fame in Europe, where she lived for 10 years, as a result of five films she made in France.

Year	Movie	Character
1965	Arizona Raiders	Brady
1971	Willard	Brandt
1976	Winterhawk	Winter Hawk
1977	The Farmer	Johnny O
1983	The Big Score	Goldy

Year	Movie	Character
1978	Big Wednesday	Sally
1979	The Main Event	Donna
1979	Time After Time	Shirley
1981	Modern Problems	Darcy
1985	Real Genius	Sherry
1988	Call Me	Cori
1988	Fresh Horses	Jean

SEVERN DARDEN

(1929 -   )

Darden attended the University of Chicago where he had originally planned to study to become a doctor, but, as he once said, he changed his mind after getting sick. The irreverent actor was well-known at the institution because he drove to classes in a 1932 Rolls-Royce, dressed in a waistcoat, black Mexican cape, white sneakers and carried a cane. A graduate of Chicago's Compass Theater and Second City troupe, he has been a fixture in film, television and theater for years.

Year	Movie	Character
1966	Dead Heat on a Merry-Go-Round	Miles Fisher
1967	The President's Analyst	Kropotkin
1968	P.J.	Shelton Quell
1969	The Mad Room	Nate
1971	Vanishing Point	J. Hovah
1972	The War Between Men and Women	Dr. Harris
1972	Conquest of the Planet of the Apes	Kolp
1973	Battle for the Planet of the Apes	Kolp
1976	Jackson County Jail	Sheriff
1979	Wanda Nevada	Merlin
1980	Hopscotch	Maddox
1980	In God We Trust	Priest
1985	Real Genius	Dr. Meredith
1986	Back to School	Dr. Barazini
1988	The Telephone	Max

JAMES DARREN

(1936 -   )

Born James Ercolani in South Philadelphia, the actor was raised in a boisterous Italian household with his parents, kid brother, three uncles, an aunt and two grandparents. A teenage idol of the 1950s and 1960s, he says it wasn't all roses: "In San Francisco a crowd of girls, 13 to 16, tore down the TV studio doors, pulled me out and pinned me to the ground, tearing my jacket, ripping my clothes off and pulling souvenir hairs from my head."

Year	Movie	Character
1960	All the Young Men	Cotton
1961	Gidget Goes Hawaiian	Jeff Mather
1961	The Guns of Navarone	Pappadimos
1962	Diamond Head	Paul Kahana
1963	Gidget Goes to Rome	Jeff
1964	For Those Who Think Young	Gardner "Ding" Pruitt III

ROBERT DAVI

(1953 -   )

A native New Yorker, Davi claims to have learned the rudiments of his craft through observing the characters and absorbing the many emotions on the city sidewalks where he grew up. Often cast as a villain, his original love was opera. He made his professional debut with Long Island's Lyric Opera Company, but switched to acting and went to Hofstra University on a drama scholarship.

Year	Movie	Character
1984	City Heat	Nino
1986	Raw Deal	Max
1987	Wild Thing	Chopper
1988	Die Hard	Big Johnson
1988	Action Jackson	Tony Moretti
1989	Licence to Kill	Franz Sanchez
1990	Predator 2	Heinemann
1990	Peacemaker	Sgt. Frank Ramos
1991	The Taking of Beverly Hills	Robert "Bat" Masterson
1993	Son of Pink Panther	Hans

KEITH DAVID

(1954 -   )

David was a student at Juilliard when he got his first professional job with the New York Shakespeare Festival understudying for *Othello*. Born in New York, he attended the High School of Performing Arts, where his interest was heightened in theater and enabled him to perform in classic works, as well as naturalistic plays. The actor may be best remembered as pro-wrestler Roddy Piper's buddy in *They Live* in which they waged a two-man war against the aliens controlling society.

Year	Movie	Character
1982	The Thing	Childs
1986	Platoon	King
1988	Off Limits	Maurice
1988	Bird	Buster Franklin
1988	They Live	Frank
1988	Stars and Bars	Teagarden
1989	Always	Powerhouse
1990	Men at Work	Louis Fedders
1990	Marked for Death	Max
1992	Final Analysis	Detective Huggins
1992	Article 99	Luther Jerome

LOLITA DAVIDOVICH

(19?? -   )

Davidovich once told an interviewer that she became an actress because she "wanted to be everything. I love being saturated with one thing at a time and then surfacing and doing something else. That's kind of how I live and operate. So acting seemed most suitable." Davidovich grew up in Ontario, Canada, the youngest of three children. Her parents emigrated from Yugoslavia and she spoke only Serbian until kindergarten.

Year	Movie	Character
1989	Blaze	Blaze Starr
1991	The Inner Circle	Anastasia Sanshin
1991	JFK	Beverly
1991	The Object of Beauty	Joan
1992	Leap of Faith	Marva
1992	Raising Cain	Jenny
1993	Boiling Point	Vikki
1993	Younger and Younger	Penelope

JIM DAVIS

(1915 - 1981)

The Edgerton, MO, native worked as a tent rigger for a circus, attended William Jewell College in Liberty, MO, and went to Hollywood as an oil salesman. Once there the husky six-foot-tall Davis played leads in grade 'B' cowboy movies and support in bigger feature films. He became famous to millions on television as Jock Ewing, head of the Ewing clan, in the soap *Dallas*. He died after surgery for a perforated ulcer.

Year	Movie	Character
1969	They Ran for Their Lives	xxx
1970	Monte Walsh	Cal Brennan
1970	Rio Lobo	Riley
1972	Bad Company	Marshal
1972	The Honkers	Mel Potter
1977	The Choirboys	Capt. Drobeck
1978	Comes a Horseman	Julie Blocker

JUDY DAVIS

(1956 -   )

Davis got the attention of international audiences with the lead in the Australian film, *My Brilliant Career*. She played an independent young woman who refused to give in to the societal norms of turn-of-the-century Australia. An independent young woman herself, Davis left school at age 17 to travel. She sang with an Italian band in Taiwan and Japan and, upon returning to her homeland, enrolled in a drama course at Sidney's National Institute of Dramatic Art.

Year	Movie	Character
1979	My Brilliant Career	Sybylla Melvyn
1984	A Passage to India	Adela Quested
1990	Alice	Vicki
1991	Barton Fink	Audrey Taylor
1991	Impromptu	George Sand
1992	Husbands and Wives	Sally

BRUCE DAVISON

(1946 -   )

A native of Pennsylvania, Davison entered Penn State as an art major, intending to earn a living as a painter. However, on a bet he auditioned for a school play and thus began his life as an actor. After only a few months of acting in New York he was cast in the film, *Last Summer,* and a succession of Hollywood movies followed.

Year	Movie	Character
1969	Last Summer	Dan
1971	Willard	Willard Stiles
1972	The Jerusalem File	David
1972	Ulzana's Raid	Lt. Garnett DeBuin
1974	Mame	Older Patrick
1976	Mother, Jugs & Speed	LeRoy
1978	Brass Target	Col. Robert Dawson
1981	High Risk	Dan
1984	Crimes of Passion	Hopper
1985	Spies Like Us	Mr. Ruby
1987	The Misfit Brigade	Porta
1990	Steel & Lace	Albert
1990	Longtime Companion	David
1993	Short Cuts	Howard Finnegan

RUBY DEE

(1924 -   )

Born in Cleveland, the daughter of a Pennsylvania Railroad porter, Dee grew up in Harlem and got her start as an actress there at the American Negro Theater. After years of appearing on stage, television and in film, she and husband, Ossie Davis, were heard on national radio on their weekly series *The Ossie Davis and Ruby Dee Story Hour* from 1974 to 1978.

Year	Movie	Character
1961	A Raisin in the Sun	Ruth
1967	The Incident	Joan Robinson
1972	Buck and the Preacher	Ruth
1982	Cat People	Female
1989	Do the Right Thing	Mother Sister
1990	Love at Large	Corrine Dart
1991	Jungle Fever	Lucinda Purify

JOHN DEHNER

(1915 - 1992)

Dehner began his Hollywood career as an animation assistant at Walt Disney Studios where he worked on *Fantasia* and *Bambi* as well as the Mickey Mouse and Donald Duck cartoons. After World War II, he worked as a radio announcer and covered the first U.N. conference in San Francisco, helping to win a Peabody award for his station. The veteran actor made his film debut in 1944 in *Thirty Seconds Over Tokyo* and went on to do about 100 pictures. He died of emphysema and diabetes.

Year	Movie	Character
1962	The Chapman Report	Geoffrey
1963	Critic's Choice	S.P. Champlain
1970	Dirty Dingus Magee	The General
1971	Support Your Local Gunfighter	Colonel Ames
1972	Slaughterhouse Five	Rumford
1976	The Killer Inside Me	Bob
1977	Mountain Man	John Muir
1977	Fun With Dick and Jane	Jane's Father
1978	The Boys from Brazil	Henry Wheelock
1980	Nothing Personal	xxx
1985	Jagged Edge	Judge Carrigan
1985	Creator	Paul

KIM DELANEY

(1963 -   )

A high school cheerleader, Delaney grew up in Roxborough, PA, a working-class suburb of Philadelphia. A modeling career opened up for her after being discovered at the front door of Resorts International in Atlantic City. Though without acting experience, she was able to land a prominent role in the daytime soap *All My Children*. Acting lessons and Hollywood soon followed.

Year	Movie	Character
1985	That Was Then, This is Now	Cathy
1986	The Delta Force	Sister Mary
1987	Campus Man	Dayna Thomas
1987	Hunter's Blood	Melanie
1988	The Drifter	Julia
1991	Body Parts	Karen Chrushank

DANNY DE LA PAZ

(19?? -   )

Perhaps best-known as Richard Yniguez's hot-headed younger brother in the barrio drama *Boulevard Nights*, De La Paz has been an actor since high school. The son of a Mexican immigrant and a Mexican-American devotes his time to community work when not acting on stage or in film and television. De La Paz hails from Whittier, CA, a suburb of Los Angeles.

Year	Movie	Character
1979	Boulevard Nights	Chuco Avila
1982	Barbarosa	Eduardo
1986	3:15	xxx
1987	Devil's Odds (The Wild Pair)	Tucker
1989	Miracle Mile	Transvestite
1992	American Me	Puppet

PATRICK DEMPSEY

(1966 -   )

Dempsey believes that acting on stage is the true test of his abilities. "I'm not taking away from film acting," he once explained. "But the people I look up to are people doing stage." He feels a play contributes to his personal growth as well: "By the end of the run, I want to feel much more secure with who I am as a person and who I am as an artist." Dempsey is from Maine.

Year	Movie	Character
1985	Heaven Help Us	Corbet
1987	Meatballs III	Rudy
1987	In the Mood	Ellsworth Wisecarver
1987	Can't Buy Me Love	Ronald Miller
1989	Happy Together	Christopher Wooden
1989	Some Girls	Michael
1989	Loverboy	Randy Bodek
1990	Run	Matthew Pogue
1990	Coupe de Ville	Bobby Libner
1991	Mobsters	Meyer Lansky
1993	Bank Robber	Billy

JEFFREY DEMUNN

(1947 -   )

DeMunn was born in Buffalo, NY, and attended upstate New York's Union College before training for the stage in Bristol, England. Commenting on his decision to do the film *Warning Sign*, he once said: "The script isn't everything. I used to think it was, but I have increasingly begun to realize that what is equally important is who you are working with...who are the people that want to make this story? That, as much as the story, is what convinced me to do this film."

Year	Movie	Character
1980	Resurrection	Joe
1982	Frances	Clifford Odets
1984	Windy City	Bobby
1985	Warning Sign	Dan Fairchild
1986	The Hitcher	Capt. Esteridge
1988	Betrayed	Flynn
1988	The Blob	Sheriff Herb Geller
1989	Blaze	Tuck

BRIAN DENNEHY

(1938 -)

Dennehy was born in Bridgeport, CT, and began acting as a student at Columbia University. After serving in Vietnam, he became a graduate student at Yale and performed in Off-Broadway and summer stock productions. Resigned at first to playing character roles in feature films, the actor has, in recent years, taken leading roles in made-for-television movies.

Year	Movie	Character
1977	Semi-Tough	T.J. Lambert
1978	Foul Play	Fergie
1978	F.I.S.T.	Frank Vasko
1979	10	Bartender
1979	Butch and Sundance: The Early Days	O.C. Hanks
1980	Little Miss Marker	Herbie
1982	Split Image	Kevin
1982	First Blood	Teasle
1983	Never Cry Wolf	Rosie
1983	Gorky Park	William Kirwill
1984	The River Rat	Doc
1984	Finders Keepers	Mayor
1985	Silverado	Cobb

(continued on page 506)

ANNE DESALVO

(1950 -)

DeSalvo was an art student at the Tyler School in Boston when she decided to try her hand at acting. She was soon performing professionally at the Boston Repertory and Harvard's Loeb Theater while teaching art during the day. She eventually abandoned art for drama and moved to New York where, although typed as "too ethnic," she managed to thrive on the stage. DeSalvo is from West Philadelphia.

Year	Movie	Character
1979	Starting Over	xxx
1982	My Favorite Year	Alice Miller
1983	D.C. Cab	Myrna
1985	Perfect	Frankie
1985	Compromising Positions	Phyllis Fleckstein
1987	Burglar	Det. Todras
1990	Taking Care of Business	Debbie

COLLEEN DEWHURST

(1926 - 1991)

A native of Montreal, Dewhurst was one of the great stage actresses, a regal star with a whiskey voice who played O'Neill's tragic women with passion. She was also busy in film and television and as the activist President of Actors Equity she spoke out on non-traditional casting and the impact of AIDs on the theater. She was twice married and twice divorced from actor George C. Scott. Dewhurst died after a long battle with cancer.

Year	Movie	Character
1960	Man on a String	Helen Benson
1966	A Fine Madness	Dr. Vera Kropotkin
1971	The Last Run	Monique
1972	The Cowboys	Kate
1974	McQ	Myra
1977	Annie Hall	Mom Hall
1978	Ice Castles	Beulah Smith
1979	When a Stranger Calls	Tracy
1980	Tribute	Gladys Petrelli
1983	The Dead Zone	Henrietta Dodd
1986	The Boy Who Could Fly	Mrs. Sherman
1989	Obsessed	xxx
1991	Dying Young	Estelle Whittier

BRAD DEXTER

(1917 -   )

Dexter was a law student at USC, but after appearing in campus plays he changed his mind about his future career, and in 1937 joined the Pasadena Playhouse. He later moved to New York where he played on the stage and on radio. His film career began when he was put under contract to Howard Hughes after serving in the U.S. Air Force during World War II. Dexter had a prominent role in Frank Sinatra's *Von Ryan's Express* as an American prisoner in that film about a mass escape across World War II Italy.

Year	Movie	Character
1960	The Magnificent Seven	Harry Luck
1962	Taras Bulba	Shilo
1963	Kings of the Sun	Ah Haleb
1964	Invitation to Gunfighter	Kenarsie
1965	None But the Brave	Sgt. Bleeker
1965	Von Ryan's Express	Sgt. Bostick
1965	Bus Riley's Back in Town	Slocum
1966	Blindfold	Harrigan
1972	Jory	Jack
1975	Shampoo	Senator
1976	Vigilante Force	Mayor
1978	House Calls	Quinn
1979	Winter Kills	Heller

CLIFF DE YOUNG

(1946 -   )

Inspired by performances by Jose Ferrer and James Dean when he was 10, De Young became convinced that "acting could be a noble profession." Nonetheless, his first foray into show business was as a lead singer and lyricist for the rock group Clear Light, which garnered modest success as an opening act for such superstars as Jimi Hendrix and Janis Joplin.

Year	Movie	Character
1974	Harry and Tonto	Junior
1981	Shock Treatment	Brad/Farley
1983	Independence Day	Les Morgan
1983	The Hunger	Tom Haver
1984	Protocol	Hilley
1984	Reckless	Phil
1985	Secret Admirer	George
1986	Flight of the Navigator	Bill Freeman
1986	F/X	Lipton
1988	Pulse	Bill
1989	Rude Awakening	Brubaker
1989	Glory	Col. James Montgomery
1990	Flashback	Sheriff Hightower
1992	Dr. Giggles	Tom Campbell

GEORGE DICENZO

(1940 -   )

DiCenzo, or more accurately, his voice, may be best known to watchers of Saturday morning cartoons. He has provided voice characterizations for such animated programs as *Scooby's Mystery Funhouse* (1985-86), *Spider-Man and His Amazing Friends* (1981-86) and *Hulk Hogan's Rock 'n' Wrestling!* (1985-87). As an actor he has appeared primarily in film and television, although he gained early experience in the play *Whitsuntide* at New York's Martinique Theater in 1972.

Year	Movie	Character
1977	The Choirboys	Lt. Grimsley
1979	The Frisco Kid	Darryl Diggs
1980	The Ninth Configuration	Captain Fairbanks
1985	Back to the Future	Sam Baines
1986	The Longshoy	DeFranco
1986	About Last Night...	Mr. Favio
1987	Omega Syndrome	Phil
1987	Walk Like a Man	xxx
1988	18 Again!	Coach
1988	The New Adventures of Pippi Longstocking	Mr. Blackhart
1989	Sing	Mr. Marowitz
1990	The Exorcist III	Stedman

BOBBY DICICCO

(1955 -   )

Growing up near Chicago, DiCicco dreamed of becoming a movie actor at an early age. High school plays, local theatrical productions and a TV-movie gave him his start. A sports lover, he told *US* magazine in 1980, "Sports give me a great sense of freedom, since they are one of the few activities entirely dependent on you, your skill, your alertness."

Year	Movie	Character
1978	I Wanna Hold Your Hand	Tony Smerko
1979	1941	xxx
1980	The Big Red One	Vinci
1982	Night Shift	Leonard
1984	Splash	Jerry
1984	Philadelphia Experiment	Jim
1987	Number One With a Bullet	Malcolm
1988	Tiger Warsaw	Tony

BRADFORD DILLMAN

(1930 -   )

Dillman's career got off to a good start when he shared the "best actor" award at Cannes in 1959 for his role as a cold-blooded killer in *Compulsion*. The son of a prominent San Francisco moneyman, he spent five years in the New York theater world before turning to films. He is a graduate of Yale and was an officer in the Marine Corps. He has played Clint Eastwood's superior officer in *The Enforcer* and *Sudden Impact*.

Year	Movie	Character
1960	Crack in the Mirror	Larnier/Claude
1961	Francis of Assisi	Francis
1968	Sergeant Ryker	Capt. Young
1968	Jigsaw	Jonathan Fields
1969	The Bridge at Remagen	Major Barnes
1971	Escape from the Planet of the Apes	Dr. Lewis Dixon
1973	The Way We Were	J.J.
1974	Gold	Manfred Steyner
1975	Bug	James
1976	The Enforcer	Capt. McKay
1978	The Swarm	Maj. Baker
1978	The Amsterdam Kill	Odums
1979	Love and Bullets	Brickman
1983	Sudden Impact	Captain Briggs

KEVIN DILLON

(1965 -   )

Resembling his more famous older brother, Matt Dillon, the actor, with no formal training, began his career with the never-aired made-for-television movie, *No Big Deal*. The director of *Heaven Help Us*, Michael Dante, once told an interviewer, "Kevin is an instinctual actor with a lot of self-confidence, which is one reason why he's so camera-smart."

Year	Movie	Character
1985	Heaven Help Us	Rooney
1986	Platoon	Bunny
1988	Remote Control	Cosmo
1988	The Blob	Brian Flagg
1988	The Rescue	J.J. Merrill
1989	Immediate Family	Sam
1989	War Party	Skitty Harris
1991	The Doors	John Densmore

MELINDA DILLON

(1939 -   )

Dillon won much praise for her role as an emotionally disturbed Catholic girl whose life is shattered by the press in *Absence of Malice*. She also had a big part in Steven Spielberg's *Close Encounters of the Third Kind* as the mother of a boy kidnapped by aliens who becomes obsessed with painting a particular mountain. Born in President Bill Clinton's hometown of Hope, AR, Dillon studied acting at the Goodman Theater School and with Lee Strasberg and has performed with Chicago's Second City troupe.

Year	Movie	Character
1969	The April Fools	Leslie Hopkins
1976	Bound for Glory	Mary Guthrie
1977	Close Encounters of the Third Kind	Jilian Guiler
1977	Slap Shot	Suzanne Hanrahan
1978	F.I.S.T.	Anna Zerinkas
1981	Absence of Malice	Teresa
1983	A Christmas Story	Mother
1984	Songwriter	Honey
1987	Harry and the Hendersons	Nancy Henderson
1989	Staying Together	Eileen McDermott
1991	The Prince of Tides	Savannah Wingo

BOB DISHY

(1934 -   )

Born in Brooklyn to a father from Beirut and a mother from Jerusalem, Dishy discovered acting in high school. Originally known as a comic actor, he honed his craft in summer stock, the U.S. Army and as a drama major at Syracuse University.

Year	Movie	Character
1967	The Tiger Makes Out	Jerry
1970	Lovers and Other Strangers	Jerry
1976	I Wonder Who's Killing Her Now?	xxx
1976	The Big Bus	Dr. Kurtz
1980	The Last Married Couple in America	Howard
1980	First Family	Vice President Shockley
1982	Author! Author!	Finestein
1986	Brighton Beach Memoirs	Jack
1987	Critical Condition	Dr. Foster
1992	Stay Tuned	Murray Seidenbaum

DONNA DIXON

(1957 -   )

Dixon's screen career began when she answered a casting call and landed a regular role in the TV hit, *Bosom Buddies* which ran from 1980 to 1984. She had been working as a model for the prestigious Wilhelmina Modeling Agency in New York. Dixon studied anthropology in college, but chose modeling as a career after winning beauty contests in Virginia and Washington, D.C. She met her future husband, Dan Aykroyd, on the set of *Doctor Detroit* and has appeared with him in *Spies Like Us* and *The Couch Trip*.

Year	Movie	Character
1983	Twilight Zone—The Movie	Jr. Stewardess (Segment 4)
1983	Doctor Detroit	Monica McNeil
1985	Spies Like Us	Karen Boyer
1988	Lucky Stiff	Cynthia Mitchell
1988	The Couch Trip	Laura Rollins
1989	Speed Zone!	Tiffany
1992	Wayne's World	the girl

PETER DONAT

(1928 -   )

Donat remains best known for his work on the stage and in television. He is the son of Robert Donat, a star of the British cinema in the 1930s and grew up in Nova Scotia. He spent several seasons with the Stratford (Ontario) Shakespeare Festival and has performed with San Francisco's American Conservatory Theater. TV viewers may remember him as Elmo Tyson in *Flamingo Road* from 1981 to 1982. His film roles include Jane Fonda's television station boss in *The China Syndrome*.

Year	Movie	Character
1975	The Hindenburg	Reed Channing
1978	F.I.S.T.	Arthur St. Claire
1979	The China Syndrome	Don Jacovich
1981	Ladies and Gentlemen, The Fabulous Stains	Harley
1985	The Bay Boy	Mr. Campbell
1988	Tucker: The Man and His Dream	Kerner
1989	The War of the Roses	Larrabee
1989	Skin Deep	Sparky
1992	The Babe	Frazee

VINCENT D'ONOFRIO

(1960 -   )

D'Onofrio is perhaps best known for his performance as the harassed and overweight (he gained 75 lbs. for the role!) private in Stanley Kubrick's *Full Metal Jacket*. He was the screenwriter in *The Player* suspected of sending the venal movie executive Griffin Mill threatening postcards. D'Onofrio grew up in Miami and studied acting with New York's American Stanislavsky Theater from the age of eighteen.

Year	Movie	Character
1987	Adventures in Babysitting	Dawson
1987	Full Metal Jacket	Pvt. Pyle
1988	Mystic Pizza	Bill Montijo
1989	Signs of Life	Daryl Monahan
1991	JFK	Bill Newman
1991	Dying Young	Gordon
1991	Fires Within	Sam
1992	The Player	David Kahane
1993	Mr. Wonderful	Dominic

PAUL DOOLEY

(1928 -   )

Dooley's early heroes were the great comedians of the silents—Chaplin, Keaton and Laurel & Hardy. He studied their routines carefully. He has said, "I don't take myself too seriously which is maybe why I've done a lot more comedy roles than anything else. I have more fun doing off-the-wall kinds of things." A native of Parkersburg, WV, Dooley enrolled at the West Virginia University School of Art, but soon switched to the drama department where he got his B.A. in Speech and Drama.

Year	Movie	Character
1970	The Out of Towners	Hotel day clerk
1972	Up the Sandbox	xxx
1977	Slap Shot	Hyannisport Announcer
1979	A Perfect Couple	Alex
1979	Breaking Away	Mr. Stohler
1979	Rich Kids	Simon Peterfreund
1979	Health	xxx
1980	Popeye	Wimpy
1981	Paternity	Kurt
1982	Endangered Species	Joe
1982	Kiss Me Goodbye	Kendall
1983	Strange Brew	Claude
1983	Going Berserk	Dr. Ted
1984	Sixteen Candles	Jim Baker
1985	Big Trouble	Noozel
1987	O.C. & Stiggs	Randall Schwab
1988	Last Rites	Father Freddie
1990	Flashback	Stark
1993	A Dangerous Woman	Tupperware Salesman

ROBERT DOQUI

(1934 -   )

Born and raised in the small town of Stillwater, OK, DoQui attended Langston University on a music scholarship. There he sang with the famous "Langstonaires." After a four-year stint in the U.S. Army, he moved to New York to pursue a career in show business. He served on the Board of Directors of the Screen Actors Guild for ten years and assisted the Guild's efforts to bring about the greater participation of women and minority groups in the media.

Year	Movie	Character
1975	Part 2, Walking Tall	Obra
1975	Nashville	Wade
1982	I'm Dancing as Fast as I Can	Teddy
1984	Cloak & Dagger	Lt. Fleming
1986	Good to Go	Max
1987	Robocop	Sgt. Reed
1989	Miracle Mile	Cook
1990	Robocop 2	Sgt. Reed
1993	Robocop 3	Sgt. Reed

MELVYN DOUGLAS

(1901 - 1981)

Born in Macon, GA, Douglas began in the 1930s as a poised, romantic lead, an old smoothie with women. He abandoned Hollywood for the stage when his lover boy days were over. After 10 years on Broadway, he returned to movies as a great character actor playing heart-of-gold old men and winning two Academy Awards for *Hud* and *Being There*. He died after a brief illness.

Year	Movie	Character
1963	Hud	Homer Bannon
1964	The Americanization of Emily	Adm. William Jessup
1964	Advance to the Rear	Col. Claude Brackenby
1967	Hotel	Trent
1972	The Candidate	John J. McKay
1972	One is a Lonely Number	Joseph
1976	The Tenant	Mr. Zy
1977	Twilight's Last Gleaming	Zachariah Guthrie
1979	Being There	Benjamin Rand
1979	The Changeling	Sen. Joe Carmichael
1979	The Seduction of Joe Tynan	Senator Birney

SARAH DOUGLAS

(1952 -   )

Born and raised in Stratford-Upon-Avon, Shakespeare's birthplace, Douglas toured throughout Europe at age 14 with Britain's prestigious National Youth Theatre. She studied drama and taught at the Rose Burford Drama School before beginning an active career in British television and theater. After two *Superman* flicks and other early feature films, she moved to L.A. to spend time on television's *Falcon Crest*.

Year	Movie	Character
1977	The People That Time Forgot	Charly
1978	Superman	Ursa
1980	Superman II	Ursa
1984	Conan the Destroyer	Queen Taramis
1986	Solarbabies	Shandray
1987	Steele Justice	Kay
1989	Return of the Swamp Thing	Dr. Lana Zurrell
1991	Beastmaster 2: Through the Portal of Time	Lyranna
1993	Return of the Living Dead 3	Sinclair

BRAD DOURIF

(1950 -)

Dourif debuted as one of Jack Nicholson's fellow patients, the acne-marked stutterer, Billy Bibbit, in *One Flew Over the Cuckoo's Nest*. Often cast as a menacing psychotic-type since then, he admits that he enjoys the challenges that violent, offbeat roles present. He was Faye Dunaway's wild-eyed driver and a murder suspect in *Eyes of Laura Mars*. A native of Huntington, WV, Dourif's acting career began with technical work and small parts at New York's Circle Repertory.

Year	Movie	Character
1975	One Flew Over the Cuckoo's Nest	Billy Bibbit
1978	Eyes of Laura Mars	Tommy Ludlow
1979	Wise Blood	Hazel Motes
1980	Heaven's Gate	Eggleston
1981	Ragtime	Younger Brother
1984	Dune	Piter DeVries
1986	Blue Velvet	Raymond
1987	Fatal Beauty	Leo Nova
1988	Child's Play	Charles Lee Ray
1988	Mississippi Burning	Deputy Pell
1990	The Exorcist III	The Gemini Killer
1991	Jungle Fever	Leslie
1991	Body Parts	Remo Lacey

LESLEY-ANNE DOWN

(1954 -)

A modeling career began for the London-born actress after being named "Britain's Most Beautiful Teenager." However, she was bitten by the acting bug and soon turned to the stage. Down was next seen on the big screen and the little screen, but it was her role as Miss Georgina on the PBS series *Upstairs, Downstairs* that caught America's eye and Hollywood soon followed.

Year	Movie	Character
1973	Scalawag	Lucy-Ann
1975	Brannigan	Luana
1976	The Pink Panther Strikes Again	Olga
1978	The Betsy	Lady Bobby Ayres
1979	The Great Train Robbery	Miriam
1979	Hanover Street	Margaret Sellinger
1980	Rough Cut	Gillian Bromley
1981	Sphinx	Erica

ROBERT DOWNEY, JR.

(1965 -   )

Downey has been described by at least one critic as the "best thing in a lot of bad movies." The bad movie cycle appeared to come to an end with 1989's *Chances Are* and *True Believer*. He often played class clown types in his early films and his Chaplin earned him an Oscar nomination. Downey is the son of the legendary underground filmmaker Robert Downey who made such films as *Putney Swope*, and *Greaser's Palace*. He got his start as a New York actor in 1982, after he dropped out of high school in California.

Year	Movie	Character
1983	Baby, It's You	Stewart
1984	First Born	Lee
1985	Weird Science	Ian
1985	Tuff Turf	Jimmy Parker
1985	To Live and Die in L.A.	Thomas
1986	Back to School	Derek
1987	The Pick-up Artist	Jack Jericho
1987	Less Than Zero	Julian
1988	Johnny Be Good	Leo Wiggins
1988	1969	Ralph
1989	Chances Are	Alex Finch
1989	True Believer	Roger Baron
1990	Air America	Billy Covington
1991	Soapdish	Jeffrey Anderson
1991	Too Much Sun	Reed Richmond
1992	Chaplin	Charlie Chaplin
1993	Heart and Souls	Thomas Reilly
1993	Short Cuts	Bill Bush

HOWARD DUFF

(1917 - 1990)

A native of Bremerton, WA, Duff was detective Sam Spade on Seattle radio station KOMO in 1935 before coming under contract to Universal. His heyday was in the 1940s and 1950s when his roles ranged from character parts to leads in "B"s. His career faltered with the end of the contract system, but he came back strong on television and in movies in the 1970s and 1980s. He died of a heart attack.

Year	Movie	Character
1962	Boys' Night Out	Doug Jackson
1977	The Late Show	Harry Regan
1979	Kramer vs. Kramer	John Shaunessy
1980	Oh, God! Book II	Dr. Whitley
1986	Double Negative	Lester Harlen
1987	No Way Out	Senator Duvall
1991	Too Much Sun	O.M. Rivers

DENNIS DUGAN

(1946 -   )

Actor/director Dugan, seen above directing 1990's *Problem Child*, once described to an interviewer how he chooses a script: "When I read a script and I get to page 30, about that time is when I've made the decision. Do I care about these people? Do I care about this story? Do I care about this at all?" Dugan has also directed episodes of *Wiseguy* and *Hunter* for television.

Year	Movie	Character
1975	Night Moves	Boy
1976	Norman, Is That You?	Garson
1976	Harry and Walter Go to New York	Lewis
1979	Unidentified Flying Oddball	Tom
1981	The Howling	Chris
1988	She's Having a Baby	Bill
1988	The New Adventures of Pippi Longstocking	Mr. Settigren
1989	Parenthood	David Brodsky

ANDREW DUGGAN

(1923 - 1988)

Duggan's 40-year career on stage, in movies and television was threatened in his mid-50s by a cancerous lump on his vocal chords. When it was removed, his voice was raspy enough to give him a new career in voiceovers and in lucrative commercials. He died at 64 of cancer in California.

Year	Movie	Character
1962	The Chapman Report	Dr. Chapman
1962	Merrill's Marauders	Major (Doc) Nemeny
1965	The Glory Guys	Gen. McCabe
1967	In Like Flint	President Trent
1968	The Secret War of Harry Frigg	Gen. Armstrong
1971	Skin Game	Calloway
1977	The Private Files of J. Edgar Hoover	Lyndon B. Johnson
1978	It Lives Again	Dr. Perry
1983	Doctor Detroit	Harmon
1987	A Return to Salem's Lot	Judge Axel

BILL DUKE

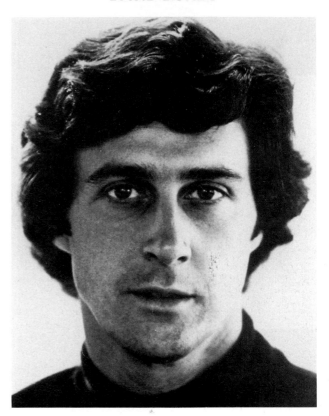

DAVID DUKES

(19?? -   )

Best known as a director, Duke is a graduate of the American Film Institute of Los Angeles. He is the director of 1991's *A Rage in Harlem* and 1992's *Deep Cover*. He has also directed episodes of television's *Knot's Landing*, *Falcon Crest* and *Flamingo Road*.

(1945 -   )

A New York stage actor, Dukes enjoys the immediate feedback of theater, but sees other advantages in front of the camera. "There's a certain kind of smallness when they come in tight, a kind of subtlety and a kind of naturalism that you can't do on the stage," he has said. "You're allowed to be very, very real and very, very spontaneous." He believes "film acting is about your motivation, it's about why you decide this or that, whereas on stage, the action is more important than the decision."

Year	Movie	Character
1985	Commando	Cooke
1987	No Man's Land	Malcolm
1987	Predator	Mac
1988	Action Jackson	Capt. Armbruster
1990	Bird on a Wire	Albert Diggs

Year	Movie	Character
1979	A Little Romance	George de Marco
1980	The First Deadly Sin	Daniel Blank
1981	Only When I Laugh	David
1983	Without a Trace	Graham Selky
1987	Date With an Angel	Ed Winston
1989	See You in the Morning	Peter Goodwin
1993	Me and the Kid	Victor Feldman

KEIR DULLEA

(1936 -)

Dullea was one of the two principal astronauts in *2001: A Space Odyssey* and co-starred with Janet Margolin in the surprisingly successful unglamorous and non-formulaic picture, *David and Lisa*. In it, he played a psychoneurotic adolescent who grows to love a schizophrenic girl while the two are institutionalized. Dullea was born in Cleveland, but considers New York City, where his Scottish-Irish parents ran a book store, to be his home. His acting career began there under the tutelage of Sanford Meisner.

Year	Movie	Character
1961	The Hoodlum Priest	Billy Lee Jackson
1962	David and Lisa	David
1964	Mail Order Bride	Lee Carey
1966	Madame X	Clay, Jr., grown up
1968	The Fox	Paul
1968	2001: A Space Odyssey	David Bowman
1973	Paperback Hero	Rick
1984	2010	Dave Bowman
1984	Blind Date	Dr. Steiger

GRIFFIN DUNNE

(1955 -)

An actor and a producer, Dunne produced his first film, *Chilly Scenes of Winter* (1979), at age 23. "Acting is what I originally wanted to do," he once explained. "Unfortunately, the business of being an actor is a lot more disheartening than the business of being a producer. As an actor, you're beholden to the material and taste of other people who are developing projects that you may or may not get in. As a producer, *you* come up with the idea." He grew up in L.A., skipped college and moved to New York at 18 to become an actor.

Year	Movie	Character
1975	The Other Side of the Mountain	Herbie Johnson
1979	Head Over Heels	Dr. Mark
1981	An American Werewolf in London	Jack
1981	The Fan	Production Asst.
1984	Almost You	Alex
1984	Johnny Dangerously	Tommy
1985	After Hours	Paul Hackett
1987	Amazon Women on the Moon	Doctor
1987	Who's That Girl?	Loudon Troff
1988	The Big Blue	Duffy
1991	My Girl	Mr. Bixler
1991	Once Around	Rob
1992	Straight Talk	Alan

MILDRED DUNNOCK

(1901 - 1991)

A Baltimore native, Dunnock gave up teaching for a stage career and made a big impression as Linda Loman, the wife of salesman Willie, in *Death of a Salesman* on Broadway and in the movies. Twice nominated for best supporting actress Oscars, she was a regular on the New York stage where she debuted in 1932.

Year	Movie	Character
1960	Butterfield 8	Mrs. Wandrous
1962	Sweet Bird of Youth	Aunt Nonnie
1964	Behold a Pale Horse	Pilar
1966	7 Women	Jane Argent
1969	Whatever Happened to Aunt Alice?	Miss Tinsley
1987	The Pick-up Artist	Nellie

CHARLES DURNING

(1933 -   )

Success in acting did not come easy to Durning. A native of Highland Falls, NY, he began his show biz career in burlesque in Buffalo. The Korean Conflict interrupted his plans and also left him temporarily blinded with badly damaged legs and a stutter. He took dance lessons to strengthen his legs and went to a drama coach for speech therapy. It was not until 1972 that his career took off when he co-starred in the Pulitzer Prize winning Off-Broadway show *That Championship Season*; it ran for two years.

Year	Movie	Character
1972	Deadhead Miles	Red Ball Rider
1973	Sisters	Joseph Larch
1973	The Sting	Lt. Snyder
1974	Front Page	Murphy
1975	The Hindenburg	Captain Pruss
1975	Dog Day Afternoon	Moretti
1976	Breakheart Pass	Frank O'Brien
1976	Harry and Walter Go to New York	Rufus T. Crisp
1977	Twilight's Last Gleaming	David T. Stevens
1977	The Choirboys	Whalen
1978	The Fury	Dr. Jim McKeever
1978	The Greek Tycoon	Michael Russell
1979	North Dallas Forty	Coach Johnson

(continued on page 506)

RICHARD DYSART

(1929 -   )

Growing up in the Kennebac Valley in Maine, Dysart worked for the local radio station, but his interests changed to acting while at Emerson College. He has spent many years on Broadway and Off-Broadway and was one of the founding members of San Francisco's American Conservatory Theater. Dysart played a ruthless mining tycoon in Clint Eastwood's *Pale Rider* and an inept, profit-hungry doctor in *The Hospital*.

Year	Movie	Character
1968	Petulia	Motel Receptionist
1969	The Lost Man	Barnes
1971	The Hospital	Dr. Welbeck
1974	The Terminal Man	Dr. John Ellis
1975	The Day of the Locust	Claude Estee
1975	The Hindenburg	Lehmann
1979	Being There	Dr. Robert Allenby
1979	Prophecy	Isely
1979	Meteor	Secretary of Defense
1982	The Thing	Dr. Copper
1985	Mask	Abe
1985	Pale Rider	Coy LaHood
1985	The Falcon and the Snowman	Dr. Lee
1985	Warning Sign	Dr. Nielsen
1987	Wall Street	Cromwell
1990	Back to the Future Part III	Barbwire Salesman

GEORGE DZUNDZA

(1945 -   )

Born in Germany, to Polish and Ukranian parents, Dzundza spent some of his childhood in displaced persons camps before he moved to Amsterdam in 1949. He arrived in New York in 1956 where he attended St. John's University as a speech and theater major. He has appeared on stage at the New York Shakespeare Festival and the Hartman Theater in Chicago and has guest-starred in many TV series. In movies, he was Michael Douglas' "regular guy" partner in *Basic Instinct*.

Year	Movie	Character
1978	The Deerhunter	John
1981	Honky Tonk Freeway	Eugene
1984	Best Defense	Loparino
1986	No Mercy	Captain Stemkowski
1987	No Way Out	Sam Hesselman
1988	The Beast	Daskal
1990	Impulse	Lt. Joe Morgan
1990	White Hunter, Black Heart	Paul Landers
1991	The Butcher's Wife	Leo Lemke
1992	Basic Instinct	Gus

JEFF EAST

(1958 -   )

East burst out of nowhere and onto movie screens in 1973 as Huck Finn in Mark Twain's *Tom Sawyer*. *Variety* wrote that he was "most effective as Huck Finn, making of that character an intriguing and contrasting personality." The movie was shot on many beautiful locations in Missouri, East's home state. The following year he reprised his role in the *Reader's Digest* version of *Huckleberry Finn*.

Year	Movie	Character
1973	Tom Sawyer	Huckleberry Finn
1974	Huckleberry Finn	Huckleberry Finn
1978	Superman	Young Clark Kent
1980	Klondike Fever	Jack London
1984	Up the Creek	Rex

CHRISTINE EBERSOLE

(1953 -   )

Ebersole launched her professional theatrical career with a 15-month run of *Oklahoma* and a year in *Camelot*, both on Broadway. Training came at New York's American Academy of Dramatic Arts which she joined after dropping out of college. The native of Winnetka, IL, spent the 1981-82 season with the late night TV program, *Saturday Night Live*.

Year	Movie	Character
1982	Tootsie	Linda
1984	Thief of Hearts	Janie Pointer
1984	Amadeus	Katerina Cavalieri
1988	Mac and Me	Janet
1990	Ghost Dad	Carol
1991	Dead Again	Lydia Larson
1992	Folks!	Arlene Aldrich

HERB EDELMAN

(1933 -   )

At 6' 5 1/2", this veteran character actor is always noticeable in his films. Edelman's entertainment career began with the USO while enlisted in the U.S. Army. After his discharge from the service, he drifted between jobs and colleges before settling into becoming an actor in New York. He is a native of Brooklyn, NY.

Year	Movie	Character
1967	Barefoot in the Park	Telephone Man
1968	P.J.	Charlie
1968	I Love You, Alice B. Toklas	Murray
1968	The Odd Couple	Murray
1972	The War Between Men and Women	Howard Mann
1973	The Way We Were	Bill Verso
1974	Front Page	Schwartz
1975	Hearts of the West	Polo
1975	The Yakuza	Wheat
1978	California Suite	Harry Michaels
1981	On the Right Track	Sam
1983	Cracking Up	Dr. Jonas Pletchick

ANTHONY EDWARDS

(1962 -   )

Edwards began acting in community theater in his hometown of Santa Barbara, CA, appearing in 25 plays before high school graduation. Work in TV commercials paid for acting studies at England's prestigious RADA. Upon his return to the U.S. he had high hopes for Hollywood, but found he had to start small: "I started doing bits on television. It was difficult and frustrating in not getting big roles, but it was for the best because I learned a lot about the camera, the people, the business, how movies are made and how to prepare for them."

Year	Movie	Character
1982	Fast Times at Ridgemont High	Stoner Bud
1983	Heart Like a Wheel	John Muldowney (15-23)
1984	Revenge of the Nerds	Gilbert
1985	Gotcha	Jonathan
1985	The Sure Thing	Lance
1986	Top Gun	Goose
1987	Summer Heat	Aaron
1987	Revenge of the Nerds II: Nerds in Paradise	Gilbert
1988	Mr. North	Theophilus North
1989	Miracle Mile	Harry Washello
1989	How I Got into College	Kip Hammet
1990	Downtown	Alex Kearney

JENNIFER EDWARDS

(1957 -)

Edwards got her first screen role, at age 10, as the title character in a television adaptation of the classic *Heidi*. At that time, the advice given to her by her famous father, the director Blake Edwards, was "to listen." She found this to be true because, as she explains, "acting is all reacting." The actress was educated in England and Switzerland, studied acting under Nina Foch and has appeared in numerous plays.

Year	Movie	Character
1969	Hook, Line & Sinker	Jennifer
1972	The Carey Treatment	Lydia Barrett
1981	S.O.B.	Lila
1983	The Man Who Loved Women	Nancy
1986	A Fine Mess	Ellen Frankenthaler
1986	That's Life!	Megan Fairchild Bartlet
1988	Sunset	Victoria Alperin
1993	Son of Pink Panther	Yussa

VINCE EDWARDS

(1928 -)

Edwards was a television star between 1961 and 1966 as Dr. Ben Casey on ABC's *Ben Casey*. One of the most popular shows in television history, its success is largely due to Edwards. The actor was discovered by Bing Crosby whose production company produced the show. He was born Vincente Eduardo Zoino and was raised in Brooklyn by Italian immigrant parents. Edwards is also a director having helmed some *Ben Casey* episodes and other TV dramas such as *Fantasy Island*.

Year	Movie	Character
1963	The Victors	Baker
1968	The Devil's Brigade	Major Cliff Bricker
1969	The Desperados	David Galt
1969	Hammerhead	Charles Hood
1982	The Seduction	Maxwell
1983	Deal of the Century	Frank Stryker
1983	Space Raiders	Hawk

LISA EICHHORN

(1952 -   )

Eichhorn grew up in Pennsylvania and finished out her college years at St. Peter's College, Oxford. Making her home in Britain she studied at RADA and went on to play many roles in British repertory theaters before being cast in John Schlesinger's *Yanks* as an English shopkeeper's daughter.

Year	Movie	Character
1979	Yanks	Jean
1979	The Europeans	Gertrude Wentworth
1981	Cutter's Way	Maureen Cutter ("Mo")
1984	Wildrose	June Lorich
1986	Opposing Force	Lt. Casey
1993	King of the Hill	Mrs. Kurlander
1993	The Vanishing	Helene

JILL EIKENBERRY

(1947 -   )

Eikenberry may be best known to television audiences as the activist lawyer, Ann Kelsey in the long-running drama, *L.A. Law*. She made her professional debut at the Arena Stage in Washington, D.C. in the production of *Moonchildren* that later went to Broadway. Wisconsin-born, she was educated at Barnard and the Yale Drama School.

Year	Movie	Character
1978	An Unmarried Woman	Claire
1979	Rich Kids	Juilliard Student
1979	Butch and Sundance: The Early Days	Mary
1980	Hide in Plain Sight	Alisa
1981	Arthur	Susan Johnson
1986	The Manhattan Project	Elizabeth Stephens

LISA EILBACHER

(1959 -)

Eilbacher grew up in Europe and the Middle East, where her father was a U.S. oil executive, and upon her return to the U.S., settled in L.A. Although unable to speak English she began working in TV commercials. She got her first real role in an episode of *Wagon Train* and was nominated for an Emmy before she was out of her teens. Eilbacher is very interested in law, particularly criminology and prison reform.

Year	Movie	Character
1972	The War Between Men and Women	Caroline Kozlenko
1981	On the Right Track	Jill
1982	An Officer and a Gentleman	Casey Seeger
1983	Ten to Midnight	Laurie Kessler
1984	Beverly Hills Cop	Jenny Summers
1989	Leviathan	Bowman

JACK ELAM

(1916 -)

Once a highly paid accountant, Elam switched to acting after being warned by his Opthamologist that bookkeeping was destroying his eyesight. He studied business and mathematics in college and, as a CPA, he grew enormously successful keeping books for, among other concerns, the Bank of America, Standard Oil of California and the Beverly Hills Hotel. Usually cast as the bad guy in films, Elam got his first role as a killer in *The Sundowners* (1950) by agreeing to find investors for the low-budget pic.

Year	Movie	Character
1961	Pocketful of Miracles	Cheesecake
1961	The Last Sunset	Ed Hobbs
1961	The Comancheros	Horseface
1966	The Rare Breed	Deke Simons
1966	The Night of the Grizzly	Hank
1967	The Way West	Weatherby
1968	Firecreek	Norman
1969	Once Upon a Time in the West	Knuckles
1969	Support Your Local Sheriff!	Jake
1970	Dirty Dingus Magee	John Wesley Hardin
1970	Rio Lobo	Phillips
1971	Hannie Caulder	Frank
1971	Support Your Local Gunfighter	Jug May
1971	The Wild Country	Thompson

(continued on page 506)

DANA ELCAR

(1927 -   )

He may be best known to TV audiences as Peter Thornton, Director of Field Operations for the Phoenix Foundation, and, otherwise, Richard Dean Anderson's contact man on the long-running hit, *MacGyver*. Elcar became afflicted with glaucoma and, although legally blind, he continued to act in the series as the producers decided to write his affliction into the show. His theatrical career began after college, producing and acting in several plays in a theater he owned and operated.

Year	Movie	Character
1968	The Boston Strangler	Luis Schubert
1969	The Learning Tree	Kirky
1971	Mrs. Pollifax—Spy	Carstairs
1971	A Gunfight	Marv Green
1973	The Sting	FBI Agent
1975	Report to the Commissioner	Chief Perna
1976	St. Ives	Charlie Blunt
1976	Baby Blue Marine	Sheriff
1979	The Champ	Hoffmaster
1980	The Nude Bomb	Chief
1981	Buddy, Buddy	Captain Hubris
1981	Condorman	Russ
1983	Blue Skies Again	Lou
1984	All of Me	Burton Schuyler
1984	2010	Dimitri Moisevitch

HECTOR ELIZONDO

(1936 -   )

Multi-talented Elizondo, in addition to his skills as an actor, is also a singer, a guitarist, and a former member of the Ballet Arts Dance Company. He has played semi-professional baseball, is an expert at Kendo (Japanese fencing) and even studied bull-fighting in Mexico! An early marriage derailed his career plans to become a history teacher. The New Yorker developed his craft as an actor in regional and Off-Broadway theaters.

Year	Movie	Character
1971	Valdez is Coming	Mexican Rider
1972	Deadhead Miles	Bad Character
1972	Pocket Money	Juan
1974	The Taking of Pelham One Two Three	Grey
1975	Report to the Commissioner	Captain d'Angelo
1979	Cuba	Ramirez
1980	American Gigolo	Sunday
1981	The Fan	Ralph Andrews
1982	Young Doctors in Love	Angelo/Angela
1984	The Flamingo Kid	Arthur Willis
1985	Private Resort	the Maestro
1986	Nothing in Common	Charlie Gargas
1989	Leviathan	Cobb
1990	Pretty Woman	Hotel Manager
1990	Taking Care of Business	The Warden
1991	Necessary Roughness	Coach Gennero
1991	Final Approach	Dr. Dio Gottlieb
1991	Frankie and Johnny	Nick

DENHOLM ELLIOTT

(1922 - 1992)

Of this scene-stealing character actor, wary actors warned: "Never act with children, dogs or Denholm Elliott." He was that good, for 47 years, winning British Academy Awards, Oscar nominations and plaudits on stage and in television. Born in London, he dropped out of RADA and into World War II as a Royal Air Force radio operator and gunner who was captured by the Germans after his plane crashed in 1942. He spent three years as a POW organizing other prisoners into a theater troupe. He died of AIDS-related TB.

Year	Movie	Character
1965	King Rat	Col. Larkin
1968	The Night They Raided Minsky's	Vance Fowler
1974	The Apprenticeship of	
	Duddy Kravitz	Friar
1976	Voyage of the Damned	Admiral Canaris
1978	The Boys from Brazil	Sidney Beynon
1979	Cuba	Skinner
1979	Saint Jack	William Leigh
1981	Raiders of the Lost Ark	Brody
1983	Trading Places	Coleman
1984	The Razor's Edge	Elliot Templeton
1985	A Room with a View	Mr. Emerson
1985	Defence of the Realm	Vernon Bayliss
1986	The Whoopee Boys	Col. Phelps
1987	September	Howard
1988	Hanna's War	xxx
1989	Indiana Jones and the	
	Last Crusade	Marcus Brody
1991	Toy Soldiers	Headmaster

SAM ELLIOTT

(1944 -   )

Introduced to movie audiences in the 1976 film *Lifeguard*, Elliott's early love of movies prompted him to try his hand at acting. Born in California and raised in Oregon, he went to college at the University of Oregon where he majored in psychology and English literature. After doing construction work in L.A., he signed a seven-year contract with 20th Century Fox.

Year	Movie	Character
1976	Lifeguard	Rick Carlson
1985	Mask	Gar
1987	Fatal Beauty	Mike Marshak
1988	Shakedown	Richie Marks
1989	Prancer	John Riggs
1989	Road House	Wade Garrett
1990	Sibling Rivalry	Charles Turner, Jr.
1991	Rush	Larry Dodd
1993	Gettysburg	Brig. Gen. John Buford

STEPHEN ELLIOTT

(1918 -   )

Elliott is a graduate of New York's Neighborhood Playhouse and began his professional career with a national tour of *The Petrified Forest*. Broadway shows led to Hollywood films and hundreds of TV appearances. He was partial to the movies, however, and commented in 1976 that television was unresolved as a medium: "It's too small. When it takes up the whole wall of a house and an image is there just as it would be on the movie screen, then it will be different."

Year	Movie	Character
1971	The Hospital	Hospital Executive
1974	Death Wish	Police Commissioner
1975	The Hindenburg	Capt. Fellows
1975	Report to the Commissioner	Police Commissioner
1981	Arthur	Burt Johnson
1981	Cutter's Way	J.J. Cord
1984	Beverly Hills Cop	Chief Hubbard
1984	Roadhouse 66	Sam
1987	Assassination	Fitzroy
1987	Walk Like a Man	xxx
1988	Arthur 2: On the Rocks	Burt Johnson
1990	Taking Care of Business	Walter Bentley

CARY ELWES

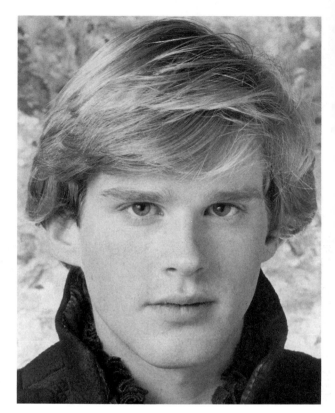

(1962 -   )

British actor Elwes moved to America after graduating from Harrow, one of England's most exclusive public schools. He moved to the U.S. to attend Sarah Lawrence College outside New York and to study acting at the Actors Studio. Early experience came with backstage work in theaters in the New York suburbs. He made his acting debut in *Equus* at New York's Greengate Theater and returned to England to complete his training at London's Drama Centre.

Year	Movie	Character
1984	Oxford Blues	Lionel
1985	The Bride	Josef
1987	The Princess Bride	Westley
1989	Glory	Maj. Cabot Forbes
1990	Days of Thunder	Russ Wheeler
1991	Hot Shots!	Kent Gregory
1992	Bram Stoker's Dracula	Lord Arthur Holmwood
1993	Robin Hood: Men in Tights	Robin Hood
1993	The Crush	Nick

ROBERT ENGLUND

(1949 -   )

You might not recognize the face, but Englund has slashed his way through six releases of *A Nightmare on Elm Street* as Freddie Krueger. The actor grew up in California's San Fernando Valley and studied acting at Cal State and UCLA. He then performed in repertory in the Midwest, where he specialized in Shakespearean clowns.

Year	Movie	Character
1974	Buster and Billie	Whitey
1976	The Great Smokey Roadblock	Beebo
1976	St. Ives	Hood
1976	A Star is Born	Marty
1976	Stay Hungry	Franklin
1981	Galaxy of Terror	Ranger
1982	Don't Cry, It's Only Thunder	Tripper
1984	A Nightmare on Elm Street	Freddy Krueger
1985	A Nightmare on Elm Street 2: Freddy's Revenge	Freddy Krueger
1987	A Nightmare on Elm Street 3: Dream Warriors	Freddy Krueger
1988	A Nightmare on Elm Street 4: The Dream Master	Freddy Krueger
1989	A Nightmare on Elm Street 5: The Dream Child	Freddy Krueger
1990	The Adventures of Ford Fairlane	Smiley
1991	Freddy's Dead: The Final Nightmare	Freddy Krueger

LEIF ERICKSON

(1911 - 1986)

Born William Wycliff Anderson in Alameda, CA, Erickson changed his name the year after his 1937 Broadway debut in *Golden Boy*. He played in movies with such stars as Bette Davis, Helen Hayes and Greta Garbo. Erickson grew up in California, but lived much of his life in the Florida Panhandle. He died of lung cancer.

Year	Movie	Character
1963	A Gathering of Eagles	General Hewitt
1964	Strait-Jacket	Bill Cutlerr
1964	Roustabout	Joe Lean
1965	I Saw What You Did	David Mannering
1965	Mirage	Major Crawford
1976	Winterhawk	Gunthrie
1977	Twilight's Last Gleaming	Ralph Whittaker

R. LEE ERMEY

(1944 -   )

The former marine's film career began as a technical advisor on Francis Ford Coppola's *Apocalypse Now* while a resident of the Philippines. Ermey enlisted in the Marines as soon as he graduated from high school with the intention of spending 30 years with the Corps. Badly wounded in Vietnam, his military career came to an end. He ran a bar on Okinawa, and then moved to the Philippines where he got married, attended college briefly and did TV commercials before meeting Coppola.

Year	Movie	Character
1978	The Boys in Company C	Sgt. Loyce
1984	Purple Hearts	Gunny
1987	Full Metal Jacket	Gny. Sgt. Hartman
1988	Mississippi Burning	Mayor Tilman
1989	Fletch Lives	Jimmy Lee Farnsworth
1989	The Siege of Firebase Gloria	Sgt. Hafner
1991	Toy Soldiers	General Kramer
1993	Hexed	Det. Ferguson

ART EVANS

(1942 -   )

Evans studied drama at the Theater of Being under the tutelage of Frank Silvera and made his professional debut in the L.A. production of *The Amen Corner*. He plays a number of musical instruments by ear and, in the role of Blind Lemon Jefferson in Gordon Parks' film *Leadbelly*, his musical and acting talents were effectively married.

Year	Movie	Character
1976	Leadbelly	Blind Lemon Jefferson
1979	The In-Laws	xxx
1979	The Main Event	xxx
1984	A Soldier's Story	Private Wilkie
1986	Jo Jo Dancer, Your Life is Calling	Arturo
1986	Native Son	Doc
1986	Ruthless People	Lt. Bender
1988	School Daze	Cedar Cloud
1989	The Mighty Quinn	Jump
1990	Die Hard 2	Barnes
1990	Downtown	Henry Coleman
1992	Trespass	Bradlee

MAURICE EVANS

(1903 - 1989)

Primarily a stage actor, Evans was known for his business acumen as well as his acting skills. The British actor/producer emigrated to the U.S. in the 1930s and became a citizen in 1941. He portrayed Romeo in his U.S. stage debut to the prestigious Katharine Cornell's Juliet. He was a hit on Broadway during the 1930s and 1940s as a producer for his ability to make Shakespeare pay at the box office. Evans died in Brighton, England, after a year of poor health.

Year	Movie	Character
1965	The War Lord	Priest
1967	Jack of Diamonds	Nicolai
1968	Planet of the Apes	Dr. Zaius
1968	Rosemary's Baby	Hutch
1970	Beneath the Planet of the Apes	Dr. Zaius
1973	Terror in the Wax Museum	Inspector

CHAD EVERETT

(1936 -   )

The popular television star decided on an acting career when, as a college student, he joined a dramatic group which travelled to India under the auspices of the U.S. Department of State. Everett spent seven years as Dr. Joe Gannon on CBS' *Medical Center* (1969-76), the longest running medical series in the history of prime-time TV. The actor has worked as a contract player for both Warner Brothers and MGM where he appeared in such TV shows as *Hawaiian Eye*, *77 Sunset Strip*, *Route 66*, *Ironside* and others.

Year	Movie	Character
1962	The Chapman Report	Water Boy
1964	Get Yourself a College Girl	Gary
1966	The Singing Nun	Robert Gerarde
1966	Made in Paris	Ted Barclay
1968	The Impossible Years	Richard Merrick
1982	Airplane II: The Sequel	Simon
1985	Fever Pitch	Dutchman

SHELLEY FABARES

(1944 -   )

Fabares is a TV veteran who started out with appearances on the shows of the early 1950s. She played Donna Reed's daughter on that star's late 50s/early 60s show and has been Craig T. Nelson's on-screen girlfriend in the popular TV sitcom *Coach* since 1989. On television continually through the 1970s and 1980s, she did a handful of teen pictures with Elvis Presley and Fabian in the mid-1960s. Modeling from age 3, she grew up in West Hollywood.

Year	Movie	Character
1964	Ride the Wild Surf	Brie Matthews
1965	Girl Happy	Valerie
1966	Spinout	Cynthia Foxhugh
1967	Clambake	Dianne Carter
1987	Hot Pursuit	Buffy Cronenberg

JEFF FAHEY

(1957 -   )

Born into a large Irish-American family in Buffalo, NY, Fahey left home at age 17 and headed for Alaska. He was soon travelling through Europe and living in a kibbutz in Israel. By age 19, he was in India. Upon his return home he attended a ballet, fell in love with dance and was eventually accepted into the Joffrey Ballet. He moved on to musicals, but after an injury, concentrated solely on drama. He spent two years on the daytime soap *One Life to Live* and then moved into feature films.

Year	Movie	Character
1985	Silverado	Tyree
1986	Psycho III	Duane
1987	Backfire	Donnie
1988	Split Decisions	Ray McGuinn
1990	White Hunter, Black Heart	Pete Verrill
1990	The Last of the Finest	Ricky Rodriguez
1990	Impulse	Stan Harris
1991	Body Parts	Chrushank
1992	The Lawnmower Man	Jobe Smith

JAMES FARENTINO

(1938 -   )

Farentino was once known as "Mr. Suspension" in Hollywood for his frequent refusals to appear in certain films while under contract to Universal and his subsequent suspensions without pay. Brooklyn-born, he studied drama in New York and came to the movie business via Broadway. He is perhaps better known on television, especially for his appearances in *The Bold Ones*.

Year	Movie	Character
1964	Ensign Pulver	Insigna
1965	The War Lord	Marc
1967	Banning	Chris
1967	Rosie!	David
1980	The Final Countdown	Cdr. Richard Owens
1989	Her Alibi	Frank Polito

ANTONIO FARGAS

(1946 -   )

Fargas, of Latin and Caribbean heritage, grew up in Manhattan. While still a student at Fashion Industries High School he won a supporting role in the film *Cool World*. Acting studies followed at such well-known institutions as the Negro Ensemble Company and the Actors Studio. His portrayal of a 90-year-old witch doctor in the Broadway production of *The Great White Hope* formally launched his adult career.

Year	Movie	Character
1971	Shaft	Bunky
1972	Across 110th Street	Henry J. Jackson
1974	Conrack	Quickfellow
1974	Busting	Stephen
1976	Next Stop, Greenwich Village	Bernstein
1978	Pretty Baby	Piano Player
1980	Up the Academy	Coach
1988	I'm Gonna Git You Sucka	Flyguy
1988	Shakedown	Nicky Carr
1991	The Borrower	Julius Caesar Roosevelt

RICHARD FARNSWORTH

(1924 -   )

Until he made his official speaking debut in *The Duchess and the Dirtwater Fox*, Farnsworth was primarily a stunt man and a bit player. Horses and wagons were his specialty. The Californian moved into this line of work after making a living as a rodeo competitor throughout the Southwest. His first job was in the 1938 Gary Cooper film *The Adventures of Marco Polo*. "I would saddle up 10 horses in the morning, ride all day as this crazy Mongolian, and then unsaddle the horses at midnight," he later recalled.

Year	Movie	Character
1978	Comes a Horseman	Dodger
1980	Resurrection	Esco
1980	Tom Horn	John Coble
1981	The Legend of the Lone Ranger	Wild Bill Hickok
1982	The Grey Fox	Bill Miner
1983	Independence Day	Evan
1984	Rhinestone	Noah
1984	The Natural	Red Blow
1985	Sylvester	Foster
1985	Into the Night	Jack Caper
1990	Misery	Buster
1990	Two Jakes	Earl Rawley
1990	Havana	Professor

SHARON FARRELL

(1949 -   )

As a teenager, Farrell spent three summers with Denver's American Ballet Theater. Stage performances followed and her dance routines became shorter while her dialogue scenes grew longer. After the New York children's theater where she was working went bankrupt, she modeled and enlisted in beauty contests. Broadway and summer stock came next and soon she found herself in Hollywood in a segment of television's *Ben Casey*.

Year	Movie	Character
1963	Forty Pounds of Trouble	Dolores
1969	The Reivers	Corrie
1969	Marlowe	Orfamay Quest
1971	The Love Machine	Maggie Stewart
1980	The Stunt Man	Denise
1983	Lone Wolf McQuade	Molly
1984	Night of the Comet	Doris
1987	Can't Buy Me Love	Mrs. Mancini
1989	One Man Force	Shirley

NORMAN FELL

(1925 -   )

Fell was born in Philadelphia, attended public schools there and probably would have followed his father into the restaurant business if it had not been for a high school play. "I enjoyed acting and marvelled that one could get paid for doing it," Fell once said. After three years as a tail gunner in the Air Force during World War II, he attended Temple University and received his B.A. in 1950. Fell began a theatrical career in New York, making the rounds of casting agents by day and studying at Stella Adler's acting school at night.

Year	Movie	Character
1960	Inherit the Wind	Radio Announcer
1963	PT 109	Edmund Drewitch
1964	The Killers	Mickey
1967	The Graduate	Mr. McCleery
1967	Fitzwilly	Oderblatz
1968	Bullitt	Baker
1968	The Secret War of Harry Frigg	Captain Stanley
1968	The Young Runaways	Mr. Donford
1968	Sergeant Ryker	Sgt. Max Winkler
1969	If It's Tuesday, This Must Be Belgium	Harve Blakely
1973	The Stone Killer	Daniels
1973	Charley Varrick	Mr. Garfinkle
1974	Airport 1975	Bill
1978	The End	Dr. Krugman
1981	Paternity	Larry
1981	On the Right Track	Mayor
1985	Transylvania 6-5000	Mac Turner
1991	For the Boys	Sam Schiff
1993	Hexed	Herschel Levine

JOSE FERRER

(1912 - 1992)

The Puerto Rican actor who graduated from Princeton started in theater as an assistant stage manager and became the long-nosed Cyrano de Bergerac in his 1946 Broadway hit, the same role that won him an Oscar in 1950. Ferrer directed several films and was seen often on television. He died after a short illness.

Year	Movie	Character
1962	Lawrence of Arabia	The Bey
1963	Nine Hours to Rama	Supt. Das
1965	The Greatest Story Ever Told	Herod Antipas
1965	Ship of Fools	Rieber
1967	Enter Laughing	Mr. Marlowe
1976	The Big Bus	Ironman
1976	Voyage of the Damned	Miguel Benitez
1977	Who Has Seen the Wind?	The Ben
1977	The Private Files of J. Edgar Hoover	Lionel McCoy
1977	The Sentinel	Robed Figure
1978	The Swarm	Dr. Andrews
1980	The Big Brawl	Dominici
1982	A Midsummer Night's Sex Comedy	Leopold
1983	To Be or Not to Be	Prof. Siletski
1984	The Evil That Men Do	Lomelin
1984	Dune	Padishah Emp. Shaddam IV
1990	Old Explorers	Warner Watney

MEL FERRER

(1912 -   )

Born Melchior Gaston Ferrer in Elberon, NJ, the actor originally began his screen career as a director in 1945 on the *Girl of the Limberlost*. He was educated at Princeton and was briefly the editor of a small newspaper in Vermont. He made his Broadway debut as a chorus dancer and then moved on to work as a radio disc jockey and a producer and director for NBC Radio. After 1960, he worked primarily in Europe as an actor, director and producer.

Year	Movie	Character
1962	The Longest Day	Major Gen. Robert Haines
1964	The Fall of the Roman Empire	Cleander
1964	Sex and the Single Girl	Rudy
1975	Brannigan	Mel Fields
1978	The Norseman	King Eurich
1979	The Visitor	Dr. Walker

BETTY FIELD

(1913 - 1973)

An intriguing character actress in drama and comedy, Field was a Boston native who attended New York's Academy of Dramatic Arts and appeared in a London play before she graduated. Her roles in Broadway comedies gave way to Hollywood traumas like *Peyton Place* and *Kings Row*. For a good part she wasn't afraid to be different instead of only pretty. She died of a cerebral hemorrhage while vacationing with her third husband on Cape Cod.

Year	Movie	Character
1960	Butterfield 8	Mrs. Fanny Thurber
1962	Birdman of Alcatraz	Stella Johnson
1966	7 Women	Florrie Pether
1968	Coogan's Bluff	Mrs. Ringerman
1968	How to Save a Marriage (And Ruin Your Life)	Thelma

FRANK FINLAY

(1927 -   )

British actor Finlay, the son of Lancashire shopkeepers, was in his twenties when he became interested in amateur dramatics. He won a scholarship to the Royal Academy of Dramatic Arts and then spent two years working in repertory. In 1963, he became a charter member, along with Laurence Olivier, in the prestigious National Theater. He is probably best known to American audiences as Iago in the 1965 film *Othello* for which he was nominated for an Academy Award.

Year	Movie	Character
1970	The Molly Maguires	Davies
1973	Shaft in Africa	Amafi
1974	The Three Musketeers	Porthos
1975	The Four Musketeers	Porthos
1978	The Wild Geese	Priest
1979	Murder by Decree	Inspector Lestrade
1985	Lifeforce	Fallada

LINDA FIORENTINO

(1960 -   )

A native of Philadelphia, when Fiorentino left college to audition for New York's prestigious Circle-in-the-Square Professional Workshop, she became one of 54 out of 1,200 applicants accepted. There she spent eight-hours-a-day on a rigorous program of voice, scene-study, technique, movement, dance and poetry. Impressed by her talents, her drama coach found her an agent and shortly thereafter she auditioned for her first screen role in *Vision Quest*.

Year	Movie	Character
1985	Vision Quest	Carla
1985	After Hours	Kiki
1985	Gotcha	Sasha
1988	The Moderns	Rachel Stone
1991	Queens Logic	Carla
1991	Shout	Molly

LARRY FISHBURNE

GERALDINE FITZGERALD

(1961 -   )

Fishburne has been acting on stage and screen since he was 10. At 14, he made an early appearance in Francis Ford Coppola's *Apocalypse Now*, a project that kept him in the Philippine jungle for two years while he was still an adolescent. The New York native is a Tony Award winner who spent four years on the soap *One Life to Live* as Josh. His lead role in John Singleton's 1991 *Boyz N the Hood* has opened many doors for Fishburne, including Broadway.

Year	Movie	Character
1979	Apocalypse Now	Clean
1983	Rumble Fish	Midget
1984	Cotton Club	Bumpy Rhodes
1986	Quicksilver	Voodoo
1987	Gardens of Stone	Flanagan
1987	A Nightmare on Elm Street 3: Dream Warriors	Max
1988	Red Heat	Lt. Stobbs
1988	School Daze	Dap Dunlap
1990	King of New York	Jimmy Jump
1991	Cadence	Stokes
1991	Class Action	Nick Holbrook
1992	Deep Cover	John Q. Hull
1993	Searching for Bobby Fischer	Vinnie
1993	What's Love Got to Do with It	Ike Turner

(1914 -   )

Considered one of the stars of the American stage, Fitzgerald is a native of Ireland. After her education in a convent school and several years of art study, she turned to the theater. Building upon her debut in Dublin and appearances in London, she came to America in a production with the newly-formed Orson Welles Mercury Theater Company. She dislikes the commercialism of Hollywood and has concentrated her efforts on the stage.

Year	Movie	Character
1965	The Pawnbroker	Marilyn Birchfield
1973	Hard Driver	Mrs. Jackson
1974	Harry and Tonto	Jessie
1981	Arthur	Martha Bach
1983	Easy Money	Mrs. Monahan
1986	Poltergeist II	Gramma Jess
1988	Arthur 2: On the Rocks	Martha Bach

PAUL FIX

(1901 - 1983)

The veteran character actor's career spanned more than 50 years and included nearly 400 movies and 200 TV productions. Often cast as a cowboy, Fix made 40 films with John Wayne and was known to TV audiences as Marshal Micah Torrance in the series *The Rifleman* starring Chuck Connors. His career began in silent films during the 1920s. Fix died of kidney failure in Santa Monica, CA.

Year	Movie	Character
1962	To Kill a Mockingbird	Judge Taylor
1964	The Outrage	Indian
1964	Mail Order Bride	Jess Linley
1965	Shenandoah	Dr. Witherspoon
1965	The Sons of Katie Elder	xxx
1966	Ride Beyond Vengeance	Hanley
1966	Nevada Smith	Sheriff Bonnell
1967	El Dorado	Doc Miller
1967	Welcome to Hard Times	Major Munn
1968	Day of the Evil Gun	Sheriff
1969	The Undefeated	General Joe Masters
1970	Dirty Dingus Magee	Chief Crazy Blanket
1971	Shootout	Brakeman
1972	Night of the Lepus	Sheriff
1973	Pat Garrett and Billy the Kid	Maxwell
1978	Grayeagle	Running Wolf
1979	Wanda Nevada	Texas Curly

ED FLANDERS

(1934 -   )

Flanders is best known to fans of the TV medical drama *St. Elsewhere* where he presided over the hospital as its chief of staff from 1982 to 1986. He took home an Emmy for the part in 1983. He was performing professionally at age 17 at San Diego's Old Globe Theater has spent his career alternating between television, the stage and movies. "I'm basically a technical actor," he once explained. "I'm not into tertiary motivations. What's more important to me is that it looks right and sounds right."

Year	Movie	Character
1977	MacArthur	President Truman
1980	The Ninth Configuration	Colonel Fell
1981	The Pursuit of D.B. Cooper	Brigadier
1981	True Confessions	Dan T. Campion
1990	The Exorcist III	Father Dyer

LOUISE FLETCHER

(1934 -   )

Fletcher played Nurse Ratched in *One Flew Over the Cuckoo's Nest* and her villainy won her critical acclaim and a best actress Oscar. A native of Birmingham, AL, she was one of three children born to an Episcopal minister and his wife, both of whom were deaf. She knew sign language as a child, but did not learn to speak until she was 3 when she spent summers with her aunt. She graduated from the University of North Carolina with a drama degree and then moved to L.A. to pursue a career in television and film.

Year	Movie	Character
1974	Thieves Like Us	Mattie
1975	One Flew Over the Cuckoo's Nest	Nurse Ratched
1977	Exorcist II: The Heretic	Dr. Gene Tuskin
1978	The Cheap Detective	Marlene DuChard
1979	The Lady in Red	Anna
1980	The Lucky Star	Loes Bakker
1983	Brainstorm	Lillian Reynolds
1983	Strange Invaders	Mrs. Benjamin
1984	Firestarter	Norma
1986	Invaders From Mars	Mrs. McKeltch
1986	Nobody's Fool	Pearl
1986	The Boy Who Could Fly	Dr. Granada
1987	Flowers in the Attic	Grandmother
1988	Two-Moon Junction	Belle
1989	Best of the Best	Mrs. Grady
1990	Blue Steel	Shirley Turner

DARLANNE FLUEGEL

(1956 -   )

Fluegel started modeling in 1974 at $100/hour with the Ford Agency and ended that career in 1981 at $300/hour. Ready for a change she moved to Hollywood to find work as an actress. Although it is always difficult to be accepted as an actress after a modeling career, Eileen Ford of the Ford Agency once explained to *People* magazine that the difference in Fluegel's case was "that she approached her acting scientifically. She worked at it and didn't let the hype go to her head. A lot of models wouldn't have done that."

Year	Movie	Character
1978	Eyes of Laura Mars	Lulu
1980	Battle Beyond the Stars	Nanelia
1984	Once Upon a Time in America	Eve
1985	To Live and Die in L.A.	Ruth Lanier
1986	Running Scared	Anna Costanzo
1986	Tough Guys	Skye Foster
1988	Bulletproof	Lt. Devon Shepard
1988	Freeway	Sarah "Sunny" Harper
1989	Lock Up	Melissa
1990	Fatal Sky	Bird McNamara

PAUL FORD

(1901 - 1976)

The homely, likeable, talented actor became famous as Col. Purdy in *Teahouse of the August Moon* in the stage, film and TV versions. Ford was well-known as Col. J.T. Hall of Phil Silvers' show *You'll Never Get Rich*, which he called "typecasting" of his character. A versatile performer, he began at age 38 in regional theater and did soap operas on radio before his first Broadway role. A resident of Manhattan, he died in Mineola, NY.

Year	Movie	Character
1962	Who's Got the Action?	Judge Boat
1962	The Music Man	Mayor Shinn
1962	Advise and Consent	Senator Danta
1963	It's a Mad Mad Mad Mad World	Col. Wilberforce
1965	Never Too Late	Harry Lambert
1966	A Big Hand for the Little Lady	Ballinger
1966	The Russians are Coming! The Russians are Coming!	Fendall Hawkins
1967	The Comedians	Smith

DEBORAH FOREMAN

(19?? -   )

Foreman's screen career got off to a good start paired with Nicolas Cage in the popular *Valley Girl*. However, her greatest critical acclaim came with her role in *My Chauffeur*. *Variety* called the "adorably spunky Deborah Foreman...a real find...[in] the mold of Goldie Hawn, Carole Lombard and Claudette Colbert. She not only can say a lot when saying nothing, she's a real pro when it comes to the difficult task of combining high-tuned dialog with physical action."

Year	Movie	Character
1983	Valley Girl	Julie
1986	My Chauffeur	Casey Meadows
1986	April Fool's Day	Muffy/Buffy
1986	3:15	Sherry Havilland
1989	The Experts	Jill

FREDERIC FORREST

(1936 -   )

Forrest's screen roles include his Oscar-nominated performance as Bette Midler's chauffeur cum boyfriend in *The Rose* and the would-be New Orleans saucier in *Apocalypse Now*. As a supporting actor, he feels "It's a continual problem when you don't have the lead—there's always the possibility you'll get cut...[you] have no control. If there's a scene with a character who isn't the lead, and if it threatens the main story or detracts from it in any way, it doesn't make a difference how good it is. It goes."

Year	Movie	Character
1974	The Conversation	Mark
1976	The Missouri Breaks	Cary
1978	It Lives Again	Eugene Scott
1979	Apocalypse Now	Chef
1979	The Rose	Dyer
1982	One From the Heart	Hank
1983	Hammett	Hammett
1983	Valley Girl	Steve
1984	The Stone Boy	Andy Jansen
1986	Where Are the Children?	Courtney Parrish
1987	Valentino Returns	Sonny Gibbs
1988	Tucker: The Man and His Dream	Eddie
1989	Music Box	Jack Burke
1989	Cat Chaser	Nolen Tyner
1990	Two Jakes	Chuck Newty
1993	Falling Down	Surplus store owner
1993	Rain Without Thunder	Walker Point Warden

STEVE FORREST

(1924 -   )

A veteran of the Battle of the Bulge in Europe during WW II, Forrest credits director George Cukor for liberating him as an actor. He once said, "George encouraged me to develop my own personal acting style, to stop imitating other actors." He believes, "If you want to continue as an actor, you must preserve a certain childlike innocence. If you cultivate this and stay as honest as you can, then the skill required beyond this is in the area of learned techniques."

Year	Movie	Character
1960	Flaming Star	Clint
1960	Heller in Pink Tights	Mabry
1960	Five Branded Women	Sgt. Keller
1971	The Wild Country	Jim
1979	North Dallas Forty	Conrad Hunter
1981	Mommie Dearest	Greg Savitt
1984	Sahara	R.J.
1985	Spies Like Us	Gen. Sline
1987	Amazon Women on the Moon	Capt. Nelson

ROBERT FORSTER

ROSEMARY FORSYTH

(1941 -   )

Forster got noticed early in his career when he portrayed a TV news cameraman, filming events at the 1968 Democratic Convention in Chicago, who managed to remain emotionally detached from his assignments, in 1969's *Medium Cool*. A native of Rochester, NY, Forster graduated from the University of Rochester with a degree in psychology in 1964. His first acting job came in a New York production of *Mrs. Dally Has a Lover* in 1965.

(1944 -   )

Forsyth enjoyed a brief screen career in the latter half of the 1960s playing the love interest to various leading men. *Variety* wrote that she gave "a compelling performance" as Doug McClure's new bride in *Shenandoah*. Charlton Heston romanced her in *The War Lord* while *Variety* wrote that she was a "nice romantic interest as a Southern coquette" with Dean Martin and Alain Delon in *Texas Across the River*.

Year	Movie	Character
1967	Reflections in a Golden Eye	Private Williams
1969	Justine	Narouz
1969	The Stalking Moon	Nick Tana
1978	Avalanche	Nick Throne
1979	The Black Hole	Captain Dan Holland
1979	The Lady in Red	xxx
1980	Alligator	David
1982	Vigilante	Eddie
1985	Hollywood Harry	Harry
1986	The Delta Force	Abdul
1990	Peacemaker	Yates
1991	29th Street	Sgt. Tartaglia

Year	Movie	Character
1965	Shenandoah	Jennie
1965	The War Lord	Bronwyn
1966	Texas Across the River	Phoebe Ann Naylor
1969	Whatever Happened to Aunt Alice?	Harriet Vaughn

MEG FOSTER

(1948 -   )

Foster started out in Hollywood in 1969 with two minor films and much TV work after two years of drama studies in New York. Unlike many actors who carefully choose roles that will enhance their career or give them personal satisafaction, she is not terribly picky. "The role I'd like to play is the role I'm doing next. I take it day by day," she admitted in 1978. The actress grew up in Rowayton, CT, and attended the exclusive Rogers Hall Boarding School in Lowell, MA.

Year	Movie	Character
1980	Carny	Gerta
1981	Ticket to Heaven	Ingrid
1983	The Osterman Weekend	Ali
1985	The Emerald Forest	Jean Markham
1987	Masters of the Universe	Evil-Lyn
1988	They Live	Holly
1989	Blind Fury	Lynn Devereaux
1989	Leviathan	Martin
1989	Relentless	Carol Dietz
1989	Stepfather II	Carol Grayland

EDWARD FOX

(1937 -   )

Fox found himself cast into the limelight following his role as a political assassin in *The Day of the Jackal*. Unimpressed with the "movie star" label, he confessed to an interviewer, "I prefer the theater because it's an actor's medium. A film belongs to the director." The winner of three British Academy Awards, Fox trained at the Royal Academy of Dramatic Art and then spent six years in repertory before making his London debut at the Royal Court Theater.

Year	Movie	Character
1973	The Day of the Jackal	"The Jackal"
1977	A Bridge Too Far	Lt. Gen. Brian Horrocks
1978	The Big Sleep	Joe Brody
1978	Force 10 from Navarone	Miller
1980	The Mirror Crack'd	Inspector Craddock
1982	Gandhi	General Dyer
1983	Never Say Never Again	M
1984	The Bounty	Capt. Greetham
1985	Wild Geese II	Alex Faulkner

JAMES FOX

(1939 -   )

The former child actor was an "overnight" sensation in the 1963 U.K. picture, *The Servant* and was named "Most Promising Young Actor of the Year" by England's Variety Club. The Britisher began his adult career with a small role in *The Loneliness of the Long Distance Runner* (1962) after a year with a large advertising firm in London. Following his role as the gangster in 1970's *Performance*, co-starring Mick Jagger, he temporarily abandoned acting to spend 12 years with a Christian group called the Navigators.

Year	Movie	Character
1965	King Rat	Flight Lt. Marlowe
1965	Those Magnificent Men in Their Flying Machines	Richard Mays
1966	The Chase	Jason "Jake" Rogers
1967	Thoroughly Modern Millie	Jimmy Smith
1968	Duffy	Stephen
1984	Greystoke: The Legend of Tarzan, Lord of the Apes	Lord Esker
1984	A Passage to India	Richard Fielding
1986	Absolute Beginners	Henley of Mayfair
1986	Whistle Blower	Lord
1989	Farewell to the King	Ferguson
1989	The Mighty Quinn	Elgin
1990	The Russia House	Ned
1992	Patriot Games	Lord Holmes
1993	The Remains of the Day	Lord Darlington

ANNE FRANCIS

(1932 -   )

Born in Ossining, NY, Francis was posing for calendar photographs when she was 6 months old. Before she had reached the age of 5, she was a fashion model and had appeared on the covers of many national magazines. Dubbed "The Little Queen of Soap Operas" she was a radio star at age 7. By age 16, she was a full-fledged Hollywood starlet having signed a contract with MGM.

Year	Movie	Character
1960	The Crowded Sky	Kitty Foster
1965	The Satan Bug	Ann
1968	Funny Girl	Georgia James
1969	Hook, Line & Sinker	Nancy
1969	More Dead Than Alive	Monica

JAMES FRANCISCUS

(1934 - 1991)

Franciscus was a handsome actor from Missouri who made school-teaching glamorous as the star of the 1960s TV series *Mr. Novak*. A natural athlete at Yale where he graduated with top academic honors, he finally stopped acting and wrote scripts. He died of emphysema.

Year	Movie	Character
1961	The Outsider	Jim Sorenson
1969	Marooned	Clayton Stone
1970	Beneath the Planet of the Apes	Brent
1976	The Amazing Dobermans	Lucky
1978	The Greek Tycoon	James Cassidy
1979	Good Guys Wear Black	Conrad Morgan
1980	When Time Ran Out...	Bob Spangler

DENNIS FRANZ

(1944 -   )

Franz is another example of an actor who plays bad guys in the movies and good guys on television. At 6' tall and weighing 200 lbs, he found himself cast as a villain early on in high school plays. The pattern continued through a succession of feature films and was only broken when he portrayed tough cop Lt. Buntz in the TV drama *Hill Street Blues*. Raised in Maywood, IL, the son of a German immigrant, he entered the U.S. Army after college and spent eleven months in the 82nd and 101st Airborne divisions in Vietnam.

Year	Movie	Character
1980	Dressed to Kill	Detective Marino
1981	Blow Out	Manny Karp
1983	Psycho II	Toomey
1984	Body Double	Rubin
1989	The Package	Milan Delich
1990	Die Hard 2	Carmine Lorenzo

KATHLEEN FREEMAN

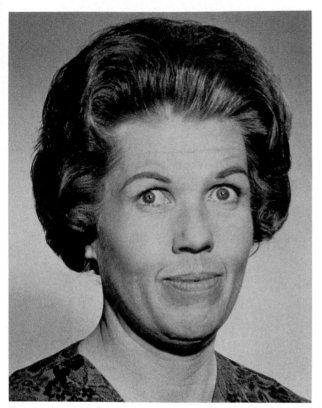

(1920 -   )

The veteran comic actress was a favorite of Jerry Lewis and appeared in several of his movies. Freeman grew up in Chicago, the daughter of vaudevillians, and became a part of their act at age two. She prefers comedy over drama and has described herself as a "confirmed lunatic." "I think comedy is more powerful than drama in the long run," she once said. "Comedy is more difficult. It's very easy to make people cry."

Year	Movie	Character
1960	North to Alaska	Lena
1961	The Errand Boy	Mrs. T. P.
1961	The Ladies' Man	Katie
1963	The Nutty Professor	Millie Lemon
1964	Mail Order Bride	Sister Sue
1964	The Disorderly Orderly	Maggie Higgins
1965	Marriage on the Rocks	Miss Blight
1965	The Rounders	Agatha Moore
1966	Three on a Couch	Murphy
1969	Hook, Line & Sinker	Baby Sitter
1970	The Ballad of Cable Hogue	Mrs. Jensen
1971	Support Your Local Gunfighter	Mrs. Perkins
1972	Where Does It Hurt?	Mrs. Mazzini
1973	Your Three Minutes Are Up	Mrs. Wilk
1978	The Norseman	Indian
1980	The Blues Brothers	Sister Mary Stigmata
1986	The Best of Times	Rosie
1987	In the Mood	Mrs. Marver
1987	Innerspace	Dream Lady
1990	Gremlins 2 The New Batch	Microwave Marge
1991	Dutch	Gritzi

VICTOR FRENCH

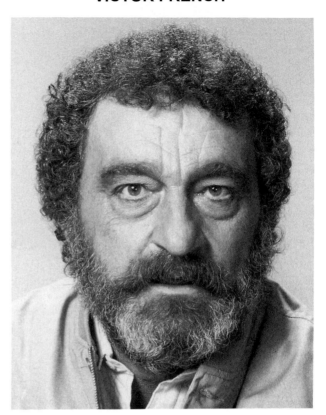

(1934 - 1989)

Early in his career French became a cowboy in TV westerns like *Gunsmoke* and *Bonanza*. A regular on *Little House on the Prarie*, he also directed stage productions and won an L.A. Drama Critics award for *12 Angry Men*. He died of lung cancer.

Year	Movie	Character
1963	Spencer's Mountain	Spencer's Brother
1969	Charro!	Vince
1970	Rio Lobo	Ketcham
1970	There Was a Crooked Man...	Whiskey
1971	The Wild Rovers	Sheriff
1972	The Other	Angelini
1981	Choices	Gary Carluccio
1982	An Officer and a Gentleman	Joe Pokrifki

MATT FREWER

(1958 -   )

Comedian Steve Martin would have called him a "wild and crazy guy" so it may be hard to believe Frewer was originally trained as a Shakespearean actor. He grew up in Ontario intending to become a professional hockey player. A thigh injury sidelined this dream, and, against his parents' wishes, he decided to pursue a theatrical career. He studied with England's prestigious Old Vic Theatre School and later became the character "Max Headroom" on television.

Year	Movie	Character
1983	The Lords of Discipline	Senior
1984	Supergirl	Truck Driver
1985	Spies Like Us	Soldier
1989	Far From Home	Charlie Cross
1989	Honey, I Shrunk the Kids	Big Russ Thompson
1989	Speed Zone!	Alec
1990	Short Time	Ernie Dills
1991	The Taking of Beverly Hills	Ed Kelvin

STEPHEN FURST

(19?? -   )

A native of Virginia, Furst migrated west with his wife upon graduation from Virginia Commonwealth University with a degree in Theater Arts. After delivering pizzas for a while, he rocketed into the public eye as Flounder in one of the most successful comedies in film history, *National Lampoon's Animal House*. His next big part was as Dr. Elliot Axelrod on NBC's popular hospital drama, *St. Elsewhere*.

Year	Movie	Character
1978	National Lampoon's Animal House	Kent Dorfman
1978	Take Down	Randy Jensen
1980	Midnight Madness	Harold
1982	National Lampoon's Class Reunion	Hubert
1982	Silent Rage	Charlie
1984	Up the Creek	Gonzer
1989	The Dream Team	Albert Ianuzzi

MAX GAIL

(1943 -   )

"I grew up watching television and think it was some kind of destiny that I became an actor," Gail told *People* magazine in 1980. His acting career didn't begin, however, until after he received an economics degree from Williams College and a masters in international finance from the University of Michigan and worked as a waiter, construction worker, teacher and piano player. Gail spent several seasons as detective Wojehowicz on the successful TV series, *Barney Miller*.

Year	Movie	Character
1971	The Organization	Rudy
1975	Night Moves	Stud
1983	D.C. Cab	Harold
1984	Heartbreakers	Charles
1986	Where Are the Children?	Clay Eldridge
1988	Judgment in Berlin	Judah Best

PETER GALLAGHER

(1955 -   )

While he'd like a crack at the leading man, or good-guy roles, Gallagher is happy when cast as the villain. "If I have a choice between a nice, bland hero or a really interesting, detestable character, I'd rather do the detestable one. Good guys can be pretty boring," he has said. "I love playing characters who celebrate the power and joy and beauty of greed. As the bad guy, you have less moral and behavioral restrictions. There's no burden of being liked. It's real freedom for the actor."

Year	Movie	Character
1980	The Idolmaker	Caesare
1982	Summer Lovers	Michael
1986	My Little Girl	Kai
1988	High Spirits	Brother Tony
1989	sex, lies and videotape	John Millaney
1991	Late for Dinner	Bob Freeman
1992	The Player	Larry Levy
1993	Watch It	John
1993	Malice	Dennis Riley
1993	Short Cuts	Stormy Weathers

RITA GAM

(1928 -   )

Gam made her film debut in 1952 with Ray Milland in *The Thief*, a picture that is considered a novelty because it contains no dialogue. Under contract to MGM at the time, she roomed with Grace Kelly and the two were best friends until the Princess' untimely death. Gam's career interests turned to writing, however, when she decided that acting was not enough. She wrote her autobiography, *Actress to Actress*, in 1986. Of French and Romanian descent, the actress was born in Pittsburgh.

Year	Movie	Character
1961	King of Kings	Herodias
1971	Klute	Trina
1971	Shootout	Emma
1987	Distortions	Mildred
1989	Midnight	Heidi

JAMES GAMMON

(1940 -   )

Gammon's screen career began behind the scenes as a cameraman and a director at television stations in Orlando, FL, in the early 1960s. He soon moved to L.A. and purchased a small theater there in 1972. At the time he stated, "My first love is theater and my acting is primarily in theater." His theater received numerous awards including the L.A. Drama Critics Circle Award of Continued Excellence. His film acting career began in earnest during the 1980s.

Year	Movie	Character
1974	Macon County Line	Elisha
1980	Urban Cowboy	Steve Strange
1983	The Ballad of Gregorio Cortez	Frank Fly
1985	Sylvester	Steve
1987	Made in Heaven	Steve Shea
1988	The Milagro Beanfield War	Horsethief Shorty
1989	Major League	Lou Brown
1990	Coupe de Ville	Doc Sturgeon
1990	I Love You to Death	Lt. Schooner
1990	Revenge	Texan
1992	CrissCross	Emmett

VINCENT GARDENIA

(1922 - 1992)

Born in Italy, the character actor came to the U.S. at age 2 with his family, made his stage debut at 5 in his father's Italian acting company, and in 1955, playing a pirate in his Broadway debut, spoke English on stage for the first time. Throughout his career Gardenia appeared in films and TV series, usually in comic roles like Archie Bunker's neighbor in *All in the Family* or Cher's father in *Moonstruck*. He won two Obies, a Tony, an Emmy, and was nominated for two best-supporting Oscars. He died of a heart attack.

Year	Movie	Character
1961	Mad Dog Coll	Schultz
1961	The Hustler	Bartender
1970	Jenny	Mr. Marsh
1970	Where's Poppa?	Coach Williams
1971	Cold Turkey	Mayor Wrappler
1972	Hickey & Boggs	Papadakis
1973	Bang the Drum Slowly	Dutch Schnell
1973	Lucky Luciano	American Colonel
1973	The Manchu Eagle Murder Caper Mystery	Big Daddy
1974	Death Wish	Frank Ochoa
1974	Front Page	Sheriff
1977	Greased Lightning	Sheriff Cotton
1978	Heaven Can Wait	Krim

(continued on page 506)

ALLEN GARFIELD

(1939 -   )

Born Allen Goorwitz in Newark, NJ, and educated at Upsala College and Anthony Mannino Studio, Garfield began his career as a journalist. He moved from copyboy to sports reporter for the Newark Star Ledger and then worked as a staff writer for Australia's Sunday Morning Herald. He has studied acting with Lee Strasberg and Elia Kazan and is a member of the Actors Studio.

Year	Movie	Character
1970	The Owl and the Pussycat	Dress Shop Proprietor
1971	The Organization	Benjy
1972	Deadhead Miles	Juicy Brucey
1972	The Candidate	Klein
1973	Slither	Vincent J. Palmer
1974	Busting	Carl Rizzo
1974	Front Page	Kruger
1974	The Conversation	Bernie Moran
1975	Nashville	Barnett
1976	Gable and Lombard	Mayer
1976	Mother, Jugs & Speed	Harry Fishbine
1978	The Brink's Job	Vinnie Costa
1980	One Trick Pony	Cal Van Damp
1980	The Stunt Man	Sam

(continued on page 507)

BEVERLY GARLAND	LORRAINE GARY

(1930 -)	(1937 -)

Garland's movie debut came in 1950 in *D.O.A.* and, after accepting several roles in low-budget horror, sci-fi and western pics, she gravitated to television, becoming familiar to audiences as the mother in *My Three Sons*. She grew up in California and Arizona and got involved in school plays at a young age. She is currently the owner and operator of the Beverly Garland Hotels in California.

Raised in L.A., Gary won a best actress award in competition at the prestigious Pasadena Playhouse at age 16. However, she declined a scholarship there in order to enroll as a political science major at Columbia University. After marrying, she followed her husband back to California, had kids and did some television work. She is perhaps best known for her roles as Roy Scheider's wife/widow in the *Jaws* pictures.

Year	Movie	Character
1968	Pretty Poison	Mrs. Stepanek
1969	The Mad Room	Mrs. Racine
1979	Roller Boogie	Mrs. Barkley
1980	It's My Turn	Emma

Year	Movie	Character
1975	Jaws	Ellen Brody
1977	I Never Promised You a Rose Garden	Mrs. Blake
1978	Jaws 2	Ellen Brody
1979	1941	Joan Douglas
1979	Just You and Me Kid	Shirl
1987	Jaws the Revenge	Ellen Brody

VITTORIO GASSMAN

(1922 -   )

The Italian actor's first attempt to break into Hollywood occurred during the 1950s after his marriage to the actress, Shelley Winters. Gassman's first four films for MGM went nowhere so he returned to Italy. Eventually, he specialized in comedy. He was born in Genoa, Italy, and, after attending law school, studied acting under Silvio D'Amico at the National Academy of Dramatic Art in Rome.

Year	Movie	Character
1967	The Tiger and the Pussycat	Francesco Vincenzini
1967	Woman Times Seven	Cenci
1979	Quintet	St. Christopher
1980	The Nude Bomb	Nino
1981	Sharky's Machine	Victor
1982	Tempest	Alonzo

JOHN GAVIN

(1935 -   )

A native of L.A., Gavin was a naval intelligence officer in Korea during the conflict and began his acting career under contract to Universal Pictures. Once President of the Screen Actors Guild, he was picked by U.S. President Ronald Reagan for the post of U.S. Ambassador to Mexico at age 51.

Year	Movie	Character
1960	A Breath of Scandal	Charlie
1960	Midnight Lace	Brian Younger
1960	Psycho	Sam Loomis
1960	Spartacus	Julius Caesar
1961	Back Street	Paul Saxon
1961	Tammy Tell Me True	Tom Freeman
1967	Thoroughly Modern Millie	Trevor Graydon

WENDY GAZELLE

(19?? -   )

Born outside of Cleveland, OH, Gazelle studied ballet until her college days at Northwestern University where she stopped dancing and began acting. Her professional career started with summer stock and Broadway and then a brief dry spell before she moved on Hollywood.

Year	Movie	Character
1987	Hot Pursuit	Lori Cronenberg
1988	The "In" Crowd	Gail Goren
1989	Triumph of the Spirit	Allegra
1989	Understudy: Graveyard Shift 2	Camilla/Patti

MICHAEL V. GAZZO

(1923 -   )

A bartender's son, Gazzo was born in Hillside, NJ, and graduated from the Dramatic Workshop of the New School for Social Research. He trained for the stage at the Actors Studio in New York. After spending World War II in the U.S. Army, he began his career on the New York stage. He has worked as a writer, a director and an acting teacher and founded the Gazzo Theater Workshop in L.A.

Year	Movie	Character
1974	The Godfather, Part II	Frankie Pentangeli
1977	Black Sunday	Muzi
1978	King of the Gypsies	Spiro Georgio
1979	Love and Bullets	Lobo
1980	Alligator	Police Chief
1981	Back Roads	Tazio
1981	Body and Soul	Frankie
1984	Fear City	Mike
1989	Cookie	Carmine Tarantino

CHRISTOPHER GEORGE

(1929 - 1983)

This stylish villain character was busy in TV-movies and series as well as in feature films. Born in Royal Oak, MN, George began to act in the mid-60's and appeared with his wife Lynda in *Chisum* and *Day of the Animals*. He died at 54 of a heart attack in L.A.

Year	Movie	Character
1967	El Dorado	Dan McLeod
1970	Chisum	Dan Nodeen
1973	I Escaped from Devil's Island	Davert
1973	The Train Robbers	Calhoun
1976	Grizzly	Kelly
1976	Midway	Lt.Cmdr. C. Wade McClusky
1980	The Exterminator	Det. Dalton

JAMI GERTZ

(1965 -   )

Acting professionally since the early 1980s, Gertz's resume of television and film credits expanded rapidly. A native of Glenview, IL, she was originally set on becoming a figure skater, but turned to acting upon winning the role of Dorothy in a grammar school production of *The Wizard of Oz*. Her big boost came with her role in television's *Square Pegs* (1982-83) as the insufferable Muffy Tepperman.

Year	Movie	Character
1981	Endless Love	Patty
1984	Alphabet City	Sophia
1984	Sixteen Candles	Robin
1985	Mischief	Rosalie
1986	Crossroads	Frances
1986	Quicksilver	Terri
1986	Solarbabies	Terra
1987	Less Than Zero	Blair
1987	The Lost Boys	Star
1989	Listen to Me	Monica Tomanski
1989	Renegades	Barbara
1990	Don't Tell Her It's Me	Emily Pear
1990	Sibling Rivalry	Jeanine

JOHN GETZ

(1947 -   )

Best known in movies as the bartender who has an affair with his boss' wife in the acclaimed *Blood Simple*, Getz started out in New York soap operas. A graduate of the University of Iowa, he spent one season with the American Conservatory Theater in San Francisco and two with the Napa Valley Theater Company. He lived for several years on a small island near New York City and spent free time on his 36-foot sailboat. "This is a better place to sail than California," he once said. "Sailing there is like driving on the freeway."

Year	Movie	Character
1984	Blood Simple	Ray
1984	Thief of Hearts	Ray Davis
1986	The Fly	Stathis Borans
1989	Born on the Fourth of July	Marine Major
1989	The Fly II	Stathis Borans
1990	Men at Work	Maxwell Potterdam III
1991	Curly Sue	Walker McCormick
1991	Don't Tell Mom the Babysitter's Dead	Gus Brandon

CYNTHIA GIBB

(1963 -   )

Hard-working and ambitious, Gibb has been an actress, a model or a dancer since she was 5. She was raised in Westport, CT, where her mother ran a dance studio. By 14, she was represented by the prestigious Ford Modeling Agency and after high school landed a role in the now-defunct daytime drama, *Search for Tomorrow*. Her acting career progressed steadily after that, even though at one point in her life, she said, "I didn't want to be an actress because I didn't want to be unemployed."

Year	Movie	Character
1986	Salvador	Cathy Moore
1986	Youngblood	Jessie Chadwick
1987	Malone	Jo Barlow
1988	Jack's Back	Christine Gibb
1988	Short Circuit 2	Sandy Banatoni
1990	Death Warrant	Amanda Beckett

JACK GILFORD

(1907 - 1990)

Born on the lower east side of Manhattan, this long time character actor and comedian played on stage and screen for more than 50 years. Gilford was most famous for his Crackerjack commercials on television, on the air from 1962 to 1973 and winner of many prizes, including a Cannes Film Festival award. He was in the first group of actors to be black-listed during the early 1950s Red Scare. He died of stomach cancer.

Year	Movie	Character
1966	A Funny Thing Happened on the Way to the Forum	Hysterium
1966	Mister Buddwing	Mr. Schwartz
1966	The Daydreamer	Papa Anderson
1967	Enter Laughing	Mr. Foreman
1967	The Incident	Sam Beckerman
1967	Who's Minding the Mint?	Avery Dugan
1970	Catch-22	Dr. Daneeka
1971	They Might Be Giants	Wilbur Peabody
1973	Save the Tiger	Phil Greene
1976	Harry and Walter Go to New York	Mischa
1980	Wholly Moses	Tailor
1981	Caveman	Gog
1985	Cocoon	Bernie Lefkowitz
1988	Arthur 2: On the Rocks	Mr. Butterworth
1988	Cocoon: The Return	Bernie Lefkowitz

ROBERT GINTY

(1948 -   )

Ginty is usually cast as an action actor and is popular in video markets outside the U.S. "I've played a very violent repertory of movies, and what they've done for me is given me an economically viable career," he once commented. Born in Brooklyn into a political family, he once played drums with Jimi Hendrix before the performer shot to stardom.

Year	Movie	Character
1976	Two Minute Warning	xxx
1978	Coming Home	Sgt. Dink Mobley
1980	The Exterminator	John Eastland
1984	Exterminator 2	Johnny
1989	Loverboy	Joe Bodek
1990	Madhouse	Dale
1991	Harley Davidson & the Marlboro Man	Thom

ANNABETH GISH

(1973 -   )

Uncertain if she is related to Lillian Gish, Annabeth grew up in Cedar Falls, IA, where her father was an English professor and her mother a teacher of 'gifted' children. Her career began at age 7, performing in university productions, community playhouses and several television commercials. At 13, she made her film debut in the critically acclaimed *Desert Bloom*.

Year	Movie	Character
1986	Desert Bloom	Rose
1987	Hiding Out	Ryan Campbell
1988	Mystic Pizza	Kat Araujo
1989	Shag	Pudge
1990	Coupe de Ville	Tammy

LILLIAN GISH

(1896 - 1993)

The enduring star began as a heroine in silent films with her sister Dorothy and continued to act throughout her life playing characters in the talkies like the 91-year-old in the 1987 *Whales of August*. In the mid-20s, Gish's contract with MGM was for $1 million for 2 years, a milestone then. In spite of her excellence, she never won an Oscar until 1970 when the Academy gave her an honorary one. She died in her sleep in her New York apartment.

Year	Movie	Character
1960	The Unforgiven	Mattilda Zachary
1967	The Comedians	Mrs. Smith
1967	Warning Shot	Alice Willows
1986	Sweet Liberty	Cecelia Burgess
1987	The Whales of August	Sarah Webber

PAUL GLEASON

(1944 -   )

A self-described "baseball bum" who spent his youth travelling from state to state, Gleason did not begin acting until he was 25. "I went into acting because I had nothing more sensible to do. However, once I began acting classes with Lee Strasberg at the Actors Studio in New York, I found it stimulating and rewarding," he once told an interviewer. Aside from his film work, he has been involved as a writer, director and actor in New York's Off-Off-Broadway movement.

Year	Movie	Character
1981	The Pursuit of D.B. Cooper	Remson
1983	Tender Mercies	Reporter
1983	Trading Places	Beeks
1985	The Breakfast Club	Richard Vernon
1987	Forever, Lulu	Robert
1988	Die Hard	Dwayne T. Robinson
1988	Johnny Be Good	Wayne Hisler
1988	She's Having a Baby	Howard
1989	Night Game	Broussard
1990	Miami Blues	Sgt. Frank Lackley
1991	Rich Girl	Marvin Wells

SCOTT GLENN

(1942 -   )

Glenn was born in Pittsburgh and attended the college of William and Mary. Before turning to acting, his many jobs included being a reporter for a Chicago area newspaper. He is a lifetime member of The Actors Studio and studied with Lee Strasberg. He performed in several Off-Broadway plays before being discovered by director James Bridges and moving to Hollywood in the late sixties.

Year	Movie	Character
1975	Nashville	Pfc. Glenn Kelly
1979	Apocalypse Now	Civilian
1979	More American Graffiti	Newt
1980	Cattle Annie and Little Britches	Bill Dalton
1980	Urban Cowboy	Wes
1982	Personal Best	Terry Tingloff
1982	The Challenge	Rick
1983	The Right Stuff	Alan Shepard
1984	The River	Joe Wade
1985	Silverado	Emmett
1985	Wild Geese II	John Haddad
1988	Off Limits	Col. Armstrong
1989	Miss Firecracker	Mac Sam
1990	The Hunt for Red October	Bart Mancuso
1991	Backdraft	John Adcox
1991	My Heroes Have Always Been Cowboys	H.D. Dalton
1991	The Silence of the Lambs	Jack Crawford

CRISPIN GLOVER

(1964 -   )

Once kicked off *The David Letterman Show* for annoying his host, Glover's offbeat personality has permeated many of his film roles including *Back to the Future* and *River's Edge*. The son of an actor and a former ballet dancer, Glover grew up in L.A. from the age of four.

Year	Movie	Character
1981	Private Lessons	xxx
1983	My Tutor	Jack
1984	Friday the 13th—	
	The Final Chapter	Jimmy
1984	Racing With the Moon	Gatsby Boy
1984	Teachers	Danny
1985	Back to the Future	George McFly
1986	At Close Range	Lucas
1986	River's Edge	Layne
1988	Twister	Howdy Cleveland
1990	Where the Heart Is	Lionel
1990	Wild at Heart	Dell
1991	The Doors	Andy Warhol

JOHN GLOVER

(1944 -   )

Enthusiastic about acting on stage as well as in movies, Glover once commented, "I would like to be able to be both a film actor and a stage actor—to be an American actor in the style of a lot of the English actors who do films. They are these wonderful actors who can do everything." Glover grew up in Maryland and spent four summers with Virginia's Barter Theater before going to New York.

Year	Movie	Character
1977	Julia	Sammy
1978	Somebody Killed Her Husband	Hubert Little
1979	Last Embrace	Richard Peabody
1979	The American Success	
	Company	Ernst
1980	Melvin and Howard	Attorney Freese
1980	The Mountain Men	Nathan
1982	A Little Sex	Walter
1984	The Evil That Men Do	Briggs
1985	White Nights	Wynn Scott
1986	52 Pick-Up	Alan Raimy
1988	Masquerade	Tony Gateworth
1988	Rocket Gibraltar	Rolo Rockwell
1988	Scrooged	Brice Cummings
1988	The Chocolate War	Brother Leon
1990	Gremlins 2 The New Batch	Daniel Clamp

VALERIA GOLINO

ARLENE GOLONKA

(1966 -   )

Born in Naples, Italy, and raised in Athens, Greece, Golino has already won the prestigious Golden Lion Award at the Venice Film Festival and Italy's version of the Oscar. A relative newcomer, she has only been living in the U.S. since 1989.

(1938 -   )

Golonka began her acting career in her hometown of Chicago with summer stock. She subsequently moved to New York and got her first breaks playing feather-brained mistresses and kooky prostitutes on the stage. She also appeared in two movies, acted in TV dramas and did commercials. She got her start in Hollywood with the production of *Penelope* for MGM.

Year	Movie	Character
1988	Big Top Pee-wee	Gina Piccolapupula
1988	Rain Man	Susanna
1991	Hot Shots!	Ramada
1991	The Indian Runner	Maria
1991	Year of the Gun	Lia Spinelli
1993	Hot Shots! Part Deux	Ramada Rodham Hayman

Year	Movie	Character
1966	Penelope	Honeysuckle Rose
1967	The Busy Body	Bobbi Brody
1967	Welcome to Hard Times	Mae
1968	Hang 'Em High	Jennifer
1977	Airport '77	Mrs. Jane Stern
1979	The In-Laws	Jean Ricardo
1980	The Last Married Couple in America	Sally
1983	My Tutor	Mrs. Chyrstal

DODY GOODMAN

(1915 -   )

Actress and comedienne, Goodman is a television veteran who was a regular on *The Jack Paar Show* in the late 1950's and spent three seasons on Norman Lear's hit *Mary Hartman, Mary Hartman*. Her entertainment career began with ballet studies at the School of American Ballet and the Metropolitan Opera Ballet School in New York. She then made the transition to comedienne and appeared often on television, in night clubs and Off-Broadway revues.

Year	Movie	Character
1964	Bedtime Story	Fanny Eubank
1978	Grease	Blanche
1982	Grease 2	Blanche
1983	Max Dugan Returns	Mrs. Litke
1984	Splash	Mrs. Stimler
1985	Private Resort	Amanda Rawlings
1991	Cool as Ice	Mae McCallister
1992	Frozen Assets	Mrs. Patterson

DON GORDON

(1926 -   )

Gordon played Steve McQueen's partner, a cop assigned to "babysit" a Chicago hood, in *Bullitt* and appeared with the star again, five years later, in *Papillon* as a returnee to the French Guyana penal colony where McQueen was a prisoner. The actor left school after the eighth grade to join the navy in 1941 after the Japanese attack on Pearl Harbor. He served aboard both the USS Saratoga and USS Yorktown. Professional acting began for him in the early television shows produced in New York and L.A.

Year	Movie	Character
1968	Bullitt	Delgetti
1970	WUSA	Bogdanovich
1973	Papillon	Julot
1973	The Mack	Hank
1981	The Final Conflict	Dean
1982	The Beast Within	Judge
1991	The Borrower	Charles Krieger

KEITH GORDON

(1961 -   )

Gordon was only 17 years old and had only one professional appearance to his credit—at the Eugene O'Neill Theater in Connecticut—when he was cast in the big budget movie *Jaws 2* . The picture took almost a year to film. Ten years later he got a chance to direct his first movie: *The Chocolate War*. The film was shot in just 24 days for $700,000. The son of an actor/teacher/director, Gordon was born in the New York borough of the Bronx and began acting at 13.

Year	Movie	Character
1978	Jaws 2	Doug
1979	All That Jazz	Young Joe
1980	Dressed to Kill	Peter Miller
1983	Christine	Arnie Cunningham
1985	The Legend of Billie Jean	Lloyd
1986	Back to School	Jason Melon

CLIFF GORMAN

(1936 -   )

Gorman had originally planned to become an artist so he went to New York's High School of Music and Art and studied for seven years at the city's Art Students League. But he gave up painting, went to college and, after graduation, became a sales rep for industrial air conditioners and water heaters. The money was good, but he was unhappy and, on the suggestion of friends, turned to acting. He may be best known for his stage and screen roles in *The Boys in the Band*.

Year	Movie	Character
1969	Justine	Toto
1978	An Unmarried Woman	Charlie
1979	All That Jazz	Davis Newman
1980	Night of the Juggler	Gus
1984	Angel	Lt. Andrews
1992	Hoffa	Solly Stein
1992	Night and the City	Phil Nassaros

HAROLD GOULD

TODD GRAFF

(1923 -   )

Gould spent the 1940s in the World War II army and studying for various higher degrees (B.A., M.A., Ph.D.). In the 1950s, he began an acting career with appearances in regional theaters and Off-Broadway. He also worked as a theater and speech instructor. His film career started in the 1960s and includes a role in *The Sting* as a fellow con-artist in the phony off-track betting joint set up by Paul Newman and Robert Redford. Gould hails from Schenectady, NY.

Year	Movie	Character
1965	The Satan Bug	Dr. Ostrer
1966	An American Dream	Ganucci's Lawyer
1966	Harper	Sheriff Spanner
1969	The Arrangement	Dr. Liebman
1971	Mrs. Pollifax—Spy	Nexdhet
1972	Where Does It Hurt?	Dr. Zerny
1973	The Sting	Kid Twist
1974	Front Page	The Mayor
1975	Love and Death	Anton
1976	Silent Movie	Engulf
1980	Seems Like Old Times	Judge
1989	Romero	Francisco Galedo

(1959 -   )

Multitalented New Yorker Graff graduated from the Professional Children's School in Manhattan in 1978 and then studied screenwriting and playwrighting at Purchase College. He has written at least three screenplays and has worked as a backup singer with such diverse artists as James Taylor, Carly Simon, Pete Seeger and Peggy Lee. He won an Emmy as a teenager in the educational television series *The Electric Company* and was nominated for a Tony for his Broadway debut in *Baby*.

Year	Movie	Character
1987	Sweet Lorraine	Leonard
1988	Dominick and Eugene	Larry Higgins
1988	Five Corners	James
1989	The Abyss	Alan "Hippy" Carnes
1990	Opportunity Knocks	Lou Pasquino
1991	City of Hope	Zip

GERRIT GRAHAM

(1948 -   )

Graham's acting debut came at age 8 in a production of *Winnie the Pooh*. He was president of the dramatic association as a high school student at Groton and general manager of the Columbia Players while studying at Columbia University. His early professional roles came in film via his association with the director, Brian De Palma and on the stage with Chicago's Second City troupe.

Year	Movie	Character
1974	Phantom of the Paradise	Beef
1976	Cannonball	Perman
1976	Tunnelvision	xxx
1977	The Demon Seed	Walter Gabler
1978	Pretty Baby	Highpockets
1980	Used Cars	Jeff
1982	National Lampoon's Class Reunion	Bob
1982	Soup for One	Brian
1985	The Annihilators	Ray
1985	The Man With One Red Shoe	Carson
1986	Band of the Hand	xxx
1986	Chopping Mall	Technician Nessler
1987	It's Alive III: Island of the Alive	Ralston
1988	Walker	xxx
1989	Police Academy 6: City Under Siege	Ace
1990	Child's Play 2	Phil Simpson
1990	Martians Go Home	Stan Garrett
1990	Night of the Cyclone	xxx

HEATHER GRAHAM

(1970 -   )

Graham's most prominent role to date has been that of Nadine, a member of Matt Dillon's druggy crew in *Drugstore Cowboy*. The young actress spent her early years quite differently than her character as she once told an interviewer: "I had a very strict Catholic childhood. My Dad was an FBI agent, so he saw a lot of bad things that were happening in the world, and he wanted to protect us from them. So we really weren't exposed to very much."

Year	Movie	Character
1988	License to Drive	Mercedes
1989	Drugstore Cowboy	Nadine
1990	I Love You to Death	Bridget
1991	Shout	Sara Benedict
1992	Diggstown	Emily Forrester
1992	Twin Peaks: Fire Walk With Me	Annie Blackburn

DAVID MARSHALL GRANT

(1955 -   )

Grant has spent most of his career on the stage and seems to prefer it. "In film you make the most money, and television is easiest because its stupid," he once said. "[But] theater is the most rewarding because you can at least try to do something worthwhile. The thing about a movie is that you basically wait all day, and it can get boring. But theater is exciting. You walk out on a stage opening night on Broadway, and, wow, you freak out! Your stage fright which you thought you left behind roars up in your head."

Year	Movie	Character
1979	French Postcards	Alex
1988	Bat 21	Ross Carver
1990	Air America	Rob Diehl
1991	Strictly Business	David
1992	Forever Young	Wilcox

RICHARD E. GRANT

(1957 -   )

Born in Swaziland, where his father was Minister of Education until independence was declared in 1968, Grant's most notable screen role to date was in *Withnail & I* (1987). After graduating from Cape Town University, he founded a small, but ambitious acting troupe. He gained further exposure to the stage upon his move to England in 1982. Hollywood followed shortly thereafter.

Year	Movie	Character
1990	Mountains of the Moon	Oliphant
1991	Hudson Hawk	Darwin Mayflower
1991	L.A. Story	Roland
1991	Warlock	Redferne
1992	Bram Stoker's Dracula	Dr. Jack Seward
1992	The Player	Tom Oakley

KERRI GREEN

(1967 -   )

A native of Fort Lee, NJ, Green began making regular trips across the Hudson River into Manhattan for modeling assignments and small guest spots on daytime dramas in her early teens. She once told a journalist, "I got a manager when I was in the eighth grade, but I didn't take it very seriously. Acting wasn't as important as cheerleading." She later became a student at Vassar.

Year	Movie	Character
1985	Summer Rental	Jennifer Chester
1985	The Goonies	Andy
1986	Lucas	Maggie
1987	Three for the Road	Robin

ELLEN GREENE

(1950 -   )

Greene's career began in the early 1970s as a cabaret singer in such famed New York night spots as Reno Sweeney's in Greenwich Village. The stage came next. "The Public Theater under Joe Papp was my real education," she once recalled. "When you walked in there, you left your ego at the door. Everybody was talented." She was Audrey, the Bowery flower shop girl, in a long run of the play *The Little Shop of Horrors* and later reprised her role in the 1986 movie version starring Rick Moranis.

Year	Movie	Character
1976	Next Stop, Greenwich Village	Sarah
1982	I'm Dancing as Fast as I Can	Karen Mulligan
1986	Little Shop of Horrors	Audrey
1988	Talk Radio	Ellen
1990	Pump Up the Volume	Jan Emerson
1991	Stepping Out	Maxine

Primarily
lege and
performi
apparent
parts are
out of a
mented a

Year N

1960 F
1962 A
1967 V
1978 C
1980 S
1982 V
1984 F

CLU GULAGER

(1928 -)

Active in the three mediums of television, stage and film, Gulager's screen appearances began in the days of live television on *The U.S. Steel Hour* in 1956. Prominent in the films *The Killers* and *The Last Picture Show*, the actor was born in Holdenville, OK, the son of a cowboy entertainer. He attended Baylor University and spent time in the U.S. Marine Corps.

Year	Movie	Character
1964	The Killers	Lee
1967	Sullivan's Empire	Juan Clemente
1969	Winning	Larry Morechek
1971	The Last Picture Show	Abilene
1974	McQ	Toms
1977	The Other Side of Midnight	Bill Fraser
1979	A Force of One	Dunne
1980	Touched by Love	Don Fielder
1984	Chattanooga Choo Choo	Sam
1985	A Nightmare on Elm Street 2: Freddy's Revenge	Mr. Walsh
1985	Into the Night	Federal Agent
1985	The Return of the Living Dead	Burt
1987	Hunter's Blood	Mason Rand
1987	Summer Heat	Will
1987	The Hidden	Ed Flynn
1988	I'm Gonna Git You Sucka	Lt. Baker
1988	Tapeheads	Norman Mart
1991	My Heroes Have Always Been Cowboys	Dark Glasses

MOSES GUNN

(1929 -)

The product of a St. Louis ghetto, Gunn attributes his success in life to his high school English teacher who took him in after his mother died. He received a scholarship to study at Tennessee State University and before graduating decided on a career as an actor. He was 32 when he arrived in New York where he subsequently received wide recognition for his performances with the Negro Ensemble Company and the New York Shakespeare Festival. Hollywood soon followed.

Year	Movie	Character
1970	Eagle in a Cage	Gen. Gourgaud
1970	The Great White Hope	Scipio
1970	WUSA	Clotho
1971	Shaft	Bumpy
1971	The Wild Rovers	Ben
1972	Shaft's Big Score!	Bumpy Jonas
1972	The Hot Rock	Dr. Amusa
1975	Rollerball	Cletus
1980	The Ninth Configuration	Major Nammack
1981	Ragtime	Booker T. Washington
1982	Amityville II: The Possession	Detective
1984	Firestarter	Dr. Pynchot
1984	The NeverEnding Story	Cairon
1986	Heartbreak Ridge	Sgt. Webster

FRED GWYNNE

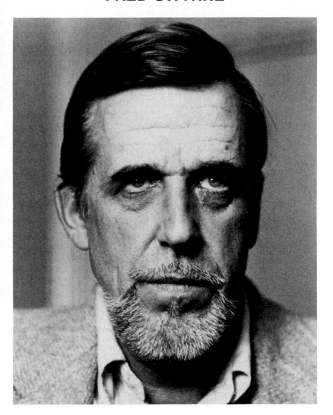

(1926 - 1993)

Beloved by TV audiences as Herman Munster in CBS's *The Munsters* (1964-1966), Gwynne grew up all over the country and was educated at Groton and Harvard. His theatrical debut came at the Brattle Theater, a professional repertory company in Cambridge, MA. After graduation from college, he spent five years as a copywriter on the Ford account at the advertising agency J. Walter Thompson. He died of complications from pancreatic cancer.

Year	Movie	Character
1966	Munster, Go Home	Herman Munster
1980	Simon	Korey
1981	So Fine	Chairman Lincoln
1984	The Cotton Club	Frenchy Demange
1986	Off Beat	Commissioner
1986	The Boy Who Could Fly	Uncle Hugo
1987	Fatal Attraction	Arthur
1987	Ironweed	Oscar Reo
1987	The Secret of My Success	Donald Davenport
1989	Disorganized Crime	Max Green
1989	Pet Sematary	Jud Crandall
1992	My Cousin Vinny	Judge Chamberlain Haller
1992	Shadows and Fog	Hacker's follower

LUKAS HAAS

(1976 -   )

Widely regarded as one of America's finest child actors, Haas made his film debut at age six. While a student at Montessori school, he announced to his parents one day that he wanted to become an actor and with his school's prompting he won a role in *Testament*.

Year	Movie	Character
1983	Testament	Scottie Wetherly
1985	Witness	Samuel
1986	Solarbabies	Daniel
1988	The Wizard of Loneliness	Wendall
1989	Music Box	Mikey Talbot
1989	See You in the Morning	Petey Goodwin
1991	Rambling Rose	Buddy
1992	Leap of Faith	Boyd

187

JOAN HACKETT

(1939 - 1983)

Playing independent women in unglamorous roles in the movies made the Broadway and Off-Broadway star a character actress in Hollywood. A successful teenage model, Hackett was discovered by television after she made the leap to legitimate theater and, in 1961, won several awards. She won an Emmy nomination for a guest-star spot in TV's *Ben Casey*, then made her film debut in 1966 in *The Group*. Nominated for a best supporting actress Oscar for *Only When I Laugh*, the dedicated social activist died of cancer.

Year	Movie	Character
1966	The Group	Dottie
1968	Assignment to Kill	Dominique
1968	Will Penny	Catherine Allen
1969	Support Your Local Sheriff!	Prudy Perkins
1973	The Last of Sheila	Lee
1974	The Terminal Man	Dr. Janet Ross
1980	One Trick Pony	Lonnie Fox
1981	Only When I Laugh	Toby
1982	The Escape Artist	Aunt Sibyl

CHARLES HAID

(1943 -   )

The actor/director/producer is known for his portrayal of Sgt. Renko on NBC's *Hill Street Blues*. Born in Palo Alto, CA, the son of an attorney, Haid spent three years in the U.S. Navy Submarine Corps, and then enrolled at Carnegie Tech where he majored in directing and acted in a wide variety of character roles. He began his professional career as a director and a teacher in the New York area. His Broadway debut came in 1972 in *Elizabeth the First*.

Year	Movie	Character
1977	The Choirboys	Yanov
1978	Oliver's Story	Stephen Simpson
1978	Who'll Stop the Rain	Eddy
1979	The House of God	Fats
1980	Altered States	Mason Parrish
1987	Cop	Whitey Haines
1988	The Rescue	Commander Howard

JACKIE EARLE HALEY

(1961 -   )

A native of Northridge, CA, Haley entered the entertainment world at age six as the voice of the animated cartoon characterization of *Dennis the Menace*. A self-taught actor who learned quickly from his "on the job" experiences, he rapidly moved into TV commercials and appearances on such series as *Marcus Welby, M.D.*, *The Waltons* and *The Carol Burnett Show*.

Year	Movie	Character
1975	The Day of the Locust	Adore
1976	The Bad News Bears	Kelly Leak
1977	Damnation Alley	Billy
1977	The Bad News Bears in Breaking Training	Kelly Leak
1978	The Bad News Bears Go to Japan	Kelly
1979	Breaking Away	Moocher
1983	Losin' It	Dave
1991	Dollman	xxx

ANTHONY MICHAEL HALL

(1968 -   )

In TV commercials from the age of eight, Hall got his big break when Steve Allen cast him as a younger version of himself in his semi-autobiographical play, *The Wake*. He went on to do steady work in television and the theater before making his film debut in *Six Pack*. Hall was born in Boston and raised in New York.

Year	Movie	Character
1982	Six Pack	Doc
1983	National Lampoon's Vacation	Rusty Griswold
1984	Sixteen Candles	Geek
1985	The Breakfast Club	Brian Johnson
1985	Weird Science	Gary
1986	Out of Bounds	Daryl Cage
1988	Johnny Be Good	Johnny Walker
1990	Edward Scissorhands	Jim
1992	Into the Sun	Tom Slade

LINDA HAMILTON

(1957 -   )

Hamilton first got movie audiences' attention in Arnold Schwarzenegger's 1984 box office smash, *The Terminator*. In it, she played a seemingly innocent woman who is the target of a murderous cyborg from the year 2029. Born and raised in Salisbury, MD, Hamilton began acting as a child with children's theater groups. She later studied at the Lee Strasberg Theater Institute in New York and made her professional debut on the daytime soap opera, *Search for Tomorrow*.

Year	Movie	Character
1984	The Stone Boy	Eva Crescent Moon Lady
1984	The Terminator	Sarah Connor
1986	Black Moon Rising	Nina
1986	King Kong Lives	Amy Franklin
1990	Mr. Destiny	Ellen Burrows
1991	Terminator 2: Judgment Day	Sarah Connor

MURRAY HAMILTON

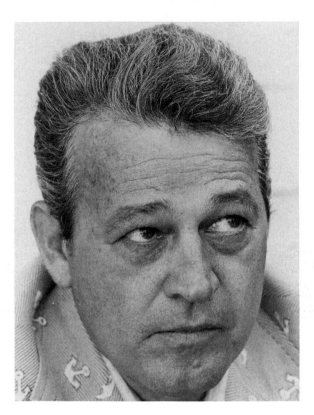

(1923 - 1986)

A native of Washington, D.C., Hamilton got his initial theatrical experience when he hitched-hiked to Hollywood, became a messenger at Warner Brothers, and acted at night with amateur theater groups. After several summer stock appearances he made his Broadway debut in *Strange Fruit*. He acted in many films and was often on television. Hamilton died of lung cancer.

Year	Movie	Character
1960	Tall Story	Coach Hardy
1961	The Hustler	Findlay
1963	The Cardinal	Lafe
1966	An American Dream	Arthur Kabot
1966	Seconds	Charlie
1967	The Graduate	Mr. Robinson
1968	No Way to Treat a Lady	Inspector Haines
1968	Sergeant Ryker	Capt. Appleton
1968	The Boston Strangler	Frank McAfee
1968	The Brotherhood	Egan
1969	If It's Tuesday, This Must Be Belgium	Fred Ferguson
1973	The Way We Were	Brooks Carpenter
1975	Jaws	Vaughn

(continued on page 507)

HARRY HAMLIN

(1951 -   )

Hamlin is remembered by TV viewers as an upstanding, young law partner in the popular *L.A. Law* series (1986-90). His film career is largely undistinguished with the exception of his best known role as the gay writer in *Making Love* who steals Kate Jackson's husband. He claims that he has "never given any thought" to image and packaging "and probably because of that, my career has rambled around." He was en route to study drama in England on a Fulbright scholarship when he was unexpectedly cast in *Movie, Movie*.

Year	Movie	Character
1978	Movie, Movie	Joey Popchik
1981	King of the Mountain	Steve
1981	Clash of the Titans	Perseus
1982	Making Love	Bart
1983	Blue Skies Again	Sandy Mendenhal
1985	Maxie	xxx

JAMES HAMPTON

(1936 -   )

Hampton's career began with appearances in TV sitcoms and supporting roles in feature films. His first starring role came in the Mulberry Square production of *Hawmps*. At the time, he said: "I'm really excited about being involved with Mulberry Square. I admire the firm's philosophies on family filmmaking and if I had my druthers, that's the only kind of film I would do. All too often, the four-letter words, sex and violence are not really necessary."

Year	Movie	Character
1974	The Longest Yard	Caretaker
1975	W.W. and the Dixie Dancekings	Junior
1976	Hawmps	Howard Clemmons
1979	The China Syndrome	Bill Gibson
1980	Hangar 18	Lew
1981	Condorman	Harry
1985	Teen Wolf	Harold Howard
1987	Teen Wolf Too	Uncle Howard

TY HARDIN

(1930 -   )

Hardin was discovered on a chance visit to the Paramount prop depart-ment to borrow a gun for a costume party. He became a television cowboy star from 1958 to 1962 in *Bronco* and was often in westerns and other actioners in the movies. He left Hollywood to work in Europe and upon his return became an ordained minister who preached regularly on television. Hardin grew up in Texas and switched his sights from football to drama after a severe leg injury.

Year	Movie	Character
1962	Merrill's Marauders	Stock
1962	The Chapman Report	Ed Kraski
1963	PT 109	Ens. Leonard J. Thom
1965	Battle of the Bulge	Schumacher
1968	Custer of the West	Maj. Marcus Reno
1990	Bad Jim	Tom Jefferd

MARK HARMON

(1951 -   )

Harmon was UCLA's star quarterback in 1972 and 1973 and gained entry to Hollywood with "beefcake" parts on television. "When someone need-ed the beefcake to swim across the pool and kiss the pretty girl, I did it," he once recalled. *People* magazine named him the "Sexiest Man Alive" in 1986. He spent three seasons on NBC's successful show *St. Elsewhere* (1983-86), but grew restless and had himself written out as TV's first het-erosexual to die of AIDS. Harmon has starred in many TV-movies.

Year	Movie	Character
1978	Comes a Horseman	Billy Joe Meynert
1979	Beyond the Poseidon Adventure	Larry Simpson
1986	Let's Get Harry	Harry
1987	Summer School	Freddy Shoop
1988	Stealing Home	Billy Wyatt
1988	The Presidio	Jay Austin
1989	Worth Winning	Taylor Worth

JESSICA HARPER

(1949 -   )

Harper fell for acting as a student at Sarah Lawrence College. "I was inter-ested in painting more than anything else, but I got bored," she once explained. "Then I studied modern dance. But I got bored. I started study-ing acting. I didn't get bored. I'd always loved the theater, but never thought I could do it until suddenly I got a part in *Hair*. It was such a fluke, it led me to think I could do it forever." Harper was born in Chicago, the daughter of a former nightclub singer and an advertising executive.

Year	Movie	Character
1974	Phantom of the Paradise	Phoenix
1975	Love and Death	Natasha
1980	Stardust Memories	Daisy
1981	Pennies From Heaven	Joan
1981	Shock Treatment	Janet Majors
1982	My Favorite Year	K.C. Downing
1986	The Imagemaker	Cynthia
1988	The Blue Iguana	Cora

TESS HARPER

(1952 -   )

Born in small-town Mammoth Spring, AR, Harper spent most of her pre-Hollywood life in Arkansas and Texas. She was cast in her first film, *Tender Mercies* with Robert Duvall, while living in Dallas doing commercials, industrial films and dinner theater. Often portraying small-town, all-American types she kept very busy in film throughout the 1980s.

Year	Movie	Character
1983	Tender Mercies	Rosa Lee
1983	Amityville 3-D	Nancy Baxter
1983	Silkwood	Linda Dawson
1984	Flashpoint	Ellen
1986	Crimes of the Heart	Chick Boyle
1987	Ishtar	Willa
1988	Far North	Rita
1989	Criminal Law	Detective Stillwell
1989	Her Alibi	Sally Blackwood
1990	Daddy's Dyin'...Who's Got the Will?	Sara Lee
1991	My Heroes Have Always Been Cowboys	Cheryl Hornby
1991	The Man in the Moon	Abigail Trant

BARBARA HARRIS

(1935 -   )

A stage actress for many years before she made her Hollywood debut, Tony Award-winner Harris was born in Chicago. She got her start there at a place called Compass, a sort of cabaret whose performers would soon form the Second City troupe. Publicity-shy, she once said that "performers should be judged only by their work on-stage—too much is made of their personal lives."

Year	Movie	Character
1965	A Thousand Clowns	Sandra
1971	Plaza Suite	Muriel Tate
1971	Who is Harry Kellerman and Why is He Saying Those Terrible Things About Me?	Allison
1972	The War Between Men and Women	Terry Kozlenko
1973	The Manchu Eagle Murder Caper Mystery	Miss Fredericks
1975	Nashville	Albuquerque
1976	Family Plot	Blanche
1977	Freaky Friday	Ellen Andrews
1978	Movie, Movie	Trixie Lane
1979	The North Avenue Irregulars	Vickie
1979	The Seduction of Joe Tynan	Ellie
1981	Second-Hand Hearts	Dinette
1986	Peggy Sue Got Married	Evelyn Kelcher
1987	Nice Girls Don't Explode	Mom
1988	Dirty Rotten Scoundrels	Fanny Eubanks

ED HARRIS

(1950 -   )

Harris became known to movie-goers for his portrayal of John Glenn in *The Right Stuff*. He's had big roles in other big pictures like *Places in the Heart* and *The Abyss*, but he often goes in for riskier projects. "I don't intentionally choose movies that aren't going to be successful commercially," he has said. "It just happens that the most interesting scripts I read are outside of the mainstream. I like characters who have an edge to them, who are going to do something unexpected."

Year	Movie	Character
1980	Borderline	Hotchkiss
1982	Creepshow	Hank
1983	The Right Stuff	John Glenn
1983	Under Fire	Oates
1984	Places in the Heart	Wayne Lomax
1984	Swing Shift	Jack Walsh
1985	Alamo Bay	Shang
1985	Code Name: Emerald	Gus Lang
1985	Sweet Dreams	Charlie Dick
1988	To Kill a Priest	Stefan
1988	Walker	xxx
1989	Jacknife	Dave
1989	The Abyss	Virgil "Bud" Brigman
1990	State of Grace	Frankie Flannery
1992	Glengarry Glen Ross	Dave Moss
1993	Needful Things	Sheriff Alan Pangborn
1993	The Firm	Wayne Tarrance

JULIE HARRIS

(1925 -   )

Harris became a Broadway star in 1950 in *The Member of the Wedding* and went on to win five Tony awards. She has emphasized the stage over Hollywood in her career, and once explained: "I was never a beauty, and to have a real movie career, the camera has to idolize you. Now I am able to cast an illusion of beauty or charm on the stage. But I'm not very good at being charming or beautiful with a camera looking right at me." Harris is known for her warmth and her generosity in welcoming fans backstage after a performance.

Year	Movie	Character
1962	Requiem for a Heavyweight	Grace Miller
1966	Harper	Betty Fraley
1966	You're a Big Boy Now	Miss Thing
1967	Reflections in a Golden Eye	Alison Langdon
1968	The Split	Gladys
1976	Voyage of the Damned	Alice Feinchild
1979	The Bell Jar	Mrs. Greenwood
1988	Gorillas in the Mist	Roz Carr
1992	HouseSitter	Edna Davis
1993	The Dark Half	Reggie Delesseps

KATHRYN HARROLD

(1950 -   )

Harrold became an actress because, as she once said: "I figured it was a way of exploring things. You get to find out about life, people, travel, research. I've hung around emergency wards, blind people, retarded children, studied LeMaze technique. For me, its not a process of hiding behind a character, but a confrontation with myself. I'll attempt to open up blocked areas in me and try to do something about them." Harrold comes from Virginia and has studied drama in New York.

Year	Movie	Character
1980	Modern Romance	Mary
1980	The Hunter	Dotty
1981	The Pursuit of D.B. Cooper	Hannah
1982	Yes, Giorgio	Pamela
1984	Heartbreakers	Cyd
1985	Into the Night	Christie
1986	Raw Deal	Monique

ELIZABETH HARTMAN

(1941 - 1987)

A native of Youngstown, OH, Hartman started acting in high school and won Ohio's "Actress of the Year" award for playing the fragile Laura in *The Glass Menagerie*. Her screen debut opposite Sidney Poitier as the blind woman in the 1965 film *A Patch of Blue* brought her an Oscar nomination. Hartman abandoned her acting career in 1983 and moved to Pittsburgh where she worked at a museum. She died at 45 after jumping from her 5th floor Pittsburgh apartment.

Year	Movie	Character
1965	A Patch of Blue	Selina D'Arcy
1966	The Group	Priss
1966	You're a Big Boy Now	Barbara Darling
1971	The Beguiled	Edwina
1973	Walking Tall	Pauline Pusser
1981	Full Moon High	Miss Montgomery

MARILYN HASSETT

(1947 -   )

Hassett's acting career began and nearly ended with TV commercials when she was stepped on by an elephant while doing an Opal ad. Miraculously recovered, she moved on to films with *The Other Side of the Mountain*. A native of Southern California, she studied drama at Cal State. She then drove a taxi in Beverly Hills, worked in a bank and photographed record album covers before getting her break.

Year	Movie	Character
1975	The Other Side of the Mountain	Jill Kinmont
1976	Shadow of the Hawk	Maureen
1976	Two Minute Warning	Lucy
1978	The Other Side of the Mountain Part 2	Jill Kinmont
1979	The Bell Jar	Esther
1988	Messenger of Death	Josephine Fabrizio

RUTGER HAUER

(1944 -   )

Often cast as a villain in action films, Hauer was born in Amsterdam, Holland. He worked for five years in a pantomine company before starting a serious acting career. He was also responsible for staging many productions, but became a national hero while playing in a Dutch television series that was shown throughout the world.

Year	Movie	Character
1981	Nighthawks	Wulfgar
1982	Blade Runner	Batty
1983	The Osterman Weekend	Tanner
1984	A Breed Apart	Jim Malden
1985	Flesh + Blood	Martin
1985	Ladyhawke	Navarre
1986	The Hitcher	John Ryder
1987	Wanted: Dead or Alive	Nick Randall
1989	Blind Fury	Nick Parker
1989	Bloodhounds of Broadway	The Brain
1992	Buffy, the Vampire Slayer	Lothos
1992	Split Second	Stone

WINGS HAUSER

(1948 -   )

Born in Hollywood, to writer Dwight Hauser, who wrote the famous *Whistler* radio series of the 1940s, Hauser's show biz career began at age 5 with a radio commercial. He excelled in sports as a teenager, particularly baseball, and was even asked to sign up as a catcher with the L.A. Dodgers. He pursued a music career for 10 years, cut two albums, but grew tired of the struggling musician's life. His acting career began with a lead role in the soap *The Young and the Restless*.

Year	Movie	Character
1982	Vice Squad	Ramrod
1983	Deadly Force	Stoney
1984	A Soldier's Story	Lt. Boyd
1986	Jo Jo Dancer, Your Life is Calling	Cliff
1987	Hostage	Sam Striker
1989	The Siege of Firebase Gloria	Corporal Di Nardo
1991	Beastmaster 2: Through the Portal of Time	Arklon

ETHAN HAWKE

(1970 -   )

As a 13-year-old growing up in New Jersey, Hawke auditioned for movie roles in New York as a lark. To his surprise he was cast in *Explorers* and spent six months in L.A. Of his chosen career, he has said: "As far as a young actor goes, there aren't that many people writing complicated parts for young actors. There's a few a year and you've got to hope that you get one of them or that you see it or that it comes your way."

Year	Movie	Character
1985	Explorers	Ben Crandall
1989	Dad	Billy Tremont
1989	Dead Poets Society	Todd Anderson
1991	Mystery Date	Tom McHugh
1991	White Fang	Jack
1993	Alive	Nando Parradon
1993	Rich in Love	Wayne Frobiness

STERLING HAYDEN

(1916 - 1986)

Tall, blonde, handsome Hayden said that he "always hated acting but I kept on like a commuter on a tinsel train." He went to sea before going to Hollywood: at 16 as a sailor in New England, at 20 around the world, at 22 as the captain of a ship going from Gloucester to Tahiti. During World War II, he won a silver star for intelligence work in Europe. In movies, he played the hero in action films. An admitted alcoholic, he died of cancer.

Year	Movie	Character
1964	Dr. Strangelove or: How I Learned to Stop Worrying and Love the Bomb	Gen. Jack D. Ripper
1969	Hard Contract	Michael Carlson
1972	The Godfather	McCluskey
1978	King of the Gypsies	King Zharko Stepanovicz
1979	The Outsider	Seamus Flaherty
1979	Winter Kills	Z.K.
1980	9 to 5	Tinsworthy

RICHARD HAYDN

(1905 - 1985)

Haydn's eccentric English manner and nasal voice made him a stand-out character actor in many Hollywood films where he specialized in playing mama's boys and later, old men. The Londoner worked as an overseer on a Jamaican banana plantation until a hurricane destroyed it. He then got a job as a make-up artist on an American movie being filmed in Jamaica before joining an English theater troupe touring the Caribbean. He went to Hollywood in the 1940s.

Year	Movie	Character
1960	Please Don't Eat the Daisies	Alfred North
1960	The Lost World	Prof. Summerlee
1962	Five Weeks in a Balloon	Sir Henry Vining
1962	Mutiny on the Bounty	Brown
1965	The Sound of Music	Max Detweiler
1974	Young Frankenstein	Herr Falkstein

ROBERT HAYS

(1947 -   )

Best known as the neurotic pilot in the comedy hit, *Airplane!*, Hays was an army brat who grew up worldwide. He discovered acting while in college and later dropped out to spent six years at $45 per week acting at San Diego's Old Globe Theater. His screen career began in television with roles in *Harry-O*, *The Love Boat*, and *Laverne and Shirley*.

Year	Movie	Character
1980	Airplane	Ted Striker
1981	Take This Job and Shove It	Frank
1982	Airplane II: The Sequel	Stryker
1983	Touched	Daniel
1983	Trenchcoat	Terry Leonard
1984	Scandalous	Frank
1985	Cat's Eye	Norris
1990	Honeymoon Academy	Sean McDonald
1993	Fifty/Fifty	Sam French

199

GLENNE HEADLY

(1955 -   )

Headly fell in love with movies early. She claims, at age eight, she watched Federico Fellini's *La Strada* ten times in one week and would walk around the house yelling 'Zampano!' just like Anthony Quinn. The actress grew up in New York's Greenwich Village, got a B.A. from the American College of Switzerland, and started acting in Chicago with the famed Steppenwolf Theater Company. She spent ten years on the boards in Chicago and New York before making her first film.

Year	Movie	Character
1981	Four Friends	Lola
1985	Eleni	Joan
1985	The Purple Rose of Cairo	Hooker
1987	Making Mr. Right	Trish
1987	Nadine	Renee
1988	Dirty Rotten Scoundrels	Janet Colgate
1988	Stars and Bars	Cora
1990	Dick Tracy	Tess Trueheart
1991	Mortal Thoughts	Joyce Urbanski

JOHN HEARD

(1946 -   )

A prolific screen actor, Heard does little television, but praises the benefits of TV acting. "Television is fast and loose," he once explained, "You have two or three takes to get your part right, and if you have a problem, well, by the time you figure it out, everyone's moved on to the next scene. It's good training, keeps you on your toes." A native of Washington, D.C., where his father worked for the Pentagon, Heard's acting career began with that city's Arena Stage and in Chicago.

Year	Movie	Character
1977	First Love	David
1979	Head Over Heels	Charles
1979	Heart Beat	Jack Kerouac
1981	Cutter's Way	Alex Cutter
1982	Cat People	Oliver
1985	After Hours	Tom the Bartender
1985	Heaven Help Us	Brother Timothy
1985	The Trip to Bountiful	Ludie Watts
1985	Too Scared to Scream	Lab Technician
1988	Beaches	John Pierce
1988	Betrayed	Michael Carnes
1988	Big	Paul
1988	The Milagro Beanfield War	Charlie Bloom
1988	The Seventh Sign	Reverend

(continued on page 507)

EILEEN HECKART

(1919 -   )

Heckart arrived in New York in the early 1940s and made her first splash on Broadway in the 1953 production of *Everybody Loves Opal*. The actress once told an interviewer: "I'm not very interesting as a person—the people I play are interesting. I think a lot of actors go into the theater for that reason. They want to be someone besides themselves." The native of Columbus, OH, was gearing up to become an actress even as a child when she would spend weekends in movie theaters with her mother.

Year	Movie	Character
1960	Heller in Pink Tights	Lorna Hathaway
1963	My Six Loves	Ethel Swenson
1967	Up the Down Staircase	Henrietta Pastorfield
1968	No Way to Treat a Lady	Mrs. Brummel
1972	Butterflies are Free	Mrs. Baker
1976	Burnt Offerings	Roz
1986	Heartbreak Ridge	Little Mary

DAN HEDAYA

(19?? -   )

Known for his role as the cuckolded husband in the now cult film *Blood Simple*, Hedaya was born and raised in Brooklyn. He attended Brooklyn Friends School, a Quaker school, and Tufts University where he studied French. After graduation he taught math and English for seven years. His early days as an actor included appearances on television's *Hill Street Blues* and *Cheers*.

Year	Movie	Character
1980	Night of the Juggler	Barnes
1981	True Confessions	Howard Terkel
1982	Endangered Species	Peck
1982	I'm Dancing as Fast as I Can	Dr. Klein
1983	The Hunger	Lt. Allegrezza
1984	Blood Simple	Julian Marty
1984	Reckless	Peter
1984	Tightrope	Detective Molinari
1985	Commando	Arius
1986	Running Scared	Captain Logan
1986	Wise Guys	Anthony Castelo
1990	Joe Versus the Volcano	Mr. Waturi
1990	Pacific Heights	Loan Officer
1991	The Addams Family	Tully Alford
1993	Benny and Joon	Thomas
1993	Boiling Point	Brady
1993	Rookie of the Year	Larry (Fish) Fisher
1993	For Love or Money	Gene Salvatore

TIPPI HEDREN

(1930 -   )

Known primarily for her roles in the two Hitchcock films *The Birds* and *Marnie*, Hedren began her career as a model. She is the mother of film star Melanie Griffith and was born in New Ulm, MN. Retrospectively, her performance in *Marnie* is often considered one of the finest performances in any of Hitchcock's films.

Year	Movie	Character
1963	The Birds	Melanie Daniels
1964	Marnie	Marnie
1967	A Countess from Hong Kong	Martha
1973	The Harrad Experiment	Margaret
1990	Pacific Heights	Florence Peters

MARILU HENNER

(1952 -   )

Best known for her work as Elaine Nardo on TV's long-running *Taxi* (1978-83), Henner is a native of Chicago whose acting career began as a student at the University of Chicago with her involvement with the original stage production of *Grease*. She ultimately appeared in both the Broadway and the national company of this show. Her film career blossomed following *Taxi*.

Year	Movie	Character
1978	Bloodbrothers	Annette
1983	Hammett	Kit Conger/ Sue Alabama
1983	The Man Who Loved Women	Agnes
1984	Cannonball Run II	Betty
1984	Johnny Dangerously	Lil
1985	Perfect	Sally
1985	Rustlers' Rhapsody	Miss Tracy
1991	L.A. Story	Trudi

LANCE HENRIKSEN

(1939 -   )

Henriksen may be better known to fans of horror films, as his gaunt appearance has led to his casting in several, including *Mansion of the Doomed*, *The Visitor* and *The Spawning*. He did not become an actor until he was in his thirties and spent much of his youth travelling. He lived in Borneo for three years, spent a year island-hopping around Fiji and Malaysia and later shipped out on a Swedish freighter sailing the Atlantic and the Caribbean. His stage debut came with a few small pantomine roles at the Boston Opera Company.

Year	Movie	Character
1975	Dog Day Afternoon	Murphy
1979	The Visitor	Raymond
1981	Prince of the City	D.A. Burano
1983	Nightmares	MacLeod
1983	The Right Stuff	Wally Schirra
1984	The Terminator	Vukovich
1985	Jagged Edge	Frank Martin
1986	Aliens	Bishop
1986	Choke Canyon	Brook Alistair
1989	Hit List	Chris Caleek
1989	Johnny Handsome	Rafe Garrett
1991	Stone Cold	Chains
1992	Alien 3	xxx
1992	Jennifer Eight	Freddy Ross
1993	Hard Target	Emil Fouchon

BUCK HENRY

(1931 -   )

Henry has been an actor for over 30 years, but remains best known for his writing abilities. His script for *The Graduate* made him famous and his co-creation (with Mel Brooks) of TV's *Get Smart* made him rich. Considered one of the best comic screenwriters, he got his start in the early 60's writing for such comedians as Steve Allen. "The good screenwriter should be able to see a movie in his head or, at the very least, hear it," he once said. "But it's not enough to have a good ear for dialogue. You have to know where the beats and pauses are."

Year	Movie	Character
1964	The Troublemaker	T.R. Kingston
1967	The Graduate	Room Clerk
1968	The Secret War of Harry Frigg	Stockade Commandant
1970	Catch-22	Lt. Col. Korn
1971	Taking Off	Larry Tyne
1976	The Man Who Fell to Earth	Oliver Farnsworth
1978	Heaven Can Wait	The Escort
1980	First Family	Father Sandstone
1980	Gloria	Jack Dawn
1982	Eating Raoul	Mr. Leech
1989	Rude Awakening	Lloyd Stoole
1991	Defending Your Life	Dick Stanley
1993	Short Cuts	Gordon Johnson

JUSTIN HENRY

(1971 -   )

Nominated for an Academy Award at age 8 for his role as Billy in *Kramer vs. Kramer*, Henry's acting career began with a bang. A native of New York, he had never acted before taking on the part. He subsequently returned to school and has made a few films sporadically in recent years.

Year	Movie	Character
1979	Kramer vs. Kramer	Billy Kramer
1984	Martin's Day	Martin
1984	Sixteen Candles	Mike Baker
1988	Sweet Hearts Dance	Kyle Boon

EDWARD HERRMANN

(1943 -   )

In 1968, Herrmann became one of four American students to win a Fulbright Scholarship to study at the London Academy of Music and Dramatic Art. Upon his return to the U.S. he set about the business of practically non-stop acting. He did TV commercials, played at the Public Theater, did the American premiere of *Moonchildren* in Washington and on Broadway, and soon started mixing movies with theater assignments. Herrmann is from Washington, D.C.

Year	Movie	Character
1973	The Paper Chase	Anderson
1974	The Great Gatsby	Klipspringer
1975	The Great Waldo Pepper	Ezra Stiles
1978	Brass Target	Col. Walter Gilchrist
1978	Take Down	Ed Branish
1978	The Betsy	Dan Weyman
1979	The North Avenue Irregulars	Michael Hill
1981	Reds	Max Eastman
1982	A Little Sex	Tommy
1982	Annie	FDR
1982	Death Valley	Paul
1984	Mrs. Soffel	Peter Soffel
1985	Compromising Positions	Bob Singer
1985	The Man With One Red Shoe	Brown
1985	The Purple Rose of Cairo	Henry
1987	Overboard	Grant Stayton III
1987	The Lost Boys	Max
1988	Big Business	Graham Sherbourne
1993	Born Yesterday	Ed Devery
1993	My Boyfriend's Back	Mr. Dingle

HOWARD HESSEMAN

(1940 -   )

Hesseman is seen above as Dr. Johnny Fever, the hip deejay of the popular TV sitcom *WKRP in Cincinnati* (1978-82). His movies are mostly comedies and began with *A Session With the Committee* (1969), a collection of live skits put on by the extremely successful San Francisco improvisation group The Committee, Hesseman's training ground. He took an interest in writing while in college, but has said he prefers "the immediate feedback of acting. I like the instant response which tells me whether or not people like what I do."

Year	Movie	Character
1973	Steelyard Blues	Frank
1975	Shampoo	xxx
1975	The Sunshine Boys	Commercial Director
1976	Jackson County Jail	David
1976	The Big Bus	Scotty's Aide Jack
1976	Tunnelvision	Sen. McMannus
1977	The Other Side of Midnight	xxx
1981	Honky Tonk Freeway	Snapper
1981	Private Lessons	Lester
1983	Doctor Detroit	Smooth Walker
1985	Clue	xxx
1985	Police Academy 2: Their First Assignment	Pete Lassard
1986	Flight of the Navigator	Dr. Faraday
1986	My Chauffeur	McBride
1987	Amazon Women on the Moon	Rupert King
1987	Heat	Pinchus Zion

WILLIAM HICKEY

(1928 -   )

Born into an Irish family in Brooklyn, Hickey began his career on radio at age 10 and a decade later appeared Off-Broadway in *Bury the Dead*. By 1950, he was running the HB Studio—named for his teachers, Uta Hagen and Herbert Berghof—and a year later got his first Broadway role as an extra in the production of *Saint Joan*. Nominated for an Oscar for his part in *Prizzi's Honor*, he continues to teach up and coming actors their craft.

Year	Movie	Character
1968	The Boston Strangler	Eugene T. Rourke
1968	The Producers	drunk in theater bar
1970	Little Big Man	Historian
1977	The Sentinel	Perry
1985	Prizzi's Honor	Don Corrado Prizzi
1985	Remo Williams: The Adventure Begins	Coney Island barker
1986	One Crazy Summer	Old Man Beckersted
1986	The Name of the Rose	Ubertino de Casale
1988	Bright Lights, Big City	Ferret Man
1988	Da	Drumm
1989	National Lampoon's Christmas Vacation	Uncle Lewis
1989	Pink Cadillac	Mr. Barton
1989	Puppetmaster	Andre Toulan
1989	Sea of Love	Frank, Sr.
1990	Any Man's Death	Schiller/Bauer
1990	My Blue Heaven	Billy Sparrow
1990	Tales From the Darkside	Drogan ("Lot 249")

DWAYNE HICKMAN

(1934 -   )

Best known as the title character in the popular series, *The Many Loves of Dobie Gillis*, Hickman enjoyed a brief film career after that show ended its four year run in 1963. The actor, who became a TV programming executive, once described Dobie as the "original yuppie." "His only ambition was to have a girl friend, a car and money. He represents the morality of the '50s."

Year	Movie	Character
1965	Cat Ballou	Jed
1965	Dr. Goldfoot and the Bikini Machine	Todd Armstrong
1965	How to Stuff a Wild Bikini	Ricky
1965	Ski Party	Craig Gamble/Nora
1967	Doctor, You've Got to Be Kidding	Hank

CATHERINE HICKS

(1951 -   )

Hicks trained in every aspect of the theater under a two-year scholarship at Cornell University before heading for New York. There, she quickly landed a part on the daytime TV drama, *Ryan's Hope*. Next came an eight month run on Broadway with Jack Lemmon in *Tribute* that preceded her Hollywood career. Hicks played one of Kathleen Turner's best friends—a beautiful, headstrong divorcee—in *Peggy Sue Got Married* and a mother who inadvertently gives her young son a murderous doll for Christmas in *Child's Play*.

Year	Movie	Character
1982	Better Late Than Never	Sable
1982	Death Valley	Sally
1984	Garbo Talks	Jane Mortimer
1984	The Razor's Edge	Isabel
1985	Fever Pitch	Flo
1986	Peggy Sue Got Married	Carol Heath
1986	Star Trek IV: The Voyage Home	Gillian
1987	Like Father, Like Son	Dr. Amy Larkin
1988	Child's Play	Karen Barclay
1989	She's Out of Control	Janet Pearson
1991	Liebestraum	Mary Parker

ARTHUR HILL

(1922 -   )

The Canadian actor started out in British films in the late 1940s, but spent most of the next decade on the stage. U.S. film roles include the family attorney in *Harper* who hires old friend Paul Newman to discover the whereabouts of the family head. In *The Andromeda Strain*, he was part of a team of four doctors investigating mysterious deaths in a desert town after a satellite crashes nearby. Hill starred in TV's *Owen Marshall, Counselor at Law* (1971-74), a popular drama that won many public-service awards.

Year	Movie	Character
1961	The Young Doctors	Tomaselli
1963	The Ugly American	Grainger
1966	Harper	Albert Graves
1966	Moment to Moment	Neil Stanton
1968	Petulia	Barney
1969	The Chairman	Shelby
1971	The Andromeda Strain	Dr. Jeremy Stone
1975	The Killer Elite	Cap Collis
1976	Futureworld	Duffy
1977	A Bridge Too Far	Tough Colonel
1979	A Little Romance	Richard King
1979	Butch and Sundance: The Early Days	Wyoming Govenor
1979	The Champ	Mike
1980	Dirty Tricks	Bert
1982	Making Love	Henry
1985	One Magic Christmas	Caleb Grainger

STEVEN HILL

(1922 -   )

Famed drama coach Lee Strasberg once called Steven Hill one of the finest actors America ever produced, but who was also very difficult to work with. Seattle-born, Hill admits he was difficult as his interpretations of scripts often clashed with those of his directors'. After a year on the TV series *Mission Impossible* (1966-67), he left Hollywood to sell real estate, to write and to study the Bible. However, he could never get show business out of his blood and returned to it after a ten-year hiatus.

Year	Movie	Character
1965	The Slender Thread	Mark Dyson
1980	It's My Turn	Jacob
1981	Eyewitness	Lt. Jacobs
1981	Rich and Famous	Jules Levi
1983	Yentl	Reb Alter Vishkower
1984	Garbo Talks	Walter Rolfe
1986	Brighton Beach Memoirs	Mr. Stroheim
1986	Heartburn	Harry
1986	Legal Eagles	Bower
1986	On Valentine's Day	George Tyler
1986	Raw Deal	Lamanski
1988	Running on Empty	Mr. Patterson
1988	The Boost	Max
1990	White Palace	Sol Horowitz
1991	Billy Bathgate	Otto Berman
1993	The Firm	F. Denton Voyles

JOHN HILLERMAN

(1932 -   )

Hillerman has had a very successful career in films during the 1970s and television in the 80's where he starred opposite Tom Selleck for eight seasons on *Magnum, P.I.* He once said the four stages of an actor's life are: "Who is John Hillerman? Get me John Hillerman. Get me a young John Hillerman. Who is John Hillerman? I want to drop dead before we get to the last one." He spent 15 years as a stage actor in New York and Washington before heading west for Hollywood.

Year	Movie	Character
1971	Lawman	Totts
1971	The Last Picture Show	Teacher
1972	Skyjacked	Walter Brandt
1972	The Carey Treatment	Jenkins
1972	What's Up, Doc?	Kaltenborn
1973	High Plains Drifter	Bootmaker
1973	Outside Man	Dept. Store Manager
1973	Paper Moon	Deputy Hardin
1973	The Thief Who Came to Dinner	Laxker
1974	Blazing Saddles	Howard Johnson
1974	Chinatown	Yelburton
1975	At Long Last Love	Rodney James
1975	Lucky Lady	Christy McTeague
1975	The Day of the Locust	Ned Grote
1979	Sunburn	Webb
1984	Up the Creek	Dean

ART HINDLE

(1948 -   )

The Canadian actor has largely avoided the Hollywood mainstream and managed to build a career around an eclectic group of movies including two Canadian-made cult horror pictures, *Black Christmas* (1975) and *The Brood* (1979). He is best known for his work as the troubled husband in the Canadian-made *The Surrogate*, the spoiled rich kid in *Say Yes* with Jonathan Winters and the sadistic-looking Dirk Winfield in the sex/murder thriller *Into the Fire*, set in a remote Canadian lodge.

Year	Movie	Character
1976	A Small Town in Texas	Boogie
1978	Invasion of the Body Snatchers	Geoffrey
1980	The Octagon	A.J.
1983	The Man Who Wasn't There	Ted
1984	The Surrogate	George Kiber
1986	Say Yes	Luke
1987	Into the Fire	Dirk Winfield
1989	Speed Zone!	Flash

PAT HINGLE

(1923 -   )

Hingle's many screen roles include an acclaimed performance in *Splendor in the Grass* as the father of Warren Beatty, one of the two young lovers. He favored Clint Eastwood with his talents as the local police chief in *Sudden Impact* who tries to bar Harry Callahan from conducting business as usual and as Eastwood's only friend on a police force out to get him in the *Gauntlet*. Hingle was born in Miami and studied acting in New York after wartime service with the navy during World War II and the Korean Conflict.

Year	Movie	Character
1961	Splendor in the Grass	Ace Stamper
1963	The Ugly American	Homer Atkins
1964	Invitation to Gunfighter	Sam Brewster
1966	Nevada Smith	Big Foot
1968	Hang 'Em High	Judge Adam Fenton
1968	Jigsaw	Lew Haley
1968	Sol Madrid	Harry Mitchell
1970	Norwood	Grady
1970	WUSA	Bingamon
1972	The Carey Treatment	Capt. Pearson
1973	Running Wild	xxx
1974	The Super Cops	Lt. Novick
1977	The Gauntlet	Josephson
1979	Norma Rae	Vernon
1983	Going Berserk	Ed

(continued on page 507)

EARL HOLLIMAN

(1928 -   )

The seventh child of a Louisiana farmer, who died shortly before his birth, Holliman was adopted when he was a week old. After a stint in the U.S. Navy, the actor settled in Hollywood where he found employment and studied drama at USC and the Pasadena Playhouse. His first recognition came in 1957 when he won the Hollywood Press Association's Golden Globe Award for Best Supporting Actor for his role as Katharine Hepburn's brother in the film, *The Rainmaker*.

Year	Movie	Character
1960	Visit to a Small Planet	Conrad
1961	Summer and Smoke	Archie Kramer
1965	The Sons of Katie Elder	Matt Elder
1968	Anzio	Sgt. Stimler
1968	The Power	Talbot Scott
1972	The Biscuit Eater	Harve McNeill
1981	Sharky's Machine	Hotchkins

CELESTE HOLM

(1919 -)

The actress has performed in movies and television since 1946, but the stage remains Holm's first love. She has even gone so far as to block the path of a bulldozer that was about to raze two Broadway theaters in order to build another skyscraper. Educated in her native New York, Chicago and Paris, her lifelong career has garnered her many awards, a knighthood and posts in many governmental arts councils. She took home a best supporting Oscar for 1947's *Gentleman's Agreement*.

Year	Movie	Character
1962	Bachelor Flat	Helen
1967	Doctor, You've Got to Be Kidding	Louise Halloran
1973	Tom Sawyer	Aunt Polly
1977	The Private Files of J. Edgar Hoover	Florence Hollister
1987	3 Men and a Baby	Jack's Mother

IAN HOLM

(1931 -)

The Britisher has spent a great deal of his career acting in Shakespearean plays and has won several awards. He studied for the stage at the Royal Academy of Dramatic Art. In films, Holm was Oscar-nominated for *Chariots of Fire* and played the Belgian captain in *Greystoke: The Legend of Tarzan, Lord of the Apes* who was first saved by Tarzan from murdering pygmies and later takes him back to England.

Year	Movie	Character
1971	Mary, Queen of Scots	David Riccio
1972	Young Winston	George Bickle
1974	Juggernaut	Nicholas Porter
1977	March or Die	El Krim
1979	Alien	Ash
1981	Chariots of Fire	Sam Mussabini
1981	Time Bandits	Napoleon
1984	Greystoke: The Legend of Tarzan, Lord of the Apes	Capt. Phillippe D'Arnot
1985	Brazil	Kurtzmann
1988	Another Woman	Ken
1990	Hamlet	Polonius
1991	Kafka	Dr. Murnav

OSCAR HOMOLKA

(1898 - 1978)

With his shaggy eyebrows and Germanic accent, the Austrian actor played leading character roles in more than 100 films and 100 TV shows. Villains, kind uncles, spies, Homolka acted them all starting on stage in Nazi Germany until he left it to work in England and the United States. Nominated for an Academy Award in 1948 for *I Remember Mama*, he died at 79 in Sussex, England.

Year	Movie	Character
1961	Mr. Sardonicus	Krull
1962	Boys' Night Out	D. Prokosch
1962	The Wonderful World of the Brothers Grimm	The Duke
1964	The Long Ships	Krok
1965	Joy in the Morning	Stan Pulaski
1966	Funeral in Berlin	Colonel Stok
1967	The Happening	Sam
1967	Billion Dollar Brain	Col. Stok
1968	Assignment to Kill	Inspector
1974	The Tamarind Seed	General Golitsyn

JAMES HONG

(1928 -   )

Hong's early show business experience came as a contestant on Groucho Marx's *Your Show of Shows* and a stint as Charlie Chan's number-one son on a British TV version of the old story in 1957. He has made over 200 TV guest appearances since then. A native of Minneapolis, Hong received an engineering degree from USC and once worked as an engineer for the city of L.A. He is the co-founder of the East West Playhouse, an Asian-American repertory company.

Year	Movie	Character
1965	The Satan Bug	Dr. Yang
1970	The Hawaiians	Ti Chong
1972	The Carey Treatment	David Tao
1974	Chinatown	Evelyn's Butler
1979	The In-Laws	Bing Wong
1982	Blade Runner	Chew
1982	Yes, Giorgio	Kwan
1983	Breathless	Grocer
1984	Missing in Action	Gen. Tran
1986	Big Trouble in Little China	Lo Pan
1986	Black Widow	Shin
1986	The Golden Child	Doctor Hong
1987	China Girl	Gung-Tu
1988	Vice Versa	Kwo
1989	Tango & Cash	Quan
1990	Two Jakes	Khan
1991	Mystery Date	Fortune Teller
1991	The Perfect Weapon	Yung
1993	Wayne's World 2	Mr. Wong

BO HOPKINS

(1942 -   )

Often playing the heavy, such as the leader of a gang of toughs in *American Graffiti*, Hopkins has had memorable "good guy" roles too. He was a daredevil driver helping out Burt Reynolds in *White Lightning* and an investigator who tries to help the young drug smuggler incarcerated in a Turkish prison in *Midnight Express*. The native of Greenwood, SC, spent two years in the army and later studied acting in New York with Stella Adler and at Desilu, which was run by Lucille Ball.

Year	Movie	Character
1969	The Wild Bunch	Crazy Lee
1970	Monte Walsh	Jumpin' Joe Joslin
1972	Culpepper Cattle Company	Dixie Brick
1972	The Getaway	Frank Jackson
1973	American Graffiti	Joe
1973	The Man Who Loved Cat Dancing	Billy
1973	White Lightning	Roy Boone
1975	The Day of the Locust	Earle Shoop
1975	The Killer Elite	Miller
1976	A Small Town in Texas	Duke
1977	Tentacles	Will
1978	Midnight Express	Tex
1979	More American Graffiti	Little Joe
1990	Big Bad John	xxx
1993	The Ballad of Little Jo	Frank Badger

BOB HOSKINS

(1942 -   )

The British actor began his acting career in the U.K., on the stage and in film and television. Prior to acting he had been a laborer, porter, window cleaner, merchant seaman, circus fire-eater, agricultural worker on a kibbutz in Israel and a truck driver. He is known to movie audiences as the disheveled, alcoholic private eye in *Who Framed Roger Rabbit* who attempts to clear his cartoon client of a murder rap. A winner of several acting awards, his outside interests include photography, listening to music and gardening.

Year	Movie	Character
1983	Beyond the Limit	Col. Perez
1984	Lassiter	Becker
1984	The Cotton Club	Owney Madden
1985	Brazil	Spoor
1986	Sweet Liberty	Stanley Gould
1988	Who Framed Roger Rabbit	Eddie Valiant
1990	Heart Condition	Jack Moony
1990	Mermaids	Lou Landsky
1991	Hook	Smee
1991	Shattered	Gus Klein
1991	The Inner Circle	Beria
1992	Passed Away	Johnny Scanlan
1993	Super Mario Brothers	Mario Mario

JOHN HOUSEMAN

(1902 - 1988)

The actor/director/producer became a popular star in his 70s as the severe Harvard Law School professor in the 1973 film *The Paper Chase*, for which he won a best supporting Oscar. Born in Rumania, and educated in England, he began a career as a grain trader in South America and New York until the Depression stopped him and he found himself directing an opera in Hartford, CT, that went to Broadway as a surprise hit. Films directed by Houseman have garnered 20 Oscar nominations and 7 wins. He died of spinal cancer.

Year	Movie	Character
1973	The Paper Chase	Kingsfield
1975	Rollerball	Bartholomew
1975	Three Days of the Condor	Mr. Wabash
1976	St. Ives	Procane
1978	The Cheap Detective	Jasper Blubber
1980	My Bodyguard	Dobbs
1980	The Fog	Machen
1980	Wholly Moses	Archangel
1988	Another Woman	Marion's Father
1988	Bright Lights, Big City	Mr. Vogel
1988	Scrooged	Himself

JERRY HOUSER

(1952 -   )

One of the "Terrible Trio" of teenage boys who rose to acclaim in the film *Summer of '42*, Houser is a native of L.A. He had no professional experience before being cast for the hit movie, but was very active in high school plays. Warner Brothers came to him while still in school and he subsequently made a series of films during the 1970s.

Year	Movie	Character
1971	Summer of '42	Oscy
1972	Bad Company	Arthur Simms
1973	Class of '44	Oscy
1977	Slap Shot	Dave "Killer" Carlson
1978	Magic	Cab Driver

ARLISS HOWARD

(1955 -   )

"When I came out to California I thought once they put you in a movie, then you become a movie star," Howard once told an interviewer. "And then a movie I did came out and noone saw it and I wasn't a movie star." He attended Missouri's Columbus College on a drama scholarship and, after graduating, worked as a ranch hand in New Mexico for a few years. Community theater led on to film and TV roles in L.A.

Year	Movie	Character
1985	Sylvester	Peter
1987	Full Metal Jacket	Cowboy
1988	Tequila Sunrise	Lindroff
1990	Men Don't Leave	Charles Simon
1991	For the Boys	Dixie's Husband
1992	CrissCross	Joe
1993	Wilder Napalm	Wilder

KEN HOWARD

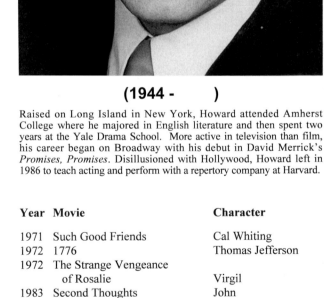

(1944 -   )

Raised on Long Island in New York, Howard attended Amherst College where he majored in English literature and then spent two years at the Yale Drama School. More active in television than film, his career began on Broadway with his debut in David Merrick's *Promises, Promises*. Disillusioned with Hollywood, Howard left in 1986 to teach acting and perform with a repertory company at Harvard.

Year	Movie	Character
1971	Such Good Friends	Cal Whiting
1972	1776	Thomas Jefferson
1972	The Strange Vengeance of Rosalie	Virgil
1983	Second Thoughts	John
1991	Oscar	Kirkwood

TREVOR HOWARD

(1916 - 1988)

"All my performances are good enough to be seen," the versatile English actor once said of his 80 film and many dramatic television roles. He began on stage in London in 1934, served four years as a paratrooper in World War II, winning the Military Cross for bravery, and later appeared in a long string of Hollywood hits. Whether he played the hero or the villain, Howard was a first-rate actor who drank too much but never gave a sloppy performance. He died of influenza and bronchitis in an English hospital.

Year	Movie	Character
1962	Mutiny on the Bounty	Captain Bligh
1964	Father Goose	Frank Houghton
1964	The Man in the Middle	Major Kensington
1965	Morituri	Colonel Statter
1965	Operation Crossbow	Prof. Lindemann
1965	Von Ryan's Express	Maj. Eric Fincham
1966	The Liquidator	Mostyn
1969	Battle of Britain	Air Vice Marshall Park
1970	Ryan's Daughter	Father Collins
1971	Mary, Queen of Scots	William Cecil
1973	The Offense	Cartwright
1977	The Last Remake of Beau Geste	Sir Hector
1978	Superman	First Elder
1979	Hurricane	Father Malone
1979	Meteor	Sir Michael Hughes
1980	The Sea Wolves	Jack Cartwright
1980	Windwalker	Windwalker
1982	Gandhi	Judge Broomfield
1988	The Unholy	Father Silva

C. THOMAS HOWELL

(1966 -   )

Although he was born into a film family in L.A., his great-grandfather was a stuntman and his father a stunt coordinator, Howell never planned a career as an actor. He initially set his sights on the rodeo circuit. A serious rodeo rider since the age of six, he was named "All-Around Cowboy" by the California Junior Rodeo Association from 1978-80. This is a prestigious and coveted award among serious, aspiring rodeo riders. He made his film debut as one of the bike-riding kids in *E.T.*

Year	Movie	Character
1982	E.T. The Extra-Terrestrial	Tyler
1983	The Outsiders	Ponyboy Curtis
1984	Grandview USA	Tim
1984	Red Dawn	Robert
1984	Tank	Billy
1985	Secret Admirer	Michael Ryan
1986	Soul Man	Mark Watson
1986	The Hitcher	Jim Halsey
1987	A Tiger's Tale	Bubber Drumm
1990	Side Out	Monroe Clark
1993	That Night	Rick

DAVID HUDDLESTON

ERNIE HUDSON

(1930 -   )

(1945 -   )

Huddleston often plays villains and once told a reporter, "Even when I play heavies I try to play them with a twinkle in my eye. Besides, it makes him seem much meaner when he does kill." The veteran character actor began his career in New York musicals after drama studies at the American Academy of Dramatic Arts. He attended Fork Military Academy and served for four years in the U.S. Air Force. He hails from Villamont, VA.

Writing plays was Hudson's first love and entry into the world of theater. He was in Vietnam, briefly in the early 1960s, with the Marine Corps, until an asthma condition got him discharged. He then attended Wayne State University and worked as a playwright with Detroit's Concept Theater East, reputed to be the oldest living black theater in America. After a short and unsatisfactory time spent in a graduate playwriting program at Yale, he moved to L.A., got a bit part in *Leadbelly*, and became an actor.

Year	Movie	Character
1970	Rio Lobo	Dr. Jones
1972	Bad Company	Big Joe
1974	Billy Two Hats	Copeland
1974	Blazing Saddles	Olson Johnson
1974	McQ	Pinky
1978	Capricorn One	Hollis Peaker
1985	Santa Claus	Claus
1988	Frantic	Peter
1993	Life with Mikey	Mr. Corcoran

Year	Movie	Character
1979	The Main Event	Killer
1982	Penitentiary II	Half Dead
1983	Going Berserk	Muhammed
1983	Spacehunter: Adventures in the Forbidden Zone	Washington
1983	Two of a Kind	Det. Staggs
1984	Ghostbusters	Winston Zeddmore
1984	Joy of Sex	Porter
1987	Weeds	Bagdad
1988	The Wrong Guys	Dawson
1989	Ghostbusters II	Winston Zeddmore
1989	Leviathan	Jones
1992	The Hand That Rocks the Cradle	Solomon

DAVID HUFFMAN

(1945 - 1985)

Huffman was born in a Chicago suburb and began acting in high school. He made his Broadway debut playing opposite the famous Gloria Swanson, and moved on to television because he could not support himself by stage acting. In 1985, Huffman was acting at the Old Globe Theater in San Diego when, one afternoon, in a nearby park, he was stabbed to death. Police later arrested a 16-year-old boy.

Year	Movie	Character
1978	F.I.S.T.	Abe Belkin
1978	Ice Castles	Brian Dockett
1980	Leo and Loree	xxx
1982	Firefox	Buckholz
1983	Last Plane Out	Jim

BARNARD HUGHES

(1915 -   )

Raised in the city and suburbs of New York by Irish-immigrant parents, Hughes inherited a love of theater from his mother and was a regular theater-goer from childhood. When older, he joined a travelling repertory company called the Shakespeare Fellowship that toured schools, church basements, community centers and country clubs in the New York area. On stage since the 1940s, he didn't move seriously into films until the late 1960s.

Year	Movie	Character
1961	The Young Doctors	Dr. Kent O'Donnell
1969	Midnight Cowboy	Towny
1970	Where's Poppa?	Colonel Hendriks
1971	Cold Turkey	Dr. Procter
1971	The Hospital	Drummond
1972	Deadhead Miles	Old Man
1972	Rage	Dr. Spencer
1973	Sisters	Mr. McLennen
1977	Oh, God!	Judge Baker
1981	First Monday in October	Chief Justice Crawford
1982	Best Friends	Tim McMullen
1982	Tron	Dr. Walter Gibbs /Dumont
1985	Maxie	Bishop Campbell
1986	Where Are the Children?	Jonathan Knowles
1987	The Lost Boys	Grandpa
1988	Da	Da
1991	Doc Hollywood	Dr. Hogue
1993	Sister Act 2: Back in the Habit	Father Maurice

217

ARTHUR HUNNICUTT

(1911 - 1979)

A veteran western character actor, Hunnicutt graduated from Arkansas State Teachers College and taught during the Depression until he saved the money to go to Cleveland's Phidela Rice School of Voice. He went from summer stock to Broadway in 1939 and in 1942 debuted in Hollywood. Television grabbed him for many series like *Bonanza* and *The Twilight Zone*. He died at 68 of cancer at the Motion Picture Country House in Woodland Hills, CA.

Year	Movie	Character
1963	The Cardinal	Sheriff Dubrow
1965	Cat Ballou	Butch Cassidy
1967	El Dorado	Bull Harris
1971	Shootout	Homer Page
1974	Harry and Tonto	Wade
1974	The Moonrunners	Uncle Jessie
1974	The Spikes Gang	Kid White
1976	Winterhawk	McClusky

GAYLE HUNNICUTT

(1943 -   )

Of Spanish-English heritage, Hunnicutt was born in Fort Worth, TX, the only daughter of a U.S. Army Reserve Colonel. As a student at UCLA, she met the French film director, Jean Renoir, whose encouragement strengthened her resolve to be an actress. She spent time in a speech clinic to rid herself of her accent and worked as a fashion model in Hollywood. Television roles came first and then a long term contract with Universal.

Year	Movie	Character
1966	The Wild Angels	Suzie
1968	P.J.	Maureen Preble
1969	Marlowe	Mavis Wald
1973	Scorpio	Susan
1985	Target	Donna Lloyd
1986	Dream Lover	Claire

HELEN HUNT

(1963 -)

Hunt began a screen career when she was just 11, appearing as Jill Prentiss in the NBC series *Amy Prentiss*. Although that program lasted only one season she was able to maintain the momentum throughout her teens acting in such TV series as *The Swiss Family Robinson* (1975-76) and *The Fitzpatricks* (1977-78). She made her film debut in 1977's *Rollercoaster*, but it was not until 1985 that things got really rolling for her. A stage actress on both coasts, the L.A. native is the daughter of the director, Gordon Hunt.

Year	Movie	Character
1977	Rollercoaster	Tracy Calder
1985	Girls Just Want to Have Fun	Lynne Stone
1986	Peggy Sue Got Married	Beth Bodell
1987	Project X	Teri
1988	Miles From Home	Jennifer
1988	Stealing Home	xxx
1989	Next of Kin	Jessie Gates
1992	Mr. Saturday Night	Annie

LINDA HUNT

(1945 -)

Best known for her Oscar-winning portrayal of the Eurasian dwarf Billy Kwan in the Australian film *The Year of Living Dangerously*, Hunt had only three weeks in which to prepare for the role. "There wasn't time for me to make some fabulous transition into being a man," she later explained. "The most I could do was work on finding the emotional center of the person and his way of thinking, and believe if that's there the other things would fall into place."

Year	Movie	Character
1980	Popeye	Mrs. Oxheart
1983	The Year of Living Dangerously	Billy Kwan
1984	Dune	Shadout Mapes
1984	The Bostonians	Dr. Prance
1985	Eleni	Katina
1985	Silverado	Stella
1989	She-Devil	Hooper
1990	Kindergarten Cop	Miss Schlowski
1991	If Looks Could Kill	Ilsa Grunt
1993	Rain Without Thunder	Atwood Society Director
1993	Younger and Younger	Frances

HOLLY HUNTER

(1958 -   )

Born and raised in Conyers, GA, Hunter began acting in her freshman year of high school. At age 16, she spent the summer with a stock company in upstate New York. The experience convinced her that her future was on the stage. After graduation from Carnegie-Mellon University in Pittsburgh, she moved to New York and, within three weeks of her arrival, landed a small part in a film. She has not stopped working since.

Year	Movie	Character
1984	Swing Shift	Jeannie Sherman
1987	Broadcast News	Jane Craig
1987	End of the Line	Charlotte
1987	Raising Arizona	Ed
1989	Always	Dorinda Durston
1989	Animal Behavior	Coral Grable
1989	Miss Firecracker	Carnelle Scott
1991	Once Around	Renata Bella
1993	The Firm	Tammy Hemphill

JEFFREY HUNTER

(1926 - 1969)

After serving in the navy and going to Northwestern University and UCLA for dramatics, the handsome Hunter started to make movies and break hearts. He acted for 20th Century Fox with heartthrob Robert Wagner and the two men rated tons of fan mail. A frequent TV performer, he died at 42 of injuries from a fall in L.A.

Year	Movie	Character
1960	Hell to Eternity	Guy Gabaldon
1961	King of Kings	Jesus Christ
1962	No Man is an Island	George R. Tweed
1962	The Longest Day	Sgt. Fuller
1968	Custer of the West	Lt. Benteen
1968	The Private Navy of Sgt. O'Farrell	Lt. (jg) Lyman P. Jones

KAKI HUNTER

(19?? -   )

She was a "regular" in the extremely popular *Porky's* series of movies, but Hunter's best performances have been elsewhere. Her debut in the Meatloaf vehicle, *Roadie*, in 1980 was a hit according to the *New York Daily News*: "The movie's strongest asset is not its rock music, but Hunter. Dressed to kill in luminous stretch pants and other outrageous combinations, she's adorably flaky as the groupie who's saving herself for the right rock star."

Year	Movie	Character
1980	Roadie	Lola
1980	Willie and Phil	Patti
1981	Porky's	Wendy
1981	Whose Life Is It Anyway?	Mary Jo
1983	Porky's II: The Next Day	Wendy
1984	Just the Way You Are	Lisa
1985	Porky's Revenge	Wendy

JOHN HURT

(1940 -   )

The English actor's career began in an opposite fashion, starting with roles in film and television before moving to theater. Hurt was Oscar-nominated for his performance as a defeated junkie in *Midnight Express* and as the misshapen, noble Victorian gentleman in *The Elephant Man*. However, it may be that his most memorable film scene occured in *Alien* when a presumed bout of indigestion turns out to be a tiny alien monster that suddenly bursts through his chest.

Year	Movie	Character
1966	A Man for All Seasons	Rich
1978	Midnight Express	Max
1979	Alien	Kane
1980	Heaven's Gate	Irvine
1980	The Elephant Man	John Merrick
1981	Night Crossing	Peter Strelzyk
1982	Partners	Kerwin
1983	The Osterman Weekend	Fassett
1986	Jake Speed	Sid
1987	From the Hip	Douglas Benoit
1987	Spaceballs	Himself
1989	Scandal	Stephen Ward
1990	Frankenstein Unbound	Dr. Joe Buchanan
1991	King Ralph	Graves

MARY BETH HURT

(1948 -   )

Hurt made her theatrical debut Off-Broadway as a 98-year-old Vietnamese man named Uncle Remus in *More Than You Deserve* in 1974. But, in movies, she has been typecast as a wifely types. "I've never been cast as a mistress," she once said. "I'm the girl men marry, not the girl they have affairs with." After leaving her hometown of Marshalltown, IA, for New York, Hurt attended the NYU School of the Arts. She later married the actor William Hurt.

Year	Movie	Character
1978	Interiors	Joey
1979	Head Over Heels	Laura
1980	A Change of Seasons	Kasey Evans
1982	The World According to Garp	Helen Holm
1985	Compromising Positions	Peg Tuccio
1985	D.A.R.Y.L.	Joyce Richardson
1989	Parents	Lily Laemle
1991	Defenseless	Ellie Seldes
1993	My Boyfriend's Back	Mrs. Dingle

JIM HUTTON

(1933 - 1979)

This film and television actor from Binghamton, N.Y., began acting while serving with the U.S. Army in Germany where he set up an English-speaking theater in Berlin. Hutton debuted in the movies in the late 50's and in television in the early 70's. The father of actor Timothy Hutton, he died at 45 of liver cancer in L.A.

Year	Movie	Character
1960	Where the Boys Are	TV Thompson
1961	Bachelor in Paradise	Larry Delavane
1961	The Honeymoon Machine	Jason Eldridge
1962	Period of Adjustment	George Haverstick
1962	The Horizontal Lieutenant	Lt. Merle Wye
1965	Major Dundee	Lt. Graham
1965	Never Too Late	Charlie Clinton
1965	The Hallelujah Trail	Capt. Paul Slater
1966	Walk, Don't Run	Steve Davis
1967	Who's Minding the Mint?	Harry Lucas
1968	The Green Berets	Sgt. Petersen
1969	Hellfighters	Greg Parker

LAUREN HUTTON

(1943 -   )

Supermodel-turned-actress Mary Laurence Hutton was born in Charleston, SC. She spent a year at a college in Florida, quit to work as a Playboy Bunny and then moved to New York to try modeling. She made the cover of *Vogue* in 1966. Commenting recently on her nearly 30 movies, Hutton said "most of them have been really bad, unseeable. I just couldn't make another movie unless I'd buy a ticket to go see it."

Year	Movie	Character
1968	Paper Lion	Kate
1970	Little Fauss and Big Halsey	Rita Nebraska
1976	Gator	Aggie Maybank
1977	Viva Knievel!	Kate Morgan
1980	American Gigolo	Michelle
1981	Paternity	Jenny
1981	Zorro, the Gay Blade	Charlotte
1984	Lassiter	Kari
1985	Once Bitten	Countess
1987	Malone	Jamie

TIMOTHY HUTTON

(1960 -   )

Hutton's co-star in *Ordinary People*, Mary Tyler Moore, described the actor as down-to-earth. "[He] doesn't appear to be driven by desire for success or ambition," she said. Considered laid-back with a natural ability to act, Hutton's interest in acting came during high school. He is the son of the late actor Jim Hutton and was raised in California.

Year	Movie	Character
1980	Ordinary People	Conrad
1981	Taps	Brian Moreland
1983	Daniel	Daniel Isaacson
1984	Iceman	Dr. Stanley Shephard
1985	The Falcon and the Snowman	Christopher Boyce
1985	Turk 182!	Jimmy Lynch
1987	Made in Heaven	Mike Shea/Elmo Barnett
1988	A Time of Destiny	Jack
1988	Betrayed	Uncle Sam
1988	Everybody's All-American	Donnie "Cake"
1990	Q & A	Al Reilly
1993	The Dark Half	Thad Beaumont/George Stark
1993	The Temp	Peter Derns

WILFRID HYDE-WHITE

(1903 - 1991)

Born in England, the character actor appeared in more than 150 British and American films after beginning his career as a magician. Hyde-White won a scholarship to RADA in London, debuted on the London stage in 1925, and was discovered and taken to Hollywood by George Cukor. During World War II, he served in the British Army. He died of heart failure.

Year	Movie	Character
1960	Let's Make Love	John Wales
1961	Ada	Sylvester Marin
1961	On the Double	Colonel Somerset
1964	My Fair Lady	Col. Pickering
1965	John Goldfarb, Please Come Home	Guz
1966	The Liquidator	The Chief
1968	P.J.	Billings Browne
1979	Battlestar: Galactica	Anton
1980	In God We Trust	Abbot
1980	Oh, God! Book II	Judge Miller
1981	Tarzan, The Ape Man	Club Member
1982	The Toy	Barkley

MARTHA HYER

(1924 -   )

A Texan, Hyer graduated from Northwestern University, where she majored in drama and speech. She was later discovered by an RKO talent scout while acting with the Pasadena Playhouse. After being screen-tested, she was signed to a long-term contract with that studio and began making pictures in 1946. She married writer-director Ray Stahl in 1951, sought her release from RKO, and spent two years circling the globe making movies. Upon her return to the US, her career lasted into the early 1970s.

Year	Movie	Character
1960	Ice Palace	Dorothy
1961	Last Time I Saw Archie	Peggy Kramer
1962	A Girl Named Tamiko	Fay Wilson
1963	The Man from the Diner's Club	Lucy
1964	Bikini Beach	Vivien Clements
1964	The Carpetbaggers	Jennie Denton
1964	First Men in the Moon	Kate Callender
1965	The Sons of Katie Elder	Mary Gordon
1966	The Chase	Mary Fuller
1966	The Night of the Grizzly	Angela Cole

JOHN IRELAND

(1914 - 1992)

Ireland was a leading man in several films during the 1940s and 1950s, but was soon appearing as tough-guys in supporting roles in westerns and actioners. Born in Canada and raised in New York, Ireland started in show biz as a professional swimmer in a water carnival. In 1954, he co-directed the famous B-movie house American International Pictures' first release titled *The Fast and the Furious* for producer Roger Corman.

Year	Movie	Character
1960	Spartacus	Crixus
1961	Wild in the Country	Phil Mac
1963	55 Days at Peking	Sergeant Harry
1964	The Fall of the Roman Empire	Ballomar
1965	I Saw What You Did	Steve Marak
1975	Farewell My Lovely	Nulty
1975	The Swiss Conspiracy	McGowan
1984	Martin's Day	Brewer
1988	Messenger of Death	Zenas Beecham

MICHAEL IRONSIDE

(1940 -   )

Born in Toronto, Ironside had always wanted to be a writer and wrote his first play at age 15 titled *The Shelter* which won first prize in a Canada-wide university contest. He mounted his own production of the play with his prize money. Ironside attended the Ontario College of Art and later studied with a National Film Board workshop for three years. Canadian television and film roles followed. He moved to L.A. in 1983.

Year	Movie	Character
1982	Visiting Hours	Colt
1984	The Surrogate	George Kyber
1986	Top Gun	Jester
1987	Extreme Prejudice	Major Paul Hackett
1987	Hello Mary Lou: Prom Night II	Principal Bill Sr.
1987	Nowhere to Hide	Ben
1990	Mind Field	Kellen O'Reilly
1990	Total Recall	Richter
1991	Highlander II: The Quickening	Katana
1991	McBain	Frank Bruce
1992	Guncrazy	Mr. Kincaid
1993	Free Willy	Dial
1993	Father Hood	Jerry

AMY IRVING

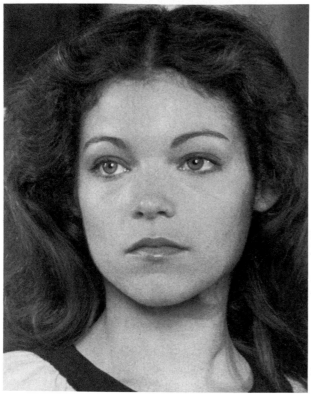

(1953 -   )

Irving studied drama at the American Conservatory Theater in San Francisco and the London Academy of Music and Art. A stage, as well as film, actress she once told an interviewer: "On stage you're in control, whereas in film you're obviously going in with a trust—the director can do anything he wants with what you do. You can give a good performance that will end up on the cutting-room floor or a terrible one that he'll fix up. But when you're out on the stage, you carry the ball from beginning to end."

Year	Movie	Character
1976	Carrie	Sue Snell
1978	The Fury	Gillian
1979	Voices	Rosemarie Lemon
1980	Honeysuckle Rose	Lily
1980	The Competition	Heidi Schoonover
1983	Yentl	Hadass
1984	Micki + Maude	Maude Salinger
1988	Crossing Delancy	Isabelle Grossman
1990	A Show of Force	Kate Ryan de Melendez
1993	Benefit of the Doubt	Karen

BILL IRWIN

(1950 -   )

A graduate of the Ringling Brothers and Barnum & Bailey Clown College, Irwin won a following as Willy the Clown in San Francisco's Pickle Family Circus for several years. Raised in California and Oklahoma, the actor/writer/comedian graduated from Oberlin College as a theater major. His medium is primarily the stage. However, he may be best known to television audiences as the mute circus performer in love with an Indian woman on *Northern Exposure*.

Year	Movie	Character
1988	Eight Men Out	Eddie Collins
1990	My Blue Heaven	Kirby
1991	Hot Shots!	Buzz Harley
1991	Scenes From a Mall	Mime
1991	Stepping Out	Geoffrey

JUDITH IVEY

(1951 -)

A Texan, Ivey discovered her love for drama in a high school production of *The Man Who Came to Dinner*. After college, she worked at the Goodman Theater in Chicago and Joseph Papp's Public Theater in New York. By 1981, however, she almost abandoned acting in New York to become a veterinarian because, as reported by the *New York Times*, "she was tired of being poor, tired of waiting in the unemployment lines between shows, and was impatient for success." Fortunately, Hollywood was just around the corner.

Year	Movie	Character
1984	Harry and Son	Sally
1984	The Lonely Guy	Iris
1984	The Woman in Red	Didi
1985	Compromising Positions	Nancy Miller
1986	Brighton Beach Memoirs	Blanche
1987	Hello Again	Zelda
1987	Sister, Sister	Charlotte Bonnard
1988	Miles From Home	Frances
1989	In Country	Anita
1990	Alice	xxx
1990	Everybody Wins	Connie

ANNE JACKSON

(1926 -)

The daughter of a Croatian socialist father and an Irish Catholic mother, Jackson grew up during the Depression years in rural Pennsylvania before moving with her family to New York . Her acting and comedic talents presented themselves early on makeshift country stages and Brooklyn street corners. High school drama classes led to studies at the Neighborhood Playhouse after graduation and her professional career began on Broadway in 1945.

Year	Movie	Character
1960	Tall Story	Myra Sullivan
1967	The Tiger Makes Out	Gloria
1968	How to Save a Marriage (And Ruin Your Life)	Muriel Laszlo
1968	The Secret Life of an American Wife	Victoria Layton
1970	Dirty Dingus Magee	Belle
1970	Lovers and Other Strangers	Cathy
1979	The Bell Jar	Dr. Nolan
1980	The Shining	Doctor
1984	Sam's Son	Harriet Orowitz
1990	Funny About Love	Adele Bergman
1992	Folks!	Mildred Aldrich

LOU JACOBI

(1913 -   )

Woody Allen once called him "the laugh machine" and built his play *Don't Drink the Water* around his comedic talents. Jacobi has been entertaining people since the 1920s with music, jokes and drama. Canadian-born, he began his career as a full-fledged performer in London's famed West End. His portrayal of a Jewish father in the stage and film versions of *The Diary of Anne Frank* ensured a steady supply of character roles for the versatile actor.

Year	Movie	Character
1963	Irma La Douce	Moustache
1966	Penelope	Ducky
1966	The Last of the Secret Agents?	Papa Leo
1972	Everything You Always Wanted to Know About Sex (But Were Afraid to Ask)	Sam
1976	Next Stop, Greenwich Village	Herb
1980	The Lucky Star	Elia Goldberg
1981	Chu Chu and the Philly Flash	Landlord
1982	My Favorite Year	Uncle Morty
1986	The Boss's Wife	Harry
1987	Amazon Women on the Moon	Murray
1990	Avalon	Gabriel Krichinsky

RICHARD JAECKEL

(1926 -   )

Following high school in California, Jaeckel got his first job as a mailman at 20th Century Fox. While there he was cast as a young marine in the 1943 war film, *Guadalcanal Diary*. So many teenagers of the day identified with his role that it probably contributed to the successful recruitment by the Marine Corps. After serving in the Merchant Marines himself, he returned to Hollywood to pursue a screen career.

Year	Movie	Character
1960	The Gallant Hours	Lt. Cmdr. Roy Webb
1967	The Dirty Dozen	Sgt. Bowren
1968	The Devil's Brigade	Omar Greco
1969	The Green Slime	Vince Elliott
1970	Chisum	Evans
1971	Never Give an Inch	Joe Ben
1972	Ulzana's Raid	Sergeant
1973	Pat Garrett and Billy the Kid	Sheriff Kip McKinney
1974	The Outfit	Chemey
1975	Part 2, Walking Tall	Stud
1976	Grizzly	Scott
1976	The Drowning Pool	Franks
1977	Twilight's Last Gleaming	Capt. Stanford Towne
1980	Herbie Goes Bananas	Shepard
1981	All the Marbles	Reno Referee
1982	Cold River	Mike
1984	Starman	George Fox
1986	Black Moon Rising	Earl Windom
1990	Delta Force 2	John Page

BRION JAMES

CLIFTON JAMES

(1945 -)

"My dad built a movie theater in Beaumont, California, [and] by the time I was two years old, I was at the movies every night," James once recalled. "I lived in books and movies. That's where I wanted to be, in that fantasy world. I started acting in school at a very early age, putting on talent shows, acting in high school plays, that kind of thing. I guess some people are just destined to do this."

(1921 -)

James is known worldwide for his role as the redneck Southern sheriff who provides comic relief in *Live and Let Die* and *The Man with the Golden Gun*, and symbolizes the lighter tone taken in the James Bond films of the 1970s. A graduate of the University of Oregon, and a member of the Actors Studio, James spent five years with the U.S. Army during World War II. He then made his Broadway debut as the warm-hearted construction foreman in William Saroyan's *The Cave Dwellers*.

Year	Movie	Character
1978	Corvette Summer	Jeff
1981	Southern Comfort	Trapper
1982	48 Hours	Kehoe
1982	Blade Runner	Leon
1983	The Ballad of Gregorio Cortez	Capt. Rogers
1984	A Breed Apart	Huey Miller
1985	Crimewave	Coddish
1985	Enemy Mine	Stubbs
1985	Flesh + Blood	Karsthans
1986	Armed and Dangerous	Anthony Lazarus
1987	Steel Dawn	Tark
1988	Cherry 2000	Stacy
1988	The Wrong Guys	Glen Grunski
1989	Red Scorpion	Krasnov
1989	Tango & Cash	ArialBold/Requin
1990	Another 48 Hours	Ben Kehoe
1992	The Player	Joel Levison

Year	Movie	Character
1962	David and Lisa	John
1967	Cool Hand Luke	Carr
1967	The Happening	O'Reilly
1968	Will Penny	Catron
1969	The Reivers	Butch Lovemaiden
1970	...tick...tick...tick...	D.J. Rankin
1972	The Biscuit Eater	Mr. Eben
1972	The New Centurions	Whitey
1973	Live and Let Die	Sheriff Pepper
1973	The Last Detail	M.A.A.
1974	Bank Shot	Frank "Bulldog" Streiger
1974	Buster and Billie	Jake
1974	The Man with the Golden Gun	J.W. Pepper
1976	Silver Streak	Sheriff Chauncey
1977	The Bad News Bears in Breaking Training	Sy Orlansky
1980	Superman II	Sheriff
1988	Eight Men Out	Charles Comiskey
1990	The Bonfire of the Vanities	Albert Fox

STEVE JAMES

(1952 -   )

Raised in a tough section of the Bronx, James fell in love with theater while in high school. After graduating from college as a theater arts and film major, he worked as a performer and manager at Manhattan's South Street Seaport Theater. He acted in TV commercials from 1976, promoting beer, cereal and life insurance, until his career took an upturn when he was hired as a stuntman for the 1979 film *The Wanderers*. Stunt work led to acting in action films where he has since solidified his career.

Year	Movie	Character
1980	The Exterminator	Michael
1984	The Brother from	
	Another Planet	Odell
1985	American Ninja	Jackson
1986	Avenging Force	Larry Richards
1986	P.O.W. The Escape	Johnston
1987	American Ninja 2:	
	The Confrontation	Jackson
1988	Hero and the Terror	Robinson
1988	I'm Gonna Git You Sucka	Kung Fu Joe
1988	Johnny Be Good	Coach Sanders
1989	American Ninja 3:	
	Blood Hunt	Jackson
1991	McBain	Eastland

LIONEL JEFFRIES

(1927 -   )

The English actor was cast by Hitchcock in his 1949 film *Stage Fright*, after the director spotted Jeffries' bald pate and wrote a part especially for him. He was billed as "The Bald-Headed Young Man." His career didn't really kick into gear, however, until the late 1950s. Told to tone down his Britishness so that the pictures would sell in the U.S., he developed, what he called, a "trans-Atlantic accent." A character player in over 150 U.K. and U.S. films, he turned his attention to directing children's films in the 1970s.

Year	Movie	Character
1961	Fanny	Monsieur Brun
1962	The Notorious Landlady	Inspector Oliphant
1963	Call Me Bwana	Ezra Larsen
1964	First Men in the Moon	Joseph Cavor
1966	Arrivederci, Baby!	Parker
1967	Camelot	King Pellinore
1967	Those Fantastic Flying Fools	Sir Charles Dillworthy
1968	Chitty, Chitty, Bang, Bang	Grandpa Potts
1970	Sudden Terror	Colonel
1979	The Prisoner of Zenda	General Sapt

DAVID JOHANSEN

(1950 -   )

Johansen was a hit as the lead singer of the 1970s glamour-rock band, The New York Dolls. He next worked as a solo artist, before becoming a lounge singer under the name, Buster Poindexter. Making the transition to acting was not hard for Johansen because, as he once said, "every singer who's worth his salt is an actor. You play different characters in different songs. Sometimes you're a romantic lead, sometimes you're this madcap party barbarian. You play all these roles, running through every aspect of emotion."

Year	Movie	Character
1988	Scrooged	Ghost of Christmas Past
1989	Let It Ride	Looney
1990	Tales From the Darkside	Halston ("Cat From Hell")
1992	Freejack	Brad Hines

GLYNIS JOHNS

(1923 -   )

The British actress comes from a theatrical family that boasts four generations in the entertainment profession. It all began when her great-grandfather formed a musical touring company in Australia called The Steele Payne Bellringers. Her career has been evenly divided between the stage and the screen. A top box-office attraction in Britain in the early 1950s, she made her Hollywood debut in a bit part in 1956 in the Danny Kaye vehicle, *The Court Jester*.

Year	Movie	Character
1960	The Sundowners	Mrs. Firth
1962	The Chapman Report	Teresa
1964	Mary Poppins	Mrs. Banks
1965	Dear Brigitte	Vina Leaf
1968	Don't Just Stand There!	Sabine Manning
1988	Zelly and Me	Co-Co

BEN JOHNSON

(1918 -   )

A stint as a rodeo rider enabled Johnson to enter films as a wrangler and a stuntman in a series of John Ford westerns in the late 1940s. A native of Foraker, OK, the actor won a best supporting Oscar for his portrayal of Sam in the 1971 blockbuster *The Last Picture Show*.

Year	Movie	Character
1961	One-Eyed Jacks	Bob Amory
1965	Major Dundee	Sgt. Chillum
1966	The Rare Breed	Jeff Harter
1968	Hang 'Em High	xxx
1968	Will Penny	Alex
1969	The Undefeated	Short Grub
1969	The Wild Bunch	Tector Gorch
1970	Chisum	James Pepper
1971	The Last Picture Show	Sam the Lion
1972	Junior Bonner	Buck Roan
1972	The Getaway	Jack Benyon
1973	Dillinger	Melvin
1973	The Train Robbers	Jesse
1974	The Sugarland Express	Capt. Tanner

(continued on page 507)

CAROLYN JONES

(1933 - 1983)

A Texas beauty, Jones started acting in an Amarillo high school and worked as a radio station deejay until she went to Hollywood after graduation. During the 1950s and 60's she acted on the stage and before the cameras in more than two dozen pictures, comedy and drama. A well-known TV actress for roles in *The Colgate Comedy Hour*, *Dragnet* and *The Schlitz Playhouse of Stars*, she died of cancer in Hollywood.

Year	Movie	Character
1960	Ice Palace	Bridie
1962	Sail a Crooked Ship	Virginia
1963	How the West Was Won	Julie Rawlings
1969	Heaven with a Gun	Madge McCloud

DEAN JONES

(1936 -   )

A familiar face in many Walt Disney movies of the 1960s, Jones launched his entertainment career as a singer while in the navy stationed in San Diego. He was soon signed by MGM and when the acting began, the singing stopped. After a ten year absence from films he was cast as an uptight corporate type in the Danny DeVito vehicle, *Other People's Money*. Jones was born in Decatur, AL.

Year	Movie	Character
1963	Under The Yum Yum Tree	David
1964	The New Interns	Lew
1966	Any Wednesday	Cass Henderson
1969	The Love Bug	Jim
1977	Herbie Goes to Monte Carlo	Jim Douglas
1991	Other People's Money	William J. Coles
1992	Beethoven	Dr. Varnick

FREDDIE JONES

(1927 -   )

Born in Stoke-On-Trent, England's pottery center, Jones was a medical laboratory technician until he was 30 years old. At that time, he took his first acting class and, as he states, "found absolute happiness." He continued to study drama at night for about a year and then auditioned for the Rose Buford College of Speech and Drama in Kent and was immediately accepted, a feat which, according to the head of the school, was unique. Well-known in England he soon began making pictures in the U.S.

Year	Movie	Character
1974	Juggernaut	Mr. Buckland
1980	The Elephant Man	Bytes
1982	Firefox	Kenneth Aubrey
1983	Krull	Ynyr
1984	Dune	Thufir Hawat
1984	Firestarter	Dr. Wanless
1985	Young Sherlock Holmes	Bragwitch
1989	Erik the Viking	Harald the Missionary
1990	Wild at Heart	George Kovich

HENRY JONES

(1912 -   )

A familiar face in movies and television, Jones knows the ropes. As an actor in the mid-70's TV series *Phyllis*, a live-audience, three-camera sitcom, he explained, "The experienced actor is needed more on television. In a feature picture, you can take someone who's limited in talent and make them look very good by reshooting the scene over and over again. On *Phyllis,* the cameras are all rolling at once and the untalented actor is going to look flat." Jones is from Philadelphia.

Year	Movie	Character
1965	Never Too Late	Dr. Kimbrough
1968	Stay Away, Joe	Hy Slager
1969	Angel in My Pocket	Will Sinclair
1969	Butch Cassdy and the Sundance	Kid Bike Salesman
1969	Support Your Local Sheriff!	Henry Jackson
1970	Dirty Dingus Magee	Reverend Green
1971	Support Your Local Gunfighter	Ez
1972	Pete 'n' Tillie	Mr. Tucker
1974	The Outfit	Doctor
1980	9 to 5	Hinkle
1982	Deathtrap	Porter Milgrim
1990	Arachnophobia	Dr. Sam Metcalf
1990	The Grifters	Simms

JEFFREY JONES

(1947 -   )

Active primarily on the stage in the early years of his career, Jones' face became better known to movie audiences from the mid-1980s. Born in Buffalo, NY, the son of an art historian, the actor received his B.A. from Lawrence University and trained for the stage at the London Academy of Music and Dramatic Arts. *Variety* praised his "delicious comic performance" in *Ferris Bueller's Day Off* "as the high school principal driven nearly out of his mind in his frustrated pursuit of Ferris."

Year	Movie	Character
1984	Amadeus	Emperor Joseph II
1985	Transylvania 6-5000	Lepescu
1986	Ferris Bueller's Day Off	Ed Rooney
1986	Howard the Duck	Dr. Jenning
1987	The Hanoi Hilton	Fischer
1988	Beetlejuice	Charles
1989	Who's Harry Crumb?	Eliot Draisen
1990	The Hunt for Red October	Skip Tyler
1992	Mom & Dad Save the World	Dick Nelson
1992	Stay Tuned	Spike

L.Q. JONES

(1927 -   )

His screen image suggests a dull-witted and rather agressive type, but veteran character actor Jones is as sharp as they come. A familiar face in countless movies, Jones was head of a profitable production company, LQ/Jaf (L.Q. Jones and friends) during the 1960s and 1970s. That company produced such films as *The Witchmaker* (1969), *Brotherhood of Satan* (1971) and *A Boy and His Dog* (1975).

Year	Movie	Character
1960	Cimarron	Millis
1962	Hell is for Heroes	Sgt. Frazer
1962	Ride the High Country	Sylvus Hammond
1965	Major Dundee	Arthur Hadley
1968	Hang 'Em High	xxx
1968	Stay Away, Joe	Bronc Hoverty
1969	The Wild Bunch	T.C.
1970	The Ballad of Cable Hogue	Taggart
1971	Brotherhood of Satan	Sheriff
1973	Pat Garrett and Billy the Kid	Black Harris
1975	White Line Fever	Buck Wessle
1976	Mother, Jugs & Speed	Davey
1976	Winterhawk	Gates
1979	Fast Charlie, The Moonbeam Rider	Floyd
1982	The Beast Within	Sheriff
1983	Lone Wolf McQuade	Dakota
1983	Sacred Ground	Tolbert
1983	Timerider	Ben Potter
1988	Bulletproof	xxx
1989	River of Death	Hiller

SAM JONES

(1954 -   )

Born in Chicago and raised in West Palm Beach, Jones' background is strictly non-show business. "I worked in health clubs. I sold athletic shoes. I sold health food. I worked on a research vessel as a scuba diver. I played semi-pro football. I drove a Pepsi truck. And I was a house painter," he once told an interviewer. However, by 1976, he was a male model and two years after that he moved on Hollywood.

Year	Movie	Character
1979	10	David
1980	Flash Gordon	Flash Gordon
1986	My Chauffeur	Battle Witherspoon
1989	One Man Force	Pete

TOMMY LEE JONES

(1946 -   )

A native of Western Texas, Jones graduated cum laude from Harvard with a degree in English. There he excelled in both football and polo. He started a career in film, television and theater in New York City. His numerous screen roles include a smooth businessman in Oliver Stone's *JFK*, a police lieutenant in *The Eyes of Laura Mars* assigned to find the killer of fashion photographer Faye Dunaway's friends and associates and Sissy Spacek's husband in *Coal Miner's Daughter*.

Year	Movie	Character
1970	Love Story	Hank
1976	Jackson County Jail	Coley
1977	Rolling Thunder	Johny Vohden
1978	Eyes of Laura Mars	John Neville
1978	The Betsy	Angelo Perino
1980	Coal Miner's Daughter	Doolittle (Mooney) Lynn
1981	Back Roads	Elmore Pratt
1983	Nate and Hayes	Capt. Bully
1984	The River Rat	Billy
1986	Black Moon Rising	Quint
1987	The Big Town	George Cole
1989	The Package	Thomas Boyette
1990	Firebirds	Brad Little
1991	JFK	Clay Shaw
1992	Under Siege	William Strannix
1993	House of Cards	Jake Beerlander
1993	The Fugitive	Sam Gerard

RICHARD JORDAN

(1938 - 1993)

Jordan was acting professionally in Connecticut summer stock while still in his teens, but it wasn't easy getting up on stage at first. He overcame his stage fright because, as he once explained, "the idea of telling a story was just fascinating to me. And the fact that people wanted stories was fascinating. And I lost all the stage fright I ever had, because I was only a participant in a group effort to tell a story." His big break came with a starring role in Joseph Papp's production of *Romeo and Juliet*. Jordan died of a brain tumor.

Year	Movie	Character
1971	Lawman	Crowe Wheelwright
1971	Valdez is Coming	R.L.
1973	The Friends of Eddie Coyle	Foley
1975	Rooster Cogburn	Hawk
1975	The Yakuza	Dusty
1976	Logan's Run	Francis
1978	Interiors	Frederick
1979	A Nightingale Sang in Berkeley Square	xxx
1980	Raise the Titanic!	Dirk Pitt
1984	Dune	Duncan Idaho
1985	The Mean Season	Alan Delous
1986	Solarbabies	Grock
1987	The Secret of My Success	Howard Prescott
1989	Romero	Father Rutilio Grande
1990	The Hunt for Red October	Jeffrey Pelt
1991	Shout	Eugene Benedict
1991	Timebomb	Col. Taylor
1993	Gettysburg	Brig. Gen. Armistead

VICTOR JORY

(1901 - 1982)

In his almost 50-year career as a character actor, Jory played in 76 feature films and more than 200 TV shows and acted on stage where he debuted in Vancouver in 1929. Often the bad guy in low-budget westerns, he also played in such classics as *Gone with the Wind*, *State Fair*, *The Miracle Worker*. He died at 79 of a probable heart attack in his Santa Monica, CA, apartment.

Year	Movie	Character
1960	The Fugitive Kind	Jabe Torrance
1962	The Miracle Worker	Capt. Keller
1964	Cheyenne Autumn	Tall Tree
1968	Jigsaw	Dr. Edward Arkroyd
1973	Papillon	Indian Chief
1980	The Mountain Men	Iron Belly

ROBERT JOY

(1951 -   )

One of Hollywood's most sought-after character actors since the early 1980s, Joy got his start as an actor, writer and composer with a comedy group that toured Canada for three years. This followed English lit studies at Oxford as a Rhodes scholar. The Montreal-native was nominated for a Genie (Canada's Oscar) for his role as a sleazy cocaine dealer in the film *Atlantic City*.

Year	Movie	Character
1981	Atlantic City	Dave
1981	Threshold	David Art
1983	Amityville 3-D	Elliott
1985	Desperately Seeking Susan	Jim
1987	Big Shots	Dickie
1989	Millennium	Sherman
1990	Longtime Companion	Ron
1992	Shadows and Fog	Hans Spiro's asst.
1993	The Dark Half	Fred Clawson

KATY JURADO

JANE KACZMAREK

(1927 -   )

A native of Mexico, Jurado was born to a wealthy cattle and orange rancher and a former opera singer. Along came a revolution and all of the family's lands were confiscated by the new government. Married to actor Ernest Borgnine for four years, Jurado was often cast as an Indian or Mexican or both.

(19?? -   )

A product of the Yale School of Drama, where she earned her MFA, Kaczmarek performed for several seasons in the Yale Repertory Theater and the nearby Williamstown and Berkshire Festivals before she tackled TV and film. On television, she has appeared on *The Paper Chase*, *Scarecrow and Mrs. King*, *Crazy Like a Fox*, *St. Elsewhere*, and *Hill Street Blues*.

Year	Movie	Character
1961	One-Eyed Jacks	Maria
1962	Barabbas	Sara
1968	Stay Away, Joe	Annie Lightcloud
1973	Pat Garrett and Billy the Kid	Mrs. Baker
1984	Under the Volcano	Senora Gregoria

Year	Movie	Character
1984	Falling In Love	Ann Raftis
1985	The Heavenly Kid	Emily
1988	D.O.A.	Gail Cornell
1988	Vice Versa	Robyn

JAMES KAREN

(1923 -   )

Karen is perhaps best known to residents in the New York-New Jersey-Philadelphia corridor as the commercial spokesman for Pathmark supermarkets. He was born in Wilkes-Barre, PA, the son of a produce dealer and a folk singer and studied acting with Sanford Meisner at the Neighborhood Playhouse. Memorable screen roles include Craig T. Nelson's unscrupulous boss in *Poltergeist*.

Year	Movie	Character
1978	F.I.S.T.	Andrews
1979	The China Syndrome	Mac Churchill
1982	Poltergeist	Teague
1982	Time Walker	Wendell
1985	Jagged Edge	Andrew Hardesty
1985	The Return of the Living Dead	Frank
1986	Invaders From Mars	Gen. Wilson
1987	Wall Street	Lynch
1988	Return of the Living Dead Part II	Ed
1990	The Closer	Ned Randall
1990	Vital Signs	Dean of Students
1991	The Unborn	Dr. Meyerling

JOHN KARLEN

(1933 -   )

Karlen played Willie Loomis for several years on ABC's supernatural soap opera *Dark Shadows* while looking for stage roles in New York. The show led to his first two movie roles. The actor has spent most of his career on the stage or television, including six seasons with the popular *Cagney & Lacey* as Tyne Daly's husband. He won an Emmy for the part in 1986 and even though it was a small one Karlen seemed satisfied. "As long as I get my 2 or 3 scenes, I'm happy," he once said.

Year	Movie	Character
1970	House of Dark Shadows	Willie
1971	The Night of Dark Shadows	Alex
1976	A Small Town in Texas	Lenny
1981	Pennies From Heaven	Detective
1984	Impulse	Bob
1984	Racing With the Moon	Mr. Nash
1986	Native Son	Max

ALEX KARRAS

(1935 -   )

A former All-Pro defensive tackle with the Detroit Lions, Karras became interested in acting during the filming of *Paper Lion*, based on George Plimpton's book about his former team. He spent three years as a commentator on ABC's Monday Night Football with Howard Cosell and made his feature film debut as a professional actor in 1973 in *The 500 Pound Jerk*.

Year	Movie	Character
1968	Paper Lion	Himself
1974	Blazing Saddles	Mongo
1978	FM	Doc Holiday
1980	When Time Ran Out...	Tiny Baker
1981	Nobody's Perfekt	Swaboda
1981	Porky's	Sheriff Wallace
1982	Victor/Victoria	Squash
1984	Against All Odds	Hank Sully

WILLIAM KATT

(1955 -   )

Katt's teenage years were spent on the Southern California beaches surfing and living the good life in the sun. He dreamed of making a career out of his interest in music and, while at Orange Coast College, he took music theory classes and played in various bands around campus. Fate and possibly genes pushed him into acting, however. Katt is the son of Barbara Hale, who played Perry Mason's secretary on film and in television and Bill Williams, TV's Kit Carson.

Year	Movie	Character
1976	Carrie	Tommy Ross
1977	First Love	Elgin Smith
1978	Big Wednesday	Jack
1979	Butch and Sundance: The Early Days	Sundance Kid
1985	Baby...Secret of the Lost Legend	George Loomis

JULIE KAVNER

(1951 -   )

Best remembered as Brenda Morgenstern, the talkative kid sister on the hit sitcom *Rhoda* (1974-78), Kavner moved into films during the 1980s, often in those of Woody Allen. A theater arts major at Cal State in San Diego, she frequently appeared in college plays and, after graduation, in community theater. Her screen outings include the nurse in *Awakenings* who assists and gives moral support to Robin Williams while he is treating encephalitis patients like Robert De Niro.

Year	Movie	Character
1985	Bad Medicine	Cookie Katz
1986	Hannah and Her Sisters	Gail
1987	Radio Days	Mother
1987	Surrender	Ronnie
1989	New York Stories	Treva
1990	Alice	Decorator
1990	Awakenings	Eleanor Costello
1992	Shadows and Fog	Alma
1992	This is My Life	Dottie Ingels

LAINIE KAZAN

(1942 -   )

A singer and an actress, Kazan began her career in nightclubs during the 1960s and at one time had her own room in New York's Playboy Club. In 1966, her debut album for MGM Records earned her the NARAS New Artist of the Year Award. Brooklyn-born, her acting career began as an understudy to Barbra Streisand in the 1964 Broadway musical *Funny Girl*. She was active in films during the 1980s.

Year	Movie	Character
1982	My Favorite Year	Belle Carroca
1982	One From the Heart	Maggie
1985	The Journey of Natty Gann	Connie
1986	The Delta Force	Sylvia Goldman
1987	Harry and the Hendersons	Irene Moffitt
1988	Beaches	Leona Bloom
1988	Out of the Dark	Hooker Nancy
1991	29th Street	Mrs. Pesce
1993	The Cemetery Club	Selma

JAMES KEACH

(1952 -   )

Actor/writer/producer/director Keach, the younger brother of actor Stacy Keach, once said that some of the best advice he ever received was from acting coach Stella Adler: "She pointed out that acting reflects life and those who have not experienced many facets of life can't truly portray it. She told us to get out there and get involved." He did just that and worked in a factory, on a fishing boat and in the lumber business before tackling the stage and screen full-time.

Year	Movie	Character
1978	FM	Lt. Reach
1979	Hurricane	Sgt. Strang
1980	The Long Riders	Jesse James
1983	Love Letters	Oliver
1984	The Razor's Edge	Gray Maturin
1985	Moving Violations	Deputy Halik
1986	Wildcats	Frank
1989	The Experts	Capt. Yuri Kuznets

STEVEN KEATS

(1945 -   )

It is often difficult to pick out the man from the characters he has played from movie to movie. Keats seems happy with this state of affairs. "I love the idea that people have a difficult time connecting me from one role to the next. It means I'm creating characters. In terms of career, however, it can pose a problem because people never know who I am," he once explained. Keats did not have much formal training when he began acting although he did spend six months at Yale Drama School.

Year	Movie	Character
1973	The Friends of Eddie Coyle	Jackie Brown
1974	Death Wish	Jack Toby
1976	The Gumball Rally	Kandinsky
1977	Black Sunday	Moshevsky
1979	The American Success Company	Rick
1980	Hangar 18	Paul
1982	Silent Rage	Dr. Spires
1985	Turk 182!	Jockamo

LILA KEDROVA

(1918 -   )

The French character actress has worked mostly in European stage and film productions. Kedrova has made Hollywood movies, however, and won a best supporting Oscar for her role in *Zorba the Greek*. In Alfred Hitchcock's *Torn Curtain*, she played a daffy Polish refugee in East Germany who helps the phony defector, Paul Newman and his companion, Julie Andrews, escape to the West. Russian-born, her theater training was in Paris with the famed actor/director Charles Dullin.

Year	Movie	Character
1964	Zorba the Greek	Madame Hortense
1965	A High Wind in Jamaica	Rosa
1966	Penelope	Sadaba
1966	Torn Curtain	Countess Kuchinska
1976	The Tenant	Mme. Gaderian
1989	Some Girls	Granny

DAVID KEITH

(1954 -   )

Keith's Hollywood career began as Fred Collins on ABC's *Happy Days* in 1978, but really got moving with his 1982 appearance in *An Officer and a Gentleman*, for which he received a best supporting Golden Globe nomination. In that movie he played Richard Gere's friend and fellow candidate in a Navy officer's training program. The following year Keith played a military school cadet in *The Lords of Discipline*. He is the son of a TVA employee and was born in Knoxville, TN.

Year	Movie	Character
1979	The Great Santini	xxx
1979	The Rose	Mal
1980	Brubaker	Larry Lee Bullen
1981	Back Roads	Mason
1981	Take This Job and Shove It	Harry
1982	An Officer and a Gentleman	Sid Worley
1983	Independence Day	Jack Parker
1983	The Lords of Discipline	Will
1984	Firestarter	Andrew
1988	Heartbreak Hotel	Elvis Presley
1990	Two Jakes	Loach, Jr.

CECIL KELLAWAY

(1893 - 1973)

A native of Capetown, South Africa, the lovable actor went to Hollywood from Australia in 1937, but returned a year later disillusioned. Kellaway went back in 1939 for a feature part in *Wuthering Heights* that marked him as a talented character player in drama or comedy. He died of natural causes at a Beverly Hills hospital at 82.

Year	Movie	Character
1961	Francis of Assisi	Cardinal Hugolino
1961	Tammy Tell Me True	Capt. Joe
1963	The Cardinal	Monsignor Monaghan
1965	Hush...Hush, Sweet Charlotte	Harry Willis
1966	Spinout	Bernard Ranley
1967	Fitzwilly	Buckmaster
1967	Guess Who's Coming to Dinner	Monsignor Ryan
1970	Getting Straight	Dr. Kasper

MARTHE KELLER

(1945 -   )

By the time Keller arrived in Hollywood, she was already a star in Europe with 15 films, 50 stage roles, a hit television show in France and both the French and German Oscars to her credit. A skiing accident at 16 forced the Basle, Switzerland native to switch careers from dance to acting. Formal training came at the Stanislavsky School in Munich while she modeled to pay the rent.

Year	Movie	Character
1976	Marathon Man	Elsa
1977	Black Sunday	Dahlia
1977	Bobby Deerfield	Lillian
1980	The Formula	Lisa

SALLY KELLERMAN

(1938 -   )

Kellerman captured national attention for her Oscar-nominated performance as Major "Hot Lips" Houlihan in Robert Altman's *M*A*S*H*. A Californian, she attended the celebrated Hollywood High School where many of the girls were starlets or professional models. Her career began in small theaters and television after training with Jeff Corey and Lee Strasberg.

Year	Movie	Character
1968	The Boston Strangler	Dianne Cluny
1969	The April Fools	Phyllis Bubaker
1970	M*A*S*H	Major Hot Lips
1973	A Reflection of Fear	Anne
1973	Lost Horizon	Sally Hughes
1973	Slither	Mary Fenaka
1975	Rafferty and the Gold Dust Twins	Mac
1976	The Big Bus	Sybil Crane
1979	A Little Romance	Kay King
1980	Foxes	Mary
1980	Loving Couples	Mrs. Liggett
1980	Serial	Martha
1985	Moving Violations	Judge Nedra Henderson

(continued on page 507)

(continued on page 507)

MIKE KELLIN

(1922 - 1983)

The stage, screen, and TV character actor was a Lt. Commander in the U.S. Navy during WW II and studied acting and playwriting at the Yale School of Drama afterwards. A varied career in serious drama and light-hearted comedy included 50 plays, 75 films, 200 TV shows. Kellin was an advisor to a prisoners' rights group and served on a blue ribbon commission on criminal justice in Rockland County, New York. He died at 61 of lung cancer in Nyack, NY.

Year	Movie	Character
1961	The Great Imposter	Thompson
1962	Hell is for Heroes	Kolinski
1964	Invitation to Gunfighter	Tom
1967	Banning	Kalielle
1967	The Incident	Harry Purvis
1968	The Boston Strangler	Julian Soshnick
1974	Freebie and the Bean	Lt. Rosen
1976	Next Stop, Greenwich Village	Mr. Lapinsky
1978	Girlfriends	Abe
1978	Midnight Express	Mr. Hayes
1980	The Jazz Singer	Leo
1981	So Fine	Sam Schlotzman

PAULA KELLY

(1939 -   )

Kelly had supporting roles in a string of movies, but her biggest parts came in the blaxploitation films of the early 1970s including *Trouble Man* (1972), *The Spook Who Sat by the Door* (1973) and *Three Tough Guys* (1974).

Year	Movie	Character
1969	Sweet Charity	Helene
1971	The Andromeda Strain	Karen Anson
1973	Soylent Green	Martha
1974	Three Tough Guys	Fay
1974	Uptown Saturday Night	Leggy Peggy
1976	Drum	Rachel
1986	Jo Jo Dancer, Your Life is Calling	Satin Doll

JEREMY KEMP

(1935 -   )

Seen mostly in British and international productions of the late 1960s/early 1970s, Kemp debuted on the London stage in 1958 in *The Chairs* at the Royal Court Theatre. Born near Chesterfield, England, the son of an engineer, he learned his craft at the Central School of Speech and Drama in London. In *The Blue Max*, Kemp played George Peppard's rival within the ranks of their air squadron and for the affection of Ursula Andress.

Year	Movie	Character
1965	Operation Crossbow	Phil Bradley
1966	The Blue Max	Willi Von Klugermann
1970	Darling Lili	Kurt von Ruger
1970	Sudden Terror	Galleria
1976	The Seven Percent Solution	Baron von Leinsdorf
1979	The Prisoner of Zenda	Duke Michael
1984	Top Secret!	Gen. Streck

ARTHUR KENNEDY

(1914 - 1990)

Kennedy started out in Hollywood in 1940 after drama studies at the Carnegie Institute of Technology and four years with a classical-repertory company in New York. He was nominated five times for an Oscar and won a Tony for his portrayal of Biff in the premiere Broadway run of Arthur Miller's *Death of a Salesman* in 1949. He was active in European films during the 60's and 70's as well as American. Kennedy died of a brain tumor in Branford, CT.

Year	Movie	Character
1960	Elmer Gantry	Jim Lefferts
1962	Lawrence of Arabia	Bentley
1962	Barabbas	Pontius Pilate
1964	Cheyenne Autumn	Doc Holliday
1965	Joy in the Morning	Patrick Brown
1966	Fantastic Voyage	Doctor Duval
1966	Nevada Smith	Bill Bowdre
1968	A Minute to Pray, a Second to Die	Roy Colby
1968	Anzio	General Lesly
1968	Day of the Evil Gun	Forbes
1969	Shark!	Doc
1977	The Sentinel	Franchino
1989	Signs of Life	Owen Coughlin

LEON ISAAC KENNEDY

(1949 -   )

To become a successful actor, Kennedy concluded early on that he needed a plan. "I decided that first I would have to be a disc jockey, then a television personality and then an actor," he once explained. By 17, he had worked as a deejay in three cities. At 18, he hosted a TV show called *Teen-Arama* in Washington, D.C. He then moved to Hollywood, where he continued his involvement with radio and TV and eventually starred in *Penitentiary*, the highest-grossing independent film in 1979.

Year	Movie	Character
1979	Penitentiary	Too Sweet
1981	Body and Soul	Leon
1982	Penitentiary II	Too Sweet Gordon
1983	Lone Wolf McQuade	Jackson
1985	Too Scared to Scream	Frank
1987	Penitentiary III	Too Sweet

VAL KILMER

(1959 -   )

Kilmer heard that England's Royal Academy of Dramatic Arts was the best place to learn acting so at 15 he went to England hoping to enroll. Rejected because of his age, he returned home and later ended up at Juilliard, considered the American RADA. The California native gained widespread attention as Tom Cruise's rival in the b.o. hit *Top Gun*.

Year	Movie	Character
1984	Top Secret!	Nick Rivers
1985	Real Genius	Chris
1986	Top Gun	Ice
1988	Willow	Madmartigan
1989	Kill Me Again	Jack Andrews
1991	The Doors	Jim Morrison
1992	Thunderheart	Ray Levoi
1993	The Real McCoy	J.T. Barker
1993	True Romance	Mentor

PERRY KING

(19?? -   )

Actor/race-car driver King was born in Alliance, OH, the son of a physician. Considered primarily a television actor, his feature film career may have been derailed by his portrayal of a homosexual in 1978's *A Different Story*. King graduated from Yale and studied briefly under John Houseman at Juilliard. He has won several auto races, including the 1986 Long Beach Grand Prix Toyota Pro-Celebrity Race.

Year	Movie	Character
1972	Slaughterhouse Five	Robert
1974	The Lords of Flatbush	Chico
1975	Mandingo	Hammond
1977	The Choirboys	Slate
1982	Class of 1984	Andy Norris
1991	Switch	Steve (the man)

KLAUS KINSKI

BRUNO KIRBY

(1926 - 1991)

Kinski's varied film career encompassed nearly 170 pictures including spaghetti westerns and the films of Werner Herzog. Essentially a character player, Kinski was born in Poland and drafted into Hitler's army during World War II at age 16. After the war, he acted on the German stage and revived the art of poetry recital before moving into films. The father of actress Nastassja Kinski, he died of natural causes in Lagunitas, CA.

Year	Movie	Character
1966	That Man in Istanbul	Schenck
1967	For a Few Dollars More	Hunchback
1977	Operation Thunderbolt	Boese
1981	Buddy, Buddy	Dr. Zuckerbrot
1982	Android	Dr. Daniel
1982	Love and Money	Frederick Stockheinz
1982	The Soldier	Dracha
1984	Little Drummer Girl	Kurtz

(1950 -   )

Born Bruno Giovanni Quidaciolu in Manhattan's Hell's Kitchen neighborhood, Kirby moved to L.A. at age 18 with his family. Often cast as a New Yorker, the actor once admitted his love for the city when he told an interviewer: "In Los Angeles, they wake you up at 5 a.m. and you drive to the studio. We're all in our cars all the time. Isolated. In New York, on the way to work, you see 200 characters you want to play."

Year	Movie	Character
1973	The Harrad Experiment	Harry
1974	The Godfather, Part II	Young Clemenza
1978	Almost Summer	Bobby
1980	Borderline	Jimmy Fante
1980	Modern Romance	Jay
1980	Where the Buffalo Roam	Marty
1984	Birdy	Renaldi
1984	This is Spinal Tap	Tommy Pischedda
1985	Flesh + Blood	Orbec
1987	Good Morning, Vietnam	Lt. Steven Hauk
1987	Tin Men	Mouse
1989	Bert Rigby, You're a Fool	Kyle DeForest
1989	We're No Angels	Deputy
1989	When Harry Met Sally...	Jess
1990	The Freshman	Victor Ray
1991	City Slickers	Ed Furillo

TOMMY KIRK

(1941 -   )

Currently managing his own business, Tom's Carpet Cleaning, Kirk was a Walt Disney child and teen star until the mid-1960s. He left the business in the early 1970s after starring in a string of low-budget beach and horror movies because as he has said, "I got sick of it, and I just stopped."

Year	Movie	Character
1960	Swiss Family Robinson	Ernst
1961	The Absent-Minded Professor	Bill Hawk
1965	Village of the Giants	Mike
1966	The Ghost in the Invisible Bikini	Chuck Phillips

SALLY KIRKLAND

(1944 -   )

An Oscar nomination for her portrayal of an exiled Czechoslovakian actress in the 1987 film *Anna* capped two decades of stage and film performances including the first nude performance Off-Broadway. The Philadelphia Main Liner trained at the Actors Studio and starred in Andy Warhol pictures early in her career.

Year	Movie	Character
1973	Cinderella Liberty	Fleet Chick
1973	The Way We Were	Pony Dunbar
1975	Bite the Bullet	Honey
1976	A Star is Born	Photography
1980	Private Benjamin	Helga
1983	Love Letters	Sally
1987	Anna	Anna
1989	Best of the Best	Wade
1989	Bull'seye!	
1989	Cold Feet	Maureen
1989	Paint It Black	
1990	Revenge	Rock Star
1991	JFK	Rose Cheramie

TERRY KISER

(1939 -   )

Kiser attended the University of Kansas on football and dramatic scholarships and graduated with a degree in Industrial Engineering in 1962. For the next 3 years, he practiced this profession in his hometown of Omaha, NE, and also managed to act in some 50 plays. New York and the Actors Studio followed as did several TV commercials. His best known movie role may be that of the corpse in the *Weekend at Bernie's* pictures.

Year	Movie	Character
1968	Rachel, Rachel	Preacher
1979	Fast Charlie, The Moonbeam Rider	Lester
1979	Rich Kids	Ralph Harris
1980	Steel	Valentino
1981	An Eye for an Eye	Davie
1982	Making Love	Harrington
1982	Six Pack	Terk
1988	Friday the 13th, Part VII— The New Blood	Dr. Crews
1989	Weekend at Bernie's	Bernie Lomax
1990	Side Out	Uncle Max
1991	Mannequin Two: On the Move	Count Spretzle
1992	Into the Sun	Mitchell Burton
1993	Weekend at Bernie's II	Bernie

SHIRLEY KNIGHT

(1937 -   )

Raised on a farm in Kansas, Knight headed west to California to begin an acting career rather than east to New York on the orders of her father who felt that the giant metropolis was a "wicked city." A graduate of the University of Wichita, she did graduate work at UCLA and while enrolled in a summer course at the Pasadena Playhouse she was spotted by a television scout and cast opposite Michael Landon on NBC's *Matinee Theater*.

Year	Movie	Character
1960	Ice Palace	Grace (at 16)
1962	Sweet Bird of Youth	Heavenly Finley
1964	Flight from Ashiya	Caroline Gordon
1966	The Group	Polly
1968	Petulia	Polo
1968	The Counterfeit Killer	Angie Peterson
1969	The Rain People	Natalie
1974	Juggernaut	Barbara Banister
1979	Beyond the Poseidon Adventure	Hannah Meredith
1981	Endless Love	Anne

PAUL KOSLO

(1944 -   )

A native of Vancouver, Koslo studied Shakespeare at Canada's National Theater School. His screen career picked up speed after he left a print at a Hollywood talent agency of a Canadian television rendition of *Crime and Punishment* that he did with Genevieve Bujold. This led to a lead in the rock musical *Hair* in New York and eventually a string of film roles.

Year	Movie	Character
1971	The Omega Man	Dutch
1971	Vanishing Point	Young Cop
1972	Joe Kidd	Roy
1972	Welcome Home, Soldier Boys	Shooter
1973	Lolly-Madonna XXX	Villum
1973	The Laughing Policeman	Haygood
1973	The Stone Killer	Langley
1974	Bootleggers	Othar Pruitt
1974	Freebie and the Bean	Whitey
1974	Mr. Majestyk	Bobby Kopas
1975	Rooster Cogburn	Luke
1979	Love and Bullets	Huntz
1980	Heaven's Gate	Mayor
1985	The Annihilators	Roy Boy
1988	A Night in the Life of Jimmy Reardon	Al Reardon
1988	Caribe	Mercenary
1990	Loose Cannons	Grimmer
1990	Robot Jox	Alexander

ELIAS KOTEAS

(1961 -   )

A graduate of the American Academy of Dramatic Arts, Montreal-born Koteas has had extensive stage experience in New York and in regional theater. Somewhat disillusioned with his craft he told an interviewer in 1987: "It's hard to keep the enthusiasm I had when I first started acting...I do get disillusioned sometimes. I love performing, but I hate the rehearsal process. All these know-it-all people always telling you what acting is all about. There's a lot of self-importance in this business."

Year	Movie	Character
1985	One Magic Christmas	Eddie
1987	Gardens of Stone	Pete Deveber
1987	Some Kind of Wonderful	Skinhead
1988	Tucker: The Man and His Dream	Alex
1990	Almost an Angel	Steve
1990	Desperate Hours	Wally Bosworth
1990	Look Who's Talking Too	Stuart
1990	Teenage Mutant Ninja Turtles	Casey Jones
1993	Teenage Mutant Ninja Turtles III	Casey Jones/Whit

YAPHET KOTTO

(1937 -   )

As a kid growing up in Harlem, Kotto's hero was John Wayne. "I thought he was the greatest thing in the world, and used to emulate him when I was a kid," the actor once said. But his mentor was Sidney Poitier. "The thing that impressed me about Poitier was he was handsome, he was black, he was a bonafide star, he had come from the tomato fields in the West Indies and became an international success—and he always carried himself with dignity."

Year	Movie	Character
1968	Five Card Stud	Little George
1968	The Thomas Crown Affair	Carl
1970	The Liberation of L.B. Jones	Sonny Boy Mosby
1972	Across 110th Street	Lt. Pope
1973	Live and Let Die	Kananga/Mr. Big
1975	Report to the Commissioner	Richard Blackstone
1975	Shark's Treasure	Ben
1976	Drum	Blaise
1978	Blue Collar	Smokey
1979	Alien	Parker
1980	Brubaker	Dickie Coombes
1982	Fighting Back	Ivanhoe
1983	The Star Chamber	Det. Harry Lowes
1985	Warning Sign	Major Connolly
1986	Eye of the Tiger	J.B. Deveraux
1987	The Running Man	Laughlin
1988	Midnight Run	Alonzo Mosely
1991	Freddy's Dead: The Final Nightmare	Doc

NANCY KOVACK

(1935 -   )

She is now Nancy Mehta, the wife of the well-known symphony conductor, Zubin Mehta; Kovack retired from the screen after her marriage in 1969. Active as an actress during the 1960s, she was born in Flint, MI, where her father was a supervisor with GM. She had her own radio show at 15 and jumped into acting upon her graduation from the University of Michigan in 1955.

Year	Movie	Character
1961	Cry for Happy	Miss Cameron
1963	Diary of a Madman	Odette
1965	The Outlaws is Coming	Annie Oakley
1966	Frankie and Johnny	Nellie Bly
1966	Tarzan and the Valley of Gold	Sophia Renault
1966	The Silencers	Barbara
1967	Enter Laughing	Miss B.
1969	Marooned	Teresa Stone

ERNIE KOVACS

(1919 - 1962)

The comedian-turned-actor came to films after making a big splash in television. His cocky humor was first noticed by executives at ABC in one of Kovac's newspaper articles. His trademark was a big cigar and he is rumored to have smoked more than a dozen a day. He was killed instantly when his station wagon struck a power pole.

Year	Movie	Character
1960	North to Alaska	Frankie Canon
1960	Strangers When We Meet	Roger Altar
1960	Wake Me When It's Over	Capt. Stark
1960	Our Man in Havana	Capt. Segura
1962	Sail a Crooked Ship	The Captain

MARTIN KOVE

(1947 -   )

Kove has been a good guy on television and a bad guy in the movies. He was Detective Isbecki, a "deskbound wimp," according to Kove, for six seasons on *Cagney & Lacey*, a show where the women got all the action. But, in films, he has been a rough-and-tumble heavy who threatened the likes of Sylvester Stallone in *Rambo* and Ralph Macchio in *The Karate Kid*. He was a struggling actor in New York before moving to L.A. in the early 1970s, where he started out as the Gaelic he-man in Irish Spring commercials.

Year	Movie	Character
1975	White Line Fever	Clem
1977	The White Buffalo	Jack McCall
1979	Seven	Skip
1984	The Karate Kid	Kreese
1985	Rambo: First Blood Part II	Ericson
1986	The Karate Kid, Part II	Kreese
1987	Steele Justice	John Steele
1989	The Karate Kid III	Kreese
1991	White Light	Sean Craig

HARLEY JANE KOZAK

(1957 -   )

Kozak began her screen career as Annabelle Reardon on the New York soap opera *Guiding Light* and then moved west to L.A. as Mary Duvall McCormack in the soap *Santa Barbara*. Roles on the big screen include the wives of Jeff Daniels, the newly-arrived town doctor in *Arachnophobia* and Rick Moranis in *Parenthood*.

Year	Movie	Character
1989	Parenthood	Susan
1989	When Harry Met Sally...	Helen
1990	Arachnophobia	Molly Jennings
1990	Side Out	Kate Jacobs
1991	All I Want for Christmas	Catherine O'Fallon
1991	Necessary Roughness	Suzanne Carter
1991	The Taking of Beverly Hills	Laura Sage

JEROEN KRABBE´

(1944 -   )

One of Holland's most popular actors, Krabbe´ is the third generation in a family of painters and that heritage inevitably led to his enrollment at the Royal Academy for Visual Arts in Amsterdam. He dropped out after only one year to train as an actor, but when filming a movie, he once told an interviewer, "I always bring my paints and brushes along. It is so boring on the set. After two or three days, you've exhausted all subjects with your colleagues."

Year	Movie	Character
1986	Jumpin' Jack Flash	Mark Van Meter
1986	No Mercy	Losad
1987	The Living Daylights	Gen. Georgi Koskov
1988	A World Apart	Gus Roth
1988	Crossing Delancy	Anton Maes
1989	Scandal	Eugene Ivanov
1989	The Punisher	Gianni Franca
1991	Kafka	Bizzlebek
1991	The Prince of Tides	Herbert Woodruff
1993	King of the Hill	Mr. Kurlander
1993	The Fugitive	Dr. Charles Nichols

JEFFREY KRAMER

ALICE KRIGE

(19?? -   )

Kramer is probably best remembered as Policeman Hendricks of the first two *Jaws* movies. The pictures brought him visibility and praise from the critics. *Variety* wrote that he was "great as (Roy) Scheider's harried assistant." Scheider played Police Chief Martin Brody in the series. Kramer had the lead in a very short-lived and unusual TV series titled *Struck by Lightning* in 1979, based on the Frankenstein story.

Year	Movie	Character
1975	Jaws	Hendricks
1978	Jaws 2	Hendricks
1981	Halloween II	Graham
1985	Santa Claus	Towzer
1988	Hero and the Terror	Dwight

(1955 -   )

Raised in the coastal resort of Port Elizabeth, near the Kalahari region of South Africa, Krige moved to London at 22 to further her education and a budding acting career. Upon graduating from London's School of Speech and Drama, she made her professional debut in the British TV drama, *The Happy Autumn Fields*. She feels, "the joy of acting is that you discover an enormous amount of information and come across subjects that you might not ordinarily encounter."

Year	Movie	Character
1981	Chariots of Fire	Sybil Gordon
1985	King David	Bathsheba
1987	Barfly	Tully
1989	See You in the Morning	Beth Goodwin
1992	Sleepwalkers	Mary Brady

JACK KRUSCHEN

(1922 -   )

Growing up in Los Angeles, Kruschen performed in radio dramas while still in high school. In 1939, he was already appearing in TV dramas on the Don Lee experimental station in L.A.; programs were beamed out to about 200 sets with 3" screens. Kruschen was nominated for an Oscar for his portrayal of the wryly philosophical Dr. Dreyfuss in *The Apartment*.

Year	Movie	Character
1960	The Apartment	Dr. Dreyfuss
1960	The Last Voyage	Second Engineer Pringle
1961	Lover Come Back	Dr. Linus Tyler
1961	The Ladies' Man	xxx
1962	Cape Fear	Dave Grafton
1962	Follow That Dream	Carmine
1963	McLintock	Birnbaum
1964	The Unsinkable Molly Brown	Christmas Morgan
1965	Dear Brigitte	Dr. Volker
1967	Caprice	Matthew Cutter
1967	The Happening	Inspector
1974	Freebie and the Bean	Red Myers
1977	Mountain Man	Madden
1979	Sunburn	Gela

DIANE LADD

(1932 -   )

Born and raised in Mississippi, the daughter of a travelling salesman, Ladd's showbiz career began on the chorus line of New York's famed Copacabana. She spent most of the early years of her career on the stage, before finding her place in film and television. In a Hollywood first, both Ladd and her daughter, Laura Dern (by first husband Bruce Dern), were nominated for Oscars in 1992 for the same movie: *Rambling Rose*.

Year	Movie	Character
1966	The Wild Angels	Gaysh
1970	WUSA	Barmaid
1973	White Lightning	Maggie
1974	Chinatown	Ida Sessions
1975	Alice Doesn't Live Here Anymore	Flo
1981	All Night Long	Helen Dupler
1983	Rumble Fish	Patty
1983	Something Wicked This Way Comes	Mrs. Nightshade
1986	Black Widow	Etta
1989	National Lampoon's Christmas Vacation	Nora Griswold
1990	Wild at Heart	Marietta Fortune
1991	A Kiss Before Dying	Mrs. Corliss
1991	Rambling Rose	Mother
1993	The Cemetery Club	Lucille Rubin
1993	Father Hood	Rita

CHRISTINE LAHTI

(1950 -   )

A native of Detroit, Lahti began her career with TV commercials in New York City. Inspired by Richard Dreyfuss' performance in *The Apprenticeship of Duddy Kravitz* she was determined to carve out an acting career that did not require her to go the glamour route.

Year	Movie	Character
1979	...And Justice For All	Gail Packer
1981	Ladies and Gentlemen, The Fabulous Stains	Aunt Linda
1981	Whose Life Is It Anyway?	Dr. Claire Scott
1984	Swing Shift	Hazel Zanussi
1986	Just Between Friends	Sandy Dunlap
1987	Housekeeping	Sylvie
1988	Running on Empty	Annie Pope
1989	Gross Anatomy	Dr. Rachel Woodruff
1990	Funny About Love	Meg Lloyd
1991	The Doctor	Anne

CHRISTOPHER LAMBERT

(1958 -   )

Born to French parents in New York, where his father was a U.N. diplomat, Lambert grew up in Geneva, Switzerland. He spent a year in the French military and then enrolled at the prestigious Paris Conservatoire Drama Academy. Shortly thereafter he was cast as Tarzan in *Greystoke: The Legend of Tarzan, Lord of the Apes*. He has worked steadily ever since.

Year	Movie	Character
1984	Greystoke: The Legend of Tarzan, Lord of the Apes	John Clayton/Tarzan
1986	Highlander	Connor MacLeod
1987	The Sicilian	Salvatore Giuliano
1988	To Kill a Priest	Father Alek
1991	Highlander II: The Quickening	Connor MacLeod
1993	Knight Moves	Sanderson
1993	Fortress	John Brennick

LAURENE LANDON

CHARLES LANE

(19?? -   )

Landon's screen career began as a member of a female wrestling duo managed by Peter Falk in *All the Marbles*. The film got a lukewarm reception, but Landon won praise as Armand Assante's secretary in her next picture, *I, the Jury*. In B-movies through the remainder of the 1980s, she starred in the Spanish-made western *Yellow Hair and the Fortress of Gold* (1984) as a part-Indian named Yellow Hair. She was the blond warrior Vena in *America 3000* (1986), a post-nuclear holocaust movie aimed at kids.

Year	Movie	Character
1981	All the Marbles	Molly
1982	I, the Jury	Velda
1986	Armed Response	Deborah Silverstein
1987	It's Alive III:	
	Island of the Alive	Sally
1989	Wicked Stepmother	Vanilla

(1905 -   )

Lane may be best-remembered by fans of the sitcom *Petticoat Junction* as Homer Bedloe (1963-68), the conniving vice president of the C.F. & W. Railroad. Born in San Francisco, he cut his acting teeth performing Shakespeare, Chekhov and Noel Coward at the Pasadena Playhouse during the 1930s. The actor enjoys listening to opera and playing golf.

Year	Movie	Character
1962	The Music Man	Constable Locke
1963	It's a Mad Mad Mad	
	Mad World	Airport Manager
1964	The Carpetbaggers	Denby
1964	Good Neighbor Sam	Jack
1964	The New Interns	xxx
1964	Billie	Coach Jones
1965	John Goldfarb, Please	
	Come Home	Editor STRIFE
		Magazine
1966	The Ghost and Mr. Chicken	xxx

DIANE LANE

(1965 -   )

One year after her film debut in *A Little Romance* Lane's picture graced the cover of *Time*. Only 14 at the time, the magazine described her as one of Hollywood's "Whiz Kids." The young actress proceeded to work steadily in pictures throughout the 1980s. Her career began as a child touring worldwide with The Great Jones Repertory Company under the direction of Andrei Serban.

Year	Movie	Character
1979	A Little Romance	Lauren
1980	Cattle Annie and Little Britches	Jenny
1980	Touched by Love	Karen
1981	Ladies and Gentlemen, The Fabulous Stains	Corinne
1982	Six Pack	Breezy
1983	The Outsiders	Cherry Valance
1984	Streets of Fire	Ellen
1984	The Cotton Club	Vera Cicero
1987	Lady Beware	Katya Yarno
1987	The Big Town	Lorry Dane
1990	Vital Signs	Gina Wyler
1992	Chaplin	Paulette Goddard
1993	Indian Summer	Beth Warden
1993	Knight Moves	Kathy Sheppard

PERRY LANG

(19?? -   )

Lang dropped out of high school in Northern California to begin an acting career, first at the Berkeley Shakespeare Festival, and then, with the Academy of Dramatic Art in L.A. His screen roles include a benchwarmer in *Eight Men Out* and one of the first of the underpaid ballplayers to agree to throw the 1919 World Series. He was a regular on the TV series *Bay City Blues* and has performed with New York's Shakespeare in the Park.

Year	Movie	Character
1980	Alligator	Kelly
1980	The Big Red One	Kaiser
1981	Body and Soul	Charles
1983	Spring Break	Adam
1984	Sahara	Andy
1987	Jocks	Jeff
1988	Eight Men Out	Fred McMullin

STEPHEN LANG

SUE ANE LANGDON

(1952 -   )

(1936 -   )

Bright, well-educated, intense and self-assured, Lang, a native New Yorker, became closely acquainted with acting as a teenager. Believing that an actor needs a firm foundation and understanding of the classics as well as training in their physical interpretation, he opted for a degree in literature during his undergraduate studies at Swarthmore. After seven years of working in regional theater, he made his Broadway debut in Sam Waterston's now famous *Hamlet* at Lincoln Center.

Langdon's career began in New York at Radio City Music Hall and progressed to film and television. She played Jackie Gleason's second TV wife (after Audrey Meadows) briefly. She grew up all over the U.S. as her father taught singing in various colleges.

Year	Movie	Character
1985	Twice in a Lifetime	Keith
1986	Band of the Hand	Joe
1986	Manhunter	Freddie
1987	Project X	Watts
1991	Another You	Rupert Dibbs
1991	The Hard Way	Party Crasher
1993	Guilty as Sin	Phil Garson
1993	Gettysburg	Maj. Gen. George E. Pickett

Year	Movie	Character
1961	The Great Imposter	Eulalie
1964	Roustabout	Madame Mijanou
1965	The Rounders	Mary
1966	A Fine Madness	Miss Walnicki
1966	Frankie and Johnny	Mitzi
1967	A Guide for the Married Man	Mrs. Johnson
1970	The Cheyenne Social Club	Opal Ann
1982	Zapped!	Rose
1989	UHF	Aunt Esther

ANTHONY LAPAGLIA

(1959 -   )

LaPaglia grew up in Australia and worked at everything from teacher to shoe salesman before he discovered acting. Hooked after seeing a performance of the 17th-century comedy *The Way of the World*, LaPaglia moved to the U.S. and found work as gun-toting and knife-wielding thugs in Hollywood films and bad New York plays. Gradually he worked his way into more substantial film roles.

Year	Movie	Character
1990	Betsy's Wedding	Stevie Dee
1991	29th Street	Frank Pesce, Jr.
1991	He Said, She Said	Mark
1991	One Good Cop	Stevie Diroma
1992	Innocent Blood	Joe Gennaro
1992	Whispers in the Dark	Det. Morgenstern
1993	So I Married an Axe Murderer	Tony Giardino

PIPER LAURIE

(1932 -   )

Best known for her work as Paul Newman's slightly damaged girl-friend in *The Hustler* and, after a 15-year hiatus from Hollywood, Sissy Spacek's fanatical mother in *Carrie*, Laurie made her first appearance on the stage before she was three. Her film career began after signing a seven-year contract with Universal at age 17.

Year	Movie	Character
1961	The Hustler	Sarah Packard
1976	Carrie	Margaret White
1985	Return to Oz	Aunt Em
1986	Children of a Lesser God	Mrs. Norman
1987	Distortions	Margot
1988	Appointment With Death	Emily Boynton
1988	Tiger Warsaw	Frances Warsaw
1989	Dream a Little Dream	Gena Ettinger
1991	Other People's Money	Bea Sullivan
1993	Rich in Love	Vera Delmage

ED LAUTER

JOHN PHILLIP LAW

(1940 -   )

Lauter made his professional debut as a nightclub comic after drama studies at the Herbert Berghof School. Next came small parts in Off-Broadway plays and work in summer stock before his Broadway debut in *The Great White Hope* in 1970. He attended C.W. Post College on a sports scholarship where he played baseball, football and basketball and received his B.A. in English. Lauter also spent two years in the army.

(1937 -   )

Law's adult film career began in Italy in the early 1960s where he moved to join friends who were working in the Maciste and gladiator films. He made three pictures there before returning to the U.S. to play the young Russian sailor who romances Eva Marie Saint's house helper in the popular comedy *The Russians are Coming! The Russians are Coming!* Born in L.A., Law moved to Hawaii with his mother after his father's death. He had his first movie role as a child in 1950 in *The Magnificent Yankee*.

Year	Movie	Character
1972	Hickey & Boggs	Ted
1972	The New Centurions	Galloway
1973	Hard Driver	Burton Colt
1973	Lolly-Madonna XXX	Hawk
1974	The Longest Yard	Captain Knauer
1974	The Midnight Man	Leroy
1976	Breakheart Pass	Maj. Claremont
1976	Family Plot	Maloney
1976	King Kong	Carnahan
1977	The Chicken Chronicles	Mr. Nastase
1977	The White Buffalo	Capt. Tom Custer
1978	Magic	Duke
1981	Death Hunt	Hazel
1983	Cujo	Joe

(continued on page 507)

Year	Movie	Character
1966	The Russians are Coming! The Russians are Coming!	Kolchin
1967	Hurry, Sundown	Rad McDowell
1968	Barbarella	Pygar
1968	Death Rides a Horse	Bill
1970	The Hawaiians	Noel Hoxworth
1971	The Love Machine	Robin Stone
1971	Von Richthofen and Brown	von Richthofen
1974	Golden Voyage of Sinbad	Sinbad
1977	Cassandra Crossing	Stack
1981	Tarzan, The Ape Man	Holt

JAMES LE GROS

(19?? -   )

Le Gros can be seen as the psychic hero in *Phantasm II* and as Matt Dillon's dull-witted buddy in *Drugstore Cowboy*. The actor spent the first two years of his career as an apprentice with the South Coast Repertory, a professional theater company in Costa Mesa, CA. Theater credits include a production of *Slab Boys* at the Back Alley Theater in Los Angeles. He has been seen on television's *Simon and Simon*, *Night Rider* and *Punky Brewster*.

Year	Movie	Character
1986	Solarbabies	Metron
1987	Fatal Beauty	Zack Jaeger
1988	Phantasm II	Mike
1989	Born on the Fourth of July	Platoon
1989	Drugstore Cowboy	Rick
1991	Blood and Concrete	Lance
1991	Point Break	Roach
1992	Guncrazy	Howard Hickock

RON LEIBMAN

(1937 -   )

Once known as Broadway's angry young man, Leibman was so obsessive and easily angered that directors shied away from working with him. Stage director Arthur Sherman once recalled, "He was just completely, totally obsessed with what he was doing. People had very little significance, particularly people who didn't take it quite as seriously as he did." He eventually mellowed and has been active in film and television for many years.

Year	Movie	Character
1970	Where's Poppa?	Sidney Hocheiser
1972	Slaughterhouse Five	Paul Lazzaro
1972	The Hot Rock	Murch
1973	Your Three Minutes Are Up	Mike
1974	The Super Cops	Greenberg
1976	Won Ton Ton, the Dog Who Saved Hollywood	Rudy Montague
1979	Norma Rae	Reuben
1980	Up the Academy	Major
1981	Zorro, the Gay Blade	Esteban
1983	Romantic Comedy	Leo
1984	Rhinestone	Freddie
1988	Seven Hours to Judgement	David Reardon

PAUL LE MAT

(1945 -   )

Le Mat is often cast as a likable middle-class American, but went memorably against type when he played Farrah Fawcett's brutal husband in the critically-acclaimed 1984 TV-movie *The Burning Bed*. After it aired, Le Mat has said, women would stop him in the street and say: 'I just hated you.' They knew he was an actor, of course, but, according to him, "they wouldn't stand that close to me either." He won a Golden Globe for the part. Le Mat is from New Jersey and began his career on the New York stage.

Year	Movie	Character
1973	American Graffiti	John
1975	Aloha, Bobby and Rose	Bobby
1979	More American Graffiti	John Milner
1980	Melvin and Howard	Melvin Dummar
1982	Death Valley	Mike
1982	Jimmy the Kid	John
1982	P.K. and the Kid	Kid Kane
1983	Strange Invaders	Charles
1987	The Hanoi Hilton	Hubman
1989	Puppetmaster	Alex

KAY LENZ

(1953 -   )

Lenz's professional acting career got off to a fast start. She debuted in a television commercial being produced by her father and went on to act on local children's and teenage television shows and more commercials. At 13, she made her legitimate stage debut acting in *Dark of the Moon* at the Pasadena Playhouse. At 14, she was regularly appearing on such network TV series as *The Monroes*, *The Andy Griffith Show* and *The Tammy Grimes Show*.

Year	Movie	Character
1975	White Line Fever	Jerri Hummer
1976	Great Scout and Cathouse Thursday	Thursday
1982	Fast Walking	Moke
1987	Death Wish 4: The Crackdown	Karen Sheldon
1989	Physical Evidence	Deborah Quinn

MICHAEL LERNER

(1937 -   )

When Lerner was assigned to portray Jack Ruby in the 1978 TV-movie *Ruby and Oswald*, he hung around with Ruby's family, went to Dallas to walk the terrain which Ruby had walked and read everything he could on the man. Such dedication to his craft began when the Brooklyn native received a master's degree in English drama from UCLA and studied for two years at the London Academy of Music and Dramatic Art. He launched his acting career in the late 1960s at the American Conservatory Theater in San Francisco.

Year	Move	Character
1972	The Candidate	Corliss
1974	Busting	Marvin
1976	St. Ives	Myron Green
1977	The Other Side of Midnight	Barbet
1977	Outlaw Blues	Hatch
1979	Goldengirl	Sternberg
1980	Borderline	Henry Lydell
1980	Coast to Coast	Dr. Froll
1980	The Baltimore Bullet	Paulie
1981	The Postman Always Rings Twice	Katz
1981	Threshold	Henry DeVici
1982	National Lampoon's Class Reunion	Dr. Young

(continued on page 507)

AL LETTIERI

(1928 - 1975)

Lettieri enjoyed a brief U.S. film career in the early 1970s in violent actioners like *The Getaway* as one of a robbery gang tracking down Steve McQueen and Ali MacGraw and in *Mr. Majestyk* as a mob killer battling it out with Charles Bronson. Most of his career was spent on Broadway and in European filmmaking, as an actor and behind the camera. He died at 47 at St. Vincent's Hospital in New York.

Year	Movie	Character
1972	Pulp	Miller
1972	The Getaway	Rudy Butler
1972	The Godfather	Sollozzo
1974	McQ	Santiago
1974	Mr. Majestyk	Frank Renda

EUGENE LEVY

(1946 -   )

Levy got his start as Earl Camembert, the announcer-newscaster on the comedy hit, *Second City TV*. The syndicated program, which ran from 1977 to 1981, satirized everything and anything on television. A writer and comedian as well as an actor, Levy was part of the Canadian branch of Chicago's famous Second City troupe that originated the show. He stayed with the show when it was picked up by NBC as *SCTV Network* (1981-83) and won Emmy awards in 1982 and 1983 for comedy writing.

Year	Movie	Character
1979	Running	Richard Rosenberg
1983	Going Berserk	Sal
1983	National Lampoon's Vacation	Car Salesman
1984	Splash	Walter Kornbluth
1986	Armed and Dangerous	Norman Kane
1986	Club Paradise	Barry Steinberg
1989	Speed Zone!	Leo Ross
1991	Father of the Bride	Auditioning singer

GEOFFREY LEWIS

(1935 -   )

Lewis once described his acting style to a reporter: "I work with the director and the other actors, but I figure that is about two inches of something that is a yard long. The other 34 inches is what I have to do myself. So far I have not conflicted with a director or writer or anybody else. But I know basically what I want to do as far as acting goes." The actor is a native New Yorker.

Year	Movie	Character
1972	Culpepper Cattle Company	Russ
1972	Welcome Home, Soldier Boys	Motel owner
1973	Dillinger	Harry
1973	High Plains Drifter	Stacey Bridges
1974	Macon County Line	Hamp
1974	Thunderbolt and Lightfoot	Goody
1975	Lucky Lady	Capt. Aaron Mosley
1975	Smile	Wilson Shears
1975	The Great Waldo Pepper	Newt
1975	The Wind and the Lion	Cummere
1976	The Return of a Man Called Horse	Zenas Morro
1978	Every Which Way But Loose	Orville
1980	Any Which Way You Can	Orville

(continued on page 507)

RICHARD LIBERTINI

(1933 -   )

Comedic actor Libertini has been seen with and without his beard on stage, film and television. He began his career in his native Chicago, where he was one of the original company of the now-famous Second City troupe. Reflecting on the actor's lot he once commented: "You do a lot of work that's just work. Then, once in a while, there's something else. An improvisation where, afterward, all you can remember is being out there some place, and having no idea what was going to happen next."

Year	Movie	Character
1968	The Night They Raided Minsky's	Pockets
1970	The Out of Towners	Boston Baggage Man
1979	The In-Laws	General Garcia
1980	Popeye	Geezil
1981	Sharky's Machine	Nosh
1982	Soup for One	Angelo
1983	Deal of the Century	Masaggi
1983	Going Berserk	Sun Yi
1984	All of Me	Prahka Lasa
1984	Unfaithfully Yours	Giuseppe
1985	Big Trouble	Dr. Lopez
1985	Fletch	Walker
1988	Betrayed	Sam Kraus
1989	Animal Behavior	Dr. Parrish
1989	Fletch Lives	Frank Walker
1990	Awakenings	Sidney
1990	The Bonfire of the Vanities	Ed Rifkin
1990	The Lemon Sisters	Nicholas Panas

VIVECA LINDFORS

(1920 -   )

The veteran Swedish actress made her Hollywood film debut more than 40 years ago opposite Errol Flynn in *The Adventures of Don Juan*. Lindfors began in modern dance at age 5 and entered Sweden's Royal Dramatic Theater at age 16. She was offered a film contract at age 25 and, after 5 years in Hollywood, moved to New York where she became a star in Broadway and Off-Broadway plays.

Year	Movie	Character
1960	The Story of Ruth	Eleilat
1961	King of Kings	Claudia
1965	Sylvia	Irma Olanski
1967	Cauldron of Blood	Tania
1973	The Way We Were	Paula Reisner
1978	Girlfriends	Beatrice
1979	Voices	Mrs. Lemon
1981	The Hand	Doctress
1982	Creepshow	Aunt Bedelia
1985	The Sure Thing	Professor Taub
1987	Lady Beware	xxx
1987	Rachel River	Harriet
1990	The Exorcist III	Nurse X
1991	Zandalee	Tatta

AUDRA LINDLEY

(1923 -   )

She once appeared in three different sitcoms on three different networks in one season. Only one of them, *Three's Company,* was a success, however. Born in Hollywood to movie actors, Lindley quit school at 15 and worked her way up from an extra to a stand-in to a stunt double to a contract player with Warner Brothers before heading east to the New York stage. Beginning in 1964, she spent five years on the daytime soap, *Another World.*

Year	Movie	Character
1971	Taking Off	Ann Lockston
1972	The Heartbreak Kid	Mrs. Corcoran
1982	Best Friends	Ann Babson
1982	Cannery Row	Fauna
1985	Desert Hearts	Frances Parker
1989	Troop Beverly Hills	Frances Temple

RAY LIOTTA

(1955 -   )

Following his graduation from the University of Miami, where he studied drama, Liotta moved to New York City and, with relative ease, fell into TV commercials and a three year stint on the soap, *Another World.* His memorable film roles include Shoeless Joe Jackson, in *Field of Dreams,* the first dead ballplayer to arrive at Kevin Costner's baseball diamond, and Melanie Griffith's sadistic ex-lover in *Something Wild.*

Year	Movie	Character
1986	Something Wild	Ray Sinclair
1988	Dominick and Eugene	Eugene Luciano
1989	Field of Dreams	Shoeless Joe Jackson
1990	Goodfellas	Henry Hill
1992	Article 99	Dr. Richard Sturgess
1992	Unlawful Entry	Officer Pete Davis

DENNIS LIPSCOMB

(19?? -   )

The stage actor is probably best known for his appearance opposite rock star Deborah Harry making her film debut in *Union City*. Lipscomb plays a paranoid businessman out to get the unknown culprit who takes a drink out of his milk bottle that is delivered each morning. A native of Brooklyn, NY, he received a master's degree from the University of Iowa and studied drama in London.

Year	Movie	Character
1980	Union City	Harlan
1983	WarGames	Watson
1984	A Soldier's Story	Captain Taylor
1986	Crossroads	Lloyd
1987	Amazing Grace and Chuck	Johnny B. Goode
1987	Sister, Sister	Cleve Doucet
1990	The First Power	Cmdr. Perkins

KATHLEEN LLOYD

(19?? -   )

Lloyd's debut came in *Missouri Breaks*, a much-discussed film starring Marlon Brando and Jack Nicholson, that did mediocre box office and received mixed reviews. Film critics praised her performance, however. *The New York Post* called her "surprisingly good, a find." Her big screen career was brief—five movies in three years—but she went on to make occasional appearances on Tom Selleck's *Magnum, P.I.* as Assistant D.A. Carol Baldwin for five seasons (1983-88).

Year	Movie	Character
1976	The Missouri Breaks	Jane Braxton
1977	The Car	Lauren
1978	It Lives Again	Judy Scott
1978	Take Down	Jill Branish

TONY LO BIANCO

CALVIN LOCKHART

(1936 -   )

The theater is Lo Bianco's first love. The Brooklyn native began by studying at the well-known Irwin Piscator Drama Workshop in New York, whose alumni include Marlon Brando and Rod Steiger. He co-founded the Triangle Theater, an experimental group which introduced young artists to the New York theater scene. In movies, he was the handsome playboy whose extravagant nightlife, yet seemingly modest income gets the attention of detectives Gene Hackman and Roy Scheider in *The French Connection*.

Year	Movie	Character
1971	The French Connection	Sal Boca
1973	The Seven-Ups	Vito
1978	Bloodbrothers	Tommy DeCoco
1978	F.I.S.T.	Babe Milano
1984	City Heat	Leon Coll
1991	City of Hope	Joe

(1934 -   )

After working on the movie *Cleopatra* in Italy, Lockhart decided to try his luck in England. It was there that he found his greatest success. He was the first black actor to play leads with the Royal Shakespeare Company and he became a familiar face in films and on TV. The British movie-going public proclaimed him "The World's Sexiest Man" in 1971. Upon his return to the U.S., the Bahamian found steady employment during the "blaxploitation" period of the early 1970s.

Year	Movie	Character
1970	Cotton Comes to Harlem	Rev. Deke O'Malley
1972	Melinda	Frankie J. Parker
1974	Uptown Saturday Night	Silky Slim
1975	Let's Do It Again	Biggie Smalls
1980	The Baltimore Bullet	Snow White
1988	Coming to America	Colonel Izzi
1990	Predator 2	King Willie
1990	Wild at Heart	Reginald Sula

ROBERT LOGAN

(1940 -   )

Logan's career began in the early 1960s as Edd "Kookie" Byrnes' replacement on ABC's *77 Sunset Strip*. After a stint on NBC's *Daniel Boone* he dropped out of showbiz for several years to roam the world. Among his adventures was a record-setting sail from L.A. to Tahiti and a documentary filming of the 1968 Russian invasion of Czechoslovakia. He returned to Hollywood in 1975 and became involved with "wilderness" pictures.

Year	Movie	Character
1975	The Adventures of the Wilderness Family	Skip
1977	Across the Great Divide	Zachariah Coop
1978	The Further Adventures of the Wilderness Family	Skip
1978	The Sea Gypsies	Travis
1983	A Night in Heaven	Whitney

ROBERT LOGGIA

(1930 -   )

Loggia began his acting career on Broadway during the 1950s, but his film career did not blossom until 1977. He usually plays the heavies, such as the Cuban cocaine kingpin in *Scarface* and the skirt-chasing Sicilian gangster in *Prizzi's Honor*. But he's had other roles like Tom Hank's toy company boss in *Big*. After a hitch in the army, he broke in with the early '50's "live" television programs *Studio One* and *Robert Montgomery Presents*. The actor was born in Staten Island to Italian immigrants.

Year	Movie	Character
1965	The Greatest Story Ever Told	Joseph
1977	First Love	John March
1978	Revenge of the Pink Panther	Marchione
1980	The Ninth Configuration	Lt. Bennish
1981	S.O.B.	Herb Maskowitz
1982	An Officer and a Gentleman	Byron Mayo
1982	Trail of the Pink Panther	Bruno
1983	Psycho II	Dr. Raymond
1983	Scarface	Frank Lopez
1983	Curse of the Pink Panther	Bruno
1985	Jagged Edge	Sam Ransom
1985	Prizzi's Honor	Eduardo Prizzi
1986	Armed and Dangerous	Michael Carlino
1986	That's Life!	Father Baragone

(continued on page 508)

HERBERT LOM

(1917 -   )

The Czech actor began his film career in England in the 1940s after fleeing his homeland and the Nazis. There, he co-starred in 1945's *The Seventh Veil*, one of the key British pictures of the 40's. He branched out into Hollywood movies in 1959 and is widely recognized by film-goers as Chief Inspector Dreyfus of the Pink Panther series.

Year	Movie	Character
1960	Spartacus	Tigranes
1961	El Cid	Ben Yussuf
1964	A Shot in the Dark	Chief Insp. Dreyfus
1966	Gambit	Shahbandar
1968	Assignment to Kill	Matt Wilson
1968	Villa Rides	Huerta
1975	Ten Little Indians	Dr. Armstrong
1975	The Return of the Pink Panther	Chief Insp. Dreyfus
1976	The Pink Panther Strikes Again	Dreyfus
1978	Revenge of the Pink Panther	Dreyfus
1979	The Lady Vanishes	Dr. Hartz
1980	Hopscotch	Mikhail Yaskov
1980	The Man with Bogart's Face	Mr. Zebra
1982	Trail of the Pink Panther	Dreyfus
1983	The Dead Zone	Dr. Sam Welzak
1983	Curse of the Pink Panther	Dreyfus
1985	King Solomon's Mines	Colonel Bockner
1989	River of Death	Col. Ricardo Diaz
1989	Ten Little Indians	Gen. Romensky
1993	Son of Pink Panther	Dreyfus

LAURENCE LUCKINBILL

(1934 -   )

Since, at the time, he was just another struggling actor, Luckinbill considers his role in Matt Crowley's successful Off-Broadway play *Boys in the Band* as the turning point in his career. When people told him that playing a homosexual would ruin his career, he replied: "What career?" The Fort Smith, AR, native has spent most of his career on the New York stage after receiving his master's degree in drama from Catholic University and spending a few years with the U.S. State Department.

Year	Movie	Character
1971	Such Good Friends	Richard Messinger
1979	The Promise	Dr. Gregson
1988	Cocktail	Mr. Mooney
1988	Messenger of Death	Homer Foxx
1989	Star Trek V: The Final Frontier	Sybok

KEYE LUKE

DOLPH LUNDGREN

(1904 - 1991)

Born in Canton, China, raised in Seattle, Luke moved to Hollywood in 1930 and became one of the most successful Asian-American character actors. He was Charlie Chan's No. 1 son in the movies and Master Po on the *Kung Fu* TV series with David Carradine. He died of a stroke.

(1959 -   )

The former world kickboxing champion is best known for his debut role as the Soviet kill-machine, Drago, who spars with Sylvester Stallone in *Rocky IV*. Lundgren's muscleman image on the screen is belied by the fact that he is a former chemical engineeer who studied at M.I.T. on a Fulbright Scholarship. The Swedish actor formed his own production company in 1993 to enable him, as he says, to "acquire new projects, portray a broader variety of characters and bring out qualities in me as an actor."

Year	Movie	Character
1969	The Chairman	Prof. Soong Li
1970	The Hawaiians	Foo Sen
1978	The Amsterdam Kill	Chung Wei
1979	Just You and Me Kid	Dr. Device
1984	Gremlins	Grandfather
1986	A Fine Mess	Ishimine
1988	Dead Heat	Mr. Thule
1989	The Mighty Quinn	Dr. Raj
1990	Alice	Dr. Yang
1990	Gremlins 2 The New Batch	Mr. Wing

Year	Movie	Character
1985	A View to a Kill	Venz
1985	Rocky IV	Drago
1987	Masters of the Universe	He-Man
1989	Red Scorpion	Lt. Nikolai
1989	The Punisher	Frank Castle
1990	I Come in Peace	Jack Caine
1991	Showdown in Little Tokyo	Det. Lundgren
1992	Universal Soldier	Scott

KELLY LYNCH

(1959 -   )

Best-known for her role as a drugstore-robbing junkie in the critically-acclaimed *Drugstore Cowboy*, Lynch moved into acting via a modeling career. After 3 1/2 years with the Elite agency in New York, she made her film debut in 1984 in a low-budget sci-fi pic shot in Mexico titled *Osa*. Lynch grew up in Minneapolis and worked briefly as an airline stewardess before becoming a model.

Year	Movie	Character
1988	Bright Lights, Big City	Elaine
1988	Cocktail	Kerry Coughlin
1989	Drugstore Cowboy	Dianne Hughes
1989	Road House	Doc (Elizabeth Clay)
1990	Desperate Hours	Nancy Breyers
1991	Curly Sue	Grey Ellison
1993	Three of Hearts	Connie

RICHARD LYNCH

(1936 -   )

Lynch got his start on the New York stage following a tour of duty with the Marine Corps. The Brooklyn-born actor won a Mercury Award from the Academy of Science Fiction and Fantasy for his role in *The Sword and the Sorcerer*.

Year	Movie	Character
1973	Scarecrow	Riley
1973	The Seven-Ups	Moon
1980	Steel	Dancer
1980	The Formula	Kladen/Tedesco
1982	The Sword and the Sorcerer	Cromwell
1985	Invasion U.S.A.	Rostov
1988	Bad Dreams	Harris
1988	Little Nikita	Scuba
1989	One Man Force	Adams
1990	The Forbidden Dance	Benjamin Maxwell

SUE LYON

(1946 -   )

Lyon burst onto the Hollwood scene at age 16 when she portrayed the title role in Stanley Kubrick's *Lolita*. Just as quickly she vanished. Born in Davenport, IA, Lyon grew up in L.A. and worked as a model before *Lolita*. She later caused a stir by marrying a convicted murderer serving two back-to-back 40-year prison sentences. The marriage ended in divorce.

Year	Movie	Character
1962	Lolita	Lolita Haze
1964	The Night of the Iguana	Charlotte Goodall
1966	7 Women	Emma Clark
1967	The Flim Flam Man	Bonnie Lee Packard
1967	Tony Rome	Diana
1980	Alligator	News Reporter

ROBERT F. LYONS

(1940 -   )

Lyons began his screen career in 1965 playing a series of heavies on television. He made his film debut as a rapist-killer in *Pendulum* with George Peppard in 1969, and got the attention of critics the next year for his part in *Getting Straight* with Elliott Gould. Lyons was a tap-dancer at age six growing up in Albany, NY, and spent his high school years in a very strict military school. He became an actor in New York following studies at the American Academy of Dramatic Arts.

Year	Movie	Character
1970	Getting Straight	Nick
1971	Shootout	Bobby Jay
1971	The Todd Killings	Skipper
1977	Black Oak Conspiracy	Harrison
1982	Death Wish II	Fred McKenzie
1985	Avenging Angel	Det. Andrews
1985	Cease Fire	Luke
1986	Murphy's Law	Art Penney
1988	Platoon Leader	Michael McNamara

JAMES MACARTHUR

(1937 -   )

Book 'em, Dano! The adopted son of famous theatrical parents, actress Helen Hayes and playwright Charles MacArthur, MacArthur was born in L.A. and was acting on stage by 1945. His screen career began with several Walt Disney productions, then took off for good when he was cast as Detective Danny Williams in the television series, *Hawaii Five-O* (1968-79).

Year	Movie	Character
1960	Swiss Family Robinson	Fritz
1962	The Interns	Dr. Lew Worship
1963	Spencer's Mountain	Clayboy
1965	Battle of the Bulge	Lt. Weaver
1965	The Bedford Incident	Ensign Ralston
1966	Ride Beyond Vengeance	Census Taker
1968	Hang 'Em High	Preacher

RALPH MACCHIO

(1961 -   )

Macchio became a teen idol after only one season as the orphaned Jeremy on TV's *Eight is Enough* (1980-81) and has maintained that image throughout much of his career after he shot to stardom as the vulnerable lead in *The Karate Kid* and its sequels. He has not had to audition for most of his movies and was able to bypass the "struggling actor" stage. The youthful-looking thesp takes his craft seriously, however. "I don't want to be known only as some guy whose poster hangs in little girls' bedrooms," he once said.

Year	Movie	Character
1980	Up the Academy	Chooch
1983	The Outsiders	Johnny Cade
1984	Teachers	Eddie
1984	The Karate Kid	Daniel
1986	Crossroads	Eugene Martone
1986	The Karate Kid, Part II	Daniel
1988	Distant Thunder	Jack Lambert
1989	The Karate Kid III	Daniel LaRusso
1991	Too Much Sun	Frank Della Rocca, Jr.
1992	My Cousin Vinny	Bill Gambini

ANDIE MACDOWELL

(1958 -   )

Breaking into movies has not been an easy matter for MacDowell. As a model, she faced all the doubts Hollywood holds of models-turned-actresses. The airhead stereotype was reinforced after her voice was erased in her debut as Jane in *Greystoke: The Legend of Tarzan, Lord of the Apes* and Glenn Close's was dubbed in. Fortunately for MacDowell, her role in *sex, lies and videotape* brought her acclaim and a near award at the Cannes Film Festival.

Year	Movie	Character
1984	Greystoke: The Legend of Tarzan, Lord of the Apes	Jane Porter
1985	St. Elmo's Fire	Dale Biberman
1989	sex, lies and videotape	Ann Millaney
1990	Green Card	Bronte Parrish
1991	Hudson Hawk	Anna Baragli
1991	The Object of Beauty	Tina
1993	Groundhog Day	Rita
1993	Short Cuts	Ann Finnigan
1993	Deception	Bessie Faro

KYLE MACLACHLAN

(1959 -   )

A favorite of filmmaker David Lynch, MacLachlan debuted in his production of *Dune* as the hero who leads the lowly residents of the Dune planet into battle against an evil empire. Born in Yakima, WA, his acting career was promoted by his mother who pushed him into a teenage community theater. He was next seen in Lynch's *Blue Velvet* as the young man who finds a disembodied, ant-covered human ear in a vacant lot.

Year	Movie	Character
1984	Dune	Paul Atreides
1986	Blue Velvet	Jeffrey Beaumont
1987	The Hidden	Lloyd Galagher
1990	Don't Tell Her It's Me	Trout
1991	The Doors	Ray Manzarek
1992	Twin Peaks: Fire Walk With Me	Special Agent Dale Cooper
1993	Rich in Love	Billy McQueen

PETER MACNICOL

(1954 -   )

MacNicol has had an extensive career on the stage, including roles in *All the Kings' Men* and *Richard II*. He has been described in the New York Times as a gentle, but "driven" actor who at times finds acting a "painful experience." Memorable film roles include the lecherous art historian in *Ghostbusters II*, who is restoring a Rembrandt-like painting and one of a group of three friends (with Meryl Streep and Kevin Kline) living in a rooming house in post-World War II Brooklyn in *Sophie's Choice*.

Year	Movie	Character
1981	Dragonslayer	Galen
1982	Sophie's Choice	Stingo
1987	Heat	Cyrus Kinnick
1989	Ghostbusters II	Janosz Poha
1992	HouseSitter	Marty
1993	Addams Family Values	Gary Granger

BILL MACY

(1922 -   )

Macy came up the theatrical ladder the hard way—driving a New York City cab by day and looking for stage roles by night. But in 1972, his late-blooming career was launched when Norman Lear hired him to play the husband in *Maude*, which was a successful television series for six years. It introduced him to many lucrative roles in movies and on stage. Born in Revere, MA, Macy had trained for the stage at New York University and in Lee Strasberg's studio.

Year	Movie	Character
1977	The Late Show	Charlie Hatter
1979	The Jerk	Stan Fox
1980	Serial	Sam
1982	My Favorite Year	Sy Benson
1985	Bad Medicine	Dr. Gerald Marx
1985	Movers and Shakers	Sid Spokane
1990	Sibling Rivalry	Pat
1991	The Doctor	Dr. Al Cade

AMY MADIGAN

(1950 -   )

Madigan earned a philosophy degree at Marquette University, but quickly decided it would count for little in the real world. She turned to acting, studying under Lee Strasberg, and has been rewarded with a series of great roles. The Chicago native can also sing and play the piano. Madigan played farmer Kevin Costner's wife in *Field of Dreams* and has an adulterous affair in *Places in the Heart* with her husband's best friend.

Year	Movie	Character
1982	Love Child	Terry Jean Moore
1983	Love Letters	Wendy
1984	Places in the Heart	Viola Kelsey
1984	Streets of Fire	McCoy
1985	Alamo Bay	Glory
1985	Twice in a Lifetime	Sunny
1987	Nowhere to Hide	Barbara Cutter
1988	The Prince of Pennsylvania	Carla Headlee
1989	Field of Dreams	Annie Kinsella
1989	Uncle Buck	Chanice Kobolowski
1993	The Dark Half	Liz Beaumont

VIRGINIA MADSEN

(1963 -   )

The theater world turned bright for Madsen one day in 1984 when she was unexpectedly selected to play Princess Irulan in *Dune*. It led on to choice roles in films and TV-movies. A Chicago native, Madsen was encouraged to perform by her mother, a documentary filmmaker. Ironically, mother and daughter found success simultaneously—on the day Virginia got the *Dune* role, her mother learned she'd been awarded an Emmy for a documentary she had made.

Year	Movie	Character
1983	Class	Lisa
1984	Dune	Princess Irulan
1984	Electric Dreams	Madeline
1985	Creator	Barbara
1986	Fire With Fire	Lisa
1988	Hot to Trot	Allison Rowe
1988	Mr. North	Sally Boffin
1989	Heart of Dixie	Delia
1990	The Hot Spot	Dolly Harshaw
1991	Highlander II: The Quickening	Louise Marcus
1992	Candyman	Helen Lyle

GEORGE MAHARIS

(1928 -   )

A rugged individualist is the way George Maharis describes himself. A native New Yorker who first tried the life of a singer on the supper club route, he took up acting under the tutelage of the famous Lee Strasberg. It was the role of the ruggedly handsome Buzz in the *Route 66* television series that brought him national prominence. That propelled him into a lucrative series of films and TV-movies.

Year	Movie	Character
1960	Exodus	Yaov
1965	Sylvia	Alan Macklin
1965	The Satan Bug	Lee Barrett
1967	The Happening	Taurus
1969	The Desperados	Jacob Galt
1982	The Sword and the Sorcerer	Machelli

JOSEPH MAHER

(1933 -   )

"I get cast frequently in aristocratic roles because I have a long nose and sound peculiar," Maher once said. The "peculiar sound" is a mixture of his various accents. He was born in Ireland, moved to London at 18, left England for Canada and somehow wound up acting in a Brendan Behan play in New York. He spent the first 15 years of his acting career on the stage and made his film debut with a bit part in Barbra Streisand's *For Pete's Sake.*

Year	Movie	Character
1974	For Pete's Sake	Mr. Coates
1978	Heaven Can Wait	Sisk
1979	Time After Time	Adams
1980	Just Tell Me What You Want	Dr. Coleson
1980	Those Lips, Those Eyes	Fibby Geyer
1981	Going Ape!	Gridley
1981	Under The Rainbow	Duke
1984	The Evil That Men Do	Moloch
1988	Funny Farm	Michael Sinclair
1988	My Stepmother Is an Alien	Dr. Lucas Budlong
1992	Sister Act	Bishop O'Hara

JOHN MAHONEY

(1940 -   )

Mahoney emigrated to the U.S. from Manchester, England at 20 looking for a better standard of living. At 37, he had a comfortable, well-paying job in Chicago, but was miserable. So, he quit his job and made his decision to become an actor after seeing stage star Leo McKern back in Manchester, first on the stage in *Uncle Vanya* and, later, in a coffee shop. "These people are not gods," he thought to himself at the time. "These people are people that sit in coffee shops, eat sausage rolls, sip tea and transform themselves in the evening."

Year	Movie	Character
1986	Streets of Gold	Lineman
1986	The Manhattan Project	Lt. Col. Conroy
1987	Moonstruck	Perry
1987	Suspect	Judge Matthew Helms
1987	Tin Men	Moe
1988	Betrayed	Shorty
1988	Eight Men Out	Kid Gleason
1988	Frantic	Williams
1989	Say Anything...	James Court
1990	The Russia House	Brady
1991	Barton Fink	W.P. Mayhew
1992	Article 99	Dr. Henry Dreyfoos
1993	In the Line of Fire	Sam Campagna
1993	Striking Distance	Vince Hardy

CHRIS MAKEPEACE

(1964 -   )

Makepeace was a much-discussed actor in his teens. He was cast as a brave, but undersized gang member in the film *My Bodyguard* when he was 16. A Montreal, Canada, native he had started making TV commercials at the age of 10. He has studied at Second City Workshop.

Year	Movie	Character
1979	Meatballs	Rudy
1980	My Bodyguard	Clifford
1981	The Last Chase	Ring
1986	Vamp	Keith
1987	Captive Hearts	Robert
1988	Aloha Summer	Mike Tognetti

MAKO

(1934 -   )

Makoto Iwamatsu (his real name) was born in Kobe, Japan, and moved to New York with his parents when he was 15. A job as a set designer lured him into the theater and he has been busily employed ever since. Mako's big breakthrough came in 1966 when he played an illiterate coolie in Steve McQueen's *The Sand Pebbles*. It won him an Academy Award nomination as best supporting actor.

Year	Movie	Character
1966	The Sand Pebbles	Po-Han
1968	The Private Navy of Sgt. O'Farrell	Calvin Coolidge Ishimuna
1969	The Great Bank Robbery	Secret Service Agent
1970	The Hawaiians	Mun Ki
1975	The Killer Elite	Yuen Chung
1980	The Big Brawl	Herbert
1981	An Eye for an Eye	Chan
1981	Under The Rainbow	Nakamuri
1982	Conan the Barbarian	Wizard
1983	Testament	Mike
1984	Conan the Destroyer	Akijiro "The Wizard"
1986	Armed Response	Akira Tanaka
1986	P.O.W. The Escape	Capt. Vinh

(continued on page 508)

JOHN MALKOVICH

(1954 -   )

By his own admission, Malkovich was a brash show-off as a kid growing up in Benton, IL. His siblings called him "mad dog." But the temperament also drew him into acting. He became a member of Chicago's Steppenwolf Theater after college and took home an Obie for his 1982 New York stage debut in Sam Shepard's *True West*. Movie roles include the photographer in *The Killing Fields*, the licentious French aristocrat in *Dangerous Liaisons* and the embittered, blind World War I veteran in *Places in the Heart*.

Year	Movie	Character
1984	The Killing Fields	Al Rockoff
1984	Places in the Heart	Mr. Will
1985	Eleni	Nick
1987	Empire of the Sun	Basie
1987	Making Mr. Right	Jeff Peters/Ulysses
1987	The Glass Menagerie	Tom
1988	Dangerous Liaisons	Vicomte de Valmont
1988	Miles From Home	Barry Maxwell
1990	The Sheltering Sky	Port Moresby
1991	Queens Logic	Eliot
1991	The Object of Beauty	Jake
1992	Jennifer Eight	St. Anne
1992	Of Mice and Men	Lennie
1992	Shadows and Fog	Clown
1993	In the Line of Fire	Mitch Leary

DOROTHY MALONE

(1925 -   )

Malone has been in films since 1943, but the role that brought her the most attention was that of Constance MacKenzie in the ABC-TV series *Peyton Place*, a show about scandals and dark secrets in a New England town. Warned that the role was not exactly a wholesome one and might ruin her career, she took it anyway because she liked the writing. It ran from 1964 to 1968, and she later appeared in NBC's movie *Peyton Place: The Next Generation*.

Year	Movie	Character
1960	The Last Voyage	Laurie Henderson
1961	The Last Sunset	Belle Breckenridge
1963	Beach Party	Marianne
1979	Winter Kills	Emma
1992	Basic Instinct	Hazel Dobkins

NICK MANCUSO

(1949 -   )

Mancuso first attracted notice as an actor in the U.S. for his role in the mini-series called *Stingray*. But behind him lay a string of successes on the stage in Canada. Born in Italy, he clothes his rugged build expensively and is all business when he talks.

Year	Movie	Character
1981	Ticket to Heaven	David
1982	Mother Lode	Jean Dupre
1984	Blame It on the Night	Chris
1984	Heartbreakers	Eli
1985	Death of an Angel	Father Angel
1992	Rapid Fire	Antonio Serrano

DINAH MANOFF

(1958 -   )

At the age of 22, Manoff saw her career take off when she won a Tony and a Theater World Award for her part in *I Ought to Be in Pictures*. She reprised her role as the young actress who hitchhikes to L.A. from Brooklyn to break into movies and see her father in the film version opposite Walter Matthau. The daughter of the actress Lee Grant, she played a babysitter murdered by Chucky, a killer doll in the popular *Child's Play*.

Year	Movie	Character
1978	Grease	Marty
1980	Ordinary People	Karen
1982	I Ought to Be in Pictures	Libby
1987	Backfire	Jill
1988	Child's Play	Maggie Peterson
1989	Staying Together	Lois Cook
1990	Welcome Home, Roxy Carmichael	Evelyn Whittacher

JOE MANTEGNA

(1947 -   )

After 15 years of musical road shows, regional plays and European tours, Mantegna arrived on Broadway in 1984 in David Mamet's *Glengarry Glen Ross*. He won a Tony for best supporting actor, the first time out. It has been through his long partnership with Mamet that Mantegna has achieved his greatest distinction as an actor. He is the Pulitzer prize-winning dramatist's favorite actor, and, according to one critic, the two have "created some of the most dazzling if despicable American male characters of the last decade."

Year	Movie	Character
1985	Compromising Positions	Dr. Bruce Fleckstein
1986	!Three Amigos!	Harry Flugelman
1986	Off Beat	Pete Peterson
1986	The Money Pit	Art Shirk
1987	Critical Condition	Chambers
1987	House of Games	Mike
1987	Suspect	Charlie Stella
1987	Weeds	Carmine
1988	Things Change	Jerry
1989	Wait Until Spring, Bandini	Svevo Bandini
1990	Alice	Joe
1990	The Godfather, Part III	Joey Zasa
1991	Bugsy	George Raft
1991	Homicide	Bobby Gold
1991	Queens Logic	Al
1993	Body of Evidence	Robert Garrett
1993	Family Prayers	Martin Jacobs
1993	Searching for Bobby Fischer	Fred Waitzkin

FREDRIC MARCH

(1897 - 1975)

Winner of two Oscars for best actor, March was a leading man in straight drama and romantic comedy in more than 65 films. With his honeyed voice and earnest manner he could play both lovers and tortured men. Born in Racine, WI, he served in an artillery unit in World War I in Texas, then worked for a New York City bank. After an emergency operation on his appendix, he decided to give up banking for Broadway. He died at 77 of cancer in an L.A. hospital.

Year	Movie	Character
1960	Inherit the Wind	Matthew Harrison Brady
1961	The Young Doctors	Dr. Joseph Pearson
1964	Seven Days in May	President Jordan Lyman
1967	Hombre	Favor
1970	...tick...tick...tick...	Mayor Jeff Parks

JANET MARGOLIN

(1943 -   )

A native New Yorker, Margolin began her life in the theater as a $9.65 a week prop girl at the Shakespeare Festival in Central Park. Things got better fast. At the age of 18, she appeared on Broadway and, two years later, achieved stardom as the schizophrenic young girl who talks backwards in rhyme in *David and Lisa*. Margolin has played opposite Woody Allen as his wife in *Take the Money and Run* and *Annie Hall*.

Year	Movie	Character
1962	David and Lisa	Lisa
1965	Bus Riley's Back in Town	Judy
1965	Morituri	Esther
1965	The Greatest Story Ever Told	Mary of Bethany
1967	Enter Laughing	Wanda
1968	Buona Sera, Mrs. Campbell	Gia
1969	Take the Money and Run	Louise
1973	Your Three Minutes Are Up	Betty
1977	Annie Hall	Robin
1979	Last Embrace	Ellie Fabian
1988	Distant Thunder	Barbara Lambert

STUART MARGOLIN

(1939 -   )

It was the role of James Garner's loyal accomplice in the long-running TV series *The Rockford Files* (1974-80) that first brought this Iowa native wide public acclaim. But his talent is varied—he has both written scripts and directed them. *Paramedics* (1988) was his feature film debut as a director. Margolin called it a "good-time, rock 'n' roll, kick-ass film."

Year	Movie	Character
1970	Kelly's Heroes	Little Joe
1973	The Stone Killer	Lawrence
1974	Death Wish	Aimes Jainchill
1976	Futureworld	Harry
1976	The Big Bus	Alex
1978	Days of Heaven	Mill Foreman
1981	S.O.B.	Gary Murdock
1983	Class	Balaban
1986	A Fine Mess	Maurice "Binky" Dzundza
1988	Iron Eagle II	Stillmore
1989	Bye Bye Blues	Slim Godfrey
1991	Guilty by Suspicion	Abe Barron

JOHN MARLEY

(1906 - 1984)

Marley was on stage and in film since he dropped out of school in Harlem, but success came late in life. He was nominated for an Oscar for his performance in *Love Story* and won a best actor award in 1968 at the Venice Film Festival for his work in *Faces*. He made his first film in 1941, appearing in *Native Land*. Marley died following open heart surgery.

Year	Movie	Character
1965	Cat Ballou	Frankie Ballou
1970	Love Story	Phil Cavilleri
1972	Jory	Roy
1972	The Godfather	Jack Woltz
1975	Framed	Sal
1977	The Car	Everett
1977	The Private Files of J. Edgar Hoover	Dave Hindley
1978	Hooper	Max Berns
1978	It Lives Again	Mallory
1980	Tribute	Lou Daniels
1981	Threshold	Edgar Fine
1982	Mother Lode	Elijah

KENNETH MARS

(1936 -   )

Mars' career began in the New York theater world in singing roles and in straight plays, often using his various accents: English, German, Russian, Irish and several American dialects. His German accents have been put to good use in his roles as the shell-shocked Nazi playwright of "Hitler in Springtime" in *The Producers*, the German poseur in *What's Up, Doc?* and the local police inspector with the arm problem in *Young Frankenstein*.

Year	Movie	Character
1968	The Producers	Franz Liebkind
1969	Butch Cassdy and the Sundance Kid	Marshal
1969	The April Fools	Don Hopkins
1971	Desperate Characters	Otto
1972	What's Up, Doc?	Hugh Simon
1974	The Parallax View	Turner
1974	Young Frankenstein	Inspector Kemp
1975	Night Moves	Nick
1979	The Apple Dumpling Gang Rides Again	Marshall
1981	Full Moon High	xxx
1983	Yellowbeard	Crisp/Verdugo
1984	Prince Jack	Lyndon

(continued on page 508)

E.G. MARSHALL

(1910 -   )

One of America's most prolific actors, Marshall spent the first 20 years of his career on the stage and the last 40 mostly on television. He was famous as the attorney Lawrence Preston in *The Defenders* (1961-65) and won an Emmy for that role in 1963. He also starred in *The New Doctors*, a hospital drama that ran from 1969 to 1973. His film debut came with a memorable performance in 1945's *The House on 92nd Street*.

Year	Movie	Character
1966	The Chase	Val Rogers
1969	The Bridge at Remagen	Brig. Gen. Shinner
1970	Tora! Tora! Tora!	Lt. Col. Bratton
1978	Interiors	Arthur
1980	Superman II	President
1982	Creepshow	Upson
1986	My Chauffeur	Witherspoon
1986	Power	Sen. Sam Hastings
1989	National Lampoon's Christmas Vacation	Art
1992	Consenting Adults	George Gordon

NAN MARTIN

(1927 -   )

Martin has acted on stage with some of the most famous American actors, including Katharine Cornell, but she appreciates the value of television—it keeps actors from being hungry. "Television keeps actors in the chips and out of the cold," she once told a reporter. She is a native of Illinois and trained for the theater at UCLA.

Year	Movie	Character
1963	Toys in the Attic	Charlotte Warkins
1965	Bus Riley's Back in Town	Mrs. Nichols
1968	For Love of Ivy	Doris Austin
1969	Goodbye, Columbus	Mrs. Patimkin
1975	The Other Side of the Mountain	June Kinmont
1978	The Other Side of the Mountain Part 2	June Kinmont
1980	Loving Couples	Walter's Nurse
1983	Doctor Detroit	Margaret
1987	A Nightmare on Elm Street 3: Dream Warriors	Nun
1989	Animal Behavior	Mrs. Norton

PAMELA SUE MARTIN

(1953 -   )

A woman of varied talents, Martin has experienced success as actress, producer and screenwriter. She debuted in films as the 17-year-old travelling with her brother on the doomed ship in *The Poseidon Adventure*. On television she was Fallon Colby in *Dynasty* and Nancy Drew in the *Nancy Drew Mysteries*. She scored a hat trick in 1984 with *Torchlight*—she wrote the film script, acted a lead part and was associate producer. Martin hails from Westport, CT.

Year	Movie	Character
1972	The Poseidon Adventure	Susan
1974	Buster and Billie	Margie Hooks
1974	Death of Her Innocence	Abby
1979	The Lady in Red	Polly
1984	Torchlight	Lillian

STROTHER MARTIN

(1919 - 1980)

This veteran character actor from Kokomo, IN, appeared in more than 100 films and 50 TV shows making a name for himself as a despicable bad guy. In the 1960s, Martin was the prison warden to Paul Newman's convict in *Cool Hand Luke* who spoke the memorable line: "What we have here is a failure to communicate." In *The Wild Bunch* he played the outlaw who dug the gold teeth out of his dead victims. He studied theater at the University of Michigan and became an NCAA champion diver. He died of a heart attack.

Year	Movie	Character
1962	The Man Who Shot Liberty Valance	Floyd
1963	McLintock	Agard
1965	Shenandoah	Engineer
1965	The Sons of Katie Elder	Jeb Ross
1966	Harper	Claude
1967	Cool Hand Luke	Captain
1967	The Flim Flam Man	Lovick
1969	Butch Cassdy and the Sundance Kid	Percy Garris
1969	The Wild Bunch	Coffer
1969	True Grit	Colonel Stonehill
1970	The Ballad of Cable Hogue	Bowen
1970	Red Sky at Morning	John Cloyd
1971	Brotherhood of Satan	Doc

(continued on page 508)

MARY STUART MASTERSON

(1967 -   )

Masterson was, as they say of many performers, born into a theatrical career. Her father, Peter Masterson, is a writer-director and her mother, an actress. Her first role came in the film *The Stepford Wives* at the age of seven. She acknowledges her parents' help, but says: "In the real world, you have to do things for yourself." Masterson played the good-hearted rural Alabama tomboy, Idgie Threadgoode, in the 1991 sleeper, *Fried Green Tomatoes*.

Year	Movie	Character
1975	The Stepford Wives	Kim
1985	Heaven Help Us	Danni
1986	At Close Range	Terry
1986	My Little Girl	Franny Bettinger
1987	Gardens of Stone	Rachel Feld
1987	Some Kind of Wonderful	Watts
1988	Mr. North	Elspeth Skeel
1989	Chances Are	Miranda Jeffries
1989	Immediate Family	Lucy Moore
1990	Funny About Love	Daphne Delillo
1991	Fried Green Tomatoes	Idgie Threadgoode
1993	Benny and Joon	Joon
1993	Married to It	Nina Bishop

MARY ELIZABETH MASTRANTONIO

(1958 -)

An Oak Park, IL, beauty with a mop of unruly, curly hair, Mastrantonio has played supporting roles with some of the top male stars of the 1980s, including Kevin Costner, Tom Cruise, Al Pacino and Paul Newman. She got an Academy Award nomination for her role as Tom Cruise's girlfriend in *The Color of Money* and played Al Pacino's sister in *Scarface*.

Year	Movie	Character
1983	Scarface	Gina
1986	The Color of Money	Carmen
1989	The Abyss	Lindsey Brigman
1989	The January Man	Bernadette Flynn
1991	Class Action	Maggie
1991	Robin Hood: Prince of Thieves	Maid Marian
1992	Consenting Adults	Priscilla Parker
1992	White Sands	Lane Bodine

RICHARD MASUR

(1948 -)

Masur, with mustache or without, is one of the most familiar faces on American television. People are always coming up to ask: "Where have I seen you?" He's had experience turning bad guys into believable people—like the child-molester in the 1981 TV-movie *Fallen Angel*. A graduate of the Yale School of Drama, Masur has appeared in many television series including *Rhoda*, *The Waltons* and *One Day at a Time*.

Year	Movie	Character
1977	Semi-Tough	Phillip Hooper
1978	Who'll Stop the Rain	Danskin
1979	Hanover Street	2nd Lt. Jerry Cimino
1980	Heaven's Gate	Cully
1982	I'm Dancing as Fast as I Can	Alan Newman
1982	The Thing	Clark
1983	Nightmares	Steven
1983	Risky Business	Rutherford
1983	Timerider	Claude Dorsett
1983	Under Fire	Hub
1985	My Science Project	Det. Nulty
1985	The Mean Season	Bill Nolan
1986	Head Office	Max Landsberger
1986	Heartburn	Arthur

(continued on page 508)

THOM MATTHEWS

(19?? -   )

Often seen in horror movies, Matthews is perhaps best remembered for his leading role in *Friday the 13th, Part VI: Jason Lives* as the boy who is first suspected of committing a rash of murders, but who is saved from jail by none other than the sheriff's cute daughter.

Year	Movie	Character
1985	The Return of the Living Dead	Freddy
1986	Friday the 13th, Part VI: Jason Lives	Tommy
1987	Down Twisted	Damalas
1988	Return of the Living Dead Part II	Joey

JOHN MATUSZAK

(1951 - 1989)

Matuszak played pro-football and led the Oakland Raiders to the Super Bowl in 1976 and 1980. Then he began his film and television career. He died of heart failure.

Year	Character	Movie
1979	North Dallas Forty	xxx
1981	Caveman	Tonda
1984	The Ice Pirates	Killjoy
1985	The Goonies	Sloth
1986	One Crazy Summer	Stain
1989	Ghost Writer	xxx
1989	One Man Force	Jake Swan
1990	Down the Drain	xxx

ELAINE MAY

(1932 -   )

May's career got started as one-half of a comedy duo with Mike Nichols doing improvisational theater at the Chicago-based Compass Theater. (Compass later became Second City.) Their sardonic performances were then seen and heard in nightclubs, on television, radio, records and finally, for one year on Broadway. They broke up in 1962. Acting only in comedies, May also wrote, directed and co-starred in *A New Leaf*.

Year	Movie	Character
1967	Enter Laughing	Angela
1971	A New Leaf	Henrietta Lowell
1978	California Suite	Millie Michaels
1990	In the Spirit	Marianne Flan

MELANIE MAYRON

(1952 -   )

Mayron has been known to say that getting an acting job is like winning a lottery. If that's so, she has been very lucky because she's had many strong roles in both television and film. Her best-known job was as the photographer, Melissa Steadman, in TV's *thirtysomething*. Her career began fast when, just out of the Academy of Dramatic Arts, she was cast for the national road show of *Godspell*. Her film credits include *Missing* in which she is seen with John Shea in a seaside resort town in Chile when a miltary coup is launched.

Year	Movie	Character
1974	Harry and Tonto	Ginger
1976	Car Wash	Marsha
1976	Gable and Lombard	Dixie
1976	The Great Smokey Roadblock	Lulu
1977	You Light Up My Life	Annie
1978	Girlfriends	Susan Weinblatt
1981	Heartbeeps	Susan
1982	Missing	Terry Simon
1986	The Boss's Wife	Janet
1988	Sticky Fingers	Lolly
1989	Checking Out	Jenny Macklin
1990	My Blue Heaven	Crystal Rybak

DIANE MCBAIN

(1941 -   )

McBain, who was born in Cleveland, was lured into acting by her grandmother who paid for a beauty course to develop poise. The grandmother guessed right because McBain went on to become a multi-talented theater artist who has produced, written and acted in films and appeared in such well-known television productions as *Marcus Welby, M.D.* and *Police Story*.

Year	Movie	Character
1960	Ice Palace	Christine
1961	Parrish	Alison Post
1963	The Caretakers	Alison
1964	A Distant Trumpet	Laura
1966	Spinout	Diana St. Clair

ANDREW MCCARTHY

(1963 -   )

The usual actor's hard luck story does not fit McCarthy. He was a drama student at NYU when he decided to kill an afternoon trying out for a part in Orion Pictures' film *Class*. He landed a plum role and suddenly was in show business. McCarthy played a wealthy nice guy who asks other-side-of-the-tracks Molly Ringwald to the senior prom in *Pretty in Pink*. As one of a group of college grad friends living in Washington, D.C., in *St. Elmo's Fire*, he had crush on his best friend's girl, Ally Sheedy.

Year	Movie	Character
1983	Class	Jonathan
1988	Fresh Horses	Larkin
1985	Heaven Help Us	Michael Dunn
1987	Less Than Zero	Clay
1987	Mannequin	Jonathan Switcher
1986	Pretty in Pink	Blane
1985	St. Elmo's Fire	Kevin
1989	Weekend at Bernie's	Larry Wilson
1991	Year of the Gun	David Raybourne
1993	Weekend at Bernie's II	Larry
1993	The Joy Luck Club	Ted

KEVIN MCCARTHY

CHRISTOPHER MCDONALD

(1914 -   )

McCarthy's screen career began when he reprised his London stage role as Biff in 1951's *Death of a Salesman*. The part didn't lead to very much, however, and he spent the rest of the 1950s on television and in a few B-movies. But one of those low-budget flicks was 1956's all-time classic chiller *Invasion of the Body Snatchers*, where he gave a riveting performance as the hero. His career picked up steam in the 1960s. He is the brother of author Mary McCarthy (*The Group*).

Year	Movie	Character
1961	The Misfits	Raymond Taber
1963	A Gathering of Eagles	General Kirby
1963	Forty Pounds of Trouble	Blanchard
1963	The Prize	Dr. John Garrett
1964	The Best Man	Dick Jensen
1965	Mirage	Josephson
1966	A Big Hand for the Little Lady	Otto Habershaw
1967	Hotel	O'Keefe
1968	The Hell with Heroes	Col. Wilson
1972	Kansas City Bomber	Burt Henry
1973	Alien Thunder	xxx
1976	Buffalo Bill and the Indians, or Sitting Bull's History Lesson	Maj. John Burke
1978	Invasion of the Body Snatchers	Running Man

(continued on page 508)

(1955 -   )

"Actors think the grass is always greener," McDonald once said. "When you do a play, you wish you could be making easy money doing a film, because you work your butt off on the stage. Then you do your television and you say, 'God, if I have to do this one more time, I'll just go crazy.' I think any actor would rather do quality work than the episodic TV which pays the rent." McDonald is from upstate New York and moved to L.A. in 1979 after studies at London's RADA.

Year	Movie	Character
1982	Grease 2	T-Bird
1984	Chattanooga Choo Choo	Paul
1988	Paramedics	Mad Mike
1989	Chances Are	Louie Jeffries
1991	Dutch	Reed
1991	Thelma & Louise	Darryl
1993	Benefit of the Doubt	Dan
1993	Fatal Instinct	Frank Kelbo

FRANCES MCDORMAND

(1958 -   )

McDormand was born in Illinois and raised in Pennsylvania, but her early roles in plays and movies were of Southern women including a deputy sheriff's wife in *Mississippi Burning*. Oscar-nominated for that role, McDormand disclaims any desire to be a celebrity; she just wants to work often and hard in the roles she gets. She earned her undergraduate degree from Bethany College in West Virginia and graduate degree from Yale.

Year	Movie	Character
1984	Blood Simple	Abby
1987	Raising Arizona	Dot
1988	Mississippi Burning	Mrs. Pell
1990	Chattahoochee	Mae Foley
1990	Darkman	Julie Hastings
1991	The Butcher's Wife	Grace
1992	Passed Away	Nora Scanlan
1993	Short Cuts	Betty Weathers

MALCOLM MCDOWELL

(1943 -   )

Best known as the leader of a band of violent, psychopathic "droogs" in the 1971 U.K. film *A Clockwork Orange,* McDowell began his working life as a salesman. He remembers it as good training for the theater. "I mean you're lying all the time, smiling, trying to make people like you," he once explained. The British actor was rescued by the Royal Shakespeare Company.

Year	Movie	Character
1971	A Clockwork Orange	Alex
1976	Voyage of the Damned	Max Gunter
1979	Time After Time	H.G. Wells
1982	Cat People	Paul Gallier
1983	Blue Thunder	Cochrane
1983	Cross Creek	Max Perkins
1983	Get Crazy	Reggie
1988	Sunset	Alfie Alperin
1989	Buy & Cell	Warden Tennant
1990	Class of 1999	Dr. Miles Langford

ANNIE MCENROE

(19?? -   )

McEnroe appeared in several 1980s films and is perhaps best remembered as the female juvenile lead in *Howling II: Your Sister is a Werewolf*, in which she and friends journeyed to Transylvania to destroy a werewolf queen.

Year	Movie	Character
1981	The Hand	Stella Roche
1982	Warlords of the 21st Century	Corlie
1983	The Survivors	Doreen
1984	Purple Hearts	Hallaway
1985	Howling II: Your Sister is a Werewolf	Jenny Templeton
1986	True Stories	Kay Culver
1987	Cop	Amy Cransfield
1987	Wall Street	Muffie Livingston
1988	Beetlejuice	Jane Butterfield

DARREN MCGAVIN

(1922 -   )

A Spokane, WA, native, McGavin has had a long and varied career as an actor, director and producer. After an extensive career on the stage, he turned to movies and in the 1950s appeared in *The Court Martial of Billy Mitchell* and *The Man With a Golden Arm*. He has headed his own film studio, Taurean Films, and on television has appeared in *The Outsider* and *Kolchak: The Night Stalker*.

Year	Movie	Character
1971	Mrs. Pollifax—Spy	Farrell
1976	No Deposit, No Return	Duke
1977	Airport '77	Stan Buchek
1978	Hot Lead and Cold Feet	Mayor Ragsdale
1980	Hangar 18	Forbes
1983	A Christmas Story	the old man
1984	The Natural	xxx
1985	Turk 182!	Detective Kowalski
1986	Raw Deal	Shannon
1987	From the Hip	Craig Duncan
1988	Dead Heat	Dr. Ernest McNab
1991	Blood and Concrete	Hank Dick

VONETTA MCGEE

(1948 -   )

A homely youngster—she was known as "Popeye" as a child—McGee bloomed into a striking actress after abandoning a planned career as a school teacher. Her first roles were in Italian films.

Year	Movie	Character
1969	The Lost Man	Diane
1972	Hammer	Lois
1972	Melinda	Melinda
1973	Shaft in Africa	Aleme
1975	Eiger Sanction	Jemima Brown
1977	Brothers	Paula Jones
1984	Repo Man	Marlene
1990	To Sleep With Anger	Pat

BRUCE MCGILL

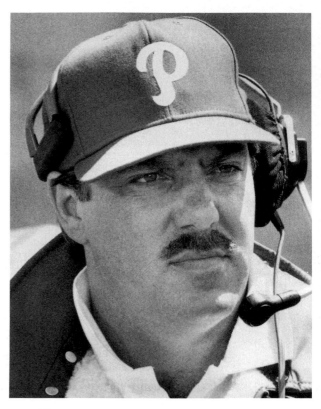

(1950 -   )

McGill's background is in Shakespearean theater: *Hamlet* at the New York Shakespeare Festival and on Broadway, as well as productions of *Othello* and *Henry V*. But his claim to cinematic fame may be his riotous performance as D-Day in *National Lampoon's Animal House*. McGill hails from San Antonio, TX, and includes playing the guitar and piano, golf and ocean sailing as his recreational hobbies.

Year	Movie	Character
1978	National Lampoon's Animal House	Daniel Simpson Day
1981	The Hand	Brian Ferguson
1983	Silkwood	Mace Hurley
1983	The Ballad of Gregorio Cortez	Reporter Blakely
1983	Tough Enough	Tony
1985	Into the Night	Charlie
1986	No Mercy	Lt. Hall
1986	Wildcats	Darwell
1987	End of the Line	Billy
1989	Three Fugitives	Charlie
1991	The Last Boy Scout	Mike Matthews
1992	My Cousin Vinny	xxx

JOHN MCGIVER

(1915 - 1975)

A prolific character actor, McGiver was a New York City school teacher who was discovered Off-Broadway and offered a role in television's *Studio One*. A regular on television and in Hollywood movies, he served in the Seventh Armored Division during World War II. His screen roles include the liberal senator and father of Laurence Harvey's girlfriend in *The Manchurian Candidate*. He died of a heart attack at his home near Albany, NY.

Year	Movie	Character
1961	Bachelor in Paradise	Austin Palfrey
1961	Breakfast at Tiffany's	Tiffany's Clerk
1962	Mr. Hobbs Takes a Vacation	Mr. Turner
1962	Period of Adjustment	Stewart P. McGill
1962	The Machurian Candidate	Senator Thomas Jordon
1962	Who's Got the Action?	Judge Fogel
1963	My Six Loves	Judge Harris
1963	Take Her, She's Mine	Hector G. Ivor
1963	Who's Minding the Store?	Mr. Tuttle
1964	Man's Favorite Sport?	William Cadwalader
1965	Marriage on the Rocks	Shad Nathan
1966	Made in Paris	Roger Barclay
1966	The Glass Bottom Boat	Ralph Goodwin
1967	Fitzwilly	Albert
1969	Midnight Cowboy	Mr. O'Daniel
1971	Lawman	Mayor Sam Bolden
1974	Mame	Mr. Babcock

STEPHEN MCHATTIE

(1947 -   )

McHattie's best known role was the critically-acclaimed lead in the 1976 TV-movie *James Dean: Portrait of a Friend*. Other actors looked more like Dean, but McHattie was chosen, according to director Robert Butler, because he "had the kind of smoldering, threatening quality that fit the part." The actor grew up in Wolfville, Nova Scotia, and made his Broadway debut in 1969 after drama studies in New York.

Year	Movie	Character
1971	Von Richthofen and Brown	Voss
1975	The Ultimate Warrior	Robert
1982	Death Valley	Hal
1986	Belizaire the Cajun	James Willoughby
1988	Call Me	Jelly Bean
1988	Caribe	Whitehale
1988	Sticky Fingers	Eddie

JOHN McINTIRE

(1907 - 1991)

McIntire is probably best remembered as wagonmaster Chris Hale on the extremely popular western TV series *Wagon Train*. He led the annual trek to California from St. Joseph, MO, from 1961 to 1965. The veteran character actor played in more than 100 films, including the part of the local sheriff in *Psycho*, plus countless roles on television and in radio. McIntire narrated the *March of Time* radio news show before World War II. He died of emphysema and cancer.

Year	Movie	Character
1960	Elmer Gantry	Rev. Pengilly
1960	Flaming Star	Pa Burton
1960	Psycho	Sheriff Chambers
1960	Who Was That Lady?	Bob Doyle
1961	Summer and Smoke	Dr. Buchanan
1961	Two Rode Together	Major Frazer
1967	Rough Night in Jericho	Ben Hickman
1974	Herbie Rides Again	Mr. Judson
1975	Rooster Cogburn	Judge Parker
1982	Honkytonk Man	Grandpa
1984	Cloak & Dagger	George MacCready
1989	Turner & Hooch	Amos Reed

TIM McINTIRE

(1943 - 1986)

A musician and composer as well as actor, McIntire was on stage in high school and worked in gas stations and men's stores to finance his theatrical career. The son of an actor, he made his film debut as James Stewart's son in *Shenandoah* and appeared four years later as Liza Minnelli's boyfriend's college roommate in *The Sterile Cuckoo*. He was co-author of several songs for the musical *Jeremiah Johnson*. McIntire died of heart failure at 42.

Year	Movie	Character
1965	Shenandoah	Henry
1969	The Sterile Cuckoo	Schumacher
1975	Aloha, Bobby and Rose	Buford
1976	The Gumball Rally	Smith
1977	The Choirboys	Roscoe Rules
1978	American Hot Wax	Alan Freed
1980	Brubaker	Huey Rauch
1982	Fast Walking	Wasco
1983	Sacred Ground	Matt

MICHAEL MCKEAN

(1947 -   )

McKean's career began as part of a zany trio, that included David L. Lander and Harry Shearer, on California radio in the early 1970s. One listener was Penny Marshall, of *Laverne and Shirley* fame, who liked the show so much that she brought McKean and Lander to *her* hit show as a pair of wonderful goofballs called Lenny and Squiggy. McKean spent seven seasons with the sitcom. Then, with former partner Shearer and others, he scripted (and co-starred in) a movie spoof of the rock 'n' roll world, *This is Spinal Tap*.

Year	Movie	Character
1980	Used Cars	Eddie
1982	Young Doctors in Love	Dr. Simon August
1984	This is Spinal Tap	David St. Hubbins
1985	Clue	Mr. Green
1985	D.A.R.Y.L.	Andy Richardson
1987	Light of Day	Bu Montgomery
1987	Planes, Trains & Automobiles	State Trooper
1988	Short Circuit 2	Fred Ritter
1989	Earth Girls Are Easy	Woody
1989	The Big Picture	Emmet Sumner
1990	Book of Love	Adult Jack Twiller
1990	Flashback	Hal
1991	Hider in the House	Phil Dryer
1991	True Identity	Harvey Cooper
1992	Man Trouble	Eddy Revere
1992	Memoirs of an Invisible Man	George Talbot
1993	Coneheads	Gorman Seedling

LONETTE MCKEE

(1954 -   )

The actress/singer was born in Detroit and has dazzled audiences on Broadway and in films. New York critics raved about McKee in the role of Billie Holiday in *Lady Day at Emerson's Bar and Grill*, a job so emotionally demanding she had to leave it for health reasons after six months.

Year	Movie	Character
1976	Sparkle	Sister
1977	Which Way is Up?	Vanetta
1979	Cuba	Therese
1984	The Cotton Club	Lila Rose Oliver
1985	Brewster's Millions	Angela Drake
1986	Round Midnight	Darcey Leigh
1987	Gardens of Stone	Betty Raie
1991	Jungle Fever	Drew
1992	Malcolm X	Louise Little

LEO MCKERN

(1920 -   )

An Australian who graduated from a technical school in Sydney, McKern has had a long and varied career in the theater. His many stage roles, including much of Shakespeare, led him to filmdom and television. He can be seen as an archaeologist in *The Omen* who advises Gregory Peck to kill his possessed son and as arch rival Professor Moriarty in *The Adventure of Sherlock Holmes' Smarter Brother.*

Year	Movie	Character
1965	Help!	Clang
1966	A Man for All Seasons	Thomas Cromwell
1968	The Shoes of the Fisherman	Cardinal Leone
1970	Ryan's Daughter	Tom Ryan
1975	The Adventure of Sherlock Holmes' Smarter Brother	Prof. Moriarty
1976	The Omen	Archaeologist
1977	Candleshoe	Bundage
1980	The Blue Lagoon	Paddy Button
1981	The French Lieutenant's Woman	Dr. Grogan
1985	Ladyhawke	Imperius

JOHN MCMARTIN

(19?? -   )

The fates have been friendly to McMartin since he left his hometown of Warsaw, IN, for New York. A versatile singer and actor, after many performances in summer stock, he got a big break to play Corporal Billy Jester in *Little Mary Sunshine* in 1959. On television McMartin has been on *Marcus Welby, M.D.* and *The Bob Newhart Show.* In Madonna's early film *Who's That Girl?*, he was Griffin Dunne's wealthy father-in-law-to-be.

Year	Movie	Character
1969	Sweet Charity	Oscar
1980	Brubaker	Senator Hite
1981	Pennies From Heaven	Mr. Warner
1986	Dream Lover	Martin
1986	Legal Eagles	Forrester
1986	Native Son	Mr. Dalton
1987	Who's That Girl?	Simon Worthington
1990	A Shock to the System	George Brewster

KENNETH McMILLAN

(1932 - 1989)

This Brooklyn native was a character actor who learned about his trade at the High School for the Performing Arts, with teachers Uta Hagen and Irene Dailey, and on the floor at Gimbels Department Store, where he was a manager. McMillan became prominent in middle age with a warm, humorous, tough guy image in films, TV and the New York stage. He died of liver disease.

Year	Movie	Character
1973	Serpico	xxx
1974	The Taking of Pelham One Two Three	Borough Commander
1978	Bloodbrothers	Banion
1978	Girlfriends	Cabbie
1978	Oliver's Story	James Francis
1979	Head Over Heels	Pete
1980	Borderline	Malcolm Wallace
1980	Carny	Heavy
1980	Hide in Plain Sight	Sam
1980	Little Miss Marker	Brannigan
1981	Eyewitness	Mr. Deever
1981	Heartbeeps	Max
1981	Ragtime	Willie Conklin

(continued on page 508)

BRIAN McNAMARA

(19?? -   )

McNamara may be best remembered for his role as the brash older brother in the 1991 teenagers' comedy, *Mystery Date*. In that one, he arranges a date for his shy kid brother with the pretty girl next door, a date which results in several near disasters. McNamara played an upper-class golfer in *Caddyshack II* and also had a part in *Arachnophobia*, which was all about the horrors of killer spiders which invade a small California town.

Year	Movie	Character
1986	Short Circuit	Frank
1988	Caddyshack II	Todd Young
1990	Arachnophobia	Chris Collins
1991	Mystery Date	Craig McHugh

FRANK MCRAE

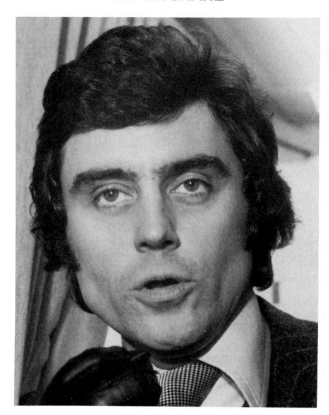

(1942 -   )

McRae got his start in pictures by the unorthodox method of standing in a production executive's parking place until he was granted a meeting. It got him a spot in *Dillinger*. The Memphis, TN, native became interested in acting after seeing his first motion picture and began taking drama classes as a teenager. He was a star athlete in high school and graduated from Tennessee State with a double major in history and drama. On television McRae has been in *Hill Street Blues* and *Trapper John, M.D.*

Year	Movie	Character
1973	Dillinger	Reed
1978	Paradise Alley	Big Glory
1980	Used Cars	Jim
1982	48 Hours	Haden
1982	Cannery Row	Hazel
1987	*batteries not included	Harry
1989	Farewell to the King	Tenga
1989	Licence to Kill	Sharkey
1989	Lock Up	Eclipse
1993	Last Action Hero	Deckker

IAN MCSHANE

(1942 -   )

The English actor abandoned a childhood desire to be a soccer player to appear on the stage at 16 and has been acting ever since. McShane played a British tour guide in *If It's Tuesday, This Must Be Belgium* more interested in his various girlfriends around Europe than his charges. In *The Last of Sheila* he was movie star Raquel Welch's manager-husband and one of six Hollywood guests invited for a cruise on the Riviera aboard the "Sheila." The son of a professional soccer player, he trained at RADA and was soon acting on the London stage.

Year	Movie	Character
1969	If It's Tuesday, This Must Be Belgium	Charlie
1973	The Last of Sheila	Antony
1983	Exposed	Greg
1984	Ordeal by Innocence	Philip
1984	Torchlight	Sidney
1985	Too Scared to Scream	Hardwick

KAY MEDFORD

(1920 - 1980)

A New Yorker, Medford was a bright light in many films as a wise-cracking comedienne. A fine character actress, Medford made her film debut in 1941 and her Broadway debut ten years later. She may be best-remembered for her portrayal of Barbra Streisand's mother in *Funny Girl*. She died after a brief illness.

Year	Movie	Character
1960	Butterfield 8	Happy
1960	The Rat Race	Soda
1964	Ensign Pulver	Head Nurse
1966	A Fine Madness	Mrs. Fish
1967	The Busy Body	Ma Norton
1968	Funny Girl	Rose Brice
1969	Angel in My Pocket	Racine

RALPH MEEKER

(1920 - 1988)

One of America's senior actors, Meeker first arrived in New York to attack Broadway with total assets of $35 in his pocket. He became a soda jerk in a drugstore that was near the Roxy Theater and later got roles in top shows including *Mister Roberts* and *Streetcar Named Desire* before moving on to Hollywood. His movie roles include a cop on the take in Frank Sinatra's *The Detective*. He died of a heart attack in Woodland Hills, CA.

Year	Movie	Character
1961	Ada	Colonel Yancey
1967	The Dirty Dozen	Capt. Stuart Kinder
1967	The St. Valentine's Day Massacre	Bugs Moran
1968	The Detective	Curran
1971	The Anderson Tapes	Delaney
1975	Brannigan	Captain Moretti
1979	Winter Kills	Baker

LEE MERIWETHER

(1935 -   )

Meriwether was in college in San Francisco when a local fraternity entered her in a beauty contest. She won, and kept on winning until she became Miss America of 1955. That led to a television debut on *Philco Playhouse* and many other film and television roles. The girl who wanted an acting career at the age of nine appeared on the *Today* show for 14 months and enjoyed a long run on television's *Barnaby Jones* in the early seventies.

Year	Movie	Character
1966	Batman	Catwoman/Kitka
1966	Namu, the Killer Whale	Kate Rand
1969	Angel in My Pocket	Mary Elizabeth
1969	The Undefeated	Margaret

DINA MERRILL

(1925 -   )

Merrill was born to riches as the daughter of E.F. Hutton and Marjorie Merriweather Post, and at the age of 6 announced she would become an actress. The big film debut came in 1957 with Spencer Tracy and Katharine Hepburn in *The Desk Set*. Sometimes described by writers as "icily beautiful," she married actor Cliff Robertson, with whom she sometimes acted. Merrill has been deeply involved in New York charity work.

Year	Movie	Character
1960	Butterfield 8	Emily Liggett
1960	The Sundowners	Jean Halstead
1961	The Young Savages	Karin Bell
1963	The Courtship of Eddie's Father	Rita Behrens
1965	I'll Take Sweden	Karin Grandstedt
1973	Running Wild	xxx
1980	Just Tell Me What You Want	Connie Herschel
1988	Caddyshack II	Cynthia Young
1991	True Colors	Joan Stiles
1992	The Player	Celia
1992	Twisted	xxx

GARY MERRILL

LAURIE METCALF

(1915 - 1990)

Sometimes tough guy character actor, other times charmer, the Hartford, CT, man performed for over 30 years on stage, screen and television. In 1950, Merrill married his co-star in *All About Eve* Bette Davis and they divorced in 1960. A Bowdoin and Trinity College student, Merrill joined the Army Air Force Special Services in 1941. He died of cancer.

(1955 -   )

Fellow actor John Mahoney once said, "Offstage [Metcalf] is really a very private, very reserved person. Onstage, she will do anything; she becomes a complete maniac." The actress has confirmed his observation. "I'm hideously shy as myself," she once said, "but onstage I can run around naked and bite the heads off fish." Metcalf spent eight years with Chicago's Steppenwolf Theater and has played Roseanne Barr's sister on the popular TV series *Roseanne*, since 1988.

Year	Movie	Character
1961	The Great Imposter	Pa Demara
1961	The Pleasure of His Company	James Dougherty
1962	A Girl Named Tamiko	Max Wilson
1966	Around the World, Under the Sea	Dr. August Boren
1966	Ride Beyond Vengeance	Dub Stokes
1967	Clambake	Sam Burton
1967	The Incident	Douglas McCann
1968	The Power	Mark Corlane
1974	Huckleberry Finn	Pap

Year	Movie	Character
1985	Desperately Seeking Susan	Leslie
1987	Making Mr. Right	Sandy
1988	Miles From Home	Exotic Dancer
1988	Stars and Bars	Melissa
1989	Uncle Buck	Marcie Dahlgren-Frost
1990	Internal Affairs	Amy Wallace
1990	Pacific Heights	Stephanie MacDonald
1991	JFK	Susie Cox
1993	A Dangerous Woman	Anita

JIM METZLER

(1951 -   )

Metzler might have spent his working life on the baseball mound instead of on the film sets. A promising pitcher at Dartmouth, he was drafted by the Boston Red Sox after college. He was soon dropped from Sox farm clubs, but decided he liked performing and turned to theatrical school.

Year	Movie	Character
1981	Four Friends	Tom Donaldson
1982	Tex	Mason McCormick
1986	River's Edge	Burkewaite
1988	976-Evil	Marty
1988	Hot to Trot	Boyd Osborne
1989	Old Gringo	Ron
1990	Circuitry Man	Danner
1990	Delusion	George O'Brien

SYLVIA MILES

(1932 -   )

If Miles were not famous for some big movie roles, she would be for the decolletage she usually displays in the numerous photos taken of her at New York parties and events. She hates being called a sex bomb, although she made her name in raunchy roles. She is proud of her serious stage roles (she has appeared in Tennessee Williams' *Night of the Iguana*). Miles got Oscar nominations for *Midnight Cowboy* and *Farewell, My Lovely*.

Year	Movie	Character
1961	Parrish	Eileen
1969	Midnight Cowboy	Cass
1975	92 in the Shade	Bella
1975	Farewell My Lovely	Mrs. Florian
1976	Great Scout and Cathouse Thursday	Mike
1977	The Sentinel	Gerde
1981	The Funhouse	Mme. Zena
1982	Evil Under the Sun	Myra Gardner
1987	Critical Condition	Maggie
1987	Wall Street	Realtor
1988	Crossing Delancy	Hannah Mandelbaum
1989	She-Devil	Mrs. Fisher

VERA MILES

(1929 -   )

In films from 1950, Miles' career was assured in 1955 when she was personally signed to a contract by Alfred Hitchcock. That event was followed by a streak of television dramas, and Hitchcock is often credited with developing her talent. The actress starred in several Walt Disney pictures in the 1960s and early 1970s. She played shower-girl Janet Leigh's sister in *Psycho*, starting the investigation into her disappearance and picked up the role 23 years later in *Psycho II*, protesting Tony Perkins' release from the mental institution.

Year	Movie	Character
1960	Five Branded Women	Daniza
1960	Psycho	Lila Crane
1961	Back Street	Liz Saxon
1962	The Man Who Shot Liberty Valance	Hallie
1964	A Tiger Walks	Dorothy Williams
1968	Sergeant Ryker	Ann Ryker
1969	Hellfighters	Madelyn Buckman
1971	The Wild Country	Kate
1977	Twilight's Last Gleaming	Victoria Stevens
1983	Psycho II	Lila
1985	Into the Night	Joan Caper

BARRY MILLER

(1958 -   )

A Hollywood boy who grew up in a theatrical family, Miller caught the screen world's attention when, at 18, he appeared as one of John Travolta's neighborhood buddies in *Saturday Night Fever*. Because he is choosy about the roles he takes, he's sometimes thought by directors to be "difficult." But that has not prevented him from winning acclaim on stage and screen. He played the school's "four-eyed worm" in *Peggy Sue Got Married* who shows up at the class reunion as a successful businessman.

Year	Movie	Character
1977	Saturday Night Fever	Bobby C
1979	Voices	Raymond Rothman
1980	Fame	Ralph
1982	The Chosen	Reuven Malter
1985	The Journey of Natty Gann	Parker
1986	Peggy Sue Got Married	Richard Norvik
1987	The Sicilian	Dr. Nattore
1990	Love at Large	Marty
1993	The Pickle	Ronnie Liebowitz

JASON MILLER

(1939 -   )

It was an unusual day for an actor. Miller was on the set making the movie *The Exorcist* in 1973 when he was called to the phone. He learned that a play he wrote, *That Championship Season*, had just won the Pulitzer Prize for drama. *The Exorcist* brought him considerable recognition as the young priest who was first called on to exorcise Linda Blair. Miller studied acting at Catholic University and while struggling to get a foothold in theater, took odd jobs, got unemployment insurance, and lived on next to nothing.

Year	Movie	Character
1973	The Exorcist	Father Karras
1980	The Ninth Configuration	Lt. Reno
1982	Monsignor	Appolini
1984	Toy Soldiers	Sarge
1987	Light of Day	Benjamin Rasnick
1990	The Exorcist III	Patient X
1993	Rudy	Ara Parseghian

PENELOPE ANN MILLER

(1964 -   )

Miller moved from her hometown of L.A. to New York to become an actress, after a brief spell in college, and was soon cast in Neil Simon's immensely successful *Biloxi Blues*. She has since acted in plays, TV shows and films, and has learned to adjust her style to fit the medium. She once said: "On the stage you have everything—your body, and the proscenium and the scenery, and two balconies. In a film, if they punch into a closeup, it makes your face 40' by 40', and you cannot be as expressive, or you will frighten many people."

Year	Movie	Character
1987	Adventures in Babysitting	Brenda
1988	Big Top Pee-wee	Winnie
1988	Biloxi Blues	Daisy Hannigan
1988	Miles From Home	Sally
1989	Dead-Bang	Linda
1990	Awakenings	Paula
1990	Downtown	Lori Mitchell
1990	Kindergarten Cop	Joyce Paulmarie
1990	The Freshman	Tina Sabatini
1991	Other People's Money	Kate Sullivan
1992	Chaplin	Edna Purviance
1992	Gun in Betty Lou's Handbag	Betty Lou
1992	Year of the Comet	Margaret Harwood
1993	Carlito's Way	Gail

JOHN MILLS

(1908 -   )

Mills was one of England's top box-office stars during the forties and fifties. He began in films with light comedies and musicals in the 1930s and came into his own during World War II when he was often called upon to show a stiff upper lip. He became a character actor in his later years. Mills' career is virtually a family institution. Both of his daughters—Hayley and Juliet—have been actresses, and his wife, Mary Hayley-Bell, has been a playwright. Mills has also worked behind the camera as a director and producer.

Year	Movie	Character
1960	Swiss Family Robinson	Father
1964	Chalk Garden	Maitland
1965	King Rat	Col. Smedley Taylor
1965	Operation Crossbow	Boyd of M.I.6
1970	Adam's Woman	Sir Philip
1970	Ryan's Daughter	Michael
1972	Young Winston	Gen. Kitchener
1973	Oklahoma Crude	Cleon
1978	The Big Sleep	Inspector Carson
1982	Gandhi	The Viceroy
1984	Sahara	Cambridge
1987	Who's That Girl?	Montgomery Bell

SAL MINEO

(1939 - 1976)

In films and on television the young actor was usually a rebel with or without a cause, a kid from the wrong neighborhood who in real life was murdered in a Hollywood alley. Two years after his stabbing death, his killer was caught. Born in the Bronx, Mineo was a troublemaker. Expelled from Catholic school at 8, he went to dancing class and by 10 he was in a Broadway play where Hollywood discovered him.

Year	Movie	Character
1960	Exodus	Dov Landau
1962	Escape from Zahrain	Ahmed
1962	The Longest Day	Pvt. Martini
1964	Cheyenne Autumn	Red Shirt
1965	The Greatest Story Ever Told	Uriah
1969	Krakatoa—East of Java	Leoncavallo
1971	Escape from the Planet of the Apes	Milo

HELEN MIRREN

(1946 -   )

Mirren is known in her native England for bouncing back and forth between Shakespearean and sexy-blonde roles. "I've hurtled from one extreme to another—very deliberately," she has said. But it was her part as a Chief of Detectives in PBS' *Prime Suspect*, one of the highest rated PBS series ever, that got America's attention. It was a heady experience for her. "An actress very rarely has to stand up in front of a room full of men and sound off," she explained. "It's very nerve-racking."

Year	Movie	Character
1980	The Fiendish Plot of Dr. Fu Manchu	Alice Rage
1981	Excalibur	Morgana
1984	2010	Tanya Kirbuk
1985	White Nights	Galina Ivanova
1986	The Mosquito Coast	Mother

MATTHEW MODINE

(1959 -   )

Modine grew up on a farm in Utah and watched a lot of movies as a kid as his father managed drive-ins in various western states. Arriving in Hollywood in the early 1980s, he has recalled: "There weren't a lot of jobs available for actors my age at that time that weren't some kind of exploitation or just silly, like *St. Elmo's Fire* or something. I was really lucky, I got the cream: *Mrs. Soffel* and *Birdy*." He also won a best actor award for his part in Robert Altman's *Streamers* (1983) at the Venice Film Festval.

Year	Movie	Character
1983	Baby, It's You	Steve
1983	Private School	Jim
1984	Birdy	Birdy
1984	Hotel New Hampshire	Chip Dove
1984	Mrs. Soffel	Jack Biddle
1985	Vision Quest	Louden Swain
1987	Full Metal Jacket	Pvt. Joker
1987	Orphans	Treat
1988	Married to the Mob	Mike Downey
1989	Gross Anatomy	Joe Slovak
1990	Pacific Heights	Drake Goodman
1990	Memphis Belle	Dennis Dearborn
1992	Wind	Will Parker
1993	Short Cuts	Dr. Ralph Wyman

DONALD MOFFAT

(1930 -)

Moffat was born in Plymouth, England, the point of departure for the Pilgrims, and started his career as a member of London's Old Vic in the early 1950s. Like the Pilgrims, he too immigrated to the U.S. He came with his American wife, whom he met while a student at RADA, in 1956, and appeared in more than twenty Shakespearean plays in those early years. Mostly on the stage until the 1970s, he is the only actor ever nominated for two best actor Tonys in the same year, which for him was 1967.

Year	Movie	Character
1968	Rachel, Rachel	Niall Cameron
1973	Showdown	Art
1974	Earthquake	Dr. Harvey Johnson
1974	The Terminal Man	Dr. Arthur McPherson
1979	Health	xxx
1979	Promises in the Dark	Dr. Walter McInerny
1979	Winter Kills	Captain
1982	The Thing	Garry
1983	The Right Stuff	Lyndon B. Johnson
1985	Alamo Bay	Wally
1986	The Best of Times	The Colonel
1988	Far North	Uncle Dane
1988	The Unbearable Lightness of Being	Chief Surgeon
1989	Music Box	Harry Talbot
1990	The Bonfire of the Vanities	Mr. McCoy
1991	Class Action	Quinn
1991	Regarding Henry	Charlie
1992	HouseSitter	George Davis

DAN MONAHAN

(1955 -)

Monahan has admitted to being a clown and a smart-aleck back in high school in Cleveland. Maybe his talent for showing off had something to do with his acting career. He was chosen from among dozens of other candidates to play the role of Pee Wee in *Porky's*. He wants to be a director some day.

Year	Movie	Character
1981	Porky's	Pee Wee
1983	Porky's II: The Next Day	Pee Wee
1984	Up the Creek	Max
1985	Porky's Revenge	Pee Wee
1987	From the Hip	Larry

BELINDA J. MONTGOMERY

(1950 -   )

Born in Winnipeg, Canada, Montgomery began her acting career early in life as a child actress on Canadian television, radio and the stage. She has had repeated successes in TV and film, both in Canada and the U.S. Television audiences have seen her in *Dynasty*, *Miami Vice* and *Murder, She Wrote*.

Year	Movie	Character
1971	The Todd Killings	Roberta
1975	The Other Side of the Mountain	Audra-Jo
1976	Breaking Point	Diana McBain
1978	The Other Side of the Mountain Part 2	Audra-Jo
1980	Stone Cold Dead	Sandy MacAuley

LEE MONTGOMERY

(1961 -   )

Montgomery comes from a family of actors in Canada. At age 11, he starred in *Ben*, the 1972 sequel to *Willard*, as a disturbed youth who befriends Ben the rat and directs him and his army of rats on a killing spree. Montgomery's television credits include *Kojak*, *The Streets of San Francisco* and *Mod Squad*.

Year	Movie	Character
1972	Pete 'n' Tillie	Robbie
1976	Baker's Hawk	Billy
1976	Burnt Offerings	David
1985	Girls Just Want to Have Fun	Jeff Malene
1987	Into the Fire	Wade Burnett

JEANNE MOREAU

(1928 -   )

In about 40 years of film acting, Moreau has appeared in some 85 productions and worked with such famed directors as Luis Bunuel and Orson Welles. She is not an introspective artist, but is known for her attention to details. Born and educated in Paris, her career began on the stage. Her performance in Louis Malle's 1958 *Les Amants* shocked movie audiences with its sexual intensity and helped to launch the New Wave movement in French Cinema.

Year	Movie	Character
1960	Five Branded Women	Ljuba
1963	The Victors	French Woman
1965	The Train	Christine
1965	The Yellow Rolls-Royce	Marchioness of Frinton
1970	Monte Walsh	Martine Bernard
1976	The Last Tycoon	Didi
1991	Until the End of the World	Edith Farber
1993	Map of the Human Heart	Sister Banville

CATHY MORIARTY

(1960 -   )

Moriarty was born in the New York borough of the Bronx, attended Lincoln High School in Yonkers and worked in many odd jobs—waitress, receptionist and telephone sales—while waiting for theatrical success. That came emphatically when she received an Oscar nomination as Robert De Niro's wife in *Raging Bull* in 1980. The following year she played Dan Aykroyd's sexy wife in *Neighbors* and the couple did their best to drive neighbor John Belushi crazy.

Year	Movie	Character
1980	Raging Bull	Vickie LaMotta
1981	Neighbors	Ramona
1990	Kindergarten Cop	Sylvester's Mother
1991	Soapdish	Montana
1992	The Mambo Kings	Lanna Lake
1993	Another Stakeout	Lu Delano
1993	Matinee	Ruth Corday
1993	Me and the Kid	Rose

MICHAEL MORIARTY

(1941 -   )

An actor and playwright, Moriarty was born in Detroit, attended Dartmouth, and trained for the stage at the London Academy of Music and Dramatic Art. He won a Tony and two other awards for his role in the 1974 play *Find Your Way Home*. He may be best remembered as the gold miner who invites gunslinger Clint Eastwood into his home in *Pale Rider*.

Year	Movie	Character
1972	Hickey & Boggs	Ballard
1973	Bang the Drum Slowly	Henry Wiggen
1973	The Last Detail	Marine O.D.
1975	Report to the Commissioner	Beauregard "Bo" Lockley
1978	Who'll Stop the Rain	John
1985	Pale Rider	Hull Barret
1986	Troll	Mr. Potter
1987	A Return to Salem's Lot	Joe Weber
1987	It's Alive III: Island of the Alive	Stephen Jarvis
1987	The Hanoi Hilton	Williamson

ANITA MORRIS

(1932 -   )

Morris achieved instant celebrity when she appeared in a see-through lace body-stocking in the Broadway musical *Nine*. She's had her share of steamy roles, mostly in Broadway musicals, but has also done movies. She played opposite George Burns in *18 Again* and got constantly sick to her stomach from inhaling his cigar smoke. Morris was Danny De Vito's mistress in the comedy hit *Ruthless People*. She is from Durham, N.C.

Year	Movie	Character
1984	Hotel New Hampshire	Ronda
1986	Blue City	Malvina Kerch
1986	Ruthless People	Carol
1986	Absolute Beginners	Dido Lament
1988	18 Again!	Madelyn
1989	Bloodhounds of Broadway	Miss Missouri Martin
1990	Martians Go Home	Dr. Jane Buchanan
1993	Me and the Kid	Mrs. Feldman

HOWARD MORRIS

(1919 -   )

Morris was a television comic before coming to the movies, where he has played supporting roles in comedies for three decades. He was a regular on Sid Caesar and Imogene Coca's famous *Your Show of Shows* (1950-54) and on its succesor comedy/variety show *Caesar's Hour* (1954-57). Perhaps his most memorable film performance was in a 1962 comedy of sexual mores in suburbia called *Boys' Night Out*. In that one, *Variety* said, Morris and Tony Randall walked off with "comedy honors."

Year	Movie	Character
1962	Boys' Night Out	Howard McIllenny
1963	Forty Pounds of Trouble	Julius
1963	The Nutty Professor	Father Kelp
1965	Fluffy	Sweeny
1966	Way ... Way Out	Schmidlap
1977	High Anxiety	Professor Lilloman
1984	Splash	Dr. Zidell
1987	End of the Line	Hobo
1991	Life Stinks	Sailor

ROBERT MORSE

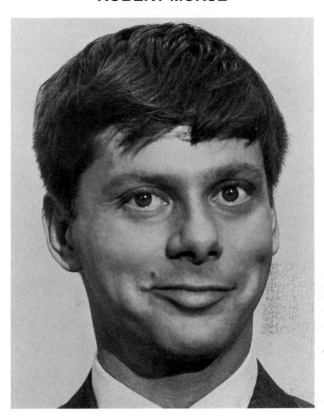

(1931 -   )

Typed as a musical-comedy performer, Morse hit his apex in the 1960s in the Broadway and film versions of *How to Succeed in Business Without Really Trying*. He made only a handful of films during that decade and once commented, "I never got an opportunity to be in the type of picture where I would be a father and have a family, where I really had to come home tired, where I could feel or show something. They were sort of superficial—except for *The Loved One*."

Year	Movie	Character
1963	The Cardinal	Bobby
1965	The Loved One	Dennis Barlow
1967	A Guide for the Married Man	Ed
1967	How to Succeed in Business Without Really Trying	J. Pierpont Finch
1968	Where Were You When the Lights Went Out?	Waldo Zane
1987	Hunk	Garrison Gaylord

JOE MORTON

(1947 -   )

Although primarily visible in films in recent years, Morton has been active on stage and in television since the late 1960s. His Broadway debut came in *Hair* and he played Hal Marshall in NBC's *Grady* during the 1975-76 season. Morton was born in New York City and studied drama at Hofstra University on Long Island. He played the ill-fated scientist in Arnold Schwarzenegger's *Terminator 2*.

Year	Movie	Character
1979	...And Justice For All	Prison Doctor
1984	The Brother from Another Planet	The Brother
1986	Crossroads	Scratch's Assistant
1987	Stranded	Sheriff McMahon
1988	The Good Mother	Frank Williams
1988	Zelly and Me	Earl
1989	Tap	Nicky
1991	City of Hope	Wynn
1991	Terminator 2: Judgment Day	Miles Dyson
1992	Forever Young	Cameron
1992	Of Mice and Men	Crooks

ROGER E. MOSLEY

(1943 -   )

Mosley is a local boy who made good. He was born and grew up in Watts, the section of L.A. where the riots erupted in the 1960s. He remembered his past by founding the Watts Repertory Theater. One of his biggest pictures was *Leadbelly*, the film biography of folk-blues composer Huddie Ledbetter.

Year	Movie	Character
1972	Hit Man	Baby Huey
1972	The New Centurions	Truck Driver
1973	The Mack	Olinga
1976	Leadbelly	Huddie Ledbetter
1976	Stay Hungry	Newton
1977	Semi-Tough	Puddin
1980	Steel	Lionel
1990	Heart Condition	Capt. Wendt
1992	Unlawful Entry	Officer Roy Cole

JOSH MOSTEL

(1946 -   )

Josh, the son of zany comic star Zero Mostel, has made his own mark in stage and screen comedy. He made his debut at 6 in a television version of *Hansel and Gretel*, and his proud father called it one of the greatest performances of the century.

Year	Movie	Character
1974	Harry and Tonto	Norman
1982	Sophie's Choice	Morris Fink
1983	Star 80	Private Detective
1984	Almost You	David
1984	Windy City	Sol
1985	Compromising Positions	Dicky Dunck
1986	The Money Pit	Jack Schnittman
1987	Matewan	Cabell
1987	Radio Days	Abe
1987	Wall Street	Ollie
1989	Animal Behavior	Mel Gorsky
1991	City Slickers	Barry Shalowitz
1991	City of Hope	Mad Anthony
1991	Little Man Tate	Physics Professor

ARMIN MUELLER-STAHL

(1930 -   )

Mueller-Stahl was a prominent actor in Germany for 25 years appearing there in more than 60 films. He was born in Tilsit, which was in East Germany after World War II, and he had frequent encounters with the old communist government there. He was once banned from filmmaking for three years for signing a manifesto the government did not like. He studied violin at Berlin Conservatory and was a concert violinist before becoming an actor.

Year	Movie	Character
1989	Music Box	Mike Laszlo
1990	Avalon	Sam Krichinsky
1991	Kafka	Inspector Grubach
1992	The Power of One	Doc
1993	Utz	Baron von Utz

RICHARD MULLIGAN

(1932 -   )

Mulligan is a familar face on television, having spent four seasons as a blue-collar type on *Soap* and five seasons (to date) as a pediatrician on *Empty Nest*. He has won Emmys for both sitcoms. His comedic talents have been put to good use in the movies as well and, since the mid-1970s, has appeared solely in comedies.

Year	Movie	Character
1966	The Group	Dick Brown
1969	The Undefeated	Dan Morse
1970	Little Big Man	Gen. George A. Custer
1976	The Big Bus	Claude Crane
1979	Scavenger Hunt	Marvin
1981	S.O.B.	Felix Farmer
1982	Trail of the Pink Panther	Clouseau Senior
1984	Meatballs II	Giddy
1984	Micki + Maude	Leo Brody
1984	Teachers	Herbert
1985	Doin' Time	Mongo
1985	The Heavenly Kid	Rafferty
1986	A Fine Mess	Wayne "Turnip" Farragalla

MICHAEL MURPHY

(1938 -   )

Although Murphy went to Hollywood with stars in his eyes he had the good fortune to link up with the director Robert Altman who inspired him to take acting seriously. He prefers to think of himself as a character actor. "I don't think of acting in terms of making a living," he once said. "What I do has to be important to me. Every time I've taken a part for the wrong reason, money or prestige, its been a disaster. I come off nervous and uptight. I just want to work with good people."

Year	Movie	Character
1967	Double Trouble	Morley
1968	Countdown	Rick
1970	Count Yorga, Vampire	Paul
1971	McCabe and Mrs. Miller	Sears
1972	What's Up, Doc?	Smith
1973	The Thief Who Came to Dinner	Ted
1975	Nashville	John Triplette
1976	The Front	Alfred Miller
1978	An Unmarried Woman	Martin
1979	Manhattan	Yale
1983	The Year of Living Dangerously	Pete Curtis
1984	Cloak & Dagger	Rice
1986	Mesmerized	Rev. Wilson
1986	Salvador	Amb. Thomas Kelly
1989	Shocker	Lt. Don Parker
1992	Batman Returns	Mayor of Gotham City
1992	Folks!	Ed

ROSEMARY MURPHY

(1925 -)

Murphy is the daughter of a U.S. diplomat who was born in Munich, Germany, and raised in Paris, France. She moved to the U.S. at the start of World War II to attend school and got her acting start in summer stock in Olney, MD, at that time. She has taken mostly supporting roles in movies and is perhaps better known for her work on the stage. She made her Broadway debut in 1957 in *Look Homeward, Angel*.

Year	Movie	Character
1961	The Young Doctors	Miss Graves
1962	To Kill a Mockingbird	Miss Maudie Atkinson
1966	Any Wednesday	Dorothy Cleves
1972	You'll Like My Mother	Mrs. Kinsolving
1973	Forty Carats	Mrs. Latham
1973	Walking Tall	Callie Hacker
1977	Julia	Dorothy Parker
1981	The Hand	Karen Wagner
1991	For the Boys	Luanna Trott

DON MURRAY

(1929 -)

Murray broke into movies in 1956 when he appeared in *Bus Stop* with Marilyn Monroe, but audiences today remember him as Sid Fairgate, the local classic car dealer, in the television serial *Knots Landing*. He has written six screenplays, including *The Hoodlum Priest*, in which he starred as the Jesuit priest in St. Louis known for his rehabilitation work with ex-cons. In *Conquest of the Planet of the Apes*, where the apes were man's slaves, Murray played their overseer.

Year	Movie	Character
1961	The Hoodlum Priest	Rev. Charles Dismas Clark
1962	Advise and Consent	Senator Anderson
1972	Conquest of the Planet of the Apes	Breck
1981	Endless Love	Hugh
1986	Peggy Sue Got Married	Jack Kelcher
1986	Radioactive Dreams	Dash Hammer
1987	Made in Heaven	Ben Chandler

TONY MUSANTE

ORNELLA MUTI

(1936 -   )

Musante has made a mini-career out of playing some not-very-nice people in film and television, ranging from mafioso to Lt. Calley of the My Lai massacre in Vietnam. He's also played the part of a Newark policeman in television's *Toma*. His film debut was in *The Incident*, in which he created the role of a terrorist, Joe Ferrone. He won a best-actor award for the role at the Mar del Plata Film Festival.

(1955 -   )

A voluptuous Italian actress, Muti had made 24 films in Europe by the age of 24. She was then discovered by Warren Beatty in a London studio where she was filming *Flash Gordon*, her first English-language film. She got her start when, at the age of 14, she accompanied her sisters to an audition and was astounded when she was selected instead of the sisters.

Year	Movie	Character
1967	The Incident	Joe Ferrone
1968	The Detective	Felix
1968	The Mercenary	Eufemio
1971	The Last Run	Paul Ricard
1984	The Pope of Greenwich Village	Pete

Year	Movie	Character
1980	Flash Gordon	Princess Aura
1982	Love and Money	Catherine Stockheinz
1989	Wait Until Spring, Bandini	Maria Bandini
1991	Oscar	Sofia Provolone
1992	Once Upon a Crime	Elena Morosco

CHARLES NAPIER

(1935 -   )

In addition to his numerous film appearances, Napier has been active on television. He portrayed Luther Sprague in *The Oregon Trail* in 1977, Major Harrison in the mini-series titled *The Blue and the Gray* in 1982 and Captain Striker in ABC's 1984 entry *The Outlaws*. One of Napier's most memorable film roles was that of a villainous U.S. Government official in *Rambo: First Blood Part II*.

Year	Movie	Character
1970	Beyond the Valley of the Dolls	Baxter Wolfe
1979	Last Embrace	Dave Quittle
1980	Melvin and Howard	Ventura
1980	The Blues Brothers	Tucker McElroy
1984	Swing Shift	Moon Willens
1985	Rambo: First Blood Part II	Murdock
1986	Something Wild	Irate Chef
1988	Married to the Mob	xxx
1989	Hit List	Tom Mitchum
1989	One Man Force	Dante
1990	Ernest Goes to Jail	Warden
1990	Miami Blues	Sgt. Bill Henderson
1990	The Grifters	Hebbing
1991	The Silence of the Lambs	Lt. Boyle

MILDRED NATWICK

(1908 -   )

This veteran character actress is known primarily for her work on the stage and has a history of being cast there as old ladies. Natwick is from Baltimore and made her Broadway debut in 1932 in *Carrie Nation*. She was Oscar-nominated for her role as Jane Fonda's mother in *Barefoot in the Park*.

Year	Movie	Character
1967	Barefoot in the Park	Mrs. Ethel Banks
1969	If It's Tuesday, This Must Be Belgium	Jenny Grant
1975	At Long Last Love	Mabel Pritchard
1982	Kiss Me Goodbye	Mrs. Reilly
1988	Dangerous Liaisons	Madame de Rosemonde

DAVID NAUGHTON

(1951 -   )

Naughton was the lead in *An American Werewolf in London*, a story about two American friends who, while bumming around Europe, are attacked by a wild animal outside a British pub. He later turns into a werewolf. A singer as well as an actor, Naughton recorded an album called *Makin' It* that reached #5 on Billboard's charts and was certified as a gold record in 1979. Born in Hartford, CT, he graduated from the University of Pennsylvania, and studied at the London Academy of Music and Dramatic Arts.

Year	Movie	Character
1980	Midnight Madness	Adam
1981	An American Werewolf in London	David
1984	Hot Dog...The Movie	Dan
1986	Separate Vacations	Richard Moore
1990	Steel & Lace	Det. Dunn

JAMES NAUGHTON

(1945 -   )

Naughton grew up in Hartford, CT, where he was blessed with what he recalls as a "very American" childhood, full of fun and sports. His parents were teachers. Naughton went to Brown University where he played baseball and contemplated a professional sports career until he decided on acting. He also sings but has decided that it's better to be "an actor who sings rather than a singer who acts." He is the brother of the actor David Naughton.

Year	Movie	Character
1973	The Paper Chase	Kevin
1982	A Stranger is Watching	Steve
1985	Cat's Eye	Hugh
1987	The Glass Menagerie	Gentleman Caller
1988	The Good Mother	Brian

LIAM NEESON

(1952 -   )

The Irish actor was discovered while working at Dublin's legendary Abby Theatre by director John Boorman and cast in his 1981 medieval adventure *Excalibur*. Neeson feels: "a big percentage of film acting is craft, knowing what the camera can do and knowing how to operate within that. All the other emotional stuff is the same as it is for stage, but for the camera it's a minimum amount for a maximum effect." The actor won acclaim for his role as the deaf, homeless, Vietnam veteran in *Suspect*.

Year	Movie	Character
1981	Excalibur	Gawain
1983	Krull	Kegan
1984	The Bounty	Churchill
1986	The Mission	Fielding
1987	Suspect	Carl Wayne Anderson
1988	High Spirits	Martin Brogan
1988	Satisfaction	Martin Falcon
1988	The Dead Pool	Peter Swan
1988	The Good Mother	Leo
1989	Next of Kin	Briar Gates
1990	Darkman	Peyton Westlake/ Darkman
1992	Husbands and Wives	Michael
1992	Leap of Faith	Will
1992	Shining Through	Franze-Otto Dietrich
1993	Ethan Frome	Ethan Frome
1993	Deception	Fergus Lamb

SAM NEILL

(1948 -   )

Neill put himself on the movie map in 1979 with his role in the popular Australian film *My Brilliant Career*. The New Zealander initially worked as a documentary filmmaker for the New Zealand Film Commission before turning to acting as there were few films being made in New Zealand. The actor claims he is best known for playing what he calls "men with cold blue eyes that can drill holes through steel at one hundred paces."

Year	Movie	Character
1979	My Brilliant Career	Harry Beecham
1981	The Final Conflict	Damien
1985	Plenty	Lazar
1988	A Cry in the Dark	Michael
1989	Dead Calm	John Ingram
1990	The Hunt for Red October	Captain Borodin
1991	Until the End of the World	Eugene Fitzpatrick
1992	Memoirs of an Invisible Man	David Jenkins
1993	Jurassic Park	Grant

KATE NELLIGAN

(1951 -   )

Nelligan left her home in Ontario, Canada, at age 15 to take a scholarship at the University of Toronto, with some idea of pursuing an academic career. But she was offered a role in *Hamlet* in a university production and was hooked. She was soon in London studying drama. One of her biggest roles was in 1981's *The Eye of the Needle*. She played the wife of a bitter paraplegic who becomes German spy Donald Sutherland's lover on a barren island during World War II.

Year	Movie	Character
1979	Dracula	Lucy
1981	Eye of the Needle	Lucy
1983	Without a Trace	Susan Selky
1985	Eleni	Eleni
1991	Frankie and Johnny	Cora
1991	The Prince of Tides	Lilia Wingo Newbury
1992	Shadows and Fog	Eve
1993	Fatal Instinct	Lana Ravine

JUDD NELSON

(1959 -   )

Nelson decided to become an actor with one year to go as a philosophy major at Haverford/Bryn Mawr College in Pennsylvania. "I chose the study of philosophy because it's very abstract," he once explained. "It doesn't instruct you as to what to do. It's more about what you know. To me, acting can be used in much the same way. I began to see a connection." So he left school and spent the next 27 months studying drama at the Stella Adler Conservatory in New York before packing for Hollywood.

Year	Movie	Character
1984	Making the Grade	Eddie
1985	The Breakfast Club	John Bender
1985	St. Elmo's Fire	Alec
1985	Fandango	Phil Hicks
1986	Blue City	Billy Turner
1987	From the Hip	Robin Weathers
1989	Relentless	Buck Taylor

FRANCO NERO

(1941 -   )

Nero, an Italian actor with a handsome face, was given so many good-guy roles in early movies that he was delighted when, finally, he got the role of a villain in *Force 10 from Navarone*, in which he plays an evil spy. His career began when he was still in high school in Parma, Italy, where he formed a singing group and crooned some Frank Sinatra bits.

Year	Movie	Character
1967	Camelot	Lancelot Du Lac
1968	The Mercenary	Bill
1978	Force 10 from Navarone	Lescovar
1980	The Man with Bogart's Face	Hakim
1981	The Salamander	Dante
1990	Die Hard 2	Esperanza

LOIS NETTLETON

(1927 -   )

Nettleton grew up in Oak Park, IL, a suburb of Chicago, where she launched her career at the age of 7: she made up her own mini-plays and acted them out in her back yard. A high school course in classic drama led her to study at Chicago's Goodman Theater. In New York, success came slowly, but persistence won her some good stage roles and they led her into television.

Year	Movie	Character
1962	Period of Adjustment	Dorothea Baitz
1964	Mail Order Bride	Annie Boley
1970	Dirty Dingus Magee	Prudence Frost
1972	The Honkers	Linda Lathrop
1982	The Best Little Whorehouse in Texas	Dulcie Mae

GEORGE NEWBERN

(19?? -   )

Newbern, usually a supporting actor, starred in the 1988 comedy *It Takes Two* and won some critical acclaim. He played a 20-year-old Texan who almost missed his own wedding while squandering his oil field earnings on a fancy new car. *Variety* called his performance "excellent and versatile."

Year	Movie	Character
1987	Adventures in Babysitting	Dan
1988	It Takes Two	Travis Rogers
1988	Paramedics	Uptown
1988	Switching Channels	Siegenthaler
1991	Father of the Bride	Bryan MacKenzie

DENISE NICHOLAS

(1944 -   )

Her screen career began as the co-star on the highly-acclaimed TV drama *Room 222* which ran from 1969-74. Besides being an actress and author, Nicholas fills out a busy life in a variety of community-action volunteer roles. Educated at the University of Michigan, she headed south in the early 1960s to become a founding member of The Free Southern Theater. In Los Angeles, she's been active in Watts.

Year	Movie	Character
1975	Let's Do It Again	Beth Foster
1975	Mr. Ricco	Irene Mapes
1977	A Piece of the Action	Lila French
1978	Capricorn One	Betty Walker
1983	Marvin and Tige	Vanessa
1990	Ghost Dad	Joan

LLOYD NOLAN

(1902 - 1985)

A San Francisco native, Nolan left Stanford to act at the Pasadena Playhouse before Hollywood discovered him and cast him in dozens of films as an intelligent tough guy. Critics usually considered him superior to the scripts he appeared in, but he made a great impact in many movies as the leading character actor. He died of lung cancer.

Year	Movie	Character
1960	Portrait in Black	Matthew Cabot
1961	Susan Slade	Roger Slade
1964	Circus World	Cap Carson
1965	Never Too Late	Mayor Crane
1966	An American Dream	Barney Kelly
1968	Ice Station Zebra	Admiral Garvey
1968	Sergeant Ryker	Gen. Amos Bailey
1970	Airport	Harry Standish
1974	Earthquake	Dr. Vance
1977	The Private Files of J. Edgar Hoover	Att. Gen. Stone
1984	Prince Jack	Joe
1986	Hannah and Her Sisters	Hannah's Father

ALAN NORTH

(1927 -   )

North hails from New York City, the son of a vaudevillian. He received an engineering degree from Columbia and spent World War II in the U.S. Navy aboard destroyers in the Pacific. He survived the sinking of one of his ships to begin an acting career in such 1950s live TV programs as *Studio One* and *Philco Playhouse*.

Year	Movie	Character
1973	Serpico	Brown
1979	...And Justice For All	Deputy Sheriff
1984	Thief of Hearts	Sweeney
1986	Billy Galvin	George
1986	Highlander	Lt. Moran
1987	Rachel River	Beske
1989	Glory	Gov. John A. Andrew
1989	Lean on Me	Mayor Don Bottman
1989	Penn & Teller Get Killed	Old Cop
1989	See No Evil, Hear No Evil	Braddock
1990	Crazy People	Judge

SHEREE NORTH

(1933 -   )

A dancer and actress, North has been described as a Marilyn Monroe look-alike. She began dancing lessons at the age of 6, and lied about her age at 13 so she could become a chorus girl. She was spotted in a Santa Monica night club by a famous choreographer who enticed her to New York for a role in a Broadway musical, which began her stage career. North plays the wealthy wife of a factory watchman in *The Organization*, Sidney Poitier's third outing as homicide detective Virgil Tibbs.

Year	Movie	Character
1968	Madigan	Jonesy
1969	The Gypsy Moths	Waitress
1969	The Trouble With Girls	Nita
1971	Lawman	Laura Selby
1971	The Organization	Mrs. Morgan
1973	Charley Varrick	Jewell Everett
1974	The Outfit	Buck's Wife
1975	Breakout	Myrna
1976	The Shootist	Serepta
1977	Telefon	Marie Wills
1991	Defenseless	Mrs. Bodeck

MICHAEL NOURI

(1945 -   )

Flashdance made him famous while his lead role in the horror/urban crime picture *The Hidden* won Nouri a Critics Choice award at a film festival in Spain. At the time, *Variety* said he turned in "the best performance of his career as the tough-but-compassionate L.A. homicide detective." He came to acting after three boring months selling insurance, a job in which he admits having been "dreadful." A native of Alpine, NJ, Nouri broke into films with a bit part in 1969's *Goodbye, Columbus*.

Year	Movie	Character
1983	Flashdance	Nick Hurley
1986	The Imagemaker	Roger Blackwell
1987	The Hidden	Tom Beck
1990	Fatal Sky	Jeff Milker

FRANCE NUYEN

(1939 -   )

Nuyen, a Eurasian, was living a quiet life in Marseilles, France, when she was picked for the role of a lifetime, that of Liat in the movie version of *South Paciific* in 1958. A photographer had spotted her while she was painting and got her picture in several magazines. She had to learn the role and the English language at the same time.

Year	Movie	Character
1961	Last Time I Saw Archie	Cindy Hamilton
1962	A Girl Named Tamiko	Tamiko
1962	Diamond Head	Mei Chen
1962	Satan Never Sleeps	Siu-Lan
1964	The Man in the Middle	Kate Davray
1971	One More Train to Rob	Toy
1993	The Joy Luck Club	Ying Ying

SIMON OAKLAND

(1922 - 1983)

Starting his career as a professional violinist, Oakland could play either heavies or nice guys and did both in 550 TV shows, many movies, and several Broadway plays. He debuted in the 1958 film, *Brothers Karamazov*. A Manhattan native, he died at 61 near Palm Springs, CA.

Year	Movie	Character
1960	Psycho	Dr. Richmond
1960	Who Was That Lady?	Belka
1961	West Side Story	Lt. Schrank
1962	Follow That Dream	Nick
1963	The Raiders	Sgt. Austin Tremaine
1965	The Satan Bug	Tesserly
1966	The Sand Pebbles	Stawski
1967	Tony Rome	Rudolph Kosterman
1968	Bullitt	Capt. Bennett
1970	On a Clear Day You Can See Forever	Dr. Conrad Fuller
1973	Emperor of the North	Policeman

WARREN OATES

(1928 - 1982)

Oates got his start as a cowboy in countless movies and television series of the 1950s and 1960s. He received acclaim for his performance and Bogart-like look in *Dillinger*. Born near the coal mines of Depoy, KY, he first broke in with live television in *Studio One* in 1957. In movies, in the 1980s, he played Roy Scheider's gruff boss in *Blue Thunder*, Bill Murray's drill sergeant in *Stripes* and Jack Nicholson's Border Patrol chief in *Border*. He died at 53 of a heart attack at home in L.A.

Year	Movie	Character
1962	Ride the High Country	Henry Hammond
1964	Mail Order Bride	Jace
1965	Major Dundee	O.W. Hadley
1966	Return of the Seven	Colbee
1967	In the Heat of the Night	Sam Wood
1967	The Shooting	Willet Gashade
1967	Welcome to Hard Times	Jenks
1968	The Split	Marty Gough
1969	The Wild Bunch	Lyle Gorch
1970	Barquero	Remy
1970	There Was a Crooked Man...	Floyd Moon
1971	Two-Lane Blacktop	G.T.O.
1973	Dillinger	Dillinger
1973	The Thief Who Came to Dinner	Dave
1973	Tom Sawyer	Muff Potter

(continued on page 508)

HUGH O'BRIAN

(1928 -   )

O'Brian played the legendary Wyatt Earp from 1955 to 1961 on television's *The Life and Legend of Wyatt Earp*. He was struggling along doing bit parts in theater and movies, trying to save money for law school, when the television career suddenly opened up. But the highlight of his life, he has said, was a nine-day visit with the humanitarian Dr. Albert Schweitzer in 1952.

Year	Movie	Character
1965	Love Has Many Faces	Hank Walker
1966	Ambush Bay	First Sgt. Steve Corey
1976	The Shootist	Pulford
1979	Game of Death	Steiner
1988	Doin' Time on Planet Earth	Richard Camalier
1988	Twins	Granger

EDMOND O'BRIEN

(1915 - 1985)

This New York City-born actor did it all—comedy, drama, westerns, thrillers—and was a leading man until he got too heavy for the roles. Then O'Brien became such a good character actor that he won an Oscar for *The Barefoot Contessa* and a nomination for *Seven Days in May*. Also a producer-director at Paramount and Columbia, he started in show biz at 10 doing magic tricks for friends that he learned from his neighbor Harry Houdini. He died from the complications of Alzheimer's Disease.

Year	Movie	Character
1960	The Last Voyage	Second Engineer Walsh
1961	The Great Imposter	Captain Glover
1962	Birdman of Alcatraz	Tom Gaddis
1962	The Man Who Shot Liberty Valance	Dutton Peabody
1964	Rio Conchos	Pardee
1964	Seven Days in May	Sen. Raymond Clark
1965	Sylvia	Oscar Stewart
1965	Synanon	Chuck Dederich
1966	Fantastic Voyage	General Carter
1969	The Wild Bunch	Sykes
1972	They Only Kill Their Masters	George
1973	Lucky Luciano	Harry J. Anslinger

ARTHUR O'CONNELL

(1908 - 1981)

O'Connell, a versatile actor, won a Tony Award for his Broadway performance in the William Inge play *Picnic* and later won an Oscar nomination for the same role in the 1955 movie. He played in stage roles for 15 years before moving into film. He was born in New York City and first performed in stock, road shows and vaudeville. O'Connell died of Alzheimer's Disease at the age of 73.

Year	Movie	Character
1960	Cimarron	Tom Wyatt
1961	A Thunder of Drums	Sgt. Carl Rodermill
1961	Pocketful of Miracles	Count Romero
1961	The Great Imposter	Warden Chandler
1962	Follow That Dream	Pop Kwimper
1964	7 Faces of Dr. Lao	Clint Stark
1964	Kissin' Cousins	Pappy Tatum
1964	Your Cheatin' Heart	Fred Rose
1965	Great Race	Henry Goodbody
1966	Fantastic Voyage	Col. Donald Reid
1966	Ride Beyond Vengeance	Narrator
1966	The Silencers	Wigman
1967	The Reluctant Astronaut	Buck Fleming
1968	The Power	Henry Hallson
1970	There Was a Crooked Man...	Mr. Lomax
1972	The Poseidon Adventure	Chaplain
1972	They Only Kill Their Masters	Ernie
1974	Huckleberry Finn	Col. Grangerford

333

DONALD O'CONNOR

(1925 -   )

This famous actor/singer/dancer was born into a circus family in Chicago—his father was a strong man and his mother an acrobat. His stage debut consisted of a vaudeville sketch with his family and, in 1938, he made his film debut in a Paramount movie called *Sing You Sinners*. After that he danced and sang his way to many big well-remembered roles.

Year	Movie	Character
1961	Cry for Happy	Murray Prince
1965	That Funny Feeling	Harvey Granson
1981	Ragtime	Evelyn's Dance Teacher
1982	Pandemonium	Special Appearance
1992	Toys	Kenneth Zevo

GLYNNIS O'CONNOR

(1956 -   )

O'Connor is the daughter of a film producer and an actress and has had an extensive career in television series and movies. She was paired twice with Robby Benson; first in *Jeremy* as the new kid in school in a tale of adolescent love and again in *Ode to Billy Joe*, as Billy Joe McAllister's (of Tallahassee Bridge fame) girlfriend in that romantic tragedy. Born in New York City, she attended the State University of New York in Purchase.

Year	Movie	Character
1973	Jeremy	Susan Rollins
1976	Baby Blue Marine	Rose
1976	Ode to Billy Joe	Bobbie Lee Hartley
1979	California Dreaming	Corky
1980	Those Lips, Those Eyes	Ramona
1981	Night Crossing	Petra Wetzel
1984	Johnny Dangerously	Sally

KEVIN J. O'CONNOR

(1964 -   )

O'Connor made a memorable film debut in *Peggy Sue Got Married* as a beatnik who takes Kathleen Turner out for a date and recites bad poetry to her in some moonlit area. He got that part immediately after four years at DePaul's Goodman School of Drama. He simply sent a videotape of himself to the William Morris Agency, which in turn passed it on to director Francis Ford Coppola, who gave him an audition. O'Connor grew up on Chicago's Southwest Side—the son of a cop and a teacher.

Year	Movie	Character
1986	Peggy Sue Got Married	Michael Fitzsimmons
1988	The Moderns	Hemingway
1989	Signs of Life	Eddie Johnson
1989	Steel Magnolias	Sammy Desoto
1990	Love at Large	Art
1991	F/X 2	Matt Neely

JACK O'HALLORAN

(19?? -   )

A native of Philadelphia, O'Halloran scored early as a professional athlete—he was a professional football player with the Philadelphia Eagles and a pro boxer. The jobs prepared him well for the roles of tough villains which he frequently played in film and television.

Year	Movie	Character
1975	Farewell My Lovely	Moose Malloy
1976	King Kong	Joe Perko
1980	Superman II	Non
1980	The Baltimore Bullet	Max
1987	Dragnet	Emil Muzz
1988	Hero and the Terror	Simon Moon

CATHERINE O'HARA

(1954 -   )

The Toronto-born actress has spent nearly as much time as a writer as she has as a performer. O'Hara got her start in the early 1970s writing and performing in satiric skits and shows with Chicago's celebrated Second City company. This led to her involvement with the popular *Second City TV* and *SCTV Network* programs, which resulted in several Emmys for writing. O'Hara is best known for her roles as Macaulay Culkin's mother in the *Home Alone* pictures and as the affected artiste Delia in *Beetlejuice*.

Year	Movie	Character
1980	Nothing Personal	Janet Samson
1985	After Hours	Gail
1986	Heartburn	Betty
1988	Beetlejuice	Delia
1990	Betsy's Wedding	Gloria Henner
1990	Dick Tracy	Texie Garcia
1990	Home Alone	Kate McCallister
1992	Home Alone 2: Lost in New York	Kate

DAN O'HERLIHY

(1919 -   )

This veteran film star made many movies on horseback—including cowboy roles, but once confessed to an an interviewer that he does not like horses and is not a very good rider. Born in Ireland, O'Herlihy had never even been inside a theater before when he was unexpectedly cast in a play at Dublin's famous Abbey Theater. Since then, O'Herlihy has made dozens of movies, on and off of horses.

Year	Movie	Character
1969	100 Rifles	Grimes
1969	The Big Cube	Charles
1971	Waterloo	Marshal Ney
1972	The Carey Treatment	J.D. Randall
1974	The Tamarind Seed	Fergus Stephenson
1977	MacArthur	President Roosevelt
1982	Halloween III: Season of the Witch	Conal
1984	The Last Starfighter	Grig
1986	The Whoopee Boys	Judge Sternhill
1987	Robocop	The Old Man
1987	The Dead	Mr. Brown
1990	Robocop 2	Old Man

MICHAEL O'KEEFE

(1955 -   )

He never considered a career as an athlete, but O'Keefe has a habit of portraying them in the movies. He was a basketball player in his Oscar-nominated debut in *The Great Santini*, a golfer in *Caddyshack*, a gymnast in *Split Image* and a baseball player in *The Slugger's Wife* with Rebecca De Mornay. O'Keefe grew up in Larchmont, NY, a prosperous suburb of New York City, and got his acting start in Colgate commercials and at Joseph Papp's Public Theater.

Year	Movie	Character
1979	The Great Santini	Ben Meechum
1980	Caddyshack	Danny
1982	Split Image	Danny
1983	Nate and Hayes	Nate Williamson
1984	Finders Keepers	Michael
1985	The Slugger's Wife	Darryl Palmer
1986	The Whoopee Boys	Jake
1987	Ironweed	Billy

GARY OLDMAN

(1958 -   )

Often portraying society's outsiders, the British actor was punk rocker Sid Vicious in *Sid and Nancy*, Lee Harvey Oswald in *JFK* and Dracula in Francis Ford Coppola's 1992 version of the classic horror tale. Oldman cites actor Malcolm McDowell as his inspiration. "I've played a lot of his kind of role. Anti-heroes. I don't do romantic leads," he has said. "A lot of what he does is controversial. For me *Clockwork Orange* is the perfect film, stylish, complete—anarchic. It's cinema—and uses the medium to its fullest extent."

Year	Movie	Character
1986	Sid and Nancy	Sid Vicious
1989	Criminal Law	Ben Chase
1990	Chattahoochee	Emmett Foley
1990	State of Grace	Jackie Flannery
1991	JFK	Lee Harvey Oswald
1992	Bram Stoker's Dracula	Dracula
1993	True Romance	Drexl Spivey

EDWARD JAMES OLMOS

(1947 -   )

Known for his Emmy-winning role as Lt. Martin Castillo in *Miami Vice*, Olmos is a Mexican-American who grew up in East L.A. He spent an extraordinary five years making and promoting the PBS special *The Ballad of Gregorio Cortez*, an endeavor which left him emotionally and financially drained. His performing career began as a singer with a band called Pacific Ocean. During the mid-1960s the combo was playing regularly at a nightclub on L.A.'s Sunset Strip.

Year	Movie	Character
1975	Aloha, Bobby and Rose	First Chicano
1981	Wolfen	Eddie Holt
1981	Zoot Suit	El Pachuco
1982	Blade Runner	Gaff
1983	The Ballad of Gregorio Cortez	Gregorio Cortez
1986	Saving Grace	Ciolino
1987	Stand and Deliver	Jaime Escalante
1989	Triumph of the Spirit	Gypsy
1991	Talent for the Game	Virgil Sweet
1992	American Me	Santana

GERALD S. O'LOUGHLIN

(1921 -   )

Remembered by fans of television's *The Rookies* (1972-76) as the hard-nosed police lieutenant, Eddie Ryker, O'Loughlin, looks, walks and talks like the tough guys he often plays. However, he is the son of a prominent New York attorney, the product of an Eastern prep school and a graduate of LaFayette College in Easton, PA, where he majored in mechanical engineering. His first acting job was at the Crystal Lake Theater in upstate New York doing repertory for $30-a-week plus room and board.

Year	Movie	Character
1964	Ensign Pulver	LaSueur
1966	A Fine Madness	Chester Quirk
1967	In Cold Blood	Harold Nye
1971	Desperate Characters	Charlie
1971	The Organization	Jack Pecora
1977	Twilight's Last Gleaming	Michael O'Rourke
1984	City Heat	Counterman Louie
1986	Quicksilver	Mr. Casey

JAMES OLSON

(1930 -   )

Olson enjoyed one of those delightful discoveries that young actors dream about. He was in a play in New York when Samuel Goldwyn, Jr. spotted him and instantly signed him for a role in a movie. Olson was born in Lake Forest, IL, and attended Northwestern University on a four-year Edgar Bergen acting fellowship. The actor's screen credits include *The Andromeda Strain*, in which he was part of a team of four doctors investigating mysterious deaths in a desert town after a satellite crashes nearby.

Year	Movie	Character
1968	Rachel, Rachel	Nick Kazlik
1971	The Andromeda Strain	Dr. Mark Hall
1981	Ragtime	Father
1982	Amityville II: The Possession	Father Adamski
1985	Commando	General Kirby
1987	Rachel River	Jack

PATRICK O'NEAL

(1927 -   )

O'Neal credits Gregory Peck for helping him decide to be an actor. Working as a grip on one of Peck's films, O'Neal asked him how to be a paid actor. Peck told him to study at the Neighborhood Playhouse in New York. So he did and a career was launched. He has been on the stage and in films and television while still finding time to operate New York restaurants with his brother Michael.

Year	Movie	Character
1960	From the Terrace	Dr. Jim Roper
1963	The Cardinal	Cecil Turner
1965	In Harm's Way	Cmdr. Neal O'Wynn
1965	King Rat	Max
1966	A Fine Madness	Dr. Oliver West
1966	Alvarez Kelly	Major Albert Stedman
1968	Assignment to Kill	Richard Cutting
1968	The Secret Life of an American Wife	Tom Layton
1968	Where Were You When the Lights Went Out?	Peter Garrison
1969	Castle Keep	Capt. Lionel Beckman
1973	The Way We Were	George Bissinger
1975	The Stepford Wives	Dale Coba
1987	Like Father, Like Son	Dr. Armbruster
1989	New York Stories	Phillip Fowler
1990	Alice	Alice's Father
1990	Q & A	Kevin Quinn
1991	For the Boys	Shephard
1992	Under Siege	Captain Adams

RON O'NEAL

MICHAEL ONTKEAN

(1937 -   )

(1946 -   )

O'Neal is best known as the Harlem drug dealer with a heart of gold in the *Superfly* movies of the early 1970s. The actor was born in Utica, NY, but grew up in Cleveland, the son of a musician who was forced to become a steelworker in the 1930s depression. Bored after only two quarters at Ohio State, he happened to see a performance of *Finian's Rainbow* and decided acting was the career for him.

A tall, rangy native of Vancouver, Ontkean could have been a professional hockey player—he once had contracts with both the Toronto Maple Leafs and the New York Rangers. He decided he did not want to get clobbered on the ice rink every night and turned to acting. A Canadian-born director spotted him in a Toronto stage production and brought him to Hollywood.

Year	Movie	Character
1971	The Organization	Joe Peralez
1972	Superfly	Priest
1973	Superfly T.N.T	Priest
1977	Brothers	Walter Nancy
1979	A Force of One	Rollins
1979	When a Stranger Calls	Lt. Charlie Garber
1980	The Final Countdown	Cdr. Dan Thurman
1984	Red Dawn	Colonel Bella
1988	Hero and the Terror	Mayor

Year	Movie	Character
1977	Slap Shot	Ned Braden
1979	Voices	Drew Rothman
1980	Willie and Phil	Willie
1982	Making Love	Zack
1984	Just the Way You Are	Peter
1987	Maid to Order	Nick McGuire
1987	The Allnighter	Mickey Leroi
1988	Clara's Heart	Bill Hart
1989	Bye Bye Blues	Teddy Cooper
1989	Street Justice	Curt Flynn
1990	Postcards From the Edge	Robert Munch

TERRY O'QUINN

(19?? -   )

O'Quinn is best known as the harmless-looking step-dad who is actually a psychotic that murdered his family in the *Stepfather* films. The Michigan native's career got started in typical fashion as a struggling actor in New York's Off-Broadway productions. His television appearances have included guest starring roles in *Remington Steele*, *The Twilight Zone* and specials such as *FDR* and *The Final Year*.

Year	Movie	Character
1980	Heaven's Gate	Capt. Minardi
1984	Mrs. Soffel	Buck McGovern
1984	Places in the Heart	Buddy Kelsey
1985	Mischief	Claude Harbrough
1985	Silver Bullet	Sheriff Joe Haller
1986	Black Widow	Bruce
1986	SpaceCamp	Launch Director
1987	The Stepfather	Jerry Blake
1988	Young Guns	Alex McSween
1989	Blind Fury	Frank Devereaux
1989	Stepfather II	Dr. Gene Clifford
1991	Company Business	Col. Grissom
1991	The Rocketeer	Howard Hughes
1992	The Cutting Edge	Jack

JERRY ORBACH

(1935 -   )

Early on, Orbach dreamed of a film career and a chance to become the next Marlon Brando or Montgomery Clift. His ability to sing, however, kept the Broadway offers coming and he eventually saw no reason to move to California. Considered one of Broadway's most bankable leading men for over twenty years, Orbach has become more active in feature films in recent years and is often cast as a tough-guy heavy.

Year	Movie	Character
1961	Mad Dog Coll	Joe
1965	John Goldfarb, Please Come Home	Pinkerton
1971	The Gang That Couldn't Shoot Straight	Kid Sally
1977	The Sentinel	Film Director
1981	Prince of the City	Gus Levy
1985	Brewster's Millions	Charley Pegler
1986	F/X	Nicholas DeFranco
1986	The Imagemaker	Byron Caine
1987	Dirty Dancing	Jake Houseman
1987	Someone to Watch Over Me	Lt. Garber
1989	Crimes and Misdemeanors	Jack Rosenthal
1990	Delusion	Larry
1991	Delirious	Lou Sherwood
1991	Out for Justice	Ronnie Donziger
1992	Mr. Saturday Night	Phil Gussman
1992	Straight Talk	Milo Jacoby
1992	Universal Soldier	Dr. Gregor

ED O'ROSS

(19?? -   )

O'Ross is a former Golden Gloves boxing champ who usually appears in tough guy roles in action/adventure pictures. His stage credits range from City Center children's theater to James Thurber's *Story Theater* to an appearance in *King Lear*. He was a drama student under Uta Hagen and Stella Adler. O'Ross has made many television appearances, including soap operas such as *Guiding Light*, and has performed in several television commercials.

Year	Movie	Character
1984	The Cotton Club	Monk
1987	Full Metal Jacket	Lt. Touchdown
1987	The Hidden	Cliff Willis
1988	Red Heat	Viktor Rostavili
1990	Another 48 Hours	Frank Cruise
1992	Universal Soldier	Colonel Perry

CLIFF OSMOND

(1937 -   )

A versatile man of theatrical trades, Osmond has been an actor, writer and director. He both scripted and directed the 1988 film *The Penitent* and, in 1977, wrote episodes of *The Hardy Boys Mysteries* for ABC. In *The Fortune Cookie*, he played an insurance investigator who uncovers a fraud perpetrated by shyster lawyer Walter Matthau.

Year	Movie	Character
1964	Kiss Me Stupid	Barney Millsap
1966	The Fortune Cookie	Mr. Purkey
1973	Oklahoma Crude	Massive Man
1974	Front Page	Jacobi
1975	Shark's Treasure	Lobo
1977	Mountain Man	McCullough, lumber foreman
1980	Hangar 18	Sheriff

ANNETTE O'TOOLE

(1952 -   )

O'Toole, as a child growing up in Houston, wanted to be a dancer and took lessons at the age of three in her mother's studio. By 16, she was dancing professionally on television and in L.A. theaters. She finally gave it up—"Dancers hardly ever get recognized," she has said—and turned to acting. She spent a year doing roles in a variety of television programs before she got a start in films, appearing as a desperate beauty pageant contestant in *Smile*. "I don't want this big stardom thing," she once said, "I just want a good script."

Year	Movie	Character
1975	Smile	Doria Houston/ Miss Anaheim
1977	One on One	Janet Hays
1978	King of the Gypsies	Sharon
1980	Foolin' Around	Susan
1982	48 Hours	Elaine
1982	Cat People	Alice
1983	Superman III	Lana Lang
1987	Cross My Heart	Kathy
1990	Love at Large	Mrs. King

JUDY PACE

(19?? -   )

Pace was intent on a professional career when her college life was interrupted by a sudden recurrence of a bone disease that threatened to leave her crippled for life. In the hospital for two months, she decided that if she recovered she would be an actress. She did recover and set out on a career that led her into movies and television parts. She grew up in L.A.

Year	Movie	Character
1968	Three in the Attic	Eulice
1970	Cotton Comes to Harlem	Iris
1970	Up in the Cellar	Harlene
1972	Cool Breeze	Obalese Eaton

GERALDINE PAGE

(1924 - 1987)

A great lady of the American theater, Page went to New York in 1950 and modeled lingerie and checked hats before she began appearing in plays by Tennessee Williams and Eugene O'Neill. In films she played Southern women down on their luck, but won the best actress Oscar in 1985 for *The Trip to Bountiful*. Married to actor Rip Torn, she died at 62 of a heart attack in New York.

Year	Movie	Character
1961	Summer and Smoke	Alma Winemiller
1962	Sweet Bird of Youth	Alexandra Del Lago
1963	Toys in the Attic	Carrie Berniers
1966	You're a Big Boy Now	Margery Chanticleer
1969	Whatever Happened to Aunt Alice?	Mrs. Marrable
1971	The Beguiled	Martha
1972	Pete 'n' Tillie	Gertrude
1975	The Day of the Locust	Big Sister
1978	Interiors	Eve
1981	Honky Tonk Freeway	Sister Mary Clarise
1982	I'm Dancing as Fast as I Can	Jean Martin
1984	The Pope of Greenwich Village	Mrs. Ritter
1985	The Bride	Mrs. Bauman
1985	The Trip to Bountiful	Mrs. Watts
1985	White Nights	Anne Wyatt
1986	My Little Girl	Grandmother Molly
1986	Native Son	Peggy

JANIS PAIGE

(1922 -   )

Paige was once known only as a pretty girl with a pretty figure and she was so pigeonholed that all she could do was win titles like "Miss Grapefruit" and "Miss Delicious Apple." But she perservered and became an accomplished actress, appearing in such well-known plays as *Please Don't Eat the Daisies*. Paige was born Donna Mae Tjaden in Tacoma, WA.

Year	Movie	Character
1960	Please Don't Eat the Daisies	Deborah Vaughn
1961	Bachelor in Paradise	Dolores Jynson
1963	The Caretakers	Marion
1967	Welcome to Hard Times	Adah

LILLI PALMER

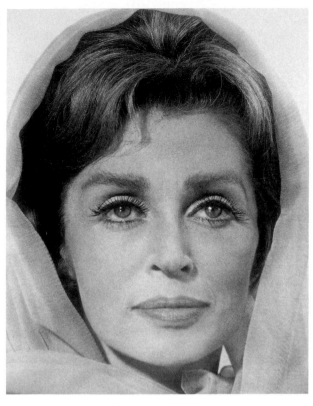

LUCIANA PALUZZI

(1914 - 1986)

The elegant actress, born in Posen, Germany, now Poland, was often cast as a mysterious Continental woman. After studying acting in Berlin, Palmer left Germany when Hitler rose to power, then appeared in Paris at the Moulin Rouge. She began her film career in Britain and during her marriage to British actor Rex Harrison, from 1943-1957, she went to Hollywood. Later she made films in Europe and played star roles into her late 40s. She died of cancer.

(1939 -   )

The red-haired Italian actress once said that she'd rather do sexpot roles than those that depict her as "sweet." The daughter of an Italian Army officer, Paluzzi's career began with a tiny role in *Three Coins in the Fountain* (1954). She had made 16 European films before being discovered for a short-lived television spy thriller called *Five Fingers* (1959).

Year	Movie	Character
1961	The Pleasure of His Company	Katharine Dougherty
1962	The Counterfeit Traitor	Marianne Mollendorf
1965	Operation Crossbow	Frieda
1967	Jack of Diamonds	xxx
1969	Hard Contract	Adrianne
1978	The Boys from Brazil	Esther Lieberman

Year	Movie	Character
1961	Return to Peyton Place	Raffaella
1964	Muscle Beach Party	Julie
1965	Thunderball	Fiona
1967	Venetian Affair	Giulia Almeranti
1969	The Green Slime	Lisa Benson

STUART PANKIN

(1946 -   )

Pankin launched his career by getting a master's degree in Fine Arts at Columbia University and studying stage acting with Jenny Egan and Peter Feldman. He's even studied fencing and juggling. Pankin's stage career includes roles in New York Shakespeare Festival productions and in many summer stock shows. His movies include *Arachnophobia*, as the sheriff of the California coastal town where the picture is set.

Year	Movie	Character
1980	The Hollywood Knights	Dudley
1986	The Dirt Bike Kid	Mr. Hodgkins
1987	Fatal Attraction	Jimmy
1987	Love at Stake	Judge John
1989	Second Sight	Preston Pickett
1990	Arachnophobia	Sheriff Parsons
1991	Life Stinks	Pritchard
1991	Mannequin Two: On the Move	Mr. James

JOHN PANKOW

(1955 -   )

Pankow achieved prominence in the role of Mozart in the Broadway production of *Amadeus* in the early 1980s. He was born in St. Louis, the sixth of nine children, and grew up in Chicago. He studied acting at the St. Nicholas School of the Theater Arts, but got his first big part almost by accident. He came to New York to visit a girl friend and was handed a role in PBS-TV's *Life on the Mississippi*.

Year	Movie	Character
1985	To Live and Die in L.A.	John Vukovich
1987	The Secret of My Success	Fred Melrose
1988	Monkey Shines: An Experiment in Fear	Geoffrey Fisher
1988	Talk Radio	Dietz
1991	Mortal Thoughts	Arthur Kellogg
1991	Year of the Gun	Italo Bianchi
1992	A Stranger Among Us	Levine

JOE PANTOLIANO

(1954 -   )

Pantoliano moved from his hometown of Hoboken, NJ, to Manhattan at 17 to study how to become a barber. He also began training for the stage and won a role with a touring company doing *One Flew Over the Cuckoo's Nest*. A journalist once described him as "down-to-earth, quick-talking with a fondness for four-letter words [and] charming." He played the bail bondsman in *Midnight Run*, Rebecca De Mornay's vicious pimp in *Risky Business* and Tommy Lee Jones' assistant in *The Fugitive*.

Year	Movie	Character
1980	The Idolmaker	Gino Pilato
1982	Monsignor	Musso
1983	Eddie and the Cruisers	Doc
1983	Risky Business	Guido
1985	The Goonies	Francis
1985	The Mean Season	Andy Porter
1986	Running Scared	Snake
1987	Amazon Women on the Moon	Sy Swerdlow
1987	Empire of the Sun	Frank Demerest
1987	La Bamba	Bob Keene
1987	The Squeeze	Norman
1988	Midnight Run	Eddie Moscone
1988	The "In" Crowd	Perry Parker
1990	Downtown	White
1990	Short Time	Scalese
1990	The Last of the Finest	Wayne Gross
1991	Zandalee	Gerri
1993	The Fugitive	Cosmo Renfro
1993	Three of Hearts	Mickey
1993	Calendar Girl	Harvey Darpinian
1993	Me and the Kid	Roy

MICHAEL PARE´

(1959 -   )

Pare´ was a chef in a Manhattan restaurant and studying acting on the side when he got started in the film business. The Brooklyn native was one of ten children and explains he took up cooking at first because he did not want to go hungry. Screen breaks then came quickly. He got his first role, in *Eddie and the Cruisers*, without even auditioning for it—a director just thought he looked right for the part.

Year	Movie	Character
1983	Eddie and the Cruisers	Eddie
1984	Philadelphia Experiment	David
1984	Streets of Fire	Tom
1988	World Gone Wild	George Landon
1989	Eddie and the Cruisers II: Eddie Lives!	Eddie Wilson/Joe West
1990	The Closer	Larry Freede
1991	Killing Streets	xxx
1992	Into the Sun	Capt. Paul Watkins

ELEANOR PARKER

(1922 -   )

It may seem that Parker made the show business big-time easily because she signed her first movie contract at the age of 19. Actually, she had been studying acting since she was 10. Parker was acclaimed as an immediate success for a role in *Mission to Moscow* (1943) with Walter Huston. She received Oscar nominations for performances in *Caged* (1950), *Detective Story* (1951) and *Interrupted Melody* (1955).

Year	Movie	Character
1960	Home from the Hill	Hannah Hunnicutt
1961	Return to Peyton Place	Connie
1965	The Sound of Music	The Baroness
1966	An American Dream	Deborah
1966	The Oscar	Sophie Cantaro
1967	The Tiger and the Pussycat	Esperia
1967	Warning Shot	Doris Ruston
1979	Sunburn	Mrs. Thoren

SARAH JESSICA PARKER

(1965 -   )

Born in Ohio, Parker had an unusual start in show business. At the age of 11 she answered an ad as a joke and won a part in a Broadway play. The play did not survive long but she did. Acting once with Vanessa Redgrave, Parker became interested in Redgrave's political activities and has since been active in many political causes, usually helping life's underdogs. "I can't get through a day without thinking I haven't done something to help someone else," she has said.

Year	Movie	Character
1983	Somewhere Tomorrow	xxx
1984	First Born	Lisa
1984	Footloose	Rusty
1985	Girls Just Want to Have Fun	Janey Glenn
1986	Flight of the Navigator	Carolyn McAdams
1991	L.A. Story	SanDee
1992	Honeymoon in Vegas	Betsy/Donna
1993	Hocus Pocus	Sarah
1993	Striking Distance	Jo Christman

MICHAEL PARKS

(1938 -   )

Signed to a long-term contract with Universal in the early 1960s and billed as the next Tony Curtis or Rock Hudson, Parks' success seemed assured. However, a string of bad pictures followed and, in 1967, Parks left the movie business for ten years. He starred, for one season, as Jim Bronson, a reporter who drops out of society and travels the country on his motorcycle, on TV's *Then Came Bronson* (1970-71). Parks got his start traveling with small theater groups in California and supporting himself as a migratory fruit picker.

Year	Movie	Character
1965	Bus Riley's Back in Town	Bus Riley
1967	The Happening	Sureshot
1977	The Private Files of J. Edgar Hoover	Robert F. Kennedy
1980	ffolkes	Shulman
1981	Hard Country	Royce
1982	Savannah Smiles	Lt. Savage
1991	The Hitman	Ronny Delaney

ESTELLE PARSONS

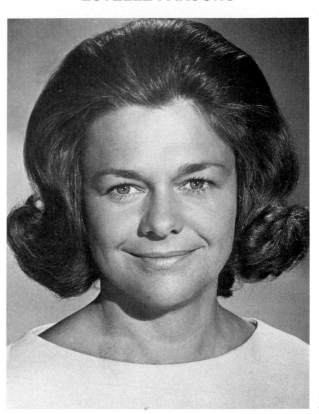

(1927 -   )

Parsons at first considered becoming a lawyer and even attended Boston University Law School, but gave it up to pursue acting. She has had an extensive career on Broadway and in regional theaters and has directed a children's theater in New York. In film, she played Gene Hackman's skittish wife in *Bonnie and Clyde* and Godfrey Cambridge's wife in 1970's *Watermelon Man*, a story of a white insurance salesman who wakes up black one morning. Parsons hails from Lynn, MA.

Year	Movie	Character
1967	Bonnie and Clyde	Blanche Barrow
1968	Rachel, Rachel	Calla Mackie
1973	Two People	Barbara
1974	For Pete's Sake	Helen
1990	Dick Tracy	Mrs. Trueheart
1990	The Lemon Sisters	Mrs. Kupchak

ADRIAN PASDAR

(1966 -   )

Pasdar began a theatrical career as a set builder at the People's Light and Theater Company in his hometown of Philadelphia. His next move was to New York and studies at the Lee Strasberg Theater Institute which he partly financed by selling Sabrett's hotdogs on the street. His audition for *Top Gun* so impressed director Tony Scott that Scott wrote a part especially for him.

Year	Movie	Character
1986	Top Gun	Chipper
1986	Solarbabies	Darstar
1986	Streets of Gold	Timmy Boyle
1989	Cookie	Vito
1989	Torn Apart	Ben Arnon
1990	Vital Signs	Michael Chatham

MANDY PATINKIN

(1952 -   )

Patinkin was born in Chicago, the son of a scrap metal dealer. His performing career began young as a singer in the choir of the Rodfi Zedek Temple. After abandoning the demanding requirements of the Juilliard School, he joined Joseph Papp's New York Shakespeare Festival where his acting career took off. He has also been a solo recording artist and concert performer. His movies include *Yentl* where he befriends Barbra Streisand at the religious school where the star is pretending to be a boy.

Year	Movie	Character
1979	French Postcards	Sayyid
1979	Last Embrace	Commuter
1980	Night of the Juggler	Cabbie
1981	Ragtime	Tateh
1983	Daniel	Paul Isaacson
1983	Yentl	Avigdor
1985	Maxie	Nick
1987	The Princess Bride	Inigo Montoya
1988	Alien Nation	Sam Francisco
1988	The House on Carroll Street	Ray Salwen
1990	Dick Tracy	88 Keys
1991	Impromptu	Alfred de Musset
1991	The Doctor	Murray
1991	True Colors	John Palmer

JASON PATRIC

(1966 -)

Patric feels the attraction of the movie-making process is about people. "You go on a movie set and you find people from 18 to 65 who have done absolutely everything," he once said. "You can put yourself in a world for four months where you can be absolutely anyone you want aside from your character...You establish a community and you use different sides of yourself which you'd never known. And then it's over and it's very sad. You become very close to someone for three months and then it's gone."

Year	Movie	Character
1986	Solarbabies	Jason
1987	The Lost Boys	Michael
1988	The Beast	Koverchenko
1990	After Dark, My Sweet	Kevin "Collie" Collins
1990	Frankenstein Unbound	Lord Byron
1991	Rush	Jim Raynor
1993	Geronimo: An American Legend	Lt. Charles Gatewood

WILL PATTON

(1954 -)

Patton came to acting by watching his father, a Lutheran preacher who traveled the South, sermonizing from a tent. Born in Charleston, SC, his interest in performing came early. "When I was a little kid, I liked getting up in front of a room. I was kind of shy unless I could get up in front of the room," he has said. "It was some kind of need I had to communicate that way since I couldn't find other ways to communicate." The actor started his career on the New York stage.

Year	Movie	Character
1983	Silkwood	Joe
1985	After Hours	Horst
1986	Belizaire the Cajun	Matthew Perry
1987	No Way Out	Scott Pritchard
1988	Stars and Bars	Duane
1989	Signs of Life	Mr. Coughlin, Sr.
1990	A Shock to the System	Lt. Laker
1990	Everybody Wins	Jerry
1991	The Rapture	Sheriff Foster

ALEXANDRA PAUL

(1963 -   )

A svelte former fashion model, Paul got into acting at the suggestion of her fashion agent. She enrolled in a theater workshop and abandoned plans to attend Stanford. Very quickly she got a spot in an ABC movie, *Paper Dolls*. She loves hiking and skiiing.

Year	Movie	Character
1983	Christine	Leigh Cabot
1984	Just the Way You Are	Bobbie
1985	American Flyers	Becky
1986	8 Million Ways to Die	Sunny
1987	Dragnet	Connie Swail

DON MICHAEL PAUL

(19?? -   )

Paul, a Californian, credits his mother with his success. A dancing instructor, she instilled professional discipline in him and developed his talents. Other talents got him his first jobs, though. He was a collegiate golfer and began his acting career in TV commercials where he plugged golf balls.

Year	Movie	Character
1984	Lovelines	Jeff
1988	Aloha Summer	Chuck Granville
1989	Heart of Dixie	Boots
1991	Rich Girl	Rick

BILL PAXTON

AMANDA PAYS

(1956 -   )

(1959 -   )

The Texas native moved to L.A. at 18 and found work as a set decorator for Roger Corman. His debut came when he was working behind the scenes on *Crazy Mama* and was offered some lines in the film by director Jonathan Demme. Paxton has appeared in theater productions, "but it was movies I had always wanted to be in," he once said. "I'm into the whole thing, not just performing. I love watching what goes on behind the camera. My heroes are Buster Keaton and Harold Lloyd—complete filmmakers."

Pays spent four years as a fashion model and then dropped out to study acting in London. She broke into film in a made-for with George Segal titled *The Cold Room*. She first became familiar to American audiences in *Max Headroom*, the innovative British TV program imported by ABC in 1987. In it, she played Theora Jones, the brilliant and erotic computer whiz. Pays was born in Berkshire, England, and was educated in a convent. She married actor Corbin Bernsen in 1988.

Year	Movie	Character
1983	The Lords of Discipline	Gilbreath
1984	Impulse	Eddie
1984	Streets of Fire	Clyde
1984	The Terminator	Punk Leader
1985	Weird Science	Chet
1986	Aliens	Private Hudson
1989	Next of Kin	Gerald Gates
1990	Navy SEALS	Dane
1990	Predator 2	Jerry
1990	The Last of the Finest	Howard "Hojo" Jones
1992	Trespass	Vince
1993	Indian Summer	Jack Belston

Year	Movie	Character
1984	Oxford Blues	Lady Victoria
1987	The Kindred	Melissa Leftridge
1988	Off Limits	Nicole
1989	Leviathan	Willie
1991	Exposure	Marie

ELIZABETH PENA

(1962 -   )

Pena is the U.S.-born daughter of Cuban parents who grew up in Cuba until age 7 when the family returned to the states. Her Latin features have largely relegated her to Hispanic roles ever since she was a senior at New York's High School of Performing Arts and was told that she couldn't play Madge in William Inge's *Picnic* as she was not the small town American type. Ever sensitive to Latin stereotypes, she has said: "There are a lot of jobs I've turned down because they wanted me to play what I call 'Miss Cuchifrito' types."

Year	Movie	Character
1980	Times Square	xxx
1981	They All Laughed	Rita
1986	Down and Out in Beverly Hills	Carmen
1987	*batteries not included	Marisa
1987	La Bamba	Rosie Morales
1988	Vibes	Consuela
1990	Blue Steel	Tracy Perez
1990	Jacob's Ladder	Jezzie

AUSTIN PENDLETON

(1940 -   )

Pendleton is both an actor and director and has also taught at the HB Studio. Born in Warren, OH, he was educated at Yale University. His stage debut was at the Phoenix Theater in New York in 1962 as Jonathan in *Oh, Dad, Poor Dad, Mama's Hung You in the Closet and I'm Feelin' So Sad.*

Year	Movie	Character
1968	Petulia	xxx
1970	Catch-22	Col. Moodus
1972	What's Up, Doc?	Frederick Larrabee
1973	The Thief Who Came to Dinner	Zukovsky
1974	Front Page	Earl Williams
1976	The Great Smokey Roadblock	Guido
1979	Starting Over	Paul
1979	The Muppet Movie	Max
1980	First Family	Alexander Grade
1980	Simon	Becker
1986	Off Beat	Gun Shop Salesman
1986	Short Circuit	Howard Marner
1987	Hello Again	Junior Lacey
1990	Mr. & Mrs. Bridge	Mr. Gadbury
1991	The Ballad of the Sad Cafe	Taylor
1992	My Cousin Vinny	Public Defender
1993	My Boyfriend's Back	Dr. Bronson
1993	Rain Without Thunder	Roman Catholic Priest

CHRISTOPHER PENN

(19?? -   )

The younger brother of Sean Penn, Christopher Penn has made a career of his own in films. He has been acting since the age of 12 and studied at the famous Loft Studio in his native Los Angeles. He once weighed in at 270 pounds and was a heavy-weight wrestler in high school. Later he became involved in karate, winning a black belt. Penn had a memorable role as the not-to-bright farm boy who befriends the new kid in town, city boy Kevin Bacon, in *Footloose*.

Year	Movie	Character
1983	All the Right Moves	Brian
1983	Rumble Fish	B.J.
1984	Footloose	Willard
1984	The Wild Life	Tom
1985	Pale Rider	Josh LaHood
1986	At Close Range	Tommy
1989	Best of the Best	Travis
1991	Mobsters	Tommy Reina
1993	Short Cuts	Jerry Kaiser

ELIZABETH PERKINS

(1960 -   )

Perkins grew up in Vermont, where she says her early theater training consisted merely of watching people on Main Street, observing how they behaved in public. She studied at the Goodman School in Chicago and performed in small theaters there before setting out for New York and a career in movies. Perkins was Tom Hanks' toy company co-worker and girl friend in *Big*. As Demi Moore's roommate in *About Last Night...* she plays a wounded veteran of the singles scene who harbors a deep resentment of men.

Year	Movie	Character
1986	About Last Night...	Joan
1987	From the Hip	Jo Ann
1988	Big	Susan
1988	Sweet Hearts Dance	Adie Nims
1990	Avalon	Ann Kaye
1990	Love at Large	Stella Wynkowski
1991	He Said, She Said	Lorie Bryer
1991	The Doctor	June
1993	Indian Summer	Jennifer Morton

MILLIE PERKINS

(1938 -   )

Perkins got the plum role of an actor's life her first time out when she made her film debut in the title role of *The Diary of Anne Frank* in 1959. She was a model in New York at the time her picture was submitted to 20th Century Fox. She at first refused the part because of her limited knowledge of acting but was eventually convinced to try it.

Year	Movie	Character
1961	Wild in the Country	Betty Lee
1964	Ensign Pulver	Scotty
1967	The Shooting	Woman
1968	Wild in the Streets	Mrs. Perkins
1983	Table for Five	Kathleen
1986	At Close Range	Julie
1987	Wall Street	Mrs. Fox
1988	Two-Moon Junction	Mrs. Delongpre

LISA JANE PERSKY

(1955 -   )

Persky was born in Atlanta, but grew up on Christopher Street in the heart of Greenwich Village. She broke into acting when a neighbor, who thought her a perfect teenager, wrote a play especially for her to perform in. It was produced in a local cafe. Persky attended NYU before beginning a real acting career. In *The Sure Thing*, she played the female half of a square college couple who offer John Cusack a ride across the country.

Year	Movie	Character
1979	The Great Santini	Mary Anne Meechum
1983	Breathless	Salesgirl
1984	The Cotton Club	Frances Flegenheimer
1985	The Sure Thing	Mary Ann Webster
1986	Peggy Sue Got Married	Delores Dodge
1987	The Big Easy	McCabe
1989	Great Balls of Fire!	Babe
1989	When Harry Met Sally...	Alice
1990	The Last of the Finest	Hariett Gross
1990	Vital Signs	Bobby
1993	Coneheads	Lisa Farber

NEHEMIAH PERSOFF

(1920 -   )

Born in Jerusalem, Persoff had a technical education and started his career as an electrician and a signal maintenance man. In New York, he studied acting under Stella Adler and Lee Strasberg. Persoff made his Off-Broadway debut in 1940 and has appeared in many plays. His favorite role, he has said, was Tom in *The Glass Menagerie*. Among his many movie roles was that of Barbra Streisand's ailing father in *Yentl*.

Year	Movie	Character
1961	The Comancheros	Graile
1964	Fate is the Hunter	Ben Sawyer
1965	The Greatest Story Ever Told	Shemiah
1968	The Power	Carl Melniker
1970	Red Sky at Morning	Amadeo Montoya
1971	Mrs. Pollifax—Spy	Berisha
1976	Voyage of the Damned	Mr. Hauser
1980	In Search of Historic Jesus	Herod Antipas
1983	Yentl	Papa
1988	Twins	Mitchell Traven

BROCK PETERS

(1927 -   )

An actor, singer and producer, Peters made an enviable Broadway debut as Jim in *Porgy and Bess* in 1943 and went on to a long career in stage, screen and television. He was born Brock Fisher in New York and attended the University of Chicago.

Year	Movie	Character
1962	To Kill a Mockingbird	Tom Robinson
1965	Major Dundee	Aesop
1965	The Pawnbroker	Rodriguez
1967	The Incident	Arnold Robinson
1968	P.J.	Waterpack
1973	Soylent Green	Hatcher
1975	Framed	Sam
1976	Two Minute Warning	Paul
1986	Star Trek IV: The Voyage Home	Admiral Cartwright
1991	Star Trek VI: The Undiscovered Country	Admiral Cartwrigh

LOU DIAMOND PHILLIPS

(1962 -   )

Hollywood producers consider Phillips to be one of the few ethnic actors who can carry a film. He's played a Mexican-American, a Navaho-Mexican, a Puerto Rican and an Eskimo. His best known role was his first, as a Chicano rock star in *La Bamba*, where he created one of the few positive images of Latinos in American films. Phillips is Scots-Irish and Cherokee on his father's side and Filipino on his mother's. He got his start in the Texas independent film industry as a screenwriter.

Year	Movie	Character
1987	La Bamba	Ritchie Valens
1987	Stand and Deliver	Angel
1988	Dakota	Dakota
1988	Young Guns	Chavez Y Chavez
1989	Disorganized Crime	Ray Forgy
1989	Renegades	Hank
1990	A Show of Force	Jesus Fuentes
1990	The First Power	Russell Logan
1990	Young Guns II	Chavez Y Chavez
1993	Shadow of the Wolf	Agaguk

RIVER PHOENIX

(1970 - 1993)

Phoenix's brief film career began with a solid performance in the kiddie picture *The Explorers*. The following year his star potential became evident as the tough boy in a group of friends looking for a corpse in the woods in *Stand by Me*. He grew up in Venezuela with his brother, Leaf, and his sisters, Rain, Summer and Liberty, where his parents were missionaries for the Children of God. Oscar-nominated for *Running on Empty*, Phoenix died of a drug overdose after collapsing in front of a West Hollywood nightclub.

Year	Movie	Character
1985	Explorers	Wolfgang Muller
1986	Stand by Me	Chris Chambers
1986	The Mosquito Coast	Charlie
1988	A Night in the Life of Jimmy Reardon	Jimmy Reardon
1988	Little Nikita	Jeff Grant
1988	Running on Empty	Danny Pope
1989	Indiana Jones and the Last Crusade	Young Indy
1990	I Love You to Death	Devo Nod
1991	Dogfight	Birdlace
1991	My Own Private Idaho	Mike Waters
1992	Sneakers	Carl
1993	The Thing Called Love	James Wright

SLIM PICKENS

(1919 - 1983)

Once a rodeo rider, Pickens appeared in countless films and TV horse operas, but his most famous role was the B-52 pilot who rode the hydrogen bomb cowboy-style down to destruction at the end of *Dr. Strangelove*. Born in California, he ran away from home at 13 to join the rodeo where, as a friend told him, he'd only get "slim pickens." He got a stage name and became a character beloved by viewers of *Wagon Train*, *Bonanza*, *Gunsmoke*. He died after surgery for a brain tumor.

Year	Movie	Character
1961	A Thunder of Drums	Trooper Erschick
1961	One-Eyed Jacks	Lon
1964	Dr. Strangelove or: How I Learned to Stop Worrying and Love the Bomb	Major T.J. "King" Kong
1965	In Harm's Way	C.P.O. Culpepper
1965	Major Dundee	Wiley
1965	The Glory Guys	Gregory
1966	Stagecoach	Buck
1967	Rough Night in Jericho	Yarbrough
1967	The Flim Flam Man	Jarvis Bates
1968	Will Penny	Ike Wallerstein
1970	The Ballad of Cable Hogue	Ben
1972	The Cowboys	Anse
1972	The Getaway	Cowboy

(continued on page 508)

WALTER PIDGEON

(1897 - 1984)

The urbane Canadian actor was always the gentleman in 53 years of making movies. "Pidge," as his friends called him, began as a singer in musicals, served with the Canadian Army and worked in a Boston bank. After signing with MGM when he was 40, he acted for the company for 20 years and became a star during the war, playing opposite Greer Garson in eight films like the hit *Mrs. Miniver*. In his later years his mellifluous voice made him an appealing character actor until he retired at 80. He died after a series of strokes.

Year	Movie	Character
1961	Voyage to the Bottom of the Sea	Admiral Nelson
1962	Advise and Consent	Senate Majority Leader
1967	Warning Shot	Orville Ames
1968	Funny Girl	Florenz Ziegfeld
1972	Skyjacked	Sen. Arne Lindner
1973	Harry in Your Pocket	Casey
1973	The Neptune Factor	Andrews
1976	Two Minute Warning	Pickpocket

MARY KAY PLACE

(1947 -   )

Place majored in radio-television at the University of Tulsa, and on the day after graduation in 1969 she jumped into her Volkswagon and headed for Hollywood. She got a clerk-typist job at CBS and landed small TV roles. Her big break was getting into the *Mary Hartman, Mary Hartman* series as Loretta. Her movies include *The Big Chill*, where she played the successful career woman who hadn't yet met the right man, but wanted to get pregnant, preferably that weekend!

Year	Movie	Character
1972	Kansas City Bomber	Lovey
1977	New York, New York	Bernice
1979	More American Graffiti	Teensa
1979	Starting Over	Marie
1980	Private Benjamin	Pvt. Mary Lou Glass
1981	Modern Problems	Lorraine
1983	The Big Chill	Meg
1985	Explorers	xxx
1988	A New Life	Donna
1991	Bright Angel	Judy
1992	Captain Ron	Katherine Harvey

TONY PLANA

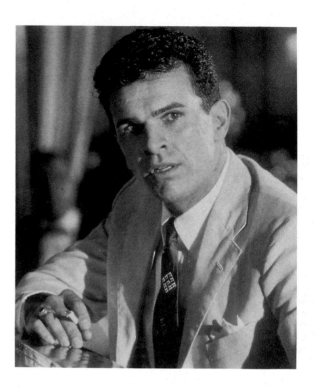

(19?? -   )

Plana was born in Cuba and studied acting at the Royal Academy of Dramatic Arts in London. He got his start when he originated the role of Rudy in the L.A. stage production of *Zoot Suit* and followed the show to Broadway. He has won five Dramalogue Awards for stage performances and has appeared in many films. He can be seen in *!Three Amigos!* as the sidekick to chief bad guy, El Guapo.

Year	Movie	Character
1982	An Officer and a Gentleman	Emiliano Della Serra
1983	Nightmares	Del Amo
1986	!Three Amigos!	Jefe
1986	Salvador	Major Max
1986	The Best of Times	Chico
1987	Born in East L.A.	Feo
1987	Disorderlies	Miguel
1989	Buy & Cell	Raoul
1989	Romero	Father Manuel Morantes
1990	Havana	Julio Ramos
1991	JFK	Carlos Bringuier
1991	One Good Cop	Beniamino

MARTHA PLIMPTON

(1970 -   )

Plimpton is the daughter of actor Keith Carradine and was born in New York. She jumped into acting early by studying at the Professional Children's School. Interested in preserving the environment, Plimpton is a member of the Nature Conservancy. Memorable film roles include that of Dianne Wiest's rebellious teenage daughter in *Parenthood* and one of the treasure-seeking "Goonies" in the film of the same name.

Year	Movie	Character
1981	Rollover	Fewster's Oldest Daughter
1984	The River Rat	Jonsy
1985	The Goonies	Stef
1986	The Mosquito Coast	Emily Spellgood
1987	Shy People	Grace
1988	Another Woman	Laura
1988	Running on Empty	Lorna Phillips
1988	Stars and Bars	Bryant
1989	Parenthood	Julie
1990	Stanley & Iris	Kelly
1993	Josh and S.A.M.	Alison

JOAN PLOWRIGHT

(1929 -   )

Primarily a British stage actress, Plowright has taken more film roles in recent years and, in 1993, won the Golden Globe Award for her part in *Enchanted April*. Plowright is the widow of Sir Laurence Olivier whom she met when the two were performing at London's Royal Court Theatre in the 1950s. The actress was born in the industrial Midlands section of England and learned her craft at the famous drama school of the Old Vic Theatre in London and in repertory theater.

Year	Movie	Character
1960	The Entertainer	Jean
1985	Revolution	Mrs. McConnahay
1990	Avalon	Eva Krichinsky
1990	I Love You to Death	Nadja
1992	Enchanted April	Mrs. Fisher
1993	Dennis the Menace	Martha Wilson
1993	Last Action Hero	Teacher

MICHAEL J. POLLARD

(1939 -   )

Often cast as criminals, clowns and the demented, Pollard commented in 1978: "For so many years I just got put in these roles. Maybe it started with *Bonnie and Clyde*, and maybe not. But even though I am that way, I shouldn't be doin' it in movies anymore. It don't do nobody no good. I play crazy people. Crazy, like killers, or sometimes just crazy people. Take that picture *Willard*. They wanted me to do that. I said, hey, man, I don't want to walk down the street and have people say 'There goes the rat man.' "

Year	Movie	Character
1963	The Stripper	Jelly
1966	The Russians are Coming!	
	The Russians are Coming!	Airplane Mechanic
1966	The Wild Angels	Pigmy
1967	Bonnie and Clyde	C.W. Moss
1967	Caprice	Barney
1967	Enter Laughing	Marvin
1968	Jigsaw	Dill
1970	Little Fauss and Big Halsey	Little Fauss
1980	Melvin and Howard	Little Red
1985	Heated Vengeance	Snake
1986	The Patriot	Howard
1987	Roxanne	Andy
1988	Scrooged	Herman
1989	Fast Food	Bud
1989	Next of Kin	Harold
1990	Dick Tracy	Bug Bailey
1990	I Come in Peace	Boner
1990	Night Visitor	Stanley Willard
1992	Split Second	The Rat Catcher

DON PORTER

(1913 -   )

Porter was a bank teller, an office manger, a salesman and a reporter before he could settle into an acting career. He was in repertory theater until 1939 when he made his first film: *The Mystery of the White Room*. Porter's favorite role was that of Petruchio in *The Taming of the Shrew*.

Year	Movie	Character
1961	Bachelor in Paradise	Thomas W. Jynson
1968	Live a Little, Love a Little	Mike Lansdown
1972	The Candidate	Jarman
1975	White Line Fever	Josh Cutler

ANNIE POTTS

(1952 -   )

Potts has lived on the French Riviera, worked as a saloon singer in Santa Fe, and been a student of the Comedie Francaise. She studied theater at Stephens College in Missouri and married a fellow student the day after graduation. Both went into show business. Potts made her film debut as an aspiring prostitute in *Corvette Summer*, played Molly Ringwald's friend in *Pretty in Pink* and was the heroes' secretary in the *Ghostbusters* pictures. Her ambition is to continue acting until she falls out of a wheelchair.

Year	Movie	Character
1978	Corvette Summer	Vanessa
1978	King of the Gypsies	Persa
1981	Heartaches	Bonnie
1984	Crimes of Passion	Amy
1984	Ghostbusters	Janine Melnitz
1986	Jumpin' Jack Flash	Liz Carlson
1986	Pretty in Pink	Iona
1989	Ghostbusters II	Janine Melnitz
1989	Who's Harry Crumb?	Helen Downing
1990	Texasville	Karla Jackson

KELLY PRESTON

(1963 -   )

Preston was born in Hawaii and moved around the world a lot with her family—her father was an international businessman. A photographer said she ought to be a model, and that led on to films. She studied drama at USC and almost immediately got a role in the soap called *Capitol*.

Year	Movie	Character
1983	Christine	Roseanne
1983	Metalstorm: The Destruction of Jared-Syn	Dhyana
1985	Mischief	Marilyn
1985	Secret Admirer	Debora
1986	52 Pick-Up	Cini
1986	SpaceCamp	Tish
1987	A Tiger's Tale	Shirley Butts
1987	Amazon Women on the Moon	Violet
1987	Love at Stake	Sara Lee
1988	Twins	Marnie Mason
1989	The Experts	Bonnie Grant
1990	Run	Karen Landers

ROBERT PRESTON

(1917 - 1987)

Preston was the legendary "Music Man" on stage and screen, a lead-ing-man type who often played character roles during a 50-year career. Born in Massachusetts and raised in Hollywood, he served in the Army Air Force during World War II, and played the charming gay nightclub showman in *Victor/Victoria* which won him an Oscar nomi-nation. A long-time smoker, he died of lung cancer in Santa Barbara.

Year	Movie	Character
1962	The Music Man	Harold Hill
1972	Junior Bonner	Ace Bonner
1974	Mame	Beauregard
1977	Semi-Tough	Big Ed Bookman
1981	S.O.B.	Dr. Irving Finegarten
1982	Victor/Victoria	Toddy
1984	The Last Starfighter	Centauri

BARRY PRIMUS

(1938 -   )

Primus grew up on the edge of Harlem, and has said, "I could easily have become a criminal if I hadn't decided to become an actor." He started off playing guitar, singing and "telling Jewish jokes like Lenny Bruce" in the Catskills. His theatrical career began as an actor on the New York stage and later expanded into writing, directing and teaching. He scripted and directed the 1992 Hollywood satire, *Mistress*, a film based on his own experience of spending several years trying to find financing for a movie about actors.

Year	Movie	Character
1968	The Brotherhood	Vido
1971	Von Richthofen and Brown	Goering
1972	Boxcar Bertha	Rake Brown
1977	New York, New York	Paul Wilson
1978	Avalanche	Mark Elliott
1979	Heartland	Jack
1979	The Rose	Dennis
1981	Absence of Malice	Waddell
1986	Jake Speed	Lawrence
1986	SpaceCamp	Brennan
1987	The Stranger	Drake
1988	Big Business	Michael
1989	Torn Apart	Arie Arnon
1991	Guilty by Suspicion	Bert Alan
1992	Night and the City	Tommy Tessler

WILLIAM PRINCE

ANDREW PRINE

(1913 -   )

One of the leading American veterans of classical stage drama, Prince came to films after a long career in New York theater, where he once acted opposite Katharine Cornell. He studied at Cornell University and trained at the famous Barter Theater in Virginia. His film appearances include the founder of TV network UBS in *Network* who loses control of the firm to Ned Beatty and his hatchet man Robert Duvall, and as a police commisioner with mob ties in *The Gauntlet*.

(1936 -   )

Prine's screen career got off to a good start as Patty Duke's troubled half-brother in 1962's *The Miracle Worker*. He spent the rest of the decade and the early 1970s on horseback in various movie and TV westerns. Since the mid-1970s, he has worked mostly in low-budget exploitation pictures. Prine originally got Hollywood's attention with a critically acclaimed Broadway performance in *Look Homeward, Angel*. The actor hails from Florida and studied drama at the University of Florida.

Year	Movie	Character
1975	The Stepford Wives	Artist
1976	Family Plot	Bishop
1976	Network	Edward George Ruddy
1977	Rollercoaster	Quinlan
1977	The Gauntlet	Blakelock
1979	The Promise	Calloway
1982	Kiss Me Goodbye	Rev. Hollis
1982	Love and Money	Ambassador Paultz
1982	The Soldier	U.S. President
1985	Spies Like Us	Mr. Keyes
1987	Nuts	Clarence Middleton
1988	Vice Versa	Avery
1989	Second Sight	Cardinal O'Hara
'91	The Taking of Beverly Hills	Mitchell Sage

Year	Movie	Character
1962	The Miracle Worker	James Keller
1964	Advance to the Rear	Pvt. Owen Selous
1966	Texas Across the River	Sibley
1968	Bandolero!	Roscoe Bookbinder
1968	The Devil's Brigade	Pvt. Theodore Ransom
1970	Chisum	Alex McSween
1976	Grizzly	Don
1977	The Town That Dreaded Sundown	Deputy Norman Rams
1982	Amityville II: The Possession	Father Tom
1993	Gettysburg	Brig. Gen. Garnett

JURGEN PROCHNOW

(1941 -)

Prochnow acted in Europe for 21 years without attracting much international attention. Then he performed in the German film *Das Boot* (1981) and became known worldwide. "All of a sudden from all over the world you get scented letters," he once said. He was born in Berlin and grew up in the Polish countryside.

Year	Movie	Character
1984	Dune	Duke Leto Atreides
1987	Beverly Hills Cop II	Maxwell Dent
1988	The Seventh Sign	The Border
1989	A Dry White Season	Captain Stolz
1990	The Fourth War	Col. N.A. Valachev
1992	Twin Peaks: Fire Walk With Me	Woodsman
1993	Body of Evidence	Dr. Alan Paley

ROBERT PROSKY

(1930 -)

For Prosky, a native of Philadelphia, the path to national attention came through Washington, D.C., where he was for two decades a fixture on the Arena Stage. His numerous film roles include the bureau chief in *Broadcast News*, the absentee landlord who torches Tom Cruise's family home in *Far and Away*, and the baseball team owner who bribes Robert Redford to blow the big game in *The Natural*. Prosky spent three seasons (1984-87) as the roll-call sergeant in NBC's *Hill Street Blues*.

Year	Movie	Character
1981	Thief	Leo
1982	Hanky Panky	Hiram Calder
1982	Monsignor	Bishop Walkmam
1983	Christine	Will Darnell
1983	The Lords of Discipline	Bear
1984	The Natural	Judge
1987	Big Shots	Keegan
1987	Broadcast News	Ernie Merriman
1987	Outrageous Fortune	Stanislov Korzenowski
1988	The Great Outdoors	Wally
1988	Things Change	Joseph Vincent
1990	Funny About Love	Emil Thomas Bergman
1990	Gremlins 2 The New Batch	Forster
1990	Loose Cannons	Curt Von Metz
1990	Green Card	Bronte's Lawyer
1992	Far and Away	Christie
1992	Hoffa	Billy Flynn
1993	Last Action Hero	Nick (the projectionist)
1993	Rudy	Father Cavanaugh
1993	Mrs. Doubtfire	Mr. Lindy

BILL PULLMAN

(1954 -   )

Pullman won attention in 1986 for his portrayal of Earl, the dim-witted extortionist, in the comedy *Ruthless People*. He grew up in Hornell, NY, and spurned college to enroll at a technical school because he liked building houses. Then he attended State University of New York at Oneonta and got a master's degree in fine arts from the University of Massachusetts. He taught in Montana before tackling the acting world in New York.

Year	Movie	Character
1986	Ruthless People	Earl
1987	Spaceballs	Lone Starr
1988	Rocket Gibraltar	Crow Black
1988	Serpent and the Rainbow	Dennis Alan
1988	The Accidental Tourist	Julian
1989	Cold Feet	Buck Latham
1990	Sibling Rivalry	Nicholas Meany
1991	Bright Angel	Bob
1991	Liebestraum	Paul Kessler
1992	A League of Their Own	Bob Hinson
1992	Newsies	Bryan Denton
1992	Singles	Dr. Jamison
1993	Sleepless in Seattle	Walter
1993	Sommersby	Orin Meecham
1993	Malice	Andy Safian

LEE PURCELL

(1947 -   )

Purcell got her start in films after being "discovered" and cast by Steve McQueen in his Solar Productions' *Adam at 6 A.M.* He chose her for the lead, after testing 500 girls, because, as he said, she "seemed to jump right out of the screen. There's no way to explain it except that this girl has soul, and it comes through loud and clear." Her career has been evenly divided between feature films and TV-movies.

Year	Movie	Character
1974	Mr. Majestyk	Wiley
1978	Almost Summer	Christine
1978	Big Wednesday	Peggy
1980	Stir Crazy	Susan
1983	Eddie Macon's Run	Jilly
1983	Valley Girl	Beth

DENVER PYLE

(1920 -   )

Pyle was lucky just to survive long enough to get into acting. He was on four ships torpedoed in the Pacific during World War II. The actor may be best known as the chubby, bearded Uncle Jesse in *The Dukes of Hazard* on CBS television.

Year	Movie	Character
1960	The Alamo	Gambler
1964	Mail Order Bride	Preacher Pope
1965	Great Race	Sheriff
1965	Shenandoah	Pastor Bjoerling
1965	The Rounders	Bull
1967	Bonnie and Clyde	Frank Hamer
1967	Tammy and the Millionaire	Grandpa
1967	Welcome to Hard Times	Alfie
1968	Bandolero!	Muncie Carter
1968	Five Card Stud	Sig Evers
1973	Cahill—U.S. Marshal	Denver
1976	Buffalo Bill and the Indians, or Sitting Bull's History Lesson	Indian Agent McLaughlin
1976	Hawmps	Col. Seymour Hawkins
1976	The Adventures of Frontier Fremont	Old Mountanian
1976	Winterhawk	Arkansas
1977	Mountain Man	Clark
1978	Return From Witch Mountain	xxx

ANTHONY QUAYLE

(1913 - 1989)

The British actor/director appeared in more than 30 films, but is primarily remembered for his achievements in British theater. As director of the precurser to the Royal Shakespeare Theatre at Stratford-on-Avon (1948-56) Quayle established its reputation as a major center of British drama by luring such actors as Laurence Olivier, Ralph Richardson, John Gielgud and others to play, despite the minimal wages. He died of cancer in London.

Year	Movie	Character
1961	The Guns of Navarone	Franklin
1964	The Fall of the Roman Empire	Verulus
1965	Operation Crossbow	Bamford
1969	Anne of the Thousand Days	Wolsey
1969	MacKenna's Gold	Englishman
1972	Everything You Always Wanted to Know About Sex (But Were Afraid to Ask)	The King
1974	The Tamarind Seed	Jack Loder
1976	The Eagle Has Landed	Adm. Wilhelm Canaris
1979	Murder by Decree	Sir Charles Warren

KATHLEEN QUINLAN

(1954 -   )

Quinlan began her film career as a stand-in, a diver, in 1972's *One is a Lonely Number*, but critical acclaim came with her portrayal of a teenaged schizophrenic in *I Never Promised You a Rose Garden*. The actress grew up in Mill Valley, CA, and trained for five years as a diver and another five years as a gymnast. She ultimately turned down an invitation to train with the national gymnastics team in order to pursue a career in Hollywood.

Year	Movie	Character
1973	American Graffiti	Peg
1976	Lifeguard	Wendy
1977	Airport '77	Julie
1977	I Never Promised You a Rose Garden	Deborah Blake
1979	The Promise	Nancy/Marie
1979	The Runner Stumbles	Sister Rita
1982	Hanky Panky	Janet Dunn
1983	Independence Day	Mary Ann Taylor
1983	Twilight Zone—The Movie	Helen (Segment 3)
1985	Warning Sign	Joanie Morse
1987	Wild Thing	Jane
1988	Clara's Heart	Leona Hart
1988	Sunset	Nancy Shoemaker
1991	The Doors	Patricia Kennealy

AIDAN QUINN

(1959 -   )

While working as a roofer in his hometown of Chicago, Quinn, not yet 20, decided to do something more with his life. An ad in a local arts weekly led him to acting classes. There, his teacher was so impressed with his natural acting ability that Quinn was awarded a scholarship. Choice parts in Chicago theatrical productions of Chekhov, Brecht and Faulkner brought him to the attention of a William Morris talent agent who introduced him to director Jim Foley. Foley cast him as Darryl Hannah's lover in *Reckless*.

Year	Movie	Character
1984	Reckless	Johnny
1985	Desperately Seeking Susan	Dez
1986	The Mission	Felipe
1987	Stakeout	Richard Montgomery
1988	Crusoe	Crusoe
1990	Avalon	Jules Kaye
1990	The Handmaid's Tale	Nick
1990	The Lemon Sisters	Frankie McGuinness
1991	At Play in the Fields of the Lord	Martin Quarrier
1993	Benny and Joon	Benny

J.C. QUINN

(1940 -)

One of the industry's very popular character actors, Quinn has been seen on a wide range of movies and television shows. He has joked that he has appeared on every police show at least once. The Philadelphia native started acting in New York in 1967 after working in a number of widely diverse fields. He appeared in *Turner & Hooch* as the boss of a fishpacking plant used to launder Panamanian drug money.

Year	Movie	Character
1980	Brubaker	xxx
1980	Times Square	Simon
1983	Silkwood	Curtis Schultz
1985	Vision Quest	Elmo
1986	At Close Range	Boyd
1986	Heartbreak Ridge	Quartermaster Sgt.
1986	Maximum Overdrive	Duncan
1987	Barfly	Jim
1989	Gross Anatomy	Papa Slovak
1989	The Abyss	"Sonny" Dawson
1989	Turner & Hooch	Walter Boyett
1991	Prayer of the Rollerboys	Jaworski
1992	CrissCross	Jetty
1992	The Babe	Jack Dunn
1992	Twisted	xxx

VICTORIA RACIMO

(1945 -)

Racimo has cheerfully admitted lying her way into the world of theater. At 13, she glibly told the Gateway Playhouse that she was 16 years old. She was put to work painting scenery, but found herself mixed in with many famous actors. She got her first minor role a few years later when she wandered up to a Broadway stage door and asked if there might be a part for her in *Flower Drum Song*. The man, who happened to be Oscar Hammerstein, said yes.

Year	Movie	Character
1979	Prophecy	Ramona
1980	The Mountain Men	Running Moon
1986	Choke Canyon	Rachel
1987	Ernest Goes to Camp	Nurse St. Cloud

CHIPS RAFFERTY

DEBORAH RAFFIN

(1909 - 1971)

This tall Australian actor first played slapstick comedy and then, during World War II, went international when he took leave from the Royal Australian Air force to perform in morale-raising films. After the war, Rafferty worked in American and Australian films, on television, and with his own film company. He made the Queen's honor list as a Member of the Order of the British Empire. He died at 62 of a heart attack in Sydney.

Year	Movie	Character
1960	The Sundowners	Quinlan
1960	The Wackiest Ship in the Army	Patterson
1967	Double Trouble	Archie Brown
1971	Outback	Jock Crawford

(1953 -)

A pretty face provided her entree into films, but Raffin pursued her craft seriously with drama coach Milton Katselas and in England with Kate Fleming at the National Theater. The TV-movie *Nightmare in Badham County* won her an Emmy nomination in 1977 and was also a huge success in China. She subsequently became the unofficial ambassador from Hollywood to China, arranging visits by Hollywood luminaries to meet with Chinese leaders and filmmakers and distributing U.S. films in China and Chinese films in the U.S.

Year	Movie	Character
1973	Forty Carats	Trina Stanley
1974	The Dove	Patti Ratterree
1975	Once is Not Enough	January
1977	The Sentinel	Jennifer
1980	Touched by Love	Lena Canada
1985	Death Wish 3	Kathryn Davis
1993	Morning Glory	Elly Dinsmore

STEVE RAILSBACK

![Steve Railsback photo]

(1947 -)

Railsback gained national attention in 1976 for his electrifying performance as Charles Manson in CBS' two-part series *Helter Skelter*. To prepare for the part, Railsback would lock himself in a closet for two hours every day. He reasoned that Manson was used to solitude from spending most of his life in institutions. "I didn't eat or talk to people much," he has said, "I just wanted to be with myself so I could understand parts of his world." Railsback is the son of a Texas oil man. His career began with acting studies in New York.

Year	Movie	Character
1980	The Stunt Man	Cameron
1984	Torchlight	Jake
1985	Lifeforce	Carlsen
1986	Armed and Dangerous	The Cowboy
1987	Distortions	Scott

HAROLD RAMIS

(1944 -)

Versatile, Ramis has been a writer, actor, director and producer. He co-scripted the box office smashes, *National Lampoon's Animal House* and *Ghostbusters* and, for a time, was the associate editor of *Playboy* magazine. The Academy of Canadian Television and Radio Artists Award for Best Writer was presented to him in 1978. Born in Chicago, Ramis was educated at Washington University.

Year	Movie	Character
1981	Stripes	Russell
1984	Ghostbusters	Dr. Egon Spengler
1987	Baby Boom	Steven Buchner
1988	Stealing Home	Alan Appleby
1989	Ghostbusters II	Dr. Egon Spengler

CHARLOTTE RAMPLING

(1946 -   )

Rampling first received notice for her acting abilities with her portrayal of Vanessa Redgrave's bitchy roommate in the international hit, *Georgy Girl*. Nine years later she achieved notoriety on both sides of the Atlantic in *The Night Porter*, a film about a Nazi officer who saves a young girl from the ovens by making her his partner in a sado-masochistic affair. The daughter of an army colonel, Rampling grew up on army bases in England and France.

Year	Movie	Character
1966	Georgy Girl	Meredith
1975	Farewell My Lovely	Mrs. Velma Grayle
1977	Orca	Rachel
1980	Stardust Memories	Dorrie
1982	The Verdict	Laura Fischer
1987	Angel Heart	Margaret Krusemark
1988	D.O.A.	Mrs. Fitzwaring

JOHN RANDOLPH

(1915 -   )

Randolph's first audition came during the depths of the Depression and he recalled there were "a lot of scared people there, women crying. If you wanted to get a job in *anything*, at the time, it was terribly tense." His passionate, left-of-center political stance put him on Hollywood's McCarthy-era blacklist from 1951 to 1965 and he did not make a movie until he was 50. He was able to make a living in Broadway shows—over 30—but never forgave those who shut the door on him. "I've never trusted Hollywood completely," he later said.

Year	Movie	Character
1966	Seconds	Arthur Hamilton
1968	Pretty Poison	Azenauer
1969	Number One	Coach Jim Southerd
1970	There Was a Crooked Man...	Cyrus McNutt
1973	Serpico	Chief Green
1976	King Kong	Captain Ross
1985	Prizzi's Honor	Angelo "Pop" Partanna
1988	The Wizard of Loneliness	Doc
1989	National Lampoon's Christmas Vacation	Clark Griswold, Sr.
1990	Sibling Rivalry	Charles Turner, Sr.

DAVID RASCHE

(1944 -   )

Rasche has played many character roles, ranging from a barefoot field-goal kicker to what he called an "insane detective" in the television series *Sledge Hammer*. He has said that all of his roles begin with his looking into himself for knowledge and imagination. Rasche comes from a family where most males became church ministers, and he once considered the religious life for his own career.

Year	Movie	Character
1980	Just Tell Me What You Want	xxx
1982	Fighting Back	Michael
1984	Best Defense	Spy
1986	Cobra	Dan
1986	Native Son	Buckley
1987	Made in Heaven	Donald Sumner
1989	An Innocent Man	Mike Parnell
1989	Wicked Stepmother	Steve
1990	Masters of Menace	Buddy
1991	Bingo	Hal Devlin
1991	Delirious	Paul and Dennis

HEATHER RATTRAY

(1965 -   )

Rattray was a child actress who enjoyed a brief film career in the 1970s, appearing in four movies in as many years. She was only 11 the day she went to a neighbor's house to help with chores. A visiting film producer spotted her and thought she might have the serene loveliness of Grace Kelly. She got her first job after a screen test the next day. Rattray grew up on a 400-acre farm in Minnesota, where she learned her favorite pastimes, riding and caring for animals.

Year	Movie	Character
1977	Across the Great Divide	Holly Smith
1978	The Further Adventures of the Wilderness Family	Jenny
1978	The Sea Gypsies	Courtney
1979	Mountain Family Robinson	Jenny

WILLIAM REDFIELD

(1927 - 1976)

Actor, writer, and talk-show panelist, Redfield did more than 2,000 performances on stage, films, TV, and radio in his career that began when he was 9 in a Broadway musical. A Manhattan native, he came from a show biz family, his mother a Ziegfield Follies girl, his father a music conductor. He was an infantryman during World War II. Redfield died at 49 of a respiratory ailment in New York.

Year	Movie	Character
1965	Morituri	Baldwin
1966	Duel at Diablo	Sgt. Ferguson
1966	Fantastic Voyage	Capt. Bill Owens
1971	A New Leaf	Beckett
1972	The Hot Rock	Lt. Hoover
1974	Death Wish	Sam Kreutzer
1974	For Pete's Sake	Fred
1975	One Flew Over the Cuckoo's Nest	Harding
1977	Mr. Billion	Leopold

JERRY REED

(1939 -   )

Originally a professional country and western singer, Reed is the son of Georgia cottonmill workers who took up the guitar as a kid because his family could not afford a piano. Burt Reynolds helped him get started in movies and he has appeared in many films with Reynolds. He has also learned to be a producer. Reed's favorite pasttimes are fishing and golf.

Year	Movie	Character
1975	W.W. and the Dixie Dancekings	Wayne
1976	Gator	Bama McCall
1977	Smokey and the Bandit	Cledus
1978	High-Ballin'	Duke
1979	Hot Stuff	Doug
1980	Smokey and the Bandit II	Cledus
1983	Smokey and the Bandit 3	Cledus/Bandit
1983	The Survivors	Jack Locke
1988	Bat 21	Col. George Walker

OLIVER REED

PAMELA REED

(1938 -   )

Reed has played a number of tough-guy roles and has come to them naturally. He has been a bouncer in a strip club, a boxer and a soldier stationed in Malaysia and Hong Kong. It was his uncle, the director Carol Reed, who steered him into acting. He was born in Wimbledon, England, the son of a sports journalist.

(1949 -   )

Trained to be a classical actress, Reed divides her time between New York plays and Hollywood movies. She graduated with a drama degree from the University of Washington, her tuition partly financed by working as a cook's helper in a camp of 300 that was building a section of the Alaska pipeline. She is the daughter of a former labor union organizer and has inherited her father's passion for left-of-center politics.

Year	Movie	Character
1968	Oliver	Bill Sikes
1970	Take a Girl Like You	Patrick
1970	The Lady in the Car With Glasses and a Gun	Michael Caldwell
1974	The Three Musketeers	Athos
1975	The Four Musketeers	Athos
1975	Ten Little Indians	Hugh
1975	Tommy	Frank Hobbs
1976	Burnt Offerings	Ben
1976	Great Scout and Cathouse Thursday	Joe
1978	The Big Sleep	Eddie Mars
1980	Dr. Heckyl and Mr. Hype	Dr. Heckyl/Mr. Hype
1981	Condorman	Krokov
1983	The Sting II	Lonnegan
1983	Two of a Kind	Beazley
1987	The Misfit Brigade	The General
1989	Outlaw of Gor	Sarm
1989	The Adventures of Baron Munchausen	Vulcan

Year	Movie	Character
1980	Melvin and Howard	Bonnie Dummar
1980	The Long Riders	Belle Starr
1981	Eyewitness	Linda
1982	Young Doctors in Love	Norine Sprockett
1983	The Right Stuff	Trudy Cooper
1984	The Goodbye People	Nancie "Shirley" Scot
1986	The Best of Times	Gigi Hightower
1986	The Clan of the Cave Bear	Iza
1987	Rachel River	Mary
1990	Cadillac Man	Tina O'Brien
1990	Chattahoochee	Earlene
1990	Kindergarten Cop	Phoebe O'Hara
1992	Bob Roberts	News Anchor
1992	Passed Away	Terry Scanlan

376

JOE REGALBUTO

(19?? -   )

Regalbuto is best known as the investigative reporter Frank Fontana on the successful TV series *Murphy Brown*. Prior to that role he had struggled to make a name for himself as a supporting player in other series, TV-movies and some features. "An actor's life is really a drag, it's really a drag," he once said, reflecting on those early days.

Year	Movie	Character
1982	Honkytonk Man	Henry Axle
1982	Missing	Frank Teruggi
1982	Six Weeks	Bob
1983	The Star Chamber	Arthur Cooms
1984	Lassiter	Breeze
1986	Raw Deal	Baxter
1987	The Sicilian	Father Doldana

KATE REID

(1930 - 1993)

On the stage and in movies and television for 40 years, Reid was not generally well-known by the public, but the theater community knew her as an actress who worked constantly. London-born, she grew up in Canada and gained her early professional experience there in stock theaters. She won critical acclaim for her part in Louis Malle's film *Atlantic City* and for her performance opposite Dustin Hoffman in the 1984 Broadway revival of *Death of a Salesman*. She died of cancer at 62 in Stratford, Ontario.

Year	Movie	Character
1966	This Property is Condemned	Hazel Starr
1971	The Andromeda Strain	Dr. Ruth Leavitt
1981	Atlantic City	Grace
1985	Heaven Help Us	Grandma
1986	Double Negative	xxx
1986	Fire With Fire	Sister Victoria
1988	Sweet Hearts Dance	Pearne Manners
1989	Bye Bye Blues	Mary Wright
1989	Signs of Life	Mrs. Wrangway
1991	Deceived	Rosalie

CARL REINER

(1922 -   )

Actor/producer/director Reiner first made his name as a comic actor on Sid Caesar's *Your Show of Shows* television program during the 1950s. He next created the hit series *The Dick Van Dyke Show* (1961-66) before working as a movie director. His debut feature was *Enter Laughing*, based on his semi-autobiographical novel, but his most popular directorial efforts came in the late 1970s with *Oh, God!* (1977) and *The Jerk* (1979).

Year	Movie	Character
1961	Gidget Goes Hawaiian	Russ Lawrence
1963	It's a Mad Mad Mad Mad World	Tower Control
1965	The Art of Love	Rodin
1966	The Russians are Coming! The Russians are Coming!	Walt Whittaker
1978	The End	Dr. Maneet
1982	Dead Men Don't Wear Plaid	Field Marshall VonKluck

JUDGE REINHOLD

(1956 -   )

Reinhold is a blunt-spoken actor who does not balk at criticizing the hands who feed him, Hollywood's movie executives. "Everything has to be put through the Stupid Department before the public sees it," he has said. "Everything must be stupidized." Reinhold studied in four East Coast acting schools before heading west to the world of film.

Year	Movie	Character
1981	Stripes	Elmo
1982	Fast Times at Ridgemont High	Brad Hamilton
1982	Pandemonium	xxx
1983	The Lords of Discipline	Macabbee
1984	Beverly Hills Cop	Det. Billy Rosewood
1984	Gremlins	Gerald
1984	Roadhouse 66	Beckman
1986	Head Office	Jack
1986	Off Beat	Joe Gower
1986	Ruthless People	Ken Kessler
1987	Beverly Hills Cop II	Billy Rosewood
1988	Vice Versa	Marshall
1990	Daddy's Dyin'...Who's Got the Will?	Harmony
1991	Zandalee	Thierry Martin
1993	Bank Robber	Officer Gross

ANN REINKING

(1949 -   )

Reinking is a dancer and singer, as well as actress, and she made it to Broadway by a traditional route—she got a job with the Rockettes. She had told her parents back in Washington State that she wanted to be an actress at age 13 and vowed not to attend college. Ballet is still her favorite dance form, but she's had experience in all kinds.

Year	Movie	Character
1978	Movie, Movie	Troubles Moran
1979	All That Jazz	Kate Jagger
1982	Annie	Grace Farrell
1984	Micki + Maude	Micki Salinger

PAUL REISER

(1957 -   )

"I always loved comedy, but I never knew it was something you could learn to do," Reiser has said. "I always thought that some people are born comedians." That idea was dispelled when he taught himself to be a successful stand-up comic, a role that led on to bigger things. Soon after breaking into some New York clubs, he was cast as one of the six buddies in the movie *Diner*. Reiser played a venal corporate exec tagging along with Sigourney Weaver in her spaceship en route to destroy some monsters in the smash sequel *Aliens*.

Year	Movie	Character
1982	Diner	Modell
1984	Beverly Hills Cop	Jeffrey
1984	Odd Jobs	Max
1986	Aliens	Burke
1987	Beverly Hills Cop II	Jeffrey Friedman
1987	Cross My Heart	Bruce
1990	Crazy People	Stephen Bachman
1991	The Marrying Man	Phil
1993	Family Prayers	Dan

JAMES REMAR

(1953 -   )

Remar got tagged for "villain" roles after appearing as the ruthless mobster Dutch Schultz in *The Cotton Club*. But he has insisted he's capable of playing all kinds of roles. "Any good actor is a character actor," he once said. Remar is an alumnus of Manhattan's Neighborhood Playhouse and made his screen debut in a project at New York University.

Year	Movie	Character
1979	The Warriors	Ajax
1980	Cruising	Gregory
1980	Windwalker	Windwalker as a young man
1982	48 Hours	Ganz
1984	The Cotton Club	Dutch Schultz
1986	Band of the Hand	Nestor
1986	The Clan of the Cave Bear	Creb
1988	Rent-a-Cop	Dancer
1989	Drugstore Cowboy	Gentry
1989	The Dream Team	Gianelli
1990	Tales From the Darkside	Preston ("Lover's Vow")
1991	White Fang	Beauty Smith
1993	Fatal Instinct	Max Shady

BERT REMSEN

(1925 -   )

Remsen seems always to be playing the role of some feisty old coot. He was a Purple Heart veteran of World War II, then came home to play ten years of summer stock. That led to Broadway which in turn led to films—his first was in *Pork Chop Hill* with Gregory Peck in 1959. Working on the TV series *No Time for Sergeants* in 1964, a falling crane struck him and nearly ended his career. He revived after two years in a hospital.

Year	Movie	Character
1971	McCabe and Mrs. Miller	xxx
1972	Fuzz	Sgt. Murchison
1974	California Split	Helen Brown
1974	Thieves Like Us	T-Dub
1975	Nashville	Star
1976	Baby Blue Marine	Mr. Hudkins
1976	Buffalo Bill and the Indians, or Sitting Bull's History Lesson	Crutch
1976	Harry and Walter Go to New York	Guard O'Meara
1979	Fast Break	Bo Winnegar
1980	Borderline	Carl Richards
1980	Carny	Delno
1980	Inside Moves	Stinky

(continued on page 509)

MICHAEL RENNIE

(1909 - 1971)

The soulful-looking British actor in films and TV preferred at first to sell cars instead of working in his father's wool mill, but he went to London to do walk-ons in a rep co. Rennie also became a movie extra and a stand-in during action scenes. After his wartime service in the Royal Air Force, he went to Hollywood in 1951 and did action films and comedy. He died at 61 of heart failure in Yorkshire, England.

Year	Movie	Character
1960	The Lost World	Lord Roxton
1966	Ride Beyond Vengeance	Brooks Durham
1967	Hotel	Duke of Lanbourne
1968	The Devil's Brigade	Lt. Gen. Mark Clark
1968	The Power	Arthur Nordlund

FERNANDO REY

(1917 -   )

Born into a well-to-do Spanish family, Rey spent three years with his father in the trenches of the Civil War, fighting against Franco. He was a compatriot of the famous director Luis Bunuel and appeared in one of Bunuel's most popular films, *The Discreet Charm of the Bourgeoise* (1972). American audiences probably know him best as the deadly drug trafficker in *The French Connection*.

Year	Movie	Character
1966	Return of the Seven	Priest
1967	Run Like a Thief	Colonel Romero
1968	Villa Rides	Fuentes
1969	Guns of the Magnificent Seven	Quintero
1971	The French Connection	Alain Charnier
1971	The Light at the Edge of the World	Captain Moriz
1975	The French Connection II	Charnier
1979	Quintet	Grigor
1980	Caboblanco	Teredo
1982	Monsignor	Satoni
1985	Rustlers' Rhapsody	Railroad Colonel
1986	Saving Grace	Cardinal Stefano Biondi
1988	Moon Over Parador	Aljandro
1992	1492: Conquest of Paradise	Marchena

VING RHAMES

(19?? -   )

A Harlem-born actor, Rhames played many stage roles and got his first major film job as an urban guerilla leader in the Paul Schrader movie *Patty Hearst*. He played the part of James Baldwin's father in the 1984 TV-movie *Go Tell It on the Mountain*. Rhames is a graduate of the High School for the Performing Arts in New York and the Juilliard School.

Year	Movie	Character
1988	Patty Hearst	Cinque
1990	Jacob's Ladder	George
1990	The Long Walk Home	Herbert Cotter
1991	Flight of the Intruder	C.P.O. Frank McRae
1991	Homicide	Randolph
1991	The People Under the Stairs	LeRoy
1993	Dave	Duane Stevenson
1993	The Saint of Fort Washington	Little Leroy

JOHN RHYS-DAVIES

(1944 -   )

Rhys-Davies was born in Salisbury, England, and graduated from the University of East Anglia with a degree in history and literature. He then taught for a year before joining RADA, from which he graduated in 1986. He has appeared on the stage in many Shakespeare productions and other classics and won an Emmy for his 1980 performance as the jovial Portuguese captain in *Shogun*. When not acting, Rhys-Davies plays chess and collects classic cars and books.

Year	Movie	Character
1981	Raiders of the Lost Ark	Sallah
1981	Sphinx	Stephanos
1982	Victor/Victoria	Cassell
1984	Sahara	Rasoul
1985	King Solomon's Mines	Dogati
1986	Firewalker	Corky Taylor
1987	The Living Daylights	Gen. Leonid Pushkin
1989	Indiana Jones and the Last Crusade	Sallah

KIM RICHARDS

(1964 -   )

Richards can claim one of the earliest ever starts—she was appearing in a diaper commercial at the age of four months. She had made 20 commercials before she was 4 1/2 when signed to be in the ABC production *Nanny and the Professor*. Richards has been in many television productions since then and has appeared in several Disney movies.

Year	Movie	Character
1976	Assault on Precinct 13	Kathy
1976	No Deposit, No Return	Tracy
1977	The Car	Lynn Marie
1978	Return From Witch Mountain	Tia
1984	Meatballs II	Cheryl
1985	Tuff Turf	Frankie Croyden

LEE RICHARDSON

(1926 -   )

Considered one of the country's leading classical repertory actors, Richardson is a founding member and repertory player in Minneapolis' Guthrie Theater. Primarily a stage actor, he got the acting bug after dropping out of college to study directing at the Goodman Theater in Chicago. He once recalled that, after enrolling, "within one month I knew I found what I should be. Nothing rational—it was just something I felt."

Year	Movie	Character
1980	Brubaker	Warden Renfro
1981	Prince of the City	Sam Heinsdorff
1985	Prizzi's Honor	Dominic Prizzi
1987	Amazing Grace and Chuck	Jeffries
1987	Sweet Lorraine	Sam
1987	The Believers	Dennis Maslow
1988	Tiger Warsaw	Mitchell Warsaw
1989	The Fly II	Anton Bartok
1990	Q & A	Leo Bloomenfeld
1990	The Exorcist III	University President
1992	A Stranger Among Us	Rebbe

PETER RIEGERT

(1947 -   )

"It never crossed my mind that acting was a legitimate way to earn a living," Riegert has said by way of explaining why he never considered the actor's life until he was 24. His appearance in the phenomenal movie hit *National Lampoon's Animal House* made him a familiar face to American movie-goers. He played a pickle dealer and Amy Irving's suitor in *Crossing Delancy*. Born in the Bronx, Riegert spent his first 8 years of acting life in War Babies, an improvisational group.

Year	Movie	Character
1978	National Lampoon's Animal House	Donald Schoenstein
1979	Americathon	Eric
1979	Head Over Heels	Sam
1983	Local Hero	Mac
1987	The Stranger	Harris Kite
1988	Crossing Delancy	Sam Posner
1990	A Shock to the System	Robert Benham
1991	Oscar	Aldo
1991	The Object of Beauty	Larry
1992	Passed Away	Peter Syracuse
1993	Utz	Marius Fischer

THELMA RITTER

(1905 - 1969)

Ritter was a very funny lady, a top character actress who saved many dull movies with her role as a sharp-tongued maid or mother. She became "box office insurance" to producers looking for a hit. In 1955, she won an Emmy for her first TV appearance in the 1955 *Catered Affair*, and in 1957 a Tony for a Broadway musical role. A Brooklyn native, she started acting at 11 as Puck in *Midsummer Night's Dream*. She died of a probable heart attack in a New York hospital.

Year	Movie	Character
1961	The Misfits	Isabelle Steers
1962	Birdman of Alcatraz	Elizabeth Stroud
1963	A New Kind of Love	Lena O'Connor
1963	For Love or Money	Chloe Brasher
1963	Move Over, Darling	Grace Arden
1965	Boeing-Boeing	Bertha
1967	The Incident	Bertha Beckerman

TIM ROBBINS

(1958 -   )

Robbins' busy film career, including well-remembered roles as pitcher "Nuke" LaLoosh in *Bull Durham* and movie exec Griffin Mill in *The Player*, is matched by his equally active involvement with the L.A.-based acting troupe The Actors' Gang. Robbins founded the avant-garde, shock theater group in 1981 and has written, directed and acted in many of its productions. The son of a folk singer, he grew up in New York's Greenwich Village and moved west to attend UCLA.

Year	Movie	Character
1984	No Small Affair	Nelson
1984	Toy Soldiers	Boe
1985	Fraternity Vacation	Larry "Mother" Tucker
1985	The Sure Thing	Gary Cooper
1986	Howard the Duck	Phil Blumburtt
1986	Top Gun	Merlin
1988	Bull Durham	Ebby Calvin LaLoosh
1988	Five Corners	Harry
1988	Tapeheads	Josh Tager
1988	Twister	xxx
1989	Erik the Viking	Erik
1989	Miss Firecracker	Delmount Williams
1990	Cadillac Man	Larry
1990	Jacob's Ladder	Jacob Singer
1991	Jungle Fever	Jerry
1992	Bob Roberts	Bob Roberts
1992	The Player	Griffin Mill
1993	Short Cuts	Gene Shepard

ERIC ROBERTS

(1956 -   )

Roberts learned his craft from his father, the founder of an actors workshop, while growing up in Atlanta and the director of *Star 80*, Bob Fosse. Especially Bob Fosse. "I learned more in eight months just watching Bob Fosse work than I did in the 10 years before that," he once said. He is the brother of actress Julia Roberts and has said that he would most like to portray Walter Brennan and Errol Flynn on film.

Year	Movie	Character
1978	King of the Gypsies	Dave Stepanovicz
1981	Raggedy Man	Teddy
1983	Star 80	Paul
1984	The Pope of Greenwich Village	Paulie
1985	Runaway Train	Buck
1986	Nobody's Fool	Riley
1989	Best of the Best	Alex
1989	Rude Awakening	Fred Wouk
1990	The Ambulance	Josh Baker
1992	Final Analysis	Jimmy Evans

TONY ROBERTS

(1939 -   )

A veteran actor with many credits from the stage, screen and television, Roberts was born in New York. Long associated with Woody Allen, his major film performances include *Play It Again, Sam* and *Annie Hall*. He won a Tony Award nomination as best actor in a musical in 1968 for *How Now, Dow Jones*. Chess, sailing and photography are his favorite pastimes.

Year	Movie	Character
1971	Star Spangled Girl	Andy Hobart
1972	Play It Again, Sam	Dick
1973	Serpico	Bob Blair
1974	The Taking of Pelham One Two Three	Warren LaSalle
1977	Annie Hall	Rob
1980	Just Tell Me What You Want	Mike Berger
1980	Stardust Memories	Tony
1982	A Midsummer Night's Sex Comedy	Maxwell
1983	Amityville 3-D	John Baxter
1985	Key Exchange	Slattery
1986	Hannah and Her Sisters	xxx
1987	Radio Days	"Silver Dollar" M.C.
1988	18 Again!	Arnold
1991	Popcorn	Mr. Davis
1991	Switch	Arnold

ALEX ROCCO

(1936 -   )

A Boston truck driver, Rocco came west to Hollywood in the 1960s and landed his first minor film role when he answered a casting agent's phone call intended for someone else. He spent a year with a speech doctor getting rid of his heavy Boston-Italian accent. After four years working with Leonard Nimoy, Rocco got a big break, a part in *The Godfather*.

Year	Movie	Character
1972	The Godfather	Moe Greene
1973	Outside Man	Miller
1973	Slither	Man with ice cream
1973	The Friends of Eddie Coyle	Scalise
1974	Freebie and the Bean	D.A.
1974	Three the Hard Way	Lt. DiNisco
1975	Hearts of the West	Earl
1975	Rafferty and the Gold Dust Twins	Vinnie
1978	Rabbit Test	Danny
1979	Voices	Frank Rothman
1980	Herbie Goes Bananas	Quinn
1980	The Stunt Man	Jake
1981	Nobody's Perfekt	Boss
1982	P.K. and the Kid	Lester
1984	Cannonball Run II	Tony
1985	Gotcha	Al
1985	Stick	Firestone
1992	Boris and Natasha	xxx

EUGENE ROCHE

(1928 -   )

Roche hails from Boston. He attended that city's Emerson College and made his professional acting debut there in *Point of No Return* at the Colonial Theater. His career got rolling in the early 1960s after training for the stage at the Actors Workshop in San Francisco. A commercial he acted in as a "professional dishwasher" aired for over 10 years and when told it would be bad for his image Roche replied, "What image? It helped support my family."

Year	Movie	Character
1967	The Happening	Motorcycle Officer
1971	They Might Be Giants	Policeman
1972	Slaughterhouse Five	Derby
1974	Newman's Law	Reardon
1975	Mr. Ricco	Detective Cronyn
1977	The Late Show	Ron Birdwell
1978	Corvette Summer	Ed McGrath
1978	Foul Play	Archbishop Thorncrest
1984	Oh, God! You Devil	Charlie Gray

CHARLES ROCKET

(1950 -   )

Rocket was a disc jockey, a rock 'n' roll musician and a demolition derby driver before getting his bigger roles as an actor. He once walked around the campus at the Rhode Island School of Design making up roles for himself to play if he ever got the chance. The part of a TV reporter in *The Investigators*, a comedy, brought him much attention.

Year	Movie	Character
1987	Down Twisted	Reno
1989	Earth Girls Are Easy	Dr. Ted Gallagher
1989	How I Got into College	Leo Whitman
1990	Dances With Wolves	Lt. Elgin
1990	Honeymoon Academy	Desbains
1991	Delirious	Ty
1993	Hocus Pocus	Dave

PAUL RODRIGUEZ

(1955 -   )

Rodriguez is a veteran television performer. He teamed up with a friend to be co-stars of a short-lived 1988 CBS series *Trial and Error*, which was the first series ever to be simulcast nationally in Spanish and English. Besides acting, Rodriguez likes to collect vintage cars. He names them after old girlfriends.

Year	Movie	Character
1983	D.C. Cab	Xavier
1986	Miracles	Juan
1986	Quicksilver	Hector
1986	The Whoopee Boys	Barney
1987	Born in East L.A.	Javier
1993	Made in America	Jose

MIMI ROGERS

(1956 -   )

Born in Coral Gables, FL, Rogers went to Hollywood in 1980 and worked her way up through minor parts to a status of a much-sought-after character actress. Not all of it has been easy—she turned down the lead in television's *Remington Steele* to act in a CBS show that never got beyond the pilot stage. Rogers was briefly married to actor Tom Cruise.

Year	Movie	Character
1983	Blue Skies Again	Liz
1986	Gung Ho	Audrey
1987	Someone to Watch Over Me	Claire Gregory
1987	Street Smart	Alison Parker
1989	The Mighty Quinn	Hadley
1990	Desperate Hours	Nora Cornell
1991	Hider in the House	Julie Dryer
1991	The Doors	Magazine photographer
1991	The Rapture	Sharon
1992	White Sands	xxx

RICHARD ROMANUS

(1943 -   )

Romanus grew up in Barre, VT, where his first paying job was delivering cold soda to the town's quarry workers. He supported himself all through college and part of law school playing guitar for campus parties. Then he quit law school to study acting under Lee Strasberg and never returned to the legal world. He made his film debut in *Mean Streets*, a Martin Scorsese film voted fifth best picture of the decade by the National Society of Film Critics.

Year	Movie	Character
1973	Mean Streets	Michael
1984	Protocol	Emir
1986	Murphy's Law	Frank Vincenzo
1988	The Couch Trip	Harvey Michaels
1991	Oscar	Vendetti

CESAR ROMERO

(1907 -   )

Romero, one of filmdom's most famous character actors, broke into movies in 1934 with Universal Studios when Hollywood was a small, cozy world of its own. His suave, debonair appearance made him a film idol for years. Before Hollywood, he had played in musicals in New York.

Year	Movie	Character
1960	Ocean's Eleven	Duke Santos
1962	If a Man Answers	Robert Swan
1963	Donovan's Reef	Marquis Andre de Lage
1965	Marriage on the Rocks	Miguel Santos
1966	Batman	The Joker
1969	A Talent for Loving	xxx
1969	Midas Run	Dodero

ISABELLA ROSSELLINI

LEO ROSSI

(1952 -   )

It was almost inevitable that Rossellini would go into film-making, because she is the daughter of Italian film-maker Roberto Rossellini and actress Ingrid Bergman. She grew up in Rome and France, but moved to New York to become a journalist for an Italian television station. She was married for several years to director Martin Scorsese.

(19?? -   )

Rossi once was cast in villain roles, despite his rugged good looks. It was in the thriller *Relentless*, in which he played a detective, that he first got the role of a good guy. He was working in his father's business in Philadelphia, feeling bored, when he got into community theater and that led on to big-time films. He played one of the cheering bystanders during the barroom rape of Jodie Foster in *The Accused*; she later rams her car repeatedly into his truck.

Year	Movie	Character
1976	A Matter of Time	Sister Pia
1985	White Nights	Darya Greenwood
1986	Blue Velvet	Dorothy Vallens
1987	Siesta	Marie
1988	Zelly and Me	Mademoiselle
1989	Cousins	Maria Hardy
1990	Wild at Heart	Perdita Durango
1992	Death Becomes Her	Lisle
1993	Fearless	Laura Klein
1993	The Innocent	Maria

Year	Movie	Character
1983	Heart Like a Wheel	Jack Muldowney
1986	River's Edge	Jim
1988	The Accused	Cliff "Scorpion" Albrect
1989	Hit List	Frank DeSalvo
1989	Relentless	Sam Dietz
1991	Fast Getaway	Sam
1991	Too Much Sun	George Bianco

RICK ROSSOVICH

(1957 -   )

Rossovich debuted as a soldier in Tom Cruise's *Losin' It* and has played a lot of military types since then. He was a cadet in *The Lords of Discipline*, a pilot in *Top Gun* and part of an elite commando unit in *Navy SEALS*. His biggest part has come in Steve Martin's *Roxanne* as Daryl Hannah's tongue-tied suitor. Critics said he was "immensely likable" and "made dim-wittedness endearing" in that updated version of the Cyrano de Bergerac tale.

Year	Movie	Character
1983	The Lords of Discipline	Pig
1983	Losin' It	Marine
1984	Streets of Fire	Cooley
1984	The Terminator	Matt
1985	Warning Sign	Bob
1986	Let's Get Harry	Kurt Klein
1986	The Morning After	Detective
1986	Top Gun	Slider
1987	Roxanne	Chris
1989	Paint It Black	Jonathan Dunbar
1990	Navy SEALS	Leary

GENA ROWLANDS

(1934 -   )

Star-struck from watching movies as a child, Rowlands moved to New York to study acting, where she met and married John Cassavetes, the late actor and film-maker. She broke into theater by applying for an apprenticeship at Provincetown Playhouse. They took her on because they thought she could sew and they needed a seamstress. A politician's daughter, she grew up in Cambria, WI.

Year	Movie	Character
1962	Lonely are the Brave	Jerri Bondi
1962	The Spiral Road	Els
1967	Tony Rome	Rita
1971	Minnie and Moskowitz	Minnie
1976	Two Minute Warning	Janet
1978	The Brink's Job	Mary Pino
1980	Gloria	Gloria Swenson
1982	Tempest	Antonia
1987	Light of Day	Jeanette Rasnick
1988	Another Woman	Marion
1991	Once Around	Marilyn Bella

SAUL RUBINEK

(1947 -   )

The first time he stepped on stage in a theater school for children, "I was like a fish in water," Rubinek has said. "It was where I belonged. I fell in love with acting immediately and it never occurred to me to do anything else." He appeared in several Canadian films before coming to his first American performance. Rubinek played English Bob's biographer, a writer of dime novels, in Clint Eastwood's *Unforgiven* and was memorable as the bumbling Asst. D.A. out to get Tom Hanks in *The Bonfire of the Vanities*.

Year	Movie	Character
1980	Nothing Personal	Peter
1981	Agency	Sam
1981	Ticket to Heaven	Larry
1982	Soup for One	Allan
1982	Young Doctors in Love	Dr. Kurtzman
1984	Against All Odds	Steve Kirsch
1984	Martin's Day	Hitchhiker
1986	Sweet Liberty	Bo Hodges
1987	Wall Street	Harold Salt
1989	Obsessed	xxx
1990	The Bonfire of the Vanities	Jed Kramer
1992	Man Trouble	Laurence Moncrief
1992	Unforgiven	W.W. Beauchamp
1993	True Romance	Lee Donowitz

ALAN RUCK

(19?? -   )

A supporting actor in several movies made for teenagers, Ruck won acclaim in *Three for the Road*, which starred Charlie Sheen. He played Sheen's literary-minded friend in this story about escorting a senator's daughter to boarding school. *Variety* called Ruck "likable and mischievous" and said he was the "only character with any spontaneity."

Year	Movie	Character
1983	Bad Boys	Carl Brennan
1983	Class	Roger
1986	Ferris Bueller's Day Off	Cameron Frye
1987	Three for the Road	T.S.
1989	Three Fugitives	Detective Tener
1990	Young Guns II	Hendry French

MERCEDES RUEHL

(19?? -   )

Ruehl is often cast as feisty, tough-talking New York women. She won an Oscar for just such a role in *The Fisher King* where she played a video store owner. She is the daughter of a schoolteacher and a former FBI agent who grew up in the Maryland suburbs of Washington, D.C., from age eight. Her first love is the theater, where she won a Tony for best actress in Neil Simon's *Lost in Yonkers*.

Year	Movie	Character
1986	Heartburn	Eve
1987	84 Charing Cross	Kay
1987	Leader of the Band	xxx
1987	Radio Days	Ad Man
1987	The Secret of My Success	Sheila
1988	Big	Mrs. Baskin
1988	Married to the Mob	Connie Russo
1990	Crazy People	Dr. Liz Baylor
1991	Another You	Elaine
1991	The Fisher King	Anne
1993	Last Action Hero	Mrs. Madigan
1993	Lost in Yonkers	Bella

JANICE RULE

(1931 -   )

Rule's professional life began as a dancer in Chicago and New York's famed Copacabana. She then turned to acting in the early 1950's making her Broadway debut in William Inge's *Picnic*. After more than two decades in films, she left Hollywood to pursue her interest in psychology and begin a third career. She ultimately received her PhD in research psycho-analysis and is currently involved in both research and clinical practice. Rule still does an occasional film.

Year	Movie	Character
1964	Invitation to Gunfighter	Ruth Adams
1966	Alvarez Kelly	Liz Pickering
1966	The Chase	Emily Stewart
1967	The Ambushers	Sheila
1967	Welcome to Hard Times	Molly Riordan
1971	Doctors' Wives	Amy
1982	Missing	Kate Newman
1985	American Flyers	Mrs. Sommers

BARBARA RUSH

(1929 -)

Rush came under contract to Paramount, Universal and Fox in the 1950s following her graduation from UC Santa Barbara and a short stint at the Pasadena Playhouse. She concentrated on a film career for the next two decades until her divorce from the actor, Jeffrey Hunter. The actress then switched her sights to the stage. Generally dissatisfied with her film roles, she once said, "I can safely say that every movie role I was ever offered that had any real quality went to someone else."

Year	Movie	Character
1960	Strangers When We Meet	Eve Coe
1960	The Bramble Bush	Mar
1963	Come Blow Your Horn	Connie
1964	Robin and the Seven Hoods	Marian
1967	Hombre	Audra Favor
1980	Can't Stop the Music	Norma White
1982	Summer Lovers	Jean

ROBERT RUSLER

(1965 -)

Rusler had a natural entrance to the cinema world—his father was a guard at Universal Studios in Hollywood and he used to hang around watching movies being made. When he told his father he wanted to be an actor, his father advised him to finish high school and grow up as a normal American teenager. Rusler played the best friend of the lead in *Nightmare on Elm Street 2*, whom he helped to defend against possession by Freddy Krueger.

Year	Movie	Character
1985	Weird Science	Max
1985	A Nightmare on Elm Street 2: Freddy's Revenge	Grady
1986	Thrashin'	Tommy Hook
1986	Vamp	A.J.
1989	Shag	Buzz

WILLIAM RUSS

(19?? -   )

Russ has played a variety of bad guys on film and in television and, as he explains, he would often come to these roles by necessity. "In L.A., when you start out you work in TV, and on TV there's the good guy who's usually someone like Don Johnson, and then there's the bad guy. On a series, all year there is only one good guy, but every week there's a different bad guy. If you can't play a bad guy, you won't work very much."

Year	Movie	Character
1979	Just You and Me Kid	Demesta
1983	The Right Stuff	Slick Goodin
1985	Beer	Merle Draggett
1987	Dead of Winter	Rob Sweeney
1987	Wanted: Dead or Alive	Danny Quintz
1988	The Unholy	Luke
1989	Disorganized Crime	Nick Bartkowski
1991	Pastime	Roy Dean Bream
1992	Traces of Red	Michael Dobson

THERESA RUSSELL

(1957 -   )

"It's easier to get to the top when you're shooting for the top," Russell once said. To prove it, she talked her way—without an agent or connections—into a casting session for *The Last Tycoon* and got the role she wanted. The Californian studied at the Lee Strasberg Institute in Hollywood and, in 1986, won the National Association of Theater Owners Award as "The Star of Tomorrow."

Year	Movie	Character
1976	The Last Tycoon	Cecilia Brady
1978	Straight Time	Jenny Mercer
1984	The Razor's Edge	Sophie
1986	Black Widow	Catharine
1989	Physical Evidence	Jenny Hudson
1990	Impulse	Lotte Mason
1991	Kafka	Gabriela

JAMES RUSSO

(1953 -   )

Russo usually gets the film roles of menacing, evil characters, such as that of the rapist in *Extremities*. He has admitted to having been a "wild thing" in his high school days, and was kicked out with only one semester to go before graduation. His film start came at New York University, where he both wrote and acted.

Year	Movie	Character
1982	Fast Times at Ridgemont High	Robber
1983	Exposed	Nick
1984	Beverly Hills Cop	Mikey Tandino
1986	Extremities	Joe
1987	China Girl	Alberto "Alby" Monte
1988	Freeway	Frank Quinn
1988	The Blue Iguana	Reno
1989	We're No Angels	Bobby
1991	A Kiss Before Dying	Dan Corelli
1991	My Own Private Idaho	Richard Waters

RENE RUSSO

(1954 -   )

Russo's early career was not an easy one—she was given to bouts of crying at the mere thought of attending auditions. But after a few minor roles, she got a part in the box office hit *Lethal Weapon 3* and her anxieties faded. In the movie, she plays a kick-boxing investigator who impresses Mel Gibson and wins his heart by stomping the bad guys. Russo was Secret Service agent Clint Eastwood's co-worker and romantic interest in *The Line of Fire*.

Year	Movie	Character
1989	Major League	Lynn Wells
1990	Mr. Destiny	Cindy Jo
1991	One Good Cop	Rita Lewis
1992	Freejack	Julie
1992	Lethal Weapon 3	Lorna Cole
1993	In the Line of Fire	Lily Raines

JOHN P. RYAN

(1938 -   )

Ryan, a native New Yorker, was graduated from the City College of New York, where he began an acting career. He spent six years in the U.S. Army and has appeared in over 90 plays. The actor played an L.A. cop in pursuit of Richard Gere in *Breathless* and a sadistic prison warden who relentlessly tracks Jon Voight in *Runaway Train*.

Year	Movie	Character
1973	Shamus	Col. Hardcore
1976	Futureworld	Schneider
1978	It Lives Again	Frank Davis
1981	The Postman Always Rings Twice	Kennedy
1983	Breathless	Lt. Parmental
1985	Runaway Train	Ranken
1986	Avenging Force	Glastenbury
1987	Death Wish 4: The Crackdown	Nathan White
1987	Fatal Beauty	Lt. Kellerman
1987	Three O'Clock High	Mr. O'Rourke
1988	Paramedics	Capt. Prescott
1988	Rent-a-Cop	Wieser
1990	Class of 1999	Mr. Hardin
1990	Delta Force 2	Gen. Taylor
1992	Hoffa	Red Bennett

MITCHELL RYAN

(1928 -   )

Ryan began his career with Shakespearean and other classics productions in New York during the 1960s. He then moved into film and television during the 1970s. He is a native of Cincinnati, OH, and has spent time in the U.S. Navy. In recent years he has been seen more often in television series and TV-movies than in film.

Year	Movie	Character
1970	Monte Walsh	Shorty Austin
1973	Electra Glide in Blue	Harve Poole
1973	High Plains Drifter	Dave Drake
1973	Magnum Force	Charlie McCoy
1973	The Friends of Eddie Coyle	Waters
1976	Two Minute Warning	Priest
1987	Lethal Weapon	The General
1989	Winter People	Drury Campbell

ROBERT RYAN

(1913 - 1973)

A serious actor whether he played the lead or a supporting role, Ryan went to Dartmouth College and was once a bill collector before breaking into Broadway in 1941, Hollywood in 1947. The Chicago native worked for political causes like campaigning for the Hollywood 10. He died of lymph cancer in New York.

Year	Movie	Character
1960	Ice Palace	Thor
1961	King of Kings	John the Baptist
1962	The Longest Day	Brig. Gen. James M. Gavin
1965	Battle of the Bulge	Gen. Grey
1966	The Professionals	Ehrengard
1967	The Busy Body	Charley Barker
1967	The Dirty Dozen	Col. Everett Dasher-Breed
1968	A Minute to Pray, a Second to Die	Gov. Lem Carter
1968	Anzio	General Carson
1968	Custer of the West	Mulligan
1969	The Wild Bunch	Thornton
1971	Lawman	Cotton Ryan
1971	The Love Machine	Gregory Austin
1973	Lolly-Madonna XXX	Pap
1974	The Outfit	Mailer

MICHAEL SACKS

(1948 -   )

Sacks went to Harvard, hated it, and dropped out to pursue acting. After a couple of false starts in minor roles, he got the break of a lifetime when an agent asked him to read a scene for the film *Slaughterhouse Five*, based on the satirical novel by Kurt Vonnegut, Jr. He got the part and was an instant success. In *Sugarland Express*, Sacks was a patrol car officer kidnapped by Goldie Hawn and William Atherton. The actor grew up in Albany, NY.

Year	Movie	Character
1972	Slaughterhouse Five	Billy Pilgrim
1974	The Sugarland Express	Maxwell Slide
1979	Hanover Street	2nd Lt. Martin Hyer
1979	The Amityville Horror	Jeff
1979	The House of God	xxx
1982	Split Image	Gabriel

WILLIAM SADLER

(1950 -   )

Born in Buffalo, Sadler attended Cornell and was graduated from the State University of New York. In 1981, he received an Obie for his part in *Limbo Tales* and one year later made his film debut with a bit part as a hotel clerk in *Hanky Panky*. Sadler has appeared in several television series and movies.

Year	Movie	Character
1987	Project X	Dr. Carroll
1990	Die Hard 2	Col. Stuart
1990	Hard to Kill	Vernon Trent
1990	The Hot Spot	Frank Sutton
1991	Bill & Ted's Bogus Journey	Death
1991	Rush	Nettle
1992	Trespass	Don
1993	Freaked	Dick Brian

RAYMOND ST. JACQUES

(1930 - 1990)

The suave Hartford, CT man was a real presence during the upsurge in black film-making in the 1960s and 70's. His playing Civil War veteran Solomon King on the *Rawhide* TV series was seen as a breakthrough for black actors on TV during the mid-60's. He was a pro on stage, film and television. St. Jacques died of cancer of the lymph glands.

Year	Movie	Character
1965	Mister Moses	Ubi
1965	The Pawnbroker	Tangee
1966	Mister Buddwing	Hank
1967	The Comedians	Cancasseur
1968	Madigan	Dr. Taylor
1968	The Green Berets	Doc McGee
1970	Cotton Comes to Harlem	Coffin Ed Johnson
1972	Come Back Charleston Blue	Coffin Ed Johnson
1972	Cool Breeze	Bill Mercer
1977	The Private Files of J. Edgar Hoover	Martin Luther King, Jr.
1984	The Evil That Men Do	Randolph
1987	Devil's Odds (The Wild Pair)	Ivory
1988	They Live	Street Preacher
1991	Timebomb	Det. Sanchez

GENE SAKS

(1921 -   )

Known mostly as a director, and especially for his long term partnership with Neil Simon (8 plays, 3 films), Saks believes: "Every actor needs a director. That director becomes a mirror. One can't look at oneself. One has to lose oneself in a part and then ask, 'Was that right, what I did? It felt right, but I'm not sure.' And the director needs an actor who brings his own imagination and inventiveness to a part, his own *creativity*. Because in the end, the part must be the actor's, not the director's."

Year	Movie	Character
1965	A Thousand Clowns	Leo
1975	The Prisoner of Second Avenue	Harry
1983	Lovesick	Frantic
1984	The Goodbye People	Marcus Soloway

THERESA SALDANA

(1955 -   )

Saldana's big break came when she was cast as Robert De Niro's sister-in-law in *Raging Bull*. However, her career almost ended in 1982 when she was nearly stabbed to death outside her West Hollywood home. She survived the attack to play in an NBC drama about stalking killers, in which she reenacted her own case. She also formed a non-profit group, Victims for Victims, in order to "lift the stigma" against victims and generally lend support to people whose lives have been turned upside-down by violent crimes.

Year	Movie	Character
1978	I Wanna Hold Your Hand	Grace Corrigan
1980	Defiance	Marsha
1980	Raging Bull	Lenore
1984	The Evil That Men Do	Rhiana
1988	The Night Before	Rhonda

MEREDITH SALENGER

ALBERT SALMI

(1970 -   )

Salenger is best known for her title role in the Disney production of *The Journey of Natty Gann*. The story, set in the mid-1930s, is about a young girl's journey across the country to find her father. To prepare for the part, Salenger watched newsreel footage and numerous movies set in the Depression and read books such as *The Ten Lost Years*, which chronicles the exploits of teenage hobo gangs in the thirties. The young actress made her debut in commercials at the age of ten.

Year	Movie	Character
1985	The Journey of Natty Gann	Natty Gann
1988	A Night in the Life of Jimmy Reardon	Lisa Bentwright
1988	The Kiss	Amy
1989	Dream a Little Dream	Lainie Diamond

(1925 - 1990)

The boy from Coney Island became a character actor on stage, screen and TV in spite of qualms about "selling out" to Hollywood. Salmi studied at Lee Strasberg's famous Actors Studio, and entered films in 1958 after his first TV work in 1956 with Paul Newman in *Bang the Drum Slowly*. He ended up with 150-plus TV credits, many westerns as well as straight roles. Salmi shot his wife, then himself in a murder-suicide death.

Year	Movie	Character
1960	The Unforgiven	Charlie Rawlins
1960	Wild River	Hank Bailey
1964	The Outrage	Sheriff
1967	The Ambushers	Ortega
1967	The Flim Flam Man	Deputy Meshaw
1971	Escape from the Planet of the Apes	E-1
1971	Lawman	Harvey Stenbaugh
1974	The Take	Dolek
1977	Black Oak Conspiracy	Sheriff
1977	Viva Knieval!	Cortland
1979	Love and Bullets	Andy Minton
1980	Brubaker	Rory Poke
1980	Steel	Tank
1981	Dragonslayer	Greil
1982	Love Child	Capt. Ellis
1984	Hard to Hold	Johnny Lawson
1989	Breaking In	Johnny Scat

LAURA SAN GIACOMO

PAUL SAND

(1962 -   )

(1935 -   )

When San Giacomo was first offered a role in the erotic film *sex, lies and videotape*, her friends warned her not to get mixed up in it. But the movie's great success rescued her from a struggling career as an Off-Broadway actress who survived by waiting tables. *Variety* wrote, "the star of the film whenever she's on is San Giacomo. Fiery, caustic and devastatingly erotic, she's the hottest thing to turn up onscreen recently." The actress played Julia Roberts' roommate in the smash *Pretty Woman*.

Sand was born in Southern California, the son of a Mexican father and a Russian mother and headed for theater work as soon as he got out of high school. Initially he spent 18 months in Paris as a mime in the famous troupe organized by Marcel Marceau. Later, hoping for talking roles, he changed his name from Sanchez to Sand and went back to school.

Year	Movie	Character
1989	sex, lies and videotape	Cynthia Bishop
1990	Pretty Woman	Kit De Luca
1990	Quigley Down Under	Crazy Cora
1990	Vital Signs	Lauren Rose
1991	Once Around	Jan Bella

Year	Movie	Character
1972	The Hot Rock	Greenberg
1979	The Main Event	David
1980	Can't Stop the Music	Steve Waits
1980	Wholly Moses	Angel of the Lord
1987	Teen Wolf Too	Coach Finstock
1992	Frozen Assets	McTaggert

JULIAN SANDS

(1958 -   )

Sands was born in Yorkshire, England, and was lured to a drama school by a girl friend. He loved acting, but was afflicted with stage fright and settled for the movies. He became somewhat famous for the nude bathing scene in the 1985 U.K. film *A Room with a View*. Sands credits his appearance in *The Killing Fields* with developing his talents.

Year	Movie	Character
1984	The Killing Fields	Jon Swain
1984	Oxford Blues	Colin
1985	A Room with a View	George Emerson
1985	The Doctor and the Devils	Dr. Murray
1987	Siesta	Kit
1988	Vibes	Dr. Harrison Steele
1990	Arachnophobia	Dr. James Atherton
1991	Impromptu	Franz Liszt
1991	Warlock	Warlock
1993	Warlock: The Armageddon	Warlock

RENI SANTONI

(1939 -   )

Santoni, probably best-remembered as Clint Eastwood's partner in *Dirty Harry*, originally envisioned a career as a sports journalist. He changed his sights to acting and gradually developed a reputation as an improvisationalist portraying off-beat characters in Off-Broadway revues. Santoni is of French and Spanish extraction and briefly played professional baseball. He hails from Sayreville, NJ.

Year	Movie	Character
1967	Enter Laughing	David Kolowitz
1968	Anzio	Movie
1969	Guns of the Magnificent Seven	Max
1971	Dirty Harry	Chico
1977	I Never Promised You a Rose Garden	Hobbs
1982	Dead Men Don't Wear Plaid	Carlos Rodriguez
1983	Bad Boys	Ramon Herrera
1986	Cobra	Gonzales
1989	The Package	Chicago Police Lieutenant

MIA SARA

(1968 -   )

Sara took up acting to cure her problem of shyness—"I'm usually foot-in-mouth Mia," she has said—and to earn pocket money. Her career began in her teens with three TV commercials and a small role on *All My Children*. Her best acting advice, she says, came from director Ridley Scott: "Play dumb, do as much as you can, and don't stop until someone says you have to."

Year	Movie	Character
1985	Legend	Lili
1986	Ferris Bueller's Day Off	Sloane Peterson
1988	Apprentice to Murder	Alie Spangler
1990	A Climate for Killing	xxx
1990	Any Man's Death	Gerlind
1992	A Stranger Among Us	Leah

CHRIS SARANDON

(1942 -   )

Sarandon's debut as Al Pacino's distraught pre-operative transsexual lover in *Dog Day Afternoon* earned him a best supporting Oscar nomination. He was so convincing that many in the industry assumed that director Sidney Lumet "found this guy on the streets of New York somewhere," Sarandon once recalled. Formerly married to actress Susan Sarandon, he grew up in the West Virginia coal town of Beckley, the son of Greek immigrants.

Year	Movie	Character
1975	Dog Day Afternoon	Leon
1977	The Sentinel	Michael Lerman
1979	Cuba	Juan Pulido
1983	The Osterman Weekend	Cardone
1984	Protocol	Michael Ransome
1985	Fright Night	Jerry Dandridge (Vampire)
1987	The Princess Bride	Prince Humperdinck
1988	Child's Play	Mike Norris
1990	Whispers	xxx

FRED SAVAGE

(1976 -   )

Savage, a child star, struck it big in ABC's hit show *The Wonder Years*, and moved with his mother, brother and sister into a house in San Fernando Valley, complete with swimming pool. He played 12-year-old Kevin Arnold in the series about growing up in suburban America during the 1960s. Acting, says this prodigy, is easy although he has been embarrassed to do a kissing scene.

Year	Movie	Character
1986	The Boy Who Could Fly	Louis
1987	The Princess Bride	The Grandson
1988	Vice Versa	Charlie
1989	Little Monsters	Brian Stevenson
1989	The Wizard	Corey Woods

JOHN SAVAGE

(1949 -   )

Movie audiences first noticed Savage as the sensitive, frightened steelworker who comes back from Vietnam without his legs in *The Deer Hunter*. His career began Off-Broadway at age 16 and has included many stage roles. "I love plays like *Of Mice and Men*," he told an interviewer in 1987. "Modern classics. They tell you so much about America, how things were. The time it's about wasn't all that long ago—50 years—but we often forget times, and things, we should remember."

Year	Movie	Character
1972	Bad Company	Loney
1973	Steelyard Blues	The Kid
1978	The Deerhunter	Steven
1979	Hair	Claude
1979	The Onion Field	Karl Hettinger
1980	Cattle Annie and Little Britches	Bittercreek Newcomb
1980	Inside Moves	Roary
1986	Salvador	John Cassady
1987	Hotel Colonial	Marco Venieri
1988	Caribe	Jeff Richardson
1989	Do the Right Thing	Clifton
1990	Any Man's Death	Leon Abrams
1990	The Godfather, Part III	Andrew Hagen

405

JOHN SAXON

(1935 -   )

As a teenager growing up in Brooklyn, Saxon saved his earnings from his delivery boy jobs to pay for acting studies. Modeling work caught Hollywood's attention and, at 17, he flew to Hollywood and signed a contract with Universal. At $150/week he was making more money than his father. The actor has said that the films he is most proud of are *War Hunt* (1962), where he played a psychotic soldier, and *The Appaloosa* (1966), where he was a Mexican soldier.

Year	Movie	Character
1960	Portrait in Black	Blake Richards
1960	The Unforgiven	Johnny Portugal
1962	Mr. Hobbs Takes a Vacation	Byron
1963	The Cardinal	Benny Rampell
1966	The Appaloosa	Chuy
1972	Joe Kidd	Luis Chama
1973	Enter the Dragon	Roper
1975	The Swiss Conspiracy	Hayes
1977	Moonshine County Express	J.B. Johnson
1979	The Electric Horseman	Hunt Sears
1980	Battle Beyond the Stars	Sador
1982	Wrong is Right	Homer Hubbard
1983	The Big Score	Davis
1984	A Nightmare on Elm Street	Lt. John Thompson
1985	Fever Pitch	Sports Editor
1987	A Nightmare on Elm Street 3: Dream Warriors	Lt. John Thompson

DIANA SCARWID

(1956 -   )

Upon her arrival in Hollywood, the Savannah, GA, native found she was not easily typecast. "I didn't fit into any mold or image, Scarwid has said. "It was somewhat of a barrier in getting jobs, but eventually I did play a variety of roles." On the demands of screen acting, she once said, "You get used to be hysterical in a scene and then you break for lunch and are expected to pick up that emotion after a meal." To do this she uses the so-called "Method" acting approach, recalling something from the past to re-create a similar emotion asked for in the scene.

Year	Movie	Character
1978	Pretty Baby	Frieda
1980	Honeysuckle Rose	Jeanne
1980	Inside Moves	Louise
1981	Mommie Dearest	Christina Crawford (Adult)
1983	Rumble Fish	Cassandra
1983	Silkwood	Angela
1983	Strange Invaders	Margaret
1986	Extremities	Terry
1986	Psycho III	Maureen
1987	Heat	Cassie
1992	Brenda Starr	Libby (Lips) Lipscomb

WILLIAM SCHALLERT

(1922 -   )

The L.A. native is one of the few actors to have been directed by Charlie Chaplin on the stage. This occurred shortly after his discharge from the army in 1945, at the start of his acting career, in a theater owned and operated by Schallert and Chaplin's son Sydney. The former president of the Screen Actors Guild once said: "I believe you shouldn't become an actor unless you *need* to. Unless you have no choice about it. Liking—even loving—acting is not enough. You have to *need* to act."

Year	Movie	Character
1962	Lonely are the Brave	Harry
1967	In the Heat of the Night	Webb Schubert
1968	Speedway	Abel Esterlake
1968	Will Penny	Dr. Fraker
1969	Sam Whiskey	Mint Supt. Perkins
1973	Charley Varrick	Sheriff Bill Horton
1976	Tunnelvision	xxx
1980	Hangar 18	Mills
1983	Twilight Zone—The Movie	Father (Segment 3)
1984	Teachers	Horn
1987	Innerspace	Dr. Greenbush
1991	House Party 2	Dean Kramer

MAXIMILIAN SCHELL

(1930 -   )

The Austrian actor started out in German pictures in 1955. After winning a best actor Oscar as a Nazi defense attorney in only his second U.S. outing *Judgement at Nuremberg*, Schell spent the remainder of the decade in a string of mediocre productions. He then found satisfaction as a director and a producer of films, commenting at the time: "It's more fulfilling than acting, but it's also more wounding to get bad reviews as a director than an actor." His first picture behind the camera was 1969's *The Castle*.

Year	Movie	Character
1961	Judgment at Nuremberg	Hans Rolfe
1964	Topkapi	William Walter
1969	Krakatoa—East of Java	Hanson
1974	The Odessa File	Eduard Roschmann
1976	St. Ives	Constable
1977	A Bridge Too Far	Lt. Gen. Wilhelm Bittrich
1977	Cross of Iron	Stransky
1977	Julia	Johann
1979	Avalanche Express	Bunin
1979	Players	Marco
1979	The Black Hole	Dr. Hans Reinhardt
1982	The Chosen	Professor Malter
1985	The Assisi Underground	Col. Mueller
1989	The Rose Garden	Aaron Reichenbacher
1990	The Freshman	Larry London
1993	A Far Off Place	Col. Mopani Theron

MICHAEL SCHOEFFLING

(1960 -   )

There was a time when Schoeffling peddled Christmas trees in a New York parking lot. Then fortune struck and he was in three major motion pictures in one year. Born in Chestnut Hill, PA, he was a high school wrestler who, in 1978, won a gold medal in a European competition. He financed his stage studies by modeling clothes in magazine ads.

Year	Movie	Character
1984	Sixteen Candles	Jake
1985	Sylvester	Matt
1985	Vision Quest	Kuch
1986	Belizaire the Cajun	Hypolite Leger
1986	Let's Get Harry	Corey
1990	Longtime Companion	Michael
1990	Mermaids	Joe
1991	Wild Hearts Can't Be Broken	Al Carver

JILL SCHOELEN

(19?? -   )

Seen most often in movies of the slasher and horror variety, Schoelen won acclaim in the 1987 suspense thriller *The Stepfather*. She played the part of Stephanie Maine, the stepdaughter of a man who is revealed as a psychotic murderer. *Variety* said she was "powerfully empathetic as the young heroine." Schoelen also played the title role in *Rich Girl* a 1991 film about the daughter of a rich Los Angeles man who rebels and finds a new life as a cocktail waitress and singer.

Year	Movie	Character
1985	That Was Then, This is Now	Angela Shepard
1987	The Stepfather	Stephanie Maine
1991	Popcorn	Maggie
1991	Rich Girl	Courtney

ANNABELLA SCIORRA

(1964 -   )

Sciorra has said that she cannot remember a time when she was not planning to be an actress. Born near Hartford, CT, she was encouraged from childhood by her family, who gave her cosmetics to work on makeup. The family later moved to Manhattan where she studied dancing. (She'd love to be in musicals, but cannot sing a note). She did odd jobs all over Manhattan until she got her start in movies with Nancy Savoca, an independent producer.

Year	Movie	Character
1989	True Love	Donna
1990	Cadillac Man	Donna
1990	Internal Affairs	Heather
1990	Reversal of Fortune	Carol
1991	Jungle Fever	Angie Tucci
1991	The Hard Way	Susan
1992	The Hand That Rocks the Cradle	Claire
1992	Whispers in the Dark	Dr. Ann Hecker
1993	The Night We Never Met	Ellen Holder
1993	Mr. Wonderful	Lee

CAMPBELL SCOTT

(1961 -   )

The son of actors George C. Scott and Colleen Dewhurst, Scott grew up in the suburbs of New York City and entered Wisconsin's Lawrence University with the goal of becoming a history teacher. There he switched his sights to acting even though at first, "I had no desire to be an actor," he once said. "Theater people were frightening to me. They were so open and expressive and wonderful, and I was this withdrawn thing." Scott may be best remembered for his co-starring role in the Julia Roberts film, *Dying Young*.

Year	Movie	Character
1990	Longtime Companion	Willy
1990	The Sheltering Sky	George Tunner
1991	Dead Again	Doug
1991	Dying Young	Victor Geddes
1992	Singles	Steve Dunne
1993	The Innocent	Leonard Markham

DONOVAN SCOTT

(19?? -   )

Scott has played mainly comic supporting roles in movies for teenagers. One of his more memorable characters was Boots in the 1982 film *Savannah Smiles*, about a rich girl who flees her home and takes up with a couple of criminals. Scott was the portly, bumbling and likable crook who befriended her and helped her get home safely. Scott also played the TV cameraman in *Sheena* starring ex-*Charlie's Angels* star, Tanya Roberts.

Year	Movie	Character
1981	Zorro, the Gay Blade	Paco
1982	Savannah Smiles	Boots
1984	Police Academy	Leslie
1984	Sheena	Fletcher
1986	The Best of Times	Eddie

JEAN SEBERG

(1938 - 1979)

The petite Iowa girl won a talent search to play the part of Joan of Arc in Otto Preminger's bomb *St. Joan*. The bad press drove Seberg to France where she had her best role in *Breathless*, a movie that began the French cinema's New Wave. Later she made films in Britain and America, had four husbands and a son and wrote her autobiography *Blue Jeans* describing her severe depression. At 40 she was found dead in her car in a Paris suburb from an overdose of barbituates.

Year	Movie	Character
1964	Lilith	Lilith Arthur
1966	A Fine Madness	Lydia
1966	Moment to Moment	Kay Stanton
1969	Paint Your Wagon	Elizabeth
1970	Airport	Tanya Livingston
1970	Macho Callahan	Alexandra Mountford

KYLE SECOR

(19?? -   )

A supporting actor in both television and movies, Secor is perhaps best remembered for his role as a contract killer in the 1990 film *Delusion*. *Variety* called his performance "striking" and "impressive".

Year	Movie	Character
1989	Heart of Dixie	Tuck
1990	Delusion	Chevy
1991	City Slickers	Jeff
1991	Late for Dinner	Leland Shakes
1991	Sleeping With the Enemy	Fleishman
1993	Untamed Heart	Howard

DAVID SELBY

(1941 -   )

The veteran stage and film actor spent most of the 1980s as Richard Channing on TV's *Falcon Crest*. Selby is a strong advocate for television, but recognizes that TV work can be hazardous creatively because of its fast pace: "There are so many setups, and so little rehearsal time, and only 7 days to do (an episode) in," he once explained. "I know that as an actor, I have to be careful not to cheat myself, or the character. I mustn't become an actor who merely delivers his lines."

Year	Movie	Character
1971	The Night of Dark Shadows	Quentin/Charles
1972	Up the Sandbox	Paul Reynolds
1974	The Super Cops	Hantz
1979	Rich Kids	Steve Sloan
1980	Raise the Titanic!	Dr. Seagram
1981	Rich and Famous	Doug Blake
1991	Dying Young	Richard Geddes

PEPE SERNA

(1944 -   )

A veteran supporting actor, Serna has made a number of films featuring crime and life in Latino gangs. Perhaps his most memorable role was that in *American Me*, a 1992 saga about a criminal gang and life in prison. Serna played Mundo, one of the gang leaders. His performance was critically well-received in that picture as well as in the 1979 movie *Walk Proud* where he also played a gang leader.

Year	Movie	Character
1971	Shootout	Pepe
1972	The New Centurions	Young Mexican
1975	The Day of the Locust	Miguel
1976	The Killer Inside Me	Johnny
1979	A Force of One	Orlando
1979	Walk Proud	Cesar
1980	Honeysuckle Rose	Rooster
1980	Inside Moves	Herrada
1982	Vice Squad	Pete
1983	Deal of the Century	Vardis
1983	Scarface	Angel
1983	The Ballad of Gregorio Cortez	Romaldo
1985	Silverado	xxx
1986	Out of Bounds	Murano
1990	Bad Jim	Virgilio Segura
1990	Postcards From the Edge	Raoul
1990	The Rookie	Lt. Ray Garcia
1992	American Me	Mundo

RAY SHARKEY

(1952 - 1993)

Sharkey was born in Brooklyn and grew up swimming around under the Brooklyn Bridge, looking at the New York skyline and wondering if he could someday be an actor in the Big Apple. He once attributed his inspiration to become an actor to Jack Lemmon's portrayal of an alcoholic in *Days of Wine and Roses*. Best remembered by fans of TV's *Wiseguy* as Sonny Steelgrave, an Atlantic City mob boss, he died of AIDs contracted from a dirty needle during five years of heroin addiction in the mid-80's.

Year	Movie	Character
1974	The Lords of Flatbush	Student
1978	Paradise Alley	Legs
1978	Who'll Stop the Rain	Smitty
1979	Heart Beat	Ira
1980	The Idolmaker	Vincent Vacarri
1980	Willie and Phil	Phil
1982	Love and Money	Byron Levin
1982	Some Kind of Hero	Vinnie
1984	Body Rock	Terrence
1986	No Mercy	Angles Ryan
1986	Wise Guy	Marco

HELEN SHAVER

(1951 -   )

Although usually cast as strong, mature and sensuous women in dramatic roles, Shaver appeared in the comedy *Best Defense* starring Dudley Moore. At the time she said, "I'd often brought a lot of comedy to roles. Whether it's drama or comedy there's a line in common with both which is, I think, the humanness of the character. We all know what we want, but we very seldom have the right behavior to get it, and if you push that in one direction it's tragic, it's Oedipus, and if you push it in the other, it's very very funny."

Year	Movie	Character
1977	Starship Invasions	Betty
1977	Who Has Seen the Wind?	Ruth Thompson
1978	High-Ballin'	Pickup
1979	The Amityville Horror	Carolyn
1982	Harry Tracy, Desperado	Catherine
1983	The Osterman Weekend	Virginia
1984	Best Defense	Clare Lewis
1985	Desert Hearts	Vivian Bell
1986	The Color of Money	Janelle
1987	The Believers	Jessica Halliday
1993	That Night	Ann O'Connor
1993	Morning Glory	Lula Peaks

STAN SHAW

(1952 -   )

Growing up in the slums of Chicago, Shaw asked his mother if he could carry a knife for protection. When she said no, he became involved with karate and judo. He earned a first-degree black belt in judo and jujitsu and a second-degree black belt in karate. His goals as an actor, he once said, were to take "roles of authority and respect with universal appeal. I want parts all people will want to see, that are marketable, and that will present a man as a man."

Year	Movie	Character
1976	Rocky	Dipper
1976	The Bingo Long Travelling All-Stars and Motor Kings	Esquire Joe Calloway
1978	The Boys in Company C	Tyrone Washington
1979	The Great Santini	Toomer Smalls
1983	Tough Enough	P.T.
1984	Runaway	Marvin
1987	The Monster Squad	Detective Sapir
1989	Harlem Nights	Jack Jenkins
1991	Fried Green Tomatoes	Big George

DICK SHAWN

(1929 - 1987)

A nightclub comedian, Shawn also had a 30-year career on Broadway and in movies and television. He worked steadily during the 1960's in such comedies as *It's a Mad Mad Mad Mad World*, as the young swinger, and *The Producers*, as a hippie-type cast as Hitler on stage. He did one big picture in the 1970s called *Love at First Bite* where he played a cop who tries to save Susan St. James from Count Dracula. Shawn worked the cabarets for years as both the opening and closing act and died doing his standup routine at UC San Diego.

Year	Movie	Character
1960	Wake Me When It's Over	Gus Brubaker
1963	It's a Mad Mad Mad Mad World	Sylvester Marcus
1965	A Very Special Favor	Arnold
1966	Penelope	Dr. Gregory Mannix
1966	Way ... Way Out	Igor
1966	What Did You Do in the War, Daddy?	Captain Cash
1968	The Producers	LSD
1979	Love at First Bite	Lt. Ferguson
1983	Young Warriors	Prof. Hoover
1984	Angel	Mae
1985	Beer	Talkshow Host
1986	The Check is in the Mail	xxx
1987	Maid to Order	Stan Starkey

WALLACE SHAWN

(1943 -   )

The actor/playwright grew up in Manhattan, studied history at Harvard and then went to Oxford, where he read in philosophy, economics and politics. The actor Shawn is best known for his role in the singular film *My Dinner with Andre*. The playwright Shawn once said: "I actually believe that what we Americans are doing in the world is wrong. So, even though I have this moderately affable personality in person, I have no interest in leaving an American audience feeling great. I don't think they should feel great."

Year	Movie	Character
1979	All That Jazz	xxx
1979	Manhattan	Jeremiah
1979	Starting Over	Workshop Member
1980	Simon	Van Dongen
1981	Atlantic City	Waiter
1981	My Dinner with Andre	Wally
1982	A Little Sex	Oliver
1983	Deal of the Century	Harold DeVoto
1983	Lovesick	Jaffe
1983	Strange Invaders	Earl
1983	The First Time	Goldfarb
1984	Crackers	Turtle
1984	Hotel New Hampshire	Freud
1984	Micki + Maude	Dr. Elliot Fibel

(continued on page 509)

414

JOHN SHEA

(1949 -   )

Best known as Sissy Spacek's kidnapped husband in Costa-Gavras' *Missing*, Shea attended Bates College in Maine on football and debate scholarships with the intention of becoming a diplomat. He switched to acting because, as he once explained, "Theater brought together the two major things in my life: debating and sports. As a debater you're speaking and communicating your ideas. As an athlete you're using your body and you're working as a team. And the theater is a perfect combination of these two things."

Year	Movie	Character
1982	Missing	Charles Horman
1984	Windy City	Danny
1988	A New Life	Doc
1988	Stealing Home	Sam Wyatt
1992	Freejack	xxx
1992	Honey, I Blew Up the Baby	Hendrickson

CRAIG SHEFFER

(1960 -   )

A native of Pennsylvania, Sheffer was born in York, where his father was a prison guard and a script writer and his mother worked in a nursing home. His acting career began in television commercials, the New York stage and appearances in ABC's *The Hamptons* and *One Life to Live*. He has been a valet to Count Basie and a member of SANE (formerly National Committee for a Sane Nuclear Policy). Leisure time includes motorcycle riding, rodeos, boxing, writing and playing guitar.

Year	Movie	Character
1985	That Was Then, This is Now	Bryon Douglas
1986	Fire With Fire	Joe
1987	Some Kind of Wonderful	Hardy Jenns
1988	Split Decisions	Eddie McGuinn
1992	A River Runs Through It	Norman Maclean
1993	Fire in the Sky	Allan Dalis
1993	The Program	Joe Kane

PAUL SHENAR

(1936 - 1989)

Shenar was an actor and teacher at the American Conservatory Theater in San Francisco from 1965-74 and was active on the L.A. stage. His screen roles include Steve Guttenberg's boss in *The Bedroom Window*. Guttenberg has an affair with his wife. The actor did commercial voiceovers in his last year and died of AIDs.

Year	Movie	Character
1983	Deadly Force	Joshua
1983	Scarface	Alejandro Sosa
1986	Dream Lover	Ben Gardner
1986	Raw Deal	Rocca
1987	Best Seller	David Madlock
1987	The Bedroom Window	Collin
1988	The Big Blue	Dr. Laurence

JAMEY SHERIDAN

(1951 -   )

The son of an Australian who settled in the U.S. after World War II, Sheridan hails from Pasadena, CA. As a college student he first saw a dance choreographed by Martha Graham and planned a career in dance. Unfortunately, a bum knee left over from his high school football days scuttled that idea and he chose acting instead.

Year	Movie	Character
1986	Jumpin' Jack Flash	New York officer
1988	Distant Thunder	Moss
1990	Quick Change	Mugger
1990	Stanley & Iris	Joe
1991	All I Want for Christmas	Michael O'Fallon
1991	Talent for the Game	Tim Weaver
1992	A Stranger Among Us	Nick
1992	Whispers in the Dark	Doug McDowell

JAMES SHIGETA

(1933 -   )

Hawaiian-born of Japanese descent, Shigeta attended New York University, served with the Marines during the Korean Conflict and, after winning on Ted Mack's Amateur Hour, embarked on a singing career. At a time when good roles for Oriental faces were scarce, Shigeta broke into film, television and theater in Japan where he spent four years. Success in the U.S. came upon his return and an appearance on TV's *Dinah Shore Show*.

Year	Movie	Character
1961	Cry for Happy	Suzuki
1961	Flower Drum Song	Wang Ta
1966	Paradise Hawaiin Style	Danny Kohana
1973	Lost Horizon	Brother To-Lenn
1976	Midway	Vice Adm. Chuichi Nagumo
1988	Die Hard	Takagi

ELISABETH SHUE

(1964 -   )

Her film career began in her family's home movies. "My father would put a bag over his head and kidnap my little brother. Then the rest of us would have to come up with the ransom," she once explained. Shue advertised hamburgers, diamonds and mayonnaise on television before she made her professional theatrical debut in the short-lived *Call to Glory* TV series in 1984.

Year	Movie	Character
1984	The Karate Kid	Ali
1987	Adventures in Babysitting	Chris
1988	Cocktail	Jordan Mooney
1989	Back to the Future Part II	Jennifer
1990	Back to the Future Part III	Jennifer
1991	Soapdish	Lori Craven
1991	The Marrying Man	Adele Horner
1993	Heart and Souls	Anne

RICHARD B. SHULL

(1929 -   )

Shull got the attention of Hollywood producers with a TV commercial broadcast during the 1972 summer Olympic Games. At the time, he said, "It's frustrating to work on stage and in movies for years and then get recognition for a commercial." The ad for a men's cologne ran for six months and starred Shull as chess champ Boris Spassky in the midst of a match. It got Shull a co-starring role on Diana Rigg's short-lived sitcom, *Diana* (1973-74).

Year	Movie	Character
1971	Klute	Sugarman
1971	The Anderson Tapes	Werner
1973	SSSSSSS	Daniels
1973	Slither	Harry Moss
1975	Hearts of the West	Fat Man
1975	The Fortune	Chief Detective
1976	The Big Bus	Emery Bush
1979	Dreamer	Taylor
1983	Lovesick	Dr. Fessner
1983	Spring Break	Eddie
1984	Garbo Talks	Shepard Plotnick
1984	Splash	Dr. Ross
1984	Unfaithfully Yours	Jess Keller
1990	Tune in Tomorrow...	Leonard Pando
1992	HouseSitter	Ralph

CASEY SIEMASZKO

(1961 -   )

Siemaszko grew up on Chicago's south side and received a fine arts degree from that city's Goodman School of Drama. At 5, he was dancing on stage with his father's Polish folk dancing group, The Kosciuszko Dancers. Later he appeared with the Ref-Ren Theater, a Polish community theater. Siemaszko has played in rock bands and supported himself clowning, juggling and riding a unicycle on the Illinois fair circuit. The actor can be seen as one of Matthew Broderick's fellow recruits in *Biloxi Blues*.

Year	Movie	Character
1983	Class	Doug
1985	Back to the Future	3-D
1985	Secret Admirer	Roger
1986	Stand by Me	Billy Tessio
1987	Gardens of Stone	Wildman
1987	Three O'Clock High	Jerry Mitchell
1988	Biloxi Blues	Don Carney
1988	Young Guns	Charley Bowdre
1989	Back to the Future Part II	3-D
1989	Breaking In	Mike
1992	Of Mice and Men	Curley

JAMES B. SIKKING

(1934 -   )

Roles in two successful TV series, Lt. Howard Hunter on *Hill Street Blues* and father David Howser on *Doogie Howser, M.D.*, have made Sikking's face more familiar to television watchers than to movie-goers. A native of L.A., Sikking studied acting at UCLA and once described his early days to a reporter: "I studied theater arts in the days when they made you learn every aspect of the theater before they would let you on stage. I learned sound, lighting, construction, painting, costuming and stage management."

Year	Movie	Character
1964	The Strangler	Artist
1969	Daddy's Gone A-Hunting	FBI Agent
1972	The New Centurions	Sgt. Anders
1974	The Terminal Man	Ralph Friedman
1979	The Electric Horseman	Dietrich
1980	Ordinary People	Ray
1980	The Competition	Brudnell
1981	Outland	Montone
1983	The Star Chamber	Dr. Harold Lewin
1984	Star Trek III: The Search for Spock	Capt. Styles
1984	Up the Creek	Tozer
1986	Soul Man	Bill Watson
1990	Narrow Margin	Nelson
1991	Final Approach	Col. Jason Halsey

HENRY SILVA

(1928 -   )

His high cheek bones and chiseled features give him a handsome, but fearsome appearance and led to his casting as a dope dealer in his Broadway debut in *Hatful of Rain*. Silva received a Tony for that role and has usually been cast as a heavy ever since. "I'm getting bored with it," he once said of his typecasting. "No, I'm not getting, I am bored with it." He grew up in New York and, at 17, was one of the youngest ever admitted to the renowned Actors Studio.

Year	Movie	Character
1960	Cinderfella	Maxmilian
1960	Ocean's Eleven	Roger Corneal
1962	Sergeants	Mountain Hawk
1962	The Machurian Candidate	Chunjin
1963	A Gathering of Eagles	Colonel Garcia
1964	The Secret Invasion	John Durrell
1966	The Hills Run Red	Mendez
1979	Buck Rogers in the 25th Century	Kane
1979	Love and Bullets	Vittorio Farroni
1980	Alligator	Col. Brock
1981	Sharky's Machine	Billy Score
1982	Megaforce	Guerera
1982	Wrong is Right	Rafeeq
1984	Cannonball Run II	Slim
1985	Code of Silence	Luis Comacho
1987	Allan Quartermain and the Lost City of Gold	Agon
1988	Above the Law	Zagon
1988	Bulletproof	Col. Kartiff
1990	Dick Tracy	Influence

RON SILVER

(1946 -   )

Silver is an actor and a political activist. He is the president of Actor's Equity and campaigned for Dukakis in the 1988 presidential race. "By inclination I am more of a politician than I am an actor," he once said. "I care more about public policy. I care more about pro-choice, the environment, homelessness, and nuclear issues than I do about any part." Silver grew up on Manhattan's lower east side, did graduate work in Chinese history in Taiwan and began an acting career in 1971 on the New York stage.

Year	Movie	Character
1976	Tunnelvision	xxx
1977	Semi-Tough	Vlada
1982	Best Friends	Larry Weisman
1982	Silent Rage	Dr. Halman
1983	Lovesick	Ted
1983	Silkwood	Paul Stone
1984	Garbo Talks	Gilbert Rolfe
1984	Oh, God! You Devil	Gary Frantz
1984	The Goodbye People	Eddie Bergson
1989	Enemies, A Love Story	Herman Broder
1990	Blue Steel	Eugene Hunt
1990	Reversal of Fortune	Alan Dershowitz
1992	Mr. Saturday Night	Larry Meyerson
1993	Married to It	Leo Rothenberg

FRANK SILVERA

(1914 - 1970)

The African-American actor/director/producer, born in Jamaica and educated in Boston, thought he wanted to be a lawyer until he made his stage debut in Boston in 1934. Silvera was not typecast as a black actor, for he played everything from *King Lear* himself to a regular on the *High Chaparral* TV series. He accidently electrocuted himself while repairing his garbage disposal at his Pasadena home at 56.

Year	Movie	Character
1960	The Mountain Road	Kwan
1966	The Appaloosa	Ramos
1967	The St. Valentine's Day Massacre	Sorello
1969	The Stalking Moon	Major
1971	Valdez is Coming	Diego

JONATHAN SILVERMAN

(1966 -   )

A native of L.A. and a graduate of Beverly Hills High, Silverman began his acting career on Broadway, as the replacement for Matthew Broderick in Neil Simon's hit play *Brighton Beach Memoirs*. He has been busy ever since with films and television. "I was raised with the work ethic," he once said. "If I hadn't been lucky enough to become an actor, I'd be working in the garment district of Los Angeles. Under no circumstances would I be idle."

Year	Movie	Character
1985	Girls Just Want to Have Fun	Drew
1986	Brighton Beach Memoirs	Eugene
1988	Caddyshack II	Harry
1988	Stealing Home	Teenage Alan Appleby
1989	Weekend at Bernie's	Richard Parker
1991	Class Action	Brian
1993	Weekend at Bernie's II	Richard

JEAN SIMMONS

(1929 -   )

Twice-nominated for Academy Awards, Simmons, of London, England, was active in U.S. films during the 1950s and 1960s. Her career began with a bang in England as the haughty and taunting Estella in the universally-loved 1946 film *Great Expectations*. She was only 17. In recent years she has done TV series and TV-movies.

Year	Movie	Character
1960	Elmer Gantry	Sister Sharon Falconer
1960	Spartacus	Varinia
1960	The Grass is Greener	Hattie
1966	Mister Buddwing	The Blonde
1967	Divorce American Style	Nancy Downes
1967	Rough Night in Jericho	Molly

NANCY SINATRA

(1940 -   )

The daughter of Frank Sinatra, Nancy enjoyed a brief career as a singer and an actress during the 1960s. She may be best remembered for her hit single *These Boots are Made for Walkin'*. After abandoning her entertainment career she spent a good part of her life working on a biography of her famous father. The book, *Frank Sinatra, My Father*, was published in 1986.

Year	Movie	Character
1964	For Those Who Think Young	Karen Cross
1964	Get Yourself a College Girl	Lynne
1965	Marriage on the Rocks	Tracy Edwards
1966	The Ghost in the Invisible Bikini	Vicki
1966	The Last of the Secret Agents?	Micheline
1966	The Oscar	Herself
1966	The Wild Angels	Mike
1968	Speedway	Susan Jacks

LORI SINGER

(1962 -   )

A concert cellist who played first chair at Juilliard, Singer starred for two years on the TV show *Fame*. Her father is Jacques Singer, a well-known symphony orchestra conductor and her brother is the actor Marc Singer. She credits Marc for her inspiration to become an actress when she recalls how he recited Shakespeare to her.

Year	Movie	Character
1984	Footloose	Ariel
1985	The Falcon and the Snowman	Lana
1985	The Man With One Red Shoe	Maddy
1987	Summer Heat	Roxy
1991	Warlock	Kassandra
1993	Short Cuts	Zoe Trainer

MARC SINGER

(1948 -   )

Although he was tricked by his father into seeing the Laurence Olivier version of *Richard II*, Singer was so excited by the film that he went home and memorized the entire soliloquy. His father was adamant about his learning to appreciate the arts and Singer made this clear when he told an interviewer: "I was trained in the classics. I find that I have recently put together my own method based on the teachings of a lot of different people. An actor must have an awareness of the form of acting and the soul of artistry."

Year	Movie	Character
1982	The Beastmaster	Dar
1988	Born to Race	Kenny Landruff
1990	Body Chemstry	Tom Redding
1991	Beastmaster 2: Through the Portal of Time	Dar

LILIA SKALA

(1907 -   )

Skala arrived by boat from Austria with her two children, penniless and unable to speak English, but free from Hitler's spreading tyranny. She left behind a prominent acting career to find refuge in the U.S. A graduate of Dresden University with the equivalent of a master's degree in architecture, Skala's religious beliefs gave her strength to overcome the difficulties of starting over in a strange land. "I owe everything in my life to my firm belief in the omnipotence of God," she once said.

Year	Movie	Character
1963	Lilies of the Field	Mother Maria
1965	Ship of Fools	Frau Hutten
1967	Caprice	Madame Piasco
1968	Charly	Dr. Anna Straus
1979	Heartland	Grandma
1983	Flashdance	Hanna Long
1983	Testament	Fania
1987	House of Games	Dr. Littauer
1991	Men of Respect	Lucia

TOM SKERRITT

(1933 -   )

Skerritt has been a busy movie actor for more than two decades. His diverse repertoire includes *Alien* and *Poltergeist III*, films that rely heavily on special effects. "It is usually the same experience, working with special effects," he once commented. "You do an awful lot of waiting and not much acting...usually something goes wrong with the electronics and they spend more time on it than they planned. They do it over and over again. So you can just sit and wait.

Year	Movie	Character
1970	M*A*S*H	Duke
1971	The Wild Rovers	John Buckman
1972	Fuzz	Det. Bert Kling
1974	Thieves Like Us	Dee Mobley
1977	The Turning Point	Wayne
1978	Ice Castles	Marcus Winston
1978	Up in Smoke	Strawberry
1979	Alien	Dallas
1981	Savage Harvest	Casey
1981	Silence of the North	Walter Reamer
1982	Fighting Back	John
1983	The Dead Zone	Sheriff Bannerman
1986	Opposing Force	Major Logan
1986	SpaceCamp	Zach

(continued on page 509)

IONE SKYE

(1971 -   )

Skye is the daughter of the 1960s pop singer Donovan and former model Enid Karl. However, she never knew her father as her parents split up before she was born. The L.A. native had not planned on an acting career, but did do some early modeling. Her photos caught the eye of director Tim Hunter who cast her as Clarissa in *River's Edge*.

Year	Movie	Character
1986	River's Edge	Clarissa
1987	Stranded	Deirdre
1988	A Night in the Life of Jimmy Reardon	Denise Hunter
1989	Say Anything...	Diane Court
1992	Guncrazy	Joy

JEREMY SLATE

(1935 -   )

Slate broke into movies in 1962 with an acclaimed supporting performance in the Elvis Presley picture *Girls! Girls! Girls!* after one season as the star of CBS' *The Aquanauts*. According to *Variety*, Slate played the villain of the plot "with a combination of crass charm and broad comedy. His is a solid performance." Supporting roles in the early 60's were followed by leads in Roger Corman biker movies and other low-budget fare. He abandoned film acting in the early 1970's, but returned to the screen 20 years later.

Year	Movie	Character
1962	Girls! Girls! Girls!	Wesley Johnson
1965	I'll Take Sweden	Erik Carlson
1965	The Sons of Katie Elder	Deputy Sheriff Latta
1968	The Devil's Brigade	Patrick O'Neill
1969	True Grit	Emmett Quincy
1990	The Dream Machine	Jack Chamberlain
1992	The Lawnmower Man	Father McKeen

HELEN SLATER

(1965 -   )

Success came early to Slater who debuted in the title role of *Supergirl* only four months out of New York's High School of Performing Arts (the so-called "Fame" school) beating out 300 seasoned actresses who wanted the part. She is also known for her role in *Ruthless People*. In that picture, she and Judge Reinhold portrayed the pair of warm-hearted, bungling kidnappers of Bette Midler. Slater grew up on Long Island, the daughter of an attorney and television executive.

Year	Movie	Character
1984	Supergirl	Supergirl/Linda Lee
1985	The Legend of Billie Jean	Billie Jean
1986	Ruthless People	Sandy Kessler
1987	The Secret of My Success	Christy Wills
1988	Sticky Fingers	Hattie
1989	Happy Together	Alexandra Page
1991	City Slickers	Bonnie Rayburn

EVERETT SLOANE

(1910 - 1965)

Sloane became one of Hollywood's most-in-demand character actors after switching to movies from a long career in radio. He divided his time between major films and television. The actor died at 55 of an overdose of sleeping pills.

Year	Movie	Character
1960	Home from the Hill	Albert Halstead
1963	The Man from the Diner's Club	Martindale
1964	The Disorderly Orderly	Mr. Tuffington
1964	The Patsy	Caryl Fergusson

ALEXIS SMITH

(1921 - 1993)

Very active in film during the 1940s and 1950s, Smith, a native of Penticton, Canada, was mostly involved with the stage and television in recent years. She received the Tony Award in 1971 for her Broadway debut in *Follies* and could be seen on TV's *Dallas* during 1984-85 as Lady Jessica Montford. She died of cancer in L.A.

Year	Movie	Character
1975	Once is Not Enough	Deidre Milford Granger
1976	The Little Girl Who Lives Down the Lane	Mrs. Hallet
1978	Casey's Shadow	Sarah Blue
1986	Tough Guys	Belle

BUBBA SMITH

(1945 -   )

Born Charles Aaron Smith, in Orange, TX, Bubba Smith was original-ly a professional football player with the Baltimore Colts, the Oakland Raiders and the Houston Oilers. He became an actor in television and film during the 1980s.

Year	Movie	Character
1983	Stroker Ace	Arnold
1984	Police Academy	Moses
1985	Police Academy 2:	
	Their First Assignment	Hightower
1986	Black Moon Rising	Johnson
1986	Police Academy 3:	
	Back in Training	Sgt. Hightower
1987	Devil's Odds (The Wild Pair)	Benny Avalon
1987	Police Academy 4:	
	Citizens on Patrol	Hightower
1988	Police Academy 5:	
	Assignment Miami Beach	Hightower
1989	Police Academy 6:	
	City Under Siege	Hightower

CHARLES MARTIN SMITH

(1953 -   )

Smith was born in Van Nuys, CA, the son of a film cartoonist and ani-mator. He spent three years of his youth in Paris where his father man-aged the English-language branch of a French animation studio. His professional career began when an agent saw him in a high school per-formance of *Man of La Mancha*. In addition to his skills as an actor, he is also an accomplished musician/songwriter, director of stage pro-ductions and screenwriter.

Year	Movie	Character
1972	Fuzz	Baby
1973	American Graffiti	Terry
1973	Pat Garrett and Billy the Kid	Bowdre
1974	The Spikes Gang	Tod
1975	Rafferty and the Gold Dust	
	Twins	Alan
1976	No Deposit, No Return	Longnecker
1978	The Buddy Holly Story	Ray Bob
1979	More American Graffiti	Terry the Toad
1980	Herbie Goes Bananas	D.J.
1983	Never Cry Wolf	Tyler
1984	Starman	Mark Shermin
1987	The Untouchables	Oscar Wallace
1989	The Experts	Bob Smith
1990	The Hot Spot	Lon Gulik
1992	Deep Cover	Jerry Carver
1993	Fifty/Fifty	Martin Sprue

KURTWOOD SMITH

(1942 -   )

Smith began acting professionally while in his 30's with the California Actors Theater in Los Gatos from 1975-79. Experience gained there, in such productions as *Plymouth Rock* and *Farces by Chekhov*, led to film and television. TV work included a season in *The Renegades* (1982-83) and guest appearances in *21 Jump Street*. He played Robocop's brutal adversary in the first picture of that series and a U.S. State Dept. official who finds Sylvester Stallone living in a monastery at the start of *Rambo III*.

Year	Movie	Character
1987	Robocop	Clarence
1988	Rambo III	Griggs
1989	Dead Poets Society	Mr. Perry
1989	Heart of Dixie	Prof. Flournoy
1989	True Believer	Robert Reynard
1990	Quick Change	Russ Crane/Lombino
1991	Company Business	Elliot Jaffe
1991	Oscar	Lt. Toomey
1991	Star Trek VI: The Undiscovered Country	Federation President
1992	Shadows and Fog	Vogel's follower
1993	The Crush	Cliff Forrester
1993	Fortress	Poe

LANE SMITH

(1935 -   )

A soft-spoken man with a slight southern drawl, Smith grew up in Memphis and, after time spent in the army, tackled the New York theater world. Of his early days as an actor he once said, "It is such a rough life in New York, living at the poverty level, driving cabs, collecting unemployment. It is frustrating, I don't know how kids today do it. I survived but I am no longer enamored of that vagabond lifestyle."

Year	Movie	Character
1973	Hard Driver	Rick Penny
1975	Rooster Cogburn	Leroy
1978	Blue Collar	Clarence Hill
1979	Over the Edge	Sloan
1981	Prince of the City	Tug Barnes
1982	Frances	Dr. Symington
1984	Purple Hearts	Cmdr. Markel
1984	Red Dawn	Mayor Bates
1987	Weeds	Claude
1990	Air America	Senator Davenport
1992	My Cousin Vinny	Jim Trotter III
1992	The Distinguished Gentleman	Dick Dodge
1992	The Mighty Ducks	Coach Reilly
1993	Son-In-Law	Walter

LOIS SMITH

(1930 -)

Primarily a stage actress on Broadway and in regional theater, Smith is the youngest of six children and was raised in Topeka, KS. Acting since she was a young girl, she once said, "I started in my father's church productions. I don't know if it was my first play, but I remember being in a dress and playing Eve—and I still have that dress."

Year	Movie	Character
1976	Next Stop, Greenwich Village	Anita
1980	Foxes	Mrs. Axman
1983	Reuben, Reuben	Mare Spofford
1984	Reckless	Mrs. Prescott
1986	Black Widow	Sara
1990	Green Card	Bronte's Mother
1991	Fried Green Tomatoes	Mama Threadgoode
1992	Twisted	xxx
1993	Falling Down	D-Fen's Mother

PAUL SMITH

(19?? -)

Smith has been in show business so long he recalls closing the last vaudeville house in Orange County, CA. He was 11 years old at the time. "I did a stand-up act in a Santa Ana theater, doing German and Italian dialects," he once said. "I became a club comic, known as 'the boy with a thousand voices'. Then I switched to the trumpet and played with four bands." His film career began in the early 1950s. Smith may be best remembered as the sadistic guard in *Midnight Express*.

Year	Movie	Character
1970	Madron	Gabe
1978	Midnight Express	Hamidou
1980	Popeye	Bluto
1981	The Salamander	Surgeon
1984	Dune	The Beast Rabban
1985	Red Sonja	Falkon
1989	Outlaw of Gor	Surbus

WILLIAM SMITH

(1931 -   )

At odds with his screen image (he is often cast as a psychotic thug) is the fact that Smith is a scholar. He speaks five languages, received a master's degree in Russian, and cites Dostoyevsky as his favorite author. Born on a cattle ranch in Missouri, Smith moved to California with his family during the Depression. He had originally planned to work for the CIA, but was unable to get clearance as his wife was a French national. Dissatisfied with teaching school, he interviewed at MGM and was put under contract.

Year	Movie	Character
1970	C.C. and Company	Moon
1972	Hammer	Brenner
1975	The Ultimate Warrior	Carrot
1976	Scorchy	Carl
1977	Twilight's Last Gleaming	Hoxey
1979	Seven	Drew
1980	Any Which Way You Can	Jack Wilson
1982	Conan the Barbarian	Conan's Father
1984	Red Dawn	Strelski
1985	Fever Pitch	Panama Hat
1985	The Mean Season	Albert O'Shaughnessy
1986	Eye of the Tiger	Blade

MADOLYN SMITH-OSBORNE

(1957 -   )

As an army brat, Smith-Osborne grew up all over, but went to high school in Albuquerque. Active in sports and ballet in her youth, she performed throughout high school. She kept up a heavy acting schedule during her days as a student at USC as well. Her first movie role, as a Texas deb in *Urban Cowboy*, came immediately upon graduation. She has worked on stage and in film and television ever since.

Year	Movie	Character
1980	Urban Cowboy	Pam
1984	2010	Caroline Floyd
1988	Funny Farm	Elizabeth
1991	Final Approach	Casey Halsey
1991	The Super	Naomi Bensinger

CARRIE SNODGRASS

(1946 -   )

Snodgrass grew up outside of Chicago and after a short spell at Northern Illinois University, she transferred to the Goodman Theater in Chicago where she studied the history of the theater, costume and art, as well as lighting, set design, make-up, dance and fencing. She left after five years with a master's degree. She was soon in Hollywood and shocked the industry with an Oscar nomination in 1970 for the title role in *Diary of a Mad Housewife*.

Year	Movie	Character
1970	Diary of a Mad Housewife	Tina Balser
1978	The Fury	Hester
1983	A Night in Heaven	Mrs. Johnson
1985	Pale Rider	Sarah Wheeler
1986	Murphy's Law	Joan Freeman
1991	Across the Tracks	Rosemary Maloney
1993	The Ballad of Little Jo	Ruth Badger

JOSEF SOMMER

(1934 -   )

Reflecting on the actor's lot, Sommer once said: "There are two things that go on in a professional actor's life. The first is finding work, making a living, pursuing a career. The other thing is the art of acting. It's so easy to lose that in the urgency of a career. Sometimes the struggle is just staying active, when you wish the struggle would be over great roles and great plays. I'm not sure you ever reconcile the two things. I guess you just remind yourself that acting is worthwhile because there is always potentially great work to be done."

Year	Movie	Character
1976	The Front	Committee Chairman
1978	Oliver's Story	Dr. Dienhart
1980	Hide in Plain Sight	Jason
1981	Absence of Malice	McAdam
1981	Reds	Official
1981	Rollover	Roy Lefcourt
1982	Hanky Panky	Adrian Pruitt
1982	Still of the Night	George Bynum
1983	Independence Day	Sam Taylor
1983	Silkwood	Max Richter
1984	Iceman	Whitman
1985	D.A.R.Y.L.	Dr. Stewart
1985	Target	Taber
1985	Witness	Schaeffer
1987	The Rosary Murders	Lt. Koznicki
1989	Bloodhounds of Broadway	Waldo Winchester
1989	Chances Are	Judge Fenwick
1992	Shadows and Fog	Priest
1992	The Mighty Ducks	The Boss
1993	Malice	Lester Adams

PAUL SORVINO

(1939 -   )

Although he has said that he prefers television over films because "the subjects have more nobility," Sorvino has been very active in film since the early 1970s. A native of Brooklyn, he is also a singer. He grew up listening to Enrico Caruso and Mario Lanza and by 15 he was studying voice in earnest. A year later he was singing in Catskill Mountain resorts. Acting began for Sorvino after winning a scholarship to study at the American Musical and Dramatic Academy.

Year	Movie	Character
1970	Where's Poppa?	xxx
1971	Made for Each Other	Giggy's Father
1971	The Panic in Needle Park	Samuels
1973	A Touch of Class	Walter Menkes
1977	Oh, God!	Rev. Willie Williams
1978	Bloodbrothers	Chubby DeCoco
1978	The Brink's Job	Jazz Maffie
1979	Lost and Found	Reilly
1980	Cruising	Capt. Edelson
1981	Reds	Louis Fraina
1982	I, the Jury	Det. Chambers
1982	That Championship Season	Phil Romano
1985	Turk 182!	Himself
1986	A Fine Mess	Tony Pazzo
1990	Dick Tracy	Lips Manlis
1990	Goodfellas	Paul Cicero
1991	The Rocketeer	Eddie Valentine

KEVIN SPACEY

(1959 -   )

Spacey won a Tony for his role in Neil Simon's comedy *Lost in Yonkers* and received high praise from the renowned playwright. "Kevin is a writer's dream," he said. "I could have used him in at least six of my plays, including Oscar in *The Odd Couple*." Expelled from California's Northridge Military Academy for hitting a classmate with a tire, he was advised by a guidance counselor to channel his combative energy into acting. "I took a drama class. And suddenly I felt at home," Spacey later recalled.

Year	Movie	Character
1988	Rocket Gibraltar	Dwayne Hanson
1988	Working Girl	Bob Speck
1989	Dad	Mario
1989	See No Evil, Hear No Evil	Kirgo
1990	A Show of Force	Frank Curtin
1992	Consenting Adults	Eddy Otis
1992	Glengarry Glen Ross	John Williamson

JAMES SPADER

(1960 -   )

Spader moved to New York after prep school in New England to pursue an acting career. He trained at the Michael Chekov Studio and, to support himself, drove trucks, loaded railway cars and worked as a stable boy at the Claremont Riding Academy. He won the best actor award at Cannes for his role as the impotent voyeur in *sex, lies and videotape*. He played Andrew McCarthy's snobby best friend in *Pretty in Pink* and a preppy department store manager in *Mannequin*.

Year	Movie	Character
1981	Endless Love	Keith
1985	Tuff Turf	Morgan Hiller
1986	Pretty in Pink	Steff
1987	Baby Boom	Ken Arrenberg
1987	Less Than Zero	Rip
1987	Mannequin	Richards
1987	Wall Street	Roger Barnes
1988	Jack's Back	John/Rick Wesford
1989	sex, lies and videotape	Graham Dalton
1990	Bad Influence	Michael Boll
1990	White Palace	Max Baron
1991	True Colors	Tim Garrity
1992	Bob Roberts	News Anchor

VINCENT SPANO

(1962 -   )

In films since his teenage years, Spano's acting career began as a ninth-grader in the play *The Shadow Box* when it premiered at the Long Wharf Theater in Connecticut. A native of Brooklyn, he has also appeared on CBS's top-rated soap *Search for Tomorrow*.

Year	Movie	Character
1979	Over the Edge	Mark
1979	The Double McGuffin	Foster
1983	Baby, It's You	Sheik
1983	Rumble Fish	Steve
1983	The Black Stallion Returns	Raj
1984	Alphabet City	Johnny
1985	Creator	Boris
1987	And God Created Woman	Billy Moran
1987	Good Morning, Babylon	Nicola
1991	City of Hope	Nick
1991	Oscar	Anthony Rossano
1993	Alive	Antonio Balbi
1993	Indian Summer	Matthew Berman

CAMILLA SPARV

(1940 -   )

The Swedish beauty came to movies via a modeling career that began when she was very young in Stockholm. She was a top fashion model in Paris for two years before being lured to New York by a large agency. Her appearances on the covers of such magazines as Vogue brought her a contract with Columbia Pictures. Sparv was once married to vacuum cleaner heir Bunker Hoover.

Year	Movie	Character
1966	Dead Heat on a Merry-Go-Round	Inger Knudson
1966	Murderer's Row	Coco Duquette
1966	The Trouble With Angels	Sister Constance
1969	Downhill Racer	Carole Stahl
1969	MacKenna's Gold	Inga
1978	The Greek Tycoon	Simi Tomasis
1980	Caboblanco	Hira

G.D. SPRADLIN

(1926 -   )

Before he ever uttered his first word of dialogue as an actor, Spradlin had struck it rich in the petroleum industry, ran for mayor of Oklahoma City and retired to the easy life on a yacht in Miami. The Oklahoma native discovered oil in his native state and was a millionaire at 35. He worked as an attorney and a college professor and discovered acting in an amateur production of Tennessee Williams' *Cat on a Hot Tin Roof* in a community theater in Oklahoma City.

Year	Movie	Character
1968	Will Penny	Anse Howard
1969	Number One	Dr. Tristler
1970	Monte Walsh	Hat Henderson
1974	The Godfather, Part II	Senator Pat Geary
1977	MacArthur	Gen. Eichelberger
1977	One on One	Coach Moreland Smith
1979	Apocalypse Now	General
1979	North Dallas Forty	B. A. Strothers
1980	The Formula	Clements
1982	Wrong is Right	Philindros
1983	The Lords of Discipline	General Durrell
1984	Tank	Sheriff Buelton
1989	The War of the Roses	Harry Thurmon

TERENCE STAMP

(1939 -   )

A leading figure in "Swinging London" during the 1960s, the British actor burst onto the scene in 1962 with his Oscar-nominated performance in *Billy Budd*. Paired with super-model Jean Shrimpton during the period, Stamp was very much in the limelight. However, with the decline of the U.K. film industry at the end of that decade Stamp seemed to vanish from sight. Actually he spent time travelling in India and working in Italian films. He reappeared during the 1980s.

Year	Movie	Character
1965	The Collector	Freddie Clegg
1967	Far from the Madding Crowd	Troy
1978	Superman	General Zod
1980	Superman II	General Zod
1986	Legal Eagles	Victor Taft
1987	The Sicilian	Prince Borsa
1987	Wall Street	Sir Larry Wildman
1988	Alien Nation	William Harcourt
1988	Young Guns	John Tunstall
1990	Genuine Risk	Paul Hellwart
1993	The Real McCoy	Jack Schmidt

LIONEL STANDER

(1908 -   )

Blunt and outspoken, Stander was blacklisted during the 50's Red Scare after not only refusing to name friends and colleagues as "communists," but attacking the HUAC for their self-righteous position. During his ten years of exile, he sold stocks on Wall Street and made films in Italy. The veteran character actor made his film debut in a silent feature at 15 and by 27 he was the highest-paid supporting actor under contract to Columbia at $3,500 per week. His career has lasted more than 60 years and includes over 200 films.

Year	Movie	Character
1965	The Loved One	The Guru Brahmin
1969	Once Upon a Time in the West	Barman
1971	The Gang That Couldn't Shoot Straight	Baccala
1972	Pulp	Ben Dinuccio
1977	Cassandra Crossing	Conductor
1977	New York, New York	Tony Harwell
1989	Cookie	Enzo Della Testa
1989	Wicked Stepmother	Sam

HARRY DEAN STANTON

(1926 -   )

The Kentucky-born character actor's sullen, dour face has served him in a wide variety of roles, especially that of burnt-out misfits living on the edge of society. Popular in the film community as a dependable performer, Stanton began with bit parts in films during the 1950s. In *Repo Man*, he played a veteran car repossessor who shows Emilio Estevez the ropes. He was Molly Ringwald's down-on-his-luck father in *Pretty in Pink* and a horse thief, part of Jack Nicholson's crew, in *The Missouri Breaks*.

Year	Movie	Character
1963	The Man from the Diner's Club	Beatnik
1967	Cool Hand Luke	Tramp
1967	The Long Ride Home	Sgt. Dan Way
1968	Day of the Evil Gun	Sgt. Parker
1970	Kelly's Heroes	Willard
1971	Two-Lane Blacktop	Oklahoma Hitchhiker
1973	Dillinger	Homer
1973	Pat Garrett and Billy the Kid	Luke
1974	The Godfather, Part II	FBI Man #1
1974	Where the Lilies Bloom	Kiser Pease
1975	92 in the Shade	Carter
1975	Farewell My Lovely	Billy Rolfe
1975	Rafferty and the Gold Dust Twins	Billy

(continued on page 509)

(continued on page 509)

MAUREEN STAPLETON

(1925 -   )

She has won two Tony Awards, one Oscar and one Emmy. Stapleton became a Broadway star in the 1951 production of Tennessee Williams' *The Rose Tatoo* for which she received her first Tony. A native of Troy, NY, she moved to New York City at 19 and has been acting on stage, television and film ever since.

Year	Movie	Character
1960	The Fugitive Kind	Vee Talbott
1963	Bye Bye Birdie	Mama
1970	Airport	Inez Guerrero
1971	Plaza Suite	Karen Nash
1978	Interiors	Pearl
1979	Lost and Found	Jemmy
1979	The Runner Stumbles	Mrs. Shandig
1981	On the Right Track	Mary/Bag Lady
1981	Reds	Emma Goldman
1981	The Fan	Belle Goldman
1984	Johnny Dangerously	Mom
1985	Cocoon	Mary Luckett
1986	Heartburn	Vera
1986	The Money Pit	Estelle
1987	Made in Heaven	Aunt Lisa
1987	Nuts	Rose Kirk
1987	Sweet Lorraine	Lillian
1988	Cocoon: The Return	Mary Luckett
1988	Doin' Time on Planet Earth	Harriett
1992	Passed Away	Mary Scanlan

MARY STEENBURGEN

(1953 -   )

Steenburgen's career took off in 1977 after being discovered and cast by Jack Nicholson in his western, *Goin' South*. Raised in Arkansas, she attributes her interest in acting to an early voracius appetite for reading. She regularly checked out 13 books a week from the local library and would often act out a few of the characters she read about. She studied acting at the Neighborhood Playhouse but then struggled in a barren New York job market for years before her fortuitous meeting with Nicholson.

Year	Movie	Character
1978	Goin' South	Julia Tate
1979	Time After Time	Amy
1980	Melvin and Howard	Lynda Dummar
1981	Ragtime	Mother
1982	A Midsummer Night's Sex Comedy	Adrian
1983	Cross Creek	Marjorie Kinnan Rawlings
1983	Romantic Comedy	Phoebe
1985	One Magic Christmas	Ginny Grainger
1987	Dead of Winter	Evelyn
1987	End of the Line	Rose
1987	The Whales of August	Young Sarah
1989	Miss Firecracker	Elain Rutledge
1989	Parenthood	Karen Buckman
1990	Back to the Future Part III	Clara Clayton
1991	The Butcher's Wife	Stella

DANIEL STERN

(1957 -   )

A very active character player in movies, Stern grew up in the Washington, D.C. suburbs. After high school, he went to D.C.'s Shakespeare Festival auditions seeking a job as a lighting technician, but ended up being cast as a musician. Next came New York, where he acted in several Off-Broadway plays. His film roles include a bungling burglar in the *Home Alone* pictures, a rookie cop flying with Roy Scheider in *Blue Thunder*, one of the guys in *Diner* (Ellen Barkin's husband) and one of the four friends in *Breaking Away*.

Year	Movie	Character
1979	Breaking Away	Cyril
1979	Starting Over	Student
1980	It's My Turn	Cooperman
1980	One Trick Pony	Hare Krishna
1980	Stardust Memories	Actor
1982	Diner	Shrevie
1982	I'm Dancing as Fast as I Can	Jim
1983	Blue Thunder	Lymangood
1983	Get Crazy	Neil
1985	Key Exchange	Michael
1986	Hannah and Her Sisters	Dusty
1986	The Boss's Wife	Joel
1987	Born in East L.A.	Jimmy
1988	D.O.A.	Hal Petersham

(continued on page 509)

FRANCES STERNHAGEN

(1932 -   )

One of New York's leading stage actresses, Sternhagen did few films prior to the 1980s because she didn't like to be away from her family on location shooting. Home and family life are very important to her (she has a husband and six kids) and she once said, "If I didn't have my family I would be so lonely. The theater and acting are so artificial that I would go crazy if that was all I had." She is from Washington, D.C., the daughter of a U.S. tax court judge and a graduate of Vassar. Acting began for her at D.C.'s Arena Stage.

Year	Movie	Character
1971	The Hospital	Mrs. Cushing
1973	Two People	Mrs. McCluskey
1979	Starting Over	Marva Potter
1981	Outland	Lazarus
1983	Independence Day	Carla Taylor
1983	Romantic Comedy	Blanche
1988	Bright Lights, Big City	Clara Tillinghast
1989	Communion	Dr. Janet Duffy
1989	See You in the Morning	Neenie
1990	Misery	Virginia
1990	Sibling Rivalry	Rose Turner
1991	Doc Hollywood	Lillian
1992	Raising Cain	Dr. Waldheim

ANDREW STEVENS

(1955 -   )

Discovered by a Hollywood agent the summer after his high school graduation, Stevens abandoned his college plans to become a professional actor. Cast as good guys and bad guys Stevens once commented, "It's an unfortunate fact of life that some of the most interesting and challenging [roles] are the most villainous. There's just so much more to work with when the character is the heavy—the audience develops really strong feelings about him right away."

Year	Movie	Character
1976	Vigilante Force	Paul
1978	The Boys in Company C	Billy Ray Pike
1978	The Fury	Robin
1981	Death Hunt	Alvin
1982	The Seduction	Derek
1983	Ten to Midnight	Paul McAnn
1990	Down the Drain	xxx

CONNIE STEVENS

(1938 -   )

The actress/singer grew up in Brooklyn and dropped out of high school to pursue a career in show business. Stevens began by singing with a rock band called the Debs and working in beach movies. Spotted by Jerry Lewis who found her an agent, she was soon seen in such TV shows as *77 Sunset Strip* and *Hawaiian Eye*. She was a teen idol in the U.S. and Japan. After a long run in the entertainment business, she started a cosmetics company and makes club appearances a few months out of the year.

Year	Movie	Character
1961	Parrish	Lucy
1961	Susan Slade	Susan Slade
1965	Never Too Late	Kate Clinton
1966	Way ... Way Out	Eileen
1976	Scorchy	Jackie
1982	Grease 2	Miss Mason
1987	Back to the Beach	Connie
1988	Tapeheads	June Tager

FISHER STEVENS

(1963 -   )

Stevens' first real ambition in life was to be a professional athlete. Famed Olympic gold medalist Jesse Owens was a neighbor in his apartment building and young Fisher idolized him. These athletic aspirations remained with him up until age 13 when he moved from Chicago to New York and discovered his physical development didn't quite keep pace with his ambitious plans. The short, slender youth found a new love in acting. He debuted in the splatter-pic *The Burning* in 1981.

Year	Movie	Character
1983	Baby, It's You	Stage Manager
1984	The Flamingo Kid	Hawk Ganz
1985	My Science Project	Vince Latello
1986	Short Circuit	Ben Jabituya
1986	The Boss's Wife	Carlos
1988	Short Circuit 2	Ben Jahrvi
1990	Reversal of Fortune	David Marriott
1991	Mystery Date	Dwight
1991	The Marrying Man	Sammy
1993	Super Mario Brothers	Iggy

INGER STEVENS

(1934 - 1970)

Born in Stockholm, Sweden, the professor's daughter moved with her family to New York at 13, then ran away from home to join the burlesque in Kansas City. After her father brought her back, Stevens started an active career on stage, screen and TV and became the star in the TV comedy *The Farmer's Daughter* (1963-66). She died at 35 in her L.A. apartment of an overdose of barbituates.

Year	Movie	Character
1964	The New Interns	Nancy
1967	A Guide for the Married Man	Ruth
1967	The Long Ride Home	Emily Biddle
1968	Firecreek	Evelyn
1968	Five Card Stud	Lily Langford
1968	Hang 'Em High	Rachel
1968	Madigan	Julia Madigan

PARKER STEVENSON

(1953 -   )

Born in Philadelphia and raised in Rye, NY, Stevenson got his start in a Clearasil ad on TV and eventually did 100 commercials plus a few feature films before he graduated from college. He moved to L.A. to continue his acting career and spent three years as a teen idol on ABC-TV's *The Hardy Boys* (1976-79). "The teen idol thing restricts where I can go," he later commented on this experience. "But it's also given me the power to do the kind of work I want."

Year	Movie	Character
1972	A Separate Peace	Gene
1974	Death of Her Innocence	Michael
1976	Lifeguard	Chris
1983	Stroker Ace	Aubrey

CATHERINE MARY STEWART

(1960 -   )

A dancer from age 7, Stewart joined a professional dance company and toured the Middle East and Europe when she was 16. "My very existence was dance," she once said. After high school, she moved to London from her native Canada and for the next two years studied dance, drama, singing, dialects, etc. She made her motion picture debut there in Peter Roth's futuristic musical *The Apple*. She was cast in a small part in *Nighthawks* before moving to L.A., where she landed a role in the soap *Days of Our Lives*.

Year	Movie	Character
1981	Nighthawks	Salesgirl
1984	Night of the Comet	Regina
1984	The Last Starfighter	Maggie Gordon
1985	Mischief	Bunny
1988	World Gone Wild	Angie
1989	Weekend at Bernie's	Gwen Saunders

DAVID OGDEN STIERS

(1952 -   )

Best known as the pompous Bostonian, Major Emerson Winchester on CBS's *M*A*S*H*, Stiers hails from Peoria, IL, and Eugene, OR, where he was often cast as the lead in high school plays. After high school graduation, he spent seven years with the California Shakespeare Festival in Santa Clara before moving to New York to study in the drama division of Juilliard. He became active in films during the mid-80's after *M*A*S*H*.

Year	Movie	Character
1977	Oh, God!	Mr. McCarthy
1978	Magic	Todson
1978	The Cheap Detective	Captain
1985	Better Off Dead	Al Myer
1985	Creator	Sid
1985	The Man With One Red Shoe	Conductor
1988	Another Woman	Young Marion's Father
1988	The Accidental Tourist	Porter
1991	Doc Hollywood	Nick Nicholson
1992	Shadows and Fog	Hacker

DEAN STOCKWELL

(1935 -   )

Stockwell was a child star under contract to MGM in the 1940s and a young leading man during the late 1950s/1960s. He then dropped out of sight for several years until his reemergence in the 1980's. Often going from one extreme to another in his choice of roles, he once said "I hate to admit it but you can't do a role unless it's somewhere in your psyche. People don't realise how vast the subconcious is. It's like infinity."

Year	Movie	Character
1962	Long Day's Journey Into Night	Edmund Tyrone
1970	The Dunwich Horror	Wilbur
1982	Wrong is Right	Hacker
1984	Dune	Dr. Wellington Yueh
1984	Paris, Texas	Walt
1985	The Legend of Billie Jean	Muldaur
1985	To Live and Die in L.A.	Bob Grimes
1986	Blue Velvet	Ben
1987	Beverly Hills Cop II	Chip Cain
1987	Gardens of Stone	Homer Thomas
1988	Married to the Mob	Tony "The Tiger" Russo
1988	The Blue Iguana	Det. Carl Strick
1988	Tucker: The Man and His Dream	Howard Hughes
1989	Backtrack	xxx
1989	Limit Up	Peter Oak
1992	The Player	Andy Civella

GUY STOCKWELL

(1934 -   )

A former school teacher who taught grades one through eight in a one-room school house in a mountain hamlet in the High Sierras, Stockwell moved to L.A. from New York with his family when his younger brother, Dean, signed a contract with MGM. He worked in theater during the late 1950s and then became a regular on *The Richard Boone Show* (1963-64), television's equivalent of repertory theater.

Year	Movie	Character
1965	The War Lord	Draco
1966	Beau Geste	Beau
1966	Blindfold	Fitzpatrick
1967	Banning	Linus
1967	Tobruk	Lt. Mohnfeld
1974	Airport 1975	Colonel Moss

JOHN STOCKWELL

(1961 -   )

Stockwell spent three years acting in Hollywood movies before trying his hand behind the camera. The co-star of *Christine* and a pilot named Cougar in *Top Gun*, he co-wrote and directed the 1987 film *Under Cover*. Born in Galveston, TX, the son of an attorney, Stockwell graduated from Harvard and studied acting at England's Royal Academy of Dramatic Arts. He was lead singer and rhythm guitarist with The Brood, a New York-based rock group.

Year	Movie	Character
1983	Christine	Dennis Guilder
1983	Losin' It	Spider
1985	My Science Project	Michael Harlan
1986	Radioactive Dreams	Phillip Marlowe
1986	Top Gun	Cougar

ERIC STOLTZ

(1961 -   )

Stoltz was born and raised in American Samoa until age 8 when his family moved back to California. His artistic talents presented themselves at age 6 when he began piano lessons. Acting followed, according to Stoltz when, "I started out as a rehearsal accompanist, playing piano for musicals, and eventually found myself on the stage in small roles—for no money, of course. I really loved being on the stage and I continued that up until college."

Year	Movie	Character
1982	Fast Times at Ridgemont High	Stoner Bud
1984	The Wild Life	Bill
1985	Code Name: Emerald	Andy Wheeler
1985	Mask	Rocky Dennis
1987	Lionheart	Robert Nerra
1987	Sister, Sister	Matt Rutledge
1987	Some Kind of Wonderful	Keith Nelson
1988	Manifesto	Christopher
1989	Say Anything...	Vahlere
1989	The Fly II	Martin Brundle
1990	Memphis Belle	Danny Daly
1993	Bodies, Rest & Motion	Sid

DEE WALLACE STONE

(1949 -   )

Stone was making a living doing TV commercials and industrial films in New York in 1974, but soon tired of that and moved to L.A. to launch a film and television career. She feels that her experience as a dancer has made a significant contribution to her acting skills, because, as she once said, "a dancer knows how to move naturally. Dancing allows me to do almost subliminal things as an actress that the audience might sense, but yet not be fully aware of."

Year	Movie	Character
1975	The Stepford Wives	xxx
1979	10	Mary Lewis
1981	The Howling	Karen
1982	E.T. The Extra-Terrestrial	Mary
1982	Jimmy the Kid	May
1983	Cujo	Donna
1985	Secret Admirer	Connie
1986	Critters	Helen Brown
1991	Popcorn	Suzanne

HAROLD J. STONE

(1911 -   )

Stone is descended from a long line of actors of the Yiddish stage and began acting himself in a Yiddish production at the age of 6. He won his first big role in Sydney Kingsley's play *The World We Make* while acting in a production called *Little Old New York* at the 1937 World's Fair. Notable movie roles include the tough Chicago nightclub owner and father of the girl Elvis Presley is supposed to keep an eye on in *Girl Happy*.

Year	Movie	Character
1960	Spartacus	David
1962	The Chapman Report	Frank Garnell
1965	Girl Happy	Big Frank
1965	The Greatest Story Ever Told	General Varus
1967	The Big Mouth	Thor
1967	The St. Valentine's Day Massacre	Frank Nitti
1981	Hardly Working	Frank

LARRY STORCH

(1923 -   )

Best-remembered as Corporal Agarn in the sixties sitcom *F Troop*, Storch is primarily a stand-up comic and nightclub performer. He had a run of films during the 1960s and then drifted into theater work that included three years on tour as "the man" in *Porgy & Bess*.

Year	Movie	Character
1960	Who Was That Lady?	Orenov
1963	Captain Newman, M.D.	Gavoni
1963	Forty Pounds of Trouble	Floyd
1964	Sex and the Single Girl	Motorcycle Cop
1964	Wild and Wonderful	Rufus
1965	A Very Special Favor	Harry
1965	Bus Riley's Back in Town	Howie
1965	Great Race	Texas Jack
1965	That Funny Feeling	Luther
1969	The Great Bank Robbery	Juan
1974	Airport 1975	Purcell
1981	S.O.B.	Guru

MADELEINE STOWE

(1958 -   )

Born and raised in L.A., Stowe was discovered at age 18 by an agent while walking up the aisle of a movie theater. A strong case of stage fright has kept her mostly in film and has even ruled out acting lessons. "I've never studied acting beyond a high school class," she once said.

Year	Movie	Character
1987	Stakeout	Maria McGuire
1989	Worth Winning	Veronica Briskow
1990	Revenge	Miryea
1990	Two Jakes	Lillian Bodine
1991	Closet Land	Woman
1992	The Last of the Mohicans	Cora
1992	Unlawful Entry	Karen Carr
1993	Another Stakeout	Maria
1993	Short Cuts	Sherri Shepard

BEATRICE STRAIGHT

MARCIA STRASSMAN

(1916 -   )

(1948 -   )

Straight has spent most of her life acting on the stage having turned down MGM's offer of a 7-year contract in 1947. It was not until her Oscar-winning role as William Holden's wife in the 1976 hit *Network* that she gained the attention of movie audiences. She has been described as "poised, gracious, unpretentious and charming." An American, she grew up in England from age 11, when her parents moved there to start Dartington Hall, a liberal progressive school that encouraged interest in theater and the arts.

The daughter of an auto parts wholesaler, Strassman grew up in New York. She auditioned for plays as a teenager because, as she once said, "I hated school and would do anything to get out of it." Her singing abilities landed her a job as a replacement to Liza Minnelli in the Off-Broadway musical *Best Foot Forward* at 15. Her acting career took off with her part as Julie Kotter in ABC's *Welcome Back, Kotter*, where she spent four not very happy years before moving into film roles.

Year	Movie	Character
1976	Network	Louise Schumacher
1979	Bloodline	Kate Erling
1979	The Promise	Marion
1980	The Formula	Kay Neeley
1981	Endless Love	Rose
1982	Poltergeist	Dr. Lesh
1983	Two of a Kind	Ruth
1986	Power	Claire Hastings
1991	Deceived	Adrienne's Mother

Year	Movie	Character
1982	Soup for One	Maria
1985	The Aviator	Rose Stiller
1989	Honey, I Shrunk the Kids	Diane Szalinski
1991	And You Thought Your Parents Were Weird	Sarah Carson
1991	Fast Getaway	Lorraine
1992	Honey, I Blew Up the Baby	Diane
1993	Another Stakeout	Pam O'Hara

DAVID STRATHAIRN

GAIL STRICKLAND

(1950 -   )

The director and actor John Sayles, known for his tight control while on a set, holds Strathairn in high regard. He often casts him in his films and once said that David Strathairn is the only actor he lets stand behind him when he is acting. The son of a surgeon, Strathairn grew up in San Francisco, graduated from Williams College in Massachusetts and worked briefly as a clown with the Ringling Brothers and Barnum & Bailey Circus.

Year	Movie	Character
1983	Lovesick	Zuckerman
1983	Silkwood	Wesley
1984	Iceman	Dr. Singe
1984	The Brother from Another Planet	man in black
1986	At Close Range	Tony Pine
1987	Matewan	Sid
1988	Call Me	Sam
1988	Dominick and Eugene	Martin Chernak
1988	Eight Men Out	Eddi Cicotte
1989	The Feud	The Stranger
1990	Memphis Belle	Commanding Officer
1991	City of Hope	Asteroid
1992	A League of Their Own	Ira Lowenstein
1992	Sneakers	Whistler
1993	Lost in Yonkers	Johnny
1993	The Firm	Ray McDeere
1993	A Dangerous Woman	Getso

(1947 -   )

In 1988, Strickland received attention when she became the first regular lesbian character in prime time television in the series *Heartbeat*. She took the role in that feminist hospital drama because, as she says, "It's not often actors get to play parts that might make a difference. The fact that somewhere, somehow, someone's perspective might be softened is important to me." Strickland was raised a Baptist in Birmingham, AL, one of five kids of a tire shop owner and a housewife. She made her Broadway debut in 1973.

Year	Movie	Character
1976	Bound for Glory	Pauline
1976	The Drowning Pool	Mavis
1977	One on One	B.J. Rudoplh
1978	Who'll Stop the Rain	Chairman
1979	Norma Rae	Bonnie Mae
1983	Uncommon Valor	Mrs. Rhodes
1984	Oxford Blues	xxx
1984	Protocol	Mrs. St. John
1991	The Man in the Moon	Marie Foster
1993	Three of Hearts	Yvonne

WOODY STRODE

(1914 -   )

A former professional wrestler, the 6-foot-4-inch Strode attended UCLA, played pro-football in Canada, and wrestled professionally for nine years. The famous director John Ford, who gave Strode his first chance in films in 1958, reportedly told the actor: "It's pretty rough to make a star out of you, but I'm going to make you a character actor and you'll make some money." A physical actor who did many of his own stunts, Strode's career truly got underway while working in the Italian film industry during the late 60's/early 70's.

Year	Movie	Character
1960	Spartacus	Draba
1960	The Last Voyage	Hank Lawson
1962	The Man Who Shot Liberty Valance	Pompey
1963	Tarzan's Three Challenges	Tarim Khan
1965	Genghis Khan	Sengal
1966	7 Women	Lean Worrior
1966	The Professionals	Jake
1968	Shalako	Chato
1969	Once Upon a Time in the West	Stony
1976	Winterhawk	Big Rude
1979	Jaguar Lives!	Sensei
1979	The Ravagers	Brown
1982	Vigilante	Rake
1983	The Black Stallion Returns	Meslar
1984	The Cotton Club	Holmes

DON STROUD

(1937 -   )

Stroud, a native of Hawaii, was the fourth-ranked surfer in the world at 19, which earned him his start in show biz riding a big wave in the opening shot of Troy Donahue's *Hawaiian Eye* TV series. Often cast as a heavy, Stroud's acting education came while he was a contract player at Universal. He credits Sidney Poitier for steering him in the right direction during his early attempts to break in.

Year	Movie	Character
1967	Games	Norman
1967	The Ballad of Josie	Bratsch
1968	Coogan's Bluff	Ringerman
1968	Madigan	Hughie
1970	...tick...tick...tick...	Bengy Springer
1972	Joe Kidd	Lamarr
1973	Scalawag	Velvet
1976	The Killer Inside Me	Elmer
1977	The Choirboys	Lyles
1978	The Buddy Holly Story	Jesse
1979	The Amityville Horror	Father Bolen
1981	The Night the Lights Went Out in Georgia	Seth
1986	Armed and Dangerous	Sgt. Rizzo
1990	Down the Drain	xxx

DAVID SUCHET

(1946 -   )

The British actor was born in London and trained for the stage at the London Academy of Music and Dramatic Arts from 1966-69. Mostly active in England, Suchet first came to the U.S. on a tour with the Royal Shakespeare Company. He has written essays on Shakespearean acting and was a visiting professor of theater at the University of Nebraska.

Year	Movie	Character
1983	Trenchcoat	Inspector Stagnos
1984	Little Drummer Girl	Mesterbein
1985	The Falcon and the Snowman	Alex
1986	Iron Eagle	Minister of Defense
1987	Harry and the Hendersons	Jacques Lafleur
1988	A World Apart	Muller
1988	To Kill a Priest	Bishop

BARRY SULLIVAN

(1912 -   )

A handsome durable actor, Sullivan was a fixture of American film and TV-movies for nearly four decades. He was prominent in many low-budget crime and western films and starred in a 1964 outlaw movie, *Stage to Thunder Rock*. He played Sheriff Horne in that story of attempted revenge. *Variety* called him "...staunch, hard and strong-willed as the lawman in a performance well suited to the role."

Year	Movie	Character
1962	Light in the Piazza	Noel Johnson
1963	A Gathering of Eagles	Colonel Fowler
1964	Stage to Thunder Rock	Sheriff Horne
1964	The Man in the Middle	General Kempton
1966	An American Dream	Roberts
1969	Shark!	Mallare
1969	Tell Them Willie Boy Is Here	Calvert
1973	Pat Garrett and Billy the Kid	xxx
1974	Earthquake	Stockle
1977	Oh, God!	Priest
1978	Caravans	Richardson

BO SVENSON

(1941 -   )

The Swedish-born actor immigrated to the U.S. in 1958 and almost immediately enlisted in the U.S. Marine Corps where he spent six years. During this time he attended the University of Meiji in Japan from 1960 to 1963 and became the Far East Heavyweight Division Judo Champion in 1961. In addition to holding a black belt in this sport he was also a professional hockey player and race car driver. His screen career began as Big Swede on ABC-TV's *Here Come the Brides* from 1968-70.

Year	Movie	Character
1975	Part 2, Walking Tall	Buford
1975	The Great Waldo Pepper	Axel Olsson
1976	Breaking Point	Michael McBain
1977	Final Chapter—Walking Tall	Buford
1979	North Dallas Forty	Jo Bob Priddy
1986	Choke Canyon	Captain
1986	Heartbreak Ridge	Roy Jennings
1986	The Delta Force	Capt. Campbell

KRISTY SWANSON

(1970 -   )

The single-minded actress from Mission Vieja, CA filed for emancipation status from her parents at 16 to be able to compete against 18-year-olds for film and TV roles. Swanson completed her high school education at home and then moved into her own Hollywood apartment. She once told an interviewer: "I've always been this strong-willed person and I've always been in love with acting. I love every aspect of show business, and that includes both the show part of it and the business part of it."

Year	Movie	Character
1986	Deadly Friend	Samantha
1987	Flowers in the Attic	Cathy
1991	Hot Shots!	Kowalski
1991	Mannequin Two: On the Move	Jessie
1992	Buffy, the Vampire Slayer	Buffy
1993	The Program	Camille

D.B. SWEENEY

(1961 -   )

Raised on Long Island, Sweeney was a baseball star throughout his teens, batting .300 and attracting the attention of pro scouts. Although he did perform in one school play, he enrolled at Tulane University where he hoped to continue to play baseball. A motorcycle accident that tore up his knee killed that dream. He transferred to NYU and switched his allegiance to drama. His acting career began immediately following graduation with a role in the Broadway production of *The Caine Mutiny Court Martial*.

Year	Movie	Character
1986	Fire With Fire	Baxter
1987	Gardens of Stone	Jackie Willow
1987	No Man's Land	Benjy Taylor
1988	Eight Men Out	"Shoeless" Joe Jackson
1990	Memphis Belle	Phil Rosenthal
1992	The Cutting Edge	Doug
1993	Fire in the Sky	Travis Walton
1993	Hear No Evil	Ben Kendall

SYLVIA SYMS

(1934 -   )

The British actress made her professional debut in a London West End production of *The Apple Cart* in 1953. Her training was at the Royal Academy of Dramatic Art and in provincial theater. After a series of British films and TV shows in the 1950s, she crossed the Atlantic to make pictures for Hollywood. She played the wife of a civil servant in *The Tamarind Seed* and William Holden's "other woman" in *The World of Suzie Wong*.

Year	Movie	Character
1960	The World of Suzie Wong	Kay
1965	Operation Crossbow	Constance Babington Smith
1968	The Fiction-Makers	xxx
1969	The Desperados	Laura
1974	The Tamarind Seed	Margaret Stephenson
1989	Shirley Valentine	Headmistress
1992	Shining Through	xxx

NITA TALBOT

(1930 -   )

Talbot signed a six-month contract with Warner Brothers while still a teenager and packed her bags for Hollywood. The studio proved unable to cast her and, therefore, did not pick up her option at the end of the term. She remained in L.A. for another one-and-a-half years to study Shakespeare under Charles Laughton before returning to her hometown of New York City. There she became active on the stage and in television in the 1950s and moved decisively into films at the end of the decade.

Year	Movie	Character
1962	Who's Got the Action?	Saturday Knight
1965	A Very Special Favor	Mickey
1965	Girl Happy	Sunny Daze
1965	That Funny Feeling	Audrey
1972	Buck and the Preacher	Madam Esther
1975	The Day of the Locust	Joan
1980	Serial	Angela
1982	Night Shift	Vivian
1982	The Concrete Jungle	Shelly Meyers
1985	Fraternity Vacation	Mrs. Ferret
1985	Movers and Shakers	Dorothy
1986	The Check is in the Mail	Mrs. Rappaport

JEFFREY TAMBOR

(19?? -   )

Very active in television during the 1980s, Tambor may be best known to fans of *Hill Street Blues* for his occasional appearances as Judge Alan Wachtel. Early acting experience was gained at the Broadhurst Theater in New York with a 1976 production of *Sly Fox*. Tambor was born in San Francisco and attended Wayne State University. He made his film debut in *...And Justice For All* as Al Pacino's jolly law partner who slowly loses his mind.

Year	Movie	Character
1979	...And Justice For All	Jay Porter
1983	Mr. Mom	Jinx
1983	The Man Who Wasn't There	Boris
1984	No Small Affair	Ken
1985	Desert Hearts	Jerry
1987	Three O'Clock High	Mr. Rice
1991	City Slickers	Lou
1991	Life Stinks	Vance Crasswell
1991	Pastime	Peter Laporte
1992	Article 99	xxx
1992	Brenda Starr	Vladimir

AKIM TAMIROFF

(1899 - 1972)

This character actor born in Russia and trained at the Moscow Art Theater school came to America in 1923 and decided to stay. After roles on Broadway, Tamiroff and his wife went to Hollywood where he was later nominated for two Oscars for *The General Died at Dawn* (1936) and *For Whom the Bell Tolls* (1943). He died in Palm Springs, CA.

Year	Movie	Character
1960	Ocean's Eleven	Spyros Acebos
1963	The Trial	Bloch
1964	Topkapi	Geven
1965	Lord Jim	Schomberg
1966	After the Fox	Okra
1966	Marco, The Magnificent	Old Man
1966	The Liquidator	Sheriek
1969	The Great Bank Robbery	Papa

LILI TAYLOR

(1967 -   )

"I like to play smart, three-dimensional women," Taylor once said. "I also like to play roles where the women are a little crazy. I just have a feel for crazy people." A native of Glencoe, IL, she made her film debut in *Mystic Pizza* as Jojo Barboza, the feisty bride-to-be who faints at the altar. She has worked on stage in Chicago at the Northlight Repertory Theater and once toured Czechoslovakia, performing the monologue "Talking With" from the play *Clear Glass Marbles*.

Year	Movie	Character
1988	Mystic Pizza	Jojo Barboza
1989	Say Anything...	Corey Flood
1991	Bright Angel	Lucy
1991	Dogfight	Rose
1993	Watch It	Brenda
1993	Short Cuts	Honey Bush
1993	Rudy	Sherry

ROD TAYLOR

(1929 -   )

Best-remembered as the Time Traveller in the film adaptation of H.G. Well's *The Time Machine* that co-starred Yvette Mimieux, Taylor was the first Australian actor to become a Hollywood star since Errol Flynn. Inspired by a performance by Sir Laurence Olivier, who was touring Australia with the Old Vic repertory company, Taylor jumped into radio soap opera. After a couple of Australian films, he moved to California in 1954 and signed a contract with Warner Brothers.

Year	Movie	Character
1960	The Time Machine	Time Traveller
1963	A Gathering of Eagles	Hollis Farr
1963	Sunday in New York	Mike Mitchell
1963	The V.I.P.s	Les Mangam
1963	The Birds	Mitch Brenner
1964	36 Hours	Major Walter Gerber
1964	Fate is the Hunter	Capt. Jack Savage
1965	Do Not Disturb	Mike Harper
1966	The Glass Bottom Boat	Bruce Templeton
1966	The Liquidator	Boysie Oakes
1967	Hotel	Peter McDermott
1968	The Hell with Heroes	Brynie MacKay
1972	The Heroes	xxx
1973	The Train Robbers	Grady
1973	Trader Horn	Trader Horn

LEIGH TAYLOR-YOUNG

(1945 -   )

Taylor-Young was born in Washington, D.C., and studied at Northwestern University where she first became interested in acting. Her big break was in ABC's *Peyton Place* during the 1966-67 season. She studied acting under Sanford Meisner and has often pursued the religious life, studying Eastern religion and living in an ashram in India.

Year	Movie	Character
1968	I Love You, Alice B. Toklas	Nancy
1970	The Adventurers	Amparo
1971	The Gang That Couldn't Shoot Straight	Angela
1973	Soylent Green	Shirl
1980	Can't Stop the Music	Claudia Walters
1981	Looker	Jennifer Long
1985	Jagged Edge	Virginia Howell
1985	Secret Admirer	Elizabeth
1990	Honeymoon Academy	Mrs. Kent

VICTORIA TENNANT

(1950 -   )

Tennant grew up in London's theatrical world, where her mother was a Russian ballerina and her father an actors' agent. She studied at the London Central School of Speech and Drama after trying unsuccessfully to become a famous ballerina like her mother. Her big break came when she was cast in the 1972 U.K. feature *The Ragman's Daughter*, which made her famous in the U.S. and England. Tennant married actor/comedian Steve Martin in 1986.

Year	Movie	Character
1984	All of Me	Terry Hoskins
1987	Best Seller	Roberta Gillian
1987	Flowers in the Attic	Mother
1990	The Handmaid's Tale	Aunt Lydia
1990	Whispers	xxx
1991	L.A. Story	Sara

RICHARD THOMAS

(1951 -   )

Thomas practically grew up on the New York stage. He first appeared on Broadway at age 7 and worked steadily in theaters until he was 17. He then did a TV-movie called *The Homecoming—A Christmas Story*, which aired in 1971, about a Depression-era family living in the Blue Ridge mountains. In it, he played John Boy and continued to do so for five seasons in the series that came out of that movie: *The Waltons*. He won an Emmy, but was eager to get back to the stage. In 1977, he did.

Year	Movie	Character
1969	Last Summer	Peter
1969	Winning	Charley
1970	Red Sky at Morning	Josh Arnold
1971	The Todd Killings	Billy
1972	You'll Like My Mother	Kenny
1977	9/30/55	Jimmy J
1980	Battle Beyond the Stars	Shad

TIM THOMERSON

(1937 -   )

In 1966, when he was 29, Thomerson was an army veteran who had no idea what to do with his life. "I thought about acting, and said 'Yeah, maybe I would like to give this a shot,' " he has said. In New York, people thought he was funny so he became a stand-up comic. That led on to TV sitcoms in the 1970s. He gradually became associated with fantasy and science fiction films.

Year	Movie	Character
1981	Take This Job and Shove It	Ray
1982	Honkytonk Man	Highway Patrolman
1983	Metalstorm: The Destruction of Jared-Syn	Rhodes
1983	Uncommon Valor	Charts
1984	Rhinestone	Barnett
1985	Volunteers	John Reynolds
1986	Iron Eagle	Ted
1987	A Tiger's Tale	Lonny
1988	Cherry 2000	Lester
1988	The Wrong Guys	Tim
1989	Who's Harry Crumb?	Vince Barnes
1990	Air America	Babo
1991	Dollman	xxx

JACK THOMPSON

(1940 -   )

Thompson abandoned formal education early to become a wanderer, railroad worker, construction man and soldier. Back in college at last, he joined a university theater group and resolved to try acting as a career for one year. An Australian, he is the son of a poet and actor. His career was made when he won the Australian Film Institute's best actor award for his part in *Breaker Morant*.

Year	Movie	Character
1971	Outback	Dick
1979	Breaker Morant	Major J. F. Thomas
1982	The Man from Snowy River	Clancy
1983	Merry Christmas, Mr. Lawrence	Hicksley-Ellis
1985	Flesh + Blood	Hawkwood
1992	Wind	Jack Neville
1993	A Far Off Place	John Ricketts
1993	Deception	Ed

LEA THOMPSON

(1962 -   )

Best known as Michael J. Fox's mother in the *Back to the Future* pictures, Thompson is both an actress and a dancer. She has danced with the Pennsylvania Ballet Company, the American Ballet Theater and the San Francisco Ballet. A native of Rochester, MN, her screen career got started with several leading roles in Burger King commercials.

Year	Movie	Character
1983	All the Right Moves	Lisa
1983	Jaws 3-D	Kelly Ann
1984	Red Dawn	Erica
1984	The Wild Life	Anita
1985	Back to the Future	Lorraine Baines
1986	Howard the Duck	Beverly Switzler
1986	SpaceCamp	Kathryn
1987	Some Kind of Wonderful	Amanda Jones
1988	Casual Sex?	Stacy
1988	The Wizard of Loneliness	Sybil
1989	Back to the Future Part II	Lorraine
1990	Back to the Future Part III	Maggie & Lorraine McFly
1992	Article 99	Dr. Robin Van Dorn
1993	Dennis the Menace	Alice Mitchell
1993	The Beverly Hillbillies	Laura

COURTNEY THORNE-SMITH

(19?? -   )

Thorne-Smith can be seen as Pam House, a cute quixotic surfer who would rather catch a wave than make the grade in Paramount's *Summer School*. Her feature film debut was in *Lucas*, as Alise, the bitchy cheerleader with a heart of gold. She was also a series regular on CBS-TV's *Fast Times at Ridgemont High* and has been seen in the Disney Sunday Movie *Thanksgiving Promise*.

Year	Movie	Character
1986	Lucas	Alise
1987	Revenge of the Nerds II: Nerds in Paradise	Sunny
1987	Summer School	Pam
1987	Welcome to 18	Lindsey
1990	Side Out	Samantha

UMA THURMAN

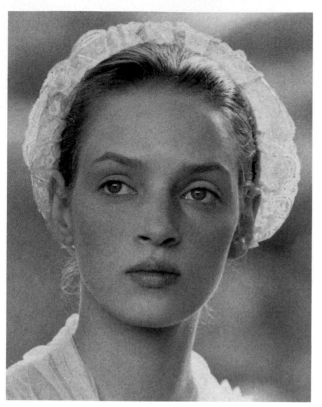

(1970 -   )

The teenage model-turned-actress was born in Boston and raised in the well-known artists' colony of Woodstock, NY. Her father is a Buddhist scholar and her mother, a former model, was once married to Timothy Leary. Thurman lived in India as a youth and attended a private boarding school in Massachusetts as well as New York's Professional Children's High School. "Uma" is the name of a Hindu goddess.

Year	Movie	Character
1988	Dangerous Liaisons	Cecile de Volanges
1988	Johnny Be Good	Georgia Elkans
1989	The Adventures of Baron Munchausen	Venus/Rose
1990	Where the Heart Is	Daphne McBain
1992	Final Analysis	Diana Baylor
1992	Jennifer Eight	Helena Robertson
1993	Mad Dog and Glory	Glory

RACHEL TICOTIN

(1958 -   )

Ticotin got her start after she was chosen from 500 hopefuls at an open casting call to play a drug-addicted nurse and Paul Newman's girlfriend in *Fort Apache, The Bronx*. She had no acting experience, but brought her skills as a dancer with the Ballet Hispanico to bear in her "O.D. walk" scene. She is her own strongest critic and didn't even watch *Fort Apache* until it aired on TV two years later. "If you care about yourself and what you do, you get nervous about it," she said in 1983. "You don't just take the money and go home."

Year	Movie	Character
1981	Fort Apache, The Bronx	Isabella
1987	Critical Condition	Rachel
1990	Total Recall	Melina
1991	F/X 2	Kim Brandon
1991	One Good Cop	Grace
1993	Falling Down	Sandra

PAMELA TIFFIN

(1942 -   )

A top model in New York, Tiffin had no desire to become an actress. However, while on vacation in California, a luncheon with the producer Hal Wallis led to her screen debut in *Summer and Smoke*. She once said that her ambition was to retire and, after a series of films during the 1960s, she did.

Year	Movie	Character
1961	Summer and Smoke	Nellie Ewell
1961	One, Two, Three	Scarlett
1962	State Fair	Margie
1964	For Those Who Think Young	Sandy Palmer
1965	The Hallelujah Trail	Louise Gearhart
1966	Harper	Miranda Sampson

JENNIFER TILLY

(1961 -   )

The younger sister of actress Meg Tilly, Jennifer is recognized as a real talent within L.A.'s theater community. But she has not been very lucky in film and has said: "I've worked with a lot of really great people on their one failure." More often than not it is her physical attributes that get emphasized rather than her acting abilities. Tilly's best-acclaimed role was in the 1989 comedy *Let It Ride*. "The real scene-stealer," said *Variety*, "is Jennifer Tilly, packed into an impossibly low-cut dress with a bombshell body and a pipsqueak voice."

Year	Movie	Character
1984	No Small Affair	Mona
1985	Moving Violations	Amy Hopkins
1987	He's My Girl	Lisa
1988	High Spirits	Miranda
1988	Johnny Be Good	Connie Hisler
1988	Remote Control	Allegra
1989	Far From Home	Amy
1989	Let It Ride	Vicki
1989	The Fabulous Baker Boys	Monica Moran
1993	Made in America	Stacy
1993	Shadow of the Wolf	Igiyook

STEPHEN TOBOLOWSKY

BEVERLY TODD

(1951 -   )

Tobolowsky grew up in Dallas, TX, with dreams of becoming a geologist or a concert pianist. As a teenager, his father found him a job at Dallas' Museum of Natural History in order to lure him away from endlessly practicing the same three piano pieces without any improvement. His focus shifted to theater while a student at SMU and he eventually ended up in L.A. Tobolowsky has directed plays in L.A. and New York and was a co-writer on David Byrne's *True Stories*.

(1946 -   )

A native of Cleveland, Todd grew up near the Karamu Theater famous for its racially integrated casting policy. After studying voice and piano, she began appearing in Karamu productions. She got her professional start when, although relatively unknown, she won a part in *No Strings*, which was being prepared for a tour of England. Todd attended Morgan State College and Kent State University.

Year	Movie	Character
1986	Nobody's Fool	Kirk
1988	Mississippi Burning	Townley
1989	Breaking In	District Attorney
1989	Great Balls of Fire!	John Phillips
1989	In Country	Pete
1990	Bird on a Wire	Joe Weyburn
1990	Funny About Love	Dr. Hugo Blatt
1990	The Grifters	Jeweler
1990	Welcome Home, Roxy Carmichael	Mayor Bill Klepler
1991	Thelma & Louise	Max
1992	Basic Instinct	xxx
1992	Memoirs of an Invisible Man	Warren Singleton
1992	Single White Female	Mitchell Myerson
1993	Groundhog Day	Ned
1993	Josh and S.A.M.	Thom Whitney
1993	The Pickle	Mike Krakower
1993	Calendar Girl	Antonio Gallo

Year	Movie	Character
1969	The Lost Man	Sally
1982	Vice Squad	Louise
1988	Clara's Heart	Dora
1988	Moving	Monica Pear
1989	Lean on Me	Ms. Levias

NANCY TRAVIS

(19?? -   )

A veteran of films and the stage, Travis has said: "They're both very different mediums to me, and I enjoy them both. Film is very technical, and it really tries your patience. What I like about film is the ability to be really spontaneous and at the same time very intimate. The camera is very close. And for the opposite reason, I like theater—and that is making an audience, a crowd of people, feel very intimate, and also being able to do a story from beginning to end, chronologically."

Year	Movie	Character
1987	3 Men and a Baby	Sylvia
1988	Married to the Mob	Karen Lutnick
1990	3 Men and a Little Lady	Sylvia
1990	Air America	Corinne Landreaux
1990	Internal Affairs	Kathleen Avilla
1990	Loose Cannons	Riva
1992	Chaplin	Joan Berry
1992	Passed Away	Cassie Slocombe
1993	So I Married an Axe Murderer	Harriet Michaels
1993	The Vanishing	Rita

CLAIRE TREVOR

(1909 -   )

Born Claire Wemlinger in Bensonhurst, NY, the actress attended Columbia University and studied for the stage at the American Academy of Dramatic Arts. Her career began in theater stock productions during the 1920's and she received Academy Award nominations for best supporting actress during the 1930s, 1940s and 1950s when she did most of her work.

Year	Movie	Character
1962	Two Weeks in Another Town	Clara
1963	The Stripper	Helen
1965	How to Murder Your Wife	Edna
1967	The Cape Town Affair	Killarney
1982	Kiss Me Goodbye	Charlotte

DOROTHY TRISTAN

(1934 -   )

Model-turned-actress Tristan was raised and educated in New York. Her acting career began on stage in the early 1960s with the touring company of *Marat/Sade* in which she played Charlotte Corday. Film roles include an ex-call girl/heroin addict in *Klute* who may be able to help Jane Fonda and Donald Sutherland solve a missing persons case.

Year	Movie	Character
1971	Klute	Arlyn Page
1973	Scarecrow	Coley
1974	Man on a Swing	Janet Tucker
1977	Rollercoaster	Helen
1979	California Dreaming	Fay

TOM TRYON

(1926 - 1991)

Famous as an actor-turned-novelist (*The Other*, *Harvest Home*), the Wethersfield, CT, boy went to Yale, served in the Navy in World War II and appeared in live TV dramas before going to Hollywood. Tryon was one of the last actors to work with Marilyn Monroe in the unfinished *Something's Got to Give*. He gave up the stage for the typewriter. Tryon died of cancer.

Year	Movie	Character
1960	The Story of Ruth	Mahlon
1962	The Longest Day	Lt. Wilson
1963	The Cardinal	Stephen Fermoyle
1965	In Harm's Way	Lt. (jg) William McConnel
1965	The Glory Guys	Demas Harrod

FORREST TUCKER

(1919 - 1986)

The Plainfield, IN, native's rugged good looks made him a popular choice for action films and westerns during the 1940s and 1950s. Tucker played villains in the forties, heroes in the fifties, and from 1965-67 he pleased a new generation as Sgt. Moran O'Rourke in the western TV series *F Troop*. He got started with the Gayety Burlesque in Washington, D.C., as a teenager and was later fired for being under-age. He died of throat cancer.

Year	Movie	Character
1968	The Night They Raided Minsky's	Trim Houlihan
1970	Barquero	Mountain Phil
1970	Chisum	Lawrence Murphy
1972	Cancel My Reservations	Reese
1977	Final Chapter—Walking Tall	Buford's Father

JOHN TURTURRO

(1957 -   )

One of Hollywood's busiest actors, Turturro's film career was launched after receiving an Obie in 1984 for his performance in *Danny and the Deep Blue Sea*. Often cast in ethnic or urban roles, the New Yorker was addicted to movies as a kid. He would make scrapbooks and write mini-biographies of his favorite movie stars: James Cagney, Edward G. Robinson, Kirk Douglas and Burt Lancaster. Turturro starred in 1991's *Barton Fink*, a picture that swept Cannes that year winning him the best actor award.

Year	Movie	Character
1985	Desperately Seeking Susan	Ray
1985	To Live and Die in L.A.	Carl Cody
1986	Gung Ho	Willie
1986	Hannah and Her Sisters	Writer
1986	Off Beat	Neil Pepper
1986	The Color of Money	Julian
1987	The Sicilian	Aspanu Pisciotta
1988	Five Corners	Heinz
1989	Backtrack	xxx
1989	Do the Right Thing	Pino
1990	Miller's Crossing	Bernie Bernbaum
1990	Mo' Better Blues	Moe Flatbush
1990	State of Grace	Nick
1991	Barton Fink	Barton Fink
1991	Jungle Fever	Paulie Carbone
1991	Men of Respect	Mike Battaglia
1993	Mac	Mac
1993	Fearless	Dr. Bill Perlman

CHARLES TYNER

(1925 -   )

Tyner came to a film career while in his early forties and could often be seen in westerns in the early years. He made his Broadway debut in *Orpheus Descending* in 1957 after training for the stage at the American Theater Wing and with Stella Adler. A World War II veteran, he hails from Danville, VA.

Year	Movie	Character
1967	Cool Hand Luke	Boss Higgins
1969	The Reivers	Edmonds
1969	The Stalking Moon	Dace
1970	Monte Walsh	Doctor
1971	Harold and Maude	Uncle Victor
1971	Lawman	Minister
1972	Bad Company	Farmer
1972	Fuzz	Pete
1972	Jeremiah Johnson	Robidoux
1972	The Cowboys	Jenkins
1973	Emperor of the North	Cracker
1973	The Stone Killer	Psychiatrist
1974	The Longest Yard	Unger
1976	Family Plot	Wheeler
1977	Pete's Dragon	Merle
1986	Hamburger...The Motion Picture	Lyman Vunk
1987	Planes, Trains & Automobiles	Gus
1988	Pulse	Old Man

SUSAN TYRRELL

(1946 -   )

Tyrrell has appeared in theater, films and television, and if that was not enough, she founded a band of the punk and new wave variety. She became its lead singer. She won critical acclaim and an Academy Award nomination in 1972 for her role in John Huston's *Fat City*. She has said: "I have the ambition of a slug. I work when I need money, which is about once a year."

Year	Movie	Character
1971	Shootout	Alma
1972	Fat City	Oma
1976	The Killer Inside Me	Joyce
1977	I Never Promised You a Rose Garden	Lee
1977	9/30/55	Melba Lou
1977	Islands in the Stream	Lil
1982	Fast Walking	Evie
1984	Angel	Mosler
1985	Avenging Angel	Sally Mosler
1985	Flesh + Blood	Celine
1988	Big Top Pee-wee	Midge Montana
1988	Tapeheads	Nikki Morton
1989	Far From Home	Agnes Reed
1990	Cry-Baby	Ramona Rickettes
1990	Rockula	Chuck the Bartender

MARY URE

RAF VALLONE

(1934 - 1975)

A native of Glasgow, Scotland, the elegant Ure played star roles in Shakespearean and modern classics on the London stage. She married playwright John Osborne who wrote *Look Back in Anger*, which she starred in, and divorced him to marry actor Robert Shaw with whom she acted in London and on Broadway. Hollywood wooed her too and she won a Best Supporting Oscar nomination for her part in *Sons and Lovers* (1960). She died from an accidental combination of champagne and barbituates.

Year	Movie	Character
1964	The Luck of Ginger Coffey	Vera
1968	Custer of the West	Elizabeth Custer
1969	Where Eagles Dare	Mary Ellison
1973	A Reflection of Fear	Katherine

(1916 -   )

Vallone was a top movie star in Italy before moving to Hollywood and came to acting after trying several other careers. He tried unsuccessfully to launch his own classical theater group, and once worked as a sports reporter and film critic. Vallone earned advanced degrees in law, literature and philosophy at the University of Turin. His screen characters include a wealthy Greek in the Sidney Sheldon potboiler *The Other Side of Midnight* and Charlton Heston's betrayer, then follower, in *El Cid*.

Year	Movie	Character
1961	El Cid	Ordonez
1963	The Cardinal	Cardinal Quarenghi
1964	The Secret Invasion	Roberto Rocca
1965	Harlow	Marino Bello
1966	Nevada Smith	Father Zaccardi
1971	A Gunfight	Francisco Alvarez
1977	The Other Side of Midnight	Constantin Demeris
1978	The Greek Tycoon	Spyros Tomasis
1979	An Almost Perfect Affair	Freddie
1990	The Godfather, Part III	Cardinal Lamberto

TRISH VAN DEVERE

(1945 -   )

Van Devere has coupled an acting career with a commitment to political causes. She graduated from Ohio Wesleyan and plunged into work with the Free Southern Theaters in the civil rights era. Later she helped organize the Poor Peoples' Theater, which produced plays in churches and community centers in New York ghetto neighborhoods.

Year	Movie	Character
1970	Where's Poppa?	Louise
1971	The Last Run	Claudie Scherrer
1972	One is a Lonely Number	Amy
1973	Harry in Your Pocket	Sandy
1978	Movie, Movie	Isobel Stuart
1979	The Changeling	Claire Norman
1988	Messenger of Death	Jastra Watson

JO VAN FLEET

(1919 -   )

Born in California, Van Fleet began her acting career with a scholarship to New York's Neighborhood Playhouse, making her stage debut in *Uncle Harry*. She is known for her desire for privacy, even when acting, and once insisted on closing a Hollywood set to outsiders while she performed. "I simply cannot create a characterization with a crowd of strangers looking at me," she said at the time.

Year	Movie	Character
1960	Wild River	Ella Garth
1967	Cool Hand Luke	Arletta
1968	I Love You, Alice B. Toklas	Mother
1971	The Gang That Couldn't Shoot Straight	Big Momma
1976	The Tenant	Mme. Dioz

JOYCE VAN PATTEN

(1934 -   )

Van Patten made her improbable debut at the age of five months—modeling a baby blanket in a Sears catalog. Her mother kept on encouraging her to perform. "It was a time when women weren't supposed to perform, but it was okay if they pushed their kids," she has recalled. "Mom did, and now I'm glad." Her brother, Dick Van Patten, is also an actor.

Year	Movie	Character
1968	I Love You, Alice B. Toklas	Joyce
1969	The Trouble With Girls	Maude
1973	The Manchu Eagle Murder Caper Mystery	Ida Mae
1974	Mame	Sally Cato
1976	The Bad News Bears	Cleveland
1985	St. Elmo's Fire	Mrs. Beamish
1986	Billy Galvin	Mae
1987	Blind Date	Nadia's Mother
1988	Monkey Shines: An Experiment in Fear	Dorothy Mann
1989	Trust Me	Nettie Brown

CHICK VENNERA

(1952 -   )

The actor, screenwriter and composer is a musician's son born in Herkimer, NY. He trained for the stage at the Pasadena Playhouse and with Milton Katselas at the Actors Lab. The actor's life began for Vennera professionally as Sonny in *Grease* during a tour of U.S. and Canadian cities from 1973-75. He is a golfer who has performed as a saxophone player and a singer in a New York City nightclub band.

Year	Movie	Character
1978	Thank God, It's Friday	Marv
1979	Yanks	Danny
1981	High Risk	Tony
1988	Last Rites	Nuzo
1988	The Milagro Beanfield War	Joe Mondragon
1991	McBain	Santos

DIANE VENORA

(1952 -   )

The only child of five to leave her hometown of Hartford, CT, Venora considers herself driven. She studied ballet at the Boston Conservatory of Music and spent four years on a drama scholarship at Juilliard. The actress received attention early in her career when she was chosen by Joseph Papp to play the lead in his 1982 production of *Hamlet*. Expected by many to fail in the role, Venora relished the risk, "I love to struggle," she said at the time. "I think life without pain is no life. I'd rather be dead than comfortable."

Year	Movie	Character
1981	Wolfen	Rebecca Neff
1984	The Cotton Club	Gloria Swanson
1986	F/X	Ellen
1987	Ironweed	Peg
1988	Bird	Chan Parker

JOHN VERNON

(1936 -   )

Vernon, a Canadian, made his Hollywood debut in 1967 after establishing himself as a stage and screen star in Canada and England. He first showed promise acting with Montreal amateur groups and then went to study in England at RADA and work in local repertory companies. He returned to Canada in 1955. The actor spent five years with Canada's Stratford Shakespearean company and was the star of the Canadian TV series *Wojeck* before appearing in his first American film, *Point Blank*.

Year	Movie	Character
1967	Point Blank	Mal Reese
1969	Justine	Nessim
1969	Tell Them Willie Boy Is Here	Hacker
1969	Topaz	Rico Parra
1971	Dirty Harry	Mayor
1971	One More Train to Rob	Timothy X. Nolan
1973	Charley Varrick	Maynard Boyle
1975	Brannigan	Larkin
1976	The Outlaw—Josey Wales	Fletcher
1978	National Lampoon's Animal House	Dean Vernon Wormer
1980	Herbie Goes Bananas	Prindle
1985	Doin' Time	Big Mac
1985	Fraternity Vacation	Chief Ferret
1987	Ernest Goes to Camp	Sherman Krader
1988	I'm Gonna Git You Sucka	Mr. Big
1988	Killer Klowns From Outer Space	Officer Mooney

ABE VIGODA

(1920 -   )

Vigoda was a stage actor for a quarter of a century before hitting the jackpot on television. The fact that he is always cast in supporting roles and is never a star apparently does not bother him. "I've always been content just to be working and making a modest living for my wife and child," he has said. Vigoda is a native New Yorker.

Year	Movie	Character
1972	The Godfather	Tessio
1974	Newman's Law	Dellanzia
1974	The Godfather, Part II	Tessio
1978	The Cheap Detective	Sgt. Rizzuto
1989	Look Who's Talking	Grandpa
1989	Prancer	Orel Benton
1990	Joe Versus the Volcano	Chief of the Waponis

JESSE VINT

(1940 -   )

Vint has been a supporting actor in several lesser-known films, but got the lead in a 1977 melodrama called *Black Oak Conspiracy*. Set in the South, it concerned a plot to cheat senior citizens out of their land. The crooks' mistake was trying to bilk the mother of Jingo Johnson, played by Vint.

Year	Movie	Character
1970	Little Big Man	Lieutenant
1971	Silent Running	Keenan
1974	Earthquake	Buck
1974	Macon County Line	Wayne Dixon
1975	Bug	Tom
1977	Black Oak Conspiracy	Jingo
1979	Fast Charlie, The Moonbeam Rider	Calvin
1990	I Come in Peace	Man in Mercedes

GEORGE VOSKOVEC

(1905 - 1981)

The Czech actor graduated from Prague's Charles University and then co-founded the Liberated Theater in the late 20's where he wrote, produced and performed. The shows got more satiric as the Nazi threat grew and the theater finally had to close down. Voskovec came to the U.S. in 1939 and broadcast radio propaganda into Czechoslovakia for the U.S. Government during the war. His U.S. stage and film career began with his Broadway debut in 1945 in *The Tempest*. He died in his home in Pearblossom, CA.

Year	Movie	Character
1960	Butterfield 8	Dr. Tredman
1965	The Spy Who Came in From the Cold	East German Def. Atty.
1966	Mister Buddwing	Shabby Old Man
1968	The Boston Strangler	Peter Hurkos
1974	Man on a Swing	Dr. Nicholas Holmar
1980	Somewhere in Time	Dr. Gerald Finney
1982	Barbarosa	Herman

KEN WAHL

(1956 -   )

A film and television actor, Wahl was born in Chicago and began acting in 1978 when he debuted in the film *The Wanderers*. He found television success as the star of CBS's long running cop show *Wiseguy*. He played Vinnie Terranova, an undercover agent for an FBI-like organization who infiltrated major mob groups. In film, he may be best remembered as Paul Newman's partner in *Fort Apache, The Bronx*.

Year	Movie	Character
1979	The Wanderers	Richie
1981	Fort Apache, The Bronx	Corelli
1982	Jinxed	Willie
1982	The Soldier	The Soldier
1984	Purple Hearts	Don
1987	Omega Syndrome	Jack Corbett
1991	The Taking of Beverly Hills	Terry "Boomer" Hayes

TOM WAITS

(1949 -   )

Waits is a songwriter and singer who turned to acting by first taking small parts in movies made by Francis Ford Coppola, including *The Cotton Club*. His gravelly Texas voice and rugged good looks have tended to guide him into tough-guy and odd-ball roles. He has summed them up: "Cops, fathers, cross-dressers, insurance investigators, limo drivers, satanist cult leaders. The usual."

Year	Movie	Character
1978	Paradise Alley	Mumbles
1983	Rumble Fish	Benny
1983	The Outsiders	Buck Merrill
1984	The Cotton Club	Irving Stark
1986	Down By Law	Zack
1987	Ironweed	Rudy
1988	Shakedown	Kelly
1989	Cold Feet	Kenny
1991	At Play in the Fields of the Lord	Wolf
1991	Queens Logic	Monte
1992	Bram Stoker's Dracula	R.M. Renfield
1993	Short Cuts	Earl Piggot

CLINT WALKER

(1927 -   )

Walker got his start as the brooding western hero in TV's *Cheyenne* from 1955 to 1963. He came to the tough-guy role naturally after a stint in the Merchant Marine, and work as a carpenter, an oil-field rough neck, a bouncer and a private detective. He was a deputy sheriff in Las Vegas when film people suggested he should become an actor and arranged a screen test.

Year	Movie	Character
1964	Send Me No Flowers	Bert
1965	None But the Brave	Capt. Bourke
1966	The Night of the Grizzly	Jim Cole
1967	The Dirty Dozen	Samson Posey
1969	More Dead Than Alive	Killer Cain
1969	Sam Whiskey	O.W. Bandy
1969	The Great Bank Robbery	Ben Quick
1976	Baker's Hawk	Dan Baker
1977	The White Buffalo	Whistling Jack Kileen

ROBERT WALKER, JR.

(1940 -   )

Walker is the son of actress Jennifer Jones and actor Robert Walker, Sr. His original plan was to become a playwright, and studied acting with Lee Strasberg as a means to this end. This led to summer stock and eventually Off-Broadway and a full-blown acting career. He was in a handful of major studio releases in the mid-60s, but eventually drifted into leading roles in low-budget films outside of the mainstream.

Year	Movie	Character
1964	Ensign Pulver	Ensign Pulver
1967	The Happening	Herby
1967	The War Wagon	Billy Hyatt
1983	The Devonsville Terror	Matthew

DEBORAH WALLEY

(1941 -   )

Walley grew up all over the country in hotels and boarding schools as both parents were professional ice skaters with the Ice Capades. She skated professionally herself at age 3. Active in the "teen" pictures of the 1960s, her film debut came in 1961 when she replaced Sandra Dee as Gidget in one film of the popular series. Walley also had the part of the married daughter in TV's *The Mothers-In-Law* from 1967 to 1969.

Year	Movie	Character
1961	Gidget Goes Hawaiian	Gidget
1965	Beach Blanket Bingo	Bonnie Graham
1965	Ski Party	Linda Hughes
1966	Spinout	Les
1966	The Ghost in the Invisible Bikini	Lili Morton
1974	Benji	Linda

J.T. WALSH

(19?? -   )

Walsh embarked on a career in acting at the age of 30, leaving a job as a salesman to join an Off-Broadway theater group. He has since become one of Hollywood's busiest supporting actors. "I always had the acting bug," he has said. "It's just that being a Catholic boy, I didn't think for a long time that it was an acceptable way to make a living." Walsh was born in San Francisco, but grew up in Germany and Ireland.

Year	Movie	Character
1986	Hannah and Her Sisters	Ed Smythe
1986	Power	Jerome Cade
1987	Good Morning, Vietnam	Sgt. Major Dickerson
1987	House of Games	The Businessman
1987	Tin Men	Wing
1988	Tequila Sunrise	Maguire
1988	Things Change	Hotel manager
1989	Dad	Dr. Santana
1989	The Big Picture	Allen Habel
1990	Crazy People	Charles F. Drucker
1990	Narrow Margin	Michael Tarlow
1990	The Grifters	Cole
1990	The Russia House	Quinn
1991	Backdraft	Martin Swayzak

(continued on page 509)

M. EMMET WALSH

(1935 -   )

Walsh is one of the most respected character actors in the business. He is a master of naturalistic acting—"you don't do anything about preparation, you just do it," he has said—and buries himself in his characters. "I don't have an ego when I get the work," he once explained. "If I'm playing a doctor I want you to see a *doctor*. I don't want you to see an *Emmet Walsh* doctor and that's, I think, been the confusion with my career. People know my work, but they don't know who *I* am. I've always had fun hiding in the character."

Year	Movie	Character
1970	Little Big Man	Shotgun Guard
1971	Cold Turkey	Art
1971	Escape from the Planet of the Apes	Aide
1971	They Might Be Giants	Sanitation Man
1972	What's Up, Doc?	Arresting Officer
1973	Serpico	Gallagher
1975	The Prisoner of Second Avenue	xxx
1976	Bound for Glory	xxx
1976	Nickelodeon	Logan
1977	Airport '77	Dr. Williams
1977	Slap Shot	Dickie Dunn
1978	Straight Time	Earl Frank
1980	Brubaker	C.P. Woodward

(continued on page 509)

473

RAY WALSTON

(1917 -   )

Walston had been a prominent stage actor for many years before making movies and television shows, but it was in TV's *My Favorite Martian* (1963-66) that he became a familiar figure to Americans. He wanted an acting career as a child, but for years was too shy to try out for parts. After finally making the leap, he was in 22 plays at the Cleveland Playhouse before making it big on Broadway.

Year	Movie	Character
1960	Portrait in Black	Cob O'Brien
1960	Tall Story	Leo Sullivan
1960	The Apartment	Mr. Dobisch
1963	Who's Minding the Store?	Mr. Quimby
1964	Kiss Me Stupid	Orville J. Spooner
1967	Caprice	Stuart Clancy
1969	Paint Your Wagon	Mad Jack Duncan
1973	The Sting	Singleton
1976	Silver Streak	Mr. Whiney
1980	Popeye	Commodore
1981	Galaxy of Terror	Kore
1982	Fast Times at Ridgemont High	Mr. Hand
1983	Private School	Chauncey
1984	Johnny Dangerously	Vendor
1987	From the Hip	1st Judge
1987	O.C. & Stiggs	Gramps
1988	Blood Relations	Charles MacLeod
1990	Ski Patrol	Pops
1991	Popcorn	Dr. Mnesyne
1992	Of Mice and Men	Candy

JESSICA WALTER

(1940 -   )

She was typecast early in her career in bitchy roles, but Walter didn't seem to mind. "It's better to be typecast in that kind of role, if you must be typecast, because I've gotten the opportunity to play some really interesting parts," she has commented. She is best known as Clint Eastwood's psychotic lover in *Play Misty For Me*, a part that required a lot of her physically and emotionally. "The emotional part was easy," she has said. "I think we all have these murderous rages lurking inside us. I just called up mine for that role."

Year	Movie	Character
1964	Lilith	Laura
1966	The Group	Libby
1966	Grand Prix	Pat Stoddard
1968	Bye Bye Braverman	Inez Braverman
1969	Number One	Julie Catlan
1971	Play Misty For Me	Evelyn
1979	Goldengirl	xxx
1981	Going Ape!	Fiona
1984	The Flamingo Kid	Phyllis Brody
1988	Tapeheads	Kay Mart

TRACEY WALTER

(1952 -   )

Born and raised in New Jersey, Walter had not thought much about becoming an actor. "I was working various odd jobs, watching people around me who couldn't wait for 5 o'clock and the weekend to come," he once said. After seeing an Off-Broadway play, he turned to acting. He started as an apprentice in summer stock and worked his way up to actor.

Year	Movie	Character
1978	Goin' South	Coogan
1980	The Hunter	Rocco Mason
1981	Raggedy Man	Arnold
1983	Rumble Fish	xxx
1983	Timerider	Carl Dorsett
1984	Conan the Destroyer	Malak
1984	Repo Man	Miller
1986	At Close Range	Patch
1986	Something Wild	The Country Squire
1988	Married to the Mob	Mr. Chicken Lickin'
1988	Out of the Dark	Lt. Meyers
1989	Batman	Bob the Goon
1989	Under the Boardwalk	Bum
1990	Delusion	Bus Ticket Cashier
1990	Two Jakes	Tyrone Otley
1991	City Slickers	Cookie
1991	The Silence of the Lambs	Lamar

SAM WANAMAKER

(1919 -   )

Wanamaker's promising stage and film career was cut short in the late 1940s when he was blacklisted by Hollywood after appearing before the House Committee on Un-American Activities (HUAC). He spent 10 years in exile in England. The actor devoted 17 years of his life in a battle with a local U.K. government council to get Shakespeare's Globe Theatre rebuilt. His goal was to build a "functioning monument" to Shakespeare and, after sacrificing much of his career, he finally won approval in 1986.

Year	Movie	Character
1962	Taras Bulba	Filipenko
1964	The Man in the Middle	Major Kaufman
1965	The Spy Who Came in From the Cold	Peters
1965	Those Magnificent Men in Their Flying Machines	George Gruber
1967	Warning Shot	Frank Sanderman
1976	Voyage of the Damned	Carl Rosen
1980	Private Benjamin	Teddy Benjamin
1980	The Competition	Erskine
1984	Irreconcilable Differences	David Kessler
1985	The Aviator	Bruno Hansen
1986	Raw Deal	Patrovita
1987	Baby Boom	Fritz Curtis
1987	Superman IV: The Quest for Peace	David Warfield
1988	Judgment in Berlin	Bernard Hellring
1991	Guilty by Suspicion	Felix Graff
1991	Pure Luck	Highsmith

FRED WARD

(1943 -   )

Ward made his film debut as Clint Eastwood's jailbreak partner in *Escape From Alcatraz*. Prior to that he demolished tenement buildings in New York, dubbed Italian films into English, made and sold jewelry in L.A., worked as a radarman in the U.S. Air Force, discovered shamanism in Morocco, studied mask and mime theater in Italy and avant-garde theater in San Francisco, was an amateur boxer, worked as a logger in the Northwest and a lumberjack in Alaska, toured the Sahara Desert, and built San Francisco's subway system.

Year	Movie	Character
1979	Escape from Alcatraz	John Anglin
1980	UFOria	xxx
1981	Southern Comfort	Reece
1983	Silkwood	Morgan
1983	The Right Stuff	Gus Grissom
1983	Timerider	Lyle Swann
1983	Uncommon Valor	Wilkes
1984	Swing Shift	Biscuits Toohey
1985	Remo Williams: The Adventure Begins	Remo Williams
1985	Secret Admirer	Lou
1988	Big Business	Roone Dimmick
1988	Off Limits	Sgt. Benjamin Dix
1988	The Prince of Pennsylvania	Gary Marshetta

(continued on page 510)

RACHEL WARD

(1957 -   )

A native of England who moved to Australia, Ward won the Australian equivalent of the Academy Award for her performance in *The Good Wife* (1986). She has also been a fashion model in New York. She married Australian actor Bryan Brown with whom she appeared in *The Thorn Birds*. "I was told by a fortune teller that I would meet Mr. Right soon," she has said. "And I bumped into Bryan on the set."

Year	Movie	Character
1981	Night School	Eleanor
1981	Sharky's Machine	Dominoe
1982	Dead Men Don't Wear Plaid	Juliet Forrest
1984	Against All Odds	Jessie Wyler
1987	Hotel Colonial	Irene
1990	After Dark, My Sweet	Fay Anderson
1993	Wide Sargasso Sea	Annette Cosway

JACK WARDEN

(1920 -   )

Born and educated in Newark, NJ, Warden spent time as a sailor, para-trooper, bouncer, bartender and prize fighter before becoming an actor. He began on the stage and has gravitated between stage, film and television throughout his long career. His burly appearance has often-caused him to be cast as tough guys, but his comedic talents were recognized by two Oscar nominations: for his work in *Shampoo* and *Heaven Can Wait*.

Year	Movie	Character
1960	Wake Me When It's Over	Doc Farrington
1962	Escape from Zahrain	Huston
1963	Donovan's Reef	Dr. Dedham
1966	Blindfold	General Pratt
1968	Bye Bye Braverman	Barnet Weiner
1971	Who is Harry Kellerman and Why is He Saying Those Terrible Things About Me?	Dr. Moses
1973	The Man Who Loved Cat Dancing	Dawes
1974	Billy Two Hats	Gifford
1974	The Apprenticeship of Duddy Kravitz	Max
1975	Shampoo	Lester

(continued on page 510)

DAVID WARNER

(1941 -   )

Warner was a well-known English actor when he made his American film debut in Sam Peckinpah's *The Ballad of Cable Hogue*. Born in Manchester, he performed in amateur productions until he was accepted into London's RADA. He spent four years with the Royal Shakespeare Company and appeared in many British films, making his debut in 1963's *Tom Jones*. Peckinpah was his favorite director and he worked with him on three films.

Year	Movie	Character
1970	The Ballad of Cable Hogue	Joshua
1971	Straw Dogs	xxx
1976	The Omen	Jennings
1977	Cross of Iron	Kiesel
1979	The Concorde—Airport '79	O'Neill
1979	Time After Time	Stevenson (The Ripper)
1980	The Island	Nau
1981	Time Bandits	Evil Genius
1982	Tron	Ed Dillinger/Sark
1983	The Man with Two Brains	Dr. Necessiter
1988	Hanna's War	Capt. Simon
1988	Mr. North	Dr. Angus McPherson
1988	My Best Friend Is a Vampire	Prof. McCarthy
1989	Star Trek V: The Final Frontier	St. John Talbot
1991	Star Trek VI: The Undiscovered Country	Klingon Chancellor
1991	Teenage Mutant Ninja Turtles II: The Secret of the Ooze	Prof. Jordan Perry
1992	Thunderheart	Jack Milton

ANN WEDGEWORTH

(1935 -   )

Wedgeworth grew up in Dallas, the daughter of strict Southern Baptists. She dreamed early of being an actress and often play-acted roles she'd seen in movies. "One day I went to see Jennifer Jones in *Ruby Gentry* and for weeks after I went around pretending I was Ruby," she once said. She was married to actor Rip Torn but they divorced. She studied at the University of Texas and Southern Methodist University and got a B.A. in drama.

Year	Movie	Character
1973	Bang the Drum Slowly	Katie
1973	Scarecrow	Frenchy
1974	Law and Disorder	Sally
1976	Birch Interval	Marie
1984	No Small Affair	Joan Cummings
1985	My Science Project	Dolores
1985	Sweet Dreams	Hilda Hensley
1987	A Tiger's Tale	Claudine
1987	Made in Heaven	Annette Shea
1988	Far North	Amy
1989	Miss Firecracker	Miss Blue
1989	Steel Magnolias	Aunt Fern
1990	Green Card	Party Guest

PETER WELLER

(1947 -   )

Weller's movie image is that of an intense man with an explosive temperment, but actually he hates violence and once admitted to having been in only two fights in his life. He has been a serious runner and ran the New York Marathon in 1986 in three hours, forty minutes. Best known as Robocop in the first two films in that series, Weller was born in Stevens Point, WI, and studied drama under Uta Hagen and Lee Strasberg.

Year	Movie	Character
1979	Butch and Sundance: The Early Days	Joe LeFors
1980	Just Tell Me What You Want	Steven Routledge
1982	Shoot the Moon	Frank Henderson
1984	First Born	Sam
1984	The Adventures of Buckaroo Banzai Across the Eighth Dimension	Buckaroo Banzai
1987	Robocop	Murphy/Robocop
1988	Shakedown	Roland Dalton
1989	Cat Chaser	George Moran
1989	Leviathan	Beck
1990	Robocop 2	Robocop
1993	Fifty/Fifty	Jake Wyer

GWEN WELLES

(1949 - 1993)

Welles was born in New York City and attended private school in Arizona and upstate New York. Her parents divorced when she was very young and she spent much of her youth commuting between homes in California and New York. She played a hooker in *California Split* and an untalented waitress in *Nashville* who is forced to strip at a stag show just to get a chance to sing. She died of cancer.

Year	Movie	Character
1974	California Split	Susan Peters
1975	Nashville	Sueleen Gay
1985	Desert Hearts	Gwen
1986	Nobody's Fool	Shirley
1988	Sticky Fingers	Marcie
1990	Eating	Sophie

VERNON WELLS

(19?? -   )

An Australian, Wells was originally a singer in a rock band until an auto accident forced him into months of recuperation. During that time, he worked as a model in Melbourne and that led to small parts on television. He soon became one of Australia's most popular actors. Hollywood has cast him as a heavy in movies like *Commando* and *Innerspace*, where he played a hired killer. He is a veteran of the war in Vietnam.

Year	Movie	Character
1985	Commando	Bennett
1985	Weird Science	Lord General
1987	Innerspace	Mr. Igoe
1990	Circuitry Man	Plughead
1990	The Shrimp on the Barbie	Bruce Woodley

ADAM WEST

(1929 -   )

West was famous in the 1960s for his television portrayal of Batman and was for a time stereotyped by the role. Producers could not see him playing any other part. They would say: "Hey, what are you guys doing. You can't put 'Batman' in bed with Faye Dunaway," he once recalled. He was born William West Anderson and grew up on a wheat farm in Walla Walla, WA.

Year	Movie	Character
1963	Tammy and the Doctor	Dr. Eric Hassler
1964	Robinson Crusoe on Mars	Col. Dan McReady
1965	The Outlaws is Coming	Kenneth Cabot
1966	Batman	Batman/Bruce Wayne
1971	The Marriage of a Young Stockbroker	Chester
1978	Hooper	Adam
1983	One Dark Night	Allan
1988	Doin' Time on Planet Earth	Charles Pinsky

JACK WESTON

(1924 -   )

A familiar face in countless supporting roles in film, Weston's career got started in the New York stage and television world of the 1950s. He followed the migration of television production to L.A. at the end of the decade and had his first sizable movie role in 1960's *Please Don't Eat the Daisies.* Weston grew up in Cleveland and was an army machine-gunner in Italy during World War II.

Year	Movie	Character
1960	Please Don't Eat the Daisies	Joe Positano
1961	All in a Night's Work	Lasker
1961	The Honeymoon Machine	Signalman Burford Taylor
1962	It's Only Money	Leopold
1965	Mirage	Lester
1965	The Cincinnati Kid	Pig
1968	The Counterfeit Killer	Randolph Riker
1968	The Thomas Crown Affair	Erwin Weaver
1969	Cactus Flower	Harvey Greenfield
1969	The April Fools	Pottie Shrader
1971	A New Leaf	Andrew McPherson
1972	Fuzz	Det. Meyer Meyer
1976	Gator	Irving Greenfield

(continued on page 510)

FRANK WHALEY

(1963 -   )

A magazine once characterized Whaley as "the sexiest man alive." His response was that comments like that "trivialize what you do. I'm very serious about what I do." Besides acting, Whaley has also played drums in a band. He is a native New Yorker whose favorite actor is Sir Laurence Olivier. He likes most playing eccentric roles far different from his own personality. Memorable film roles include that of Matthew Broderick's NYU roommate in *The Freshman*.

Year	Movie	Character
1989	Born on the Fourth of July	Timmy
1989	Field of Dreams	Archie Graham
1989	Little Monsters	Boy
1990	The Freshman	Steve Bushak
1991	Career Opportunities	Jim Dodge
1991	JFK	Oswald imposter
1991	The Doors	Robby Krieger
1992	Hoffa	Young Kid
1993	Swing Kids	Arvid

JOANNE WHALLEY-KILMER

(1964 -   )

Whalley-Kilmer found fame in her native England for her perfomance in *Scandal*, the true story of Christine Keeler, a young showgirl who has an affair with the cabinet minister John Profumo in 1963 that helps to bring down England's conservative government. Whalley-Kilmer loved reading stories as a child and began taking classes in improvisation at the age of 12. Her professional career began with television. The actress played a beautiful TV reporter in 1990's *Navy SEALS*.

Year	Movie	Character
1988	To Kill a Priest	Anna
1988	Willow	Sorsha
1989	Kill Me Again	Fay Forrester
1989	Scandal	Christine Keeler
1990	Navy SEALS	Claire Verens
1991	Shattered	Jenny Scott

FOREST WHITAKER

(1961 -   )

Whitaker, who achieved great popularity for playing jazzman Charlie Parker in the movie *Bird*, grew up in Los Angeles, the son of a teacher and insurance salesman. He began acting in college and by his sophmore year was working professionally in television, films and stage. A John Gielgud scholarship allowed him to study at the Drama Studio in London, a school that teaches both American and British acting styles. He made his directing debut in the 1993 HBO production of *Strapped*.

Year	Movie	Character
1982	Fast Times at Ridgemont High	Charles Jefferson
1985	Vision Quest	Balldozer
1986	Platoon	Big Harold
1986	The Color of Money	Amos
1987	Bloodsport	Rawlins
1987	Good Morning, Vietnam	Edward Garlick
1987	Stakeout	Jack Pismo
1988	Bird	Charlie "Bird" Parker
1989	Johnny Handsome	Dr. Steven Resher
1990	Downtown	Dennis Curren
1991	A Rage in Harlem	Jackson
1992	Article 99	Dr. Sid Handleman
1992	Consenting Adults	David Duttonville
1992	The Crying Game	Jody
1993	Bank Robber	Officer Battle

JAMES WHITMORE

(1921 -   )

A two-time Oscar nominee (*Give 'Em Hell, Harry* (1975) and *Battleground* (1949)) Whitmore began his career as a stage actor and won a Tony for his first Broadway role in *Command Decision*. In recent years, he has played nationally and won acclaim for his one-man-show portrayals of Will Rogers, Harry Truman and Teddy Roosevelt. He grew up in Buffalo, played football for Yale and spent four years in the Marine Corps before hitting the boards in the late 1940s.

Year	Movie	Character
1960	Who Was That Lady?	Harry Powell
1967	Waterhole #3	Captain Shipley
1968	Madigan	Chief Inspector Kane
1968	Planet of the Apes	President of the Assembly
1968	The Split	Herb Sutro
1969	Guns of the Magnificent Seven	Levi
1970	Tora! Tora! Tora!	Admiral Halsey
1973	The Harrad Experiment	Philip
1980	The First Deadly Sin	Dr. Sanford Ferguson
1987	Nuts	Judge Stanley Murdoch
1990	Old Explorers	Leinen Roth

MARGARET WHITTON

(1950 -   )

The daughter of a military officer and a nurse, Whitton was born in Philadelphia. Between acting and high school in Fort Lauderdale, she has worked variously as a bicycle messenger, a cab driver and a dog walker. Her memorable film roles include the baseball team owner in *Major League* who assembles a sad sack team of players in hopes that they will lose so that she can get out of the stadium lease. In *The Secret of My Success* she plays the neglected wife who seduces Michael J. Fox.

Year	Movie	Character
1986	Nine 1/2 Weeks	Molly
1986	The Best of Times	Darla
1987	Ironweed	Katrina
1987	The Secret of My Success	Vera Prescott
1989	Little Monsters	Holly Stevenson
1989	Major League	Rachel Phelps
1993	The Man Without a Face	Catherine

MARY WICKES

(1912 -   )

Very active in films during the forties, fifties and sixties, Wickes has concentrated on television in recent years with intermittent excursions to the stage. A banker's daughter from St. Louis she received her B.A. from Washington University and did graduate work in theater arts at UCLA. She has worked as a drama teacher and has become involved in health issues such as cancer and crippled children.

Year	Movie	Character
1965	How to Murder Your Wife	Harold's Secretary
1966	The Trouble With Angels	Sister Clarissa
1968	Where Angels Go...Trouble Follows	Sister Clarissa
1980	Touched by Love	Margaret
1990	Postcards From the Edge	Grandma
1992	Sister Act	Sister Mary Lazarus
1993	Sister Act 2: Back in the Habit	Sister Mary Lazarus

DIANNE WIEST

(1948 -   )

"I'd like to play a real cold, mean, mass-murderer," Wiest once said. "Some cruel, hard-bitten women, like the roles that Glenn Close gets, just to show that I am capable of *not* being vulnerable and *not* being fragile onscreen." The actress has felt typecast as fragile or neurotic women, especially since her Oscar win as Mia Farrow's insecure sister in *Hannah and Her Sisters*. However, 1990 saw her cast as the cheery Avon lady in *Edward Scissorhands* who takes the man-made boy into her home.

Year	Movie	Character
1980	It's My Turn	Gail
1982	I'm Dancing as Fast as I Can	Julie Addison
1983	Independence Day	Nancy Morgan
1984	Falling In Love	Isabelle
1984	Footloose	Vi Moore
1985	The Purple Rose of Cairo	Emma
1986	Hannah and Her Sisters	Holly
1987	Radio Days	Bea
1987	September	Stephanie
1987	The Lost Boys	Lucy
1988	Bright Lights, Big City	Mother
1989	Cookie	Lenore
1989	Parenthood	Helen
1990	Edward Scissorhands	Peg Boggs
1991	Little Man Tate	Jane Grierson

CORNEL WILDE

(1915 - 1989)

The handsome Hungarian-American actor gave a memorable performance as Chopin in the 1945 *A Song to Remember*. Wilde was also Robin Hood in the 1947 *Bandit of Sherwood Forest*. As a swashbuckler or romantic lead, he got a lot of fan mail. He made many movies for film and television, appeared on Broadway, fenced well enough to make the U.S. Olympics Team, and became a successful producer-director during the 1950s. He died of leukemia.

Year	Movie	Character
1966	The Naked Prey	Man
1967	Beach Red	Capt. MacDonald
1975	Shark's Treasure	Jim
1978	The Norseman	Ragnar

KATHLEEN WILHOITE

FRED WILLARD

(19?? -   )

Wilhoite played teenager and college girl roles in the 1980s. She may be best remembered as Molly Gibson, the stern, moralistic college newspaper editor in the 1987 film *Campus Man*. It was the story of a college athlete who is kicked off the swimming team for posing semi-nude in a calendar picture.

(1940 -   )

Willard has spent most of the last 20 years working in film and television. The Shaker Heights, OH, native debuted on the small screen in 1973 as a regular on *The Burns and Schreiber Comedy Hour*. He is a graduate of the Virginia Military Institute and a member of Chicago's famous Second City troupe and an improvisational comedy troupe, the Ace Trucking Company, in San Francisco.

Year	Movie	Character
1983	Private School	Betsy
1986	Murphy's Law	Arabella McGee
1986	The Morning After	Red
1987	Angel Heart	Nurse
1987	Campus Man	Molly Gibson
1987	Under Cover	Corinne Armor
1989	Road House	Carrie Ann Nash
1990	Bad Influence	Leslie
1990	Everybody Wins	Amy
1992	Brenda Starr	xxx
1992	Lorenzo's Oil	Deirdre

Year	Movie	Character
1976	Silver Streak	Jerry Jarvis
1979	Americathon	Vanderhoof
1980	First Family	Pres. Asst. Feebleman
1980	How to Beat the High Co$t of Living	Robert
1985	Moving Violations	Terrence "Doc" Williams
1987	Roxanne	Mayor Deebs

CINDY WILLIAMS

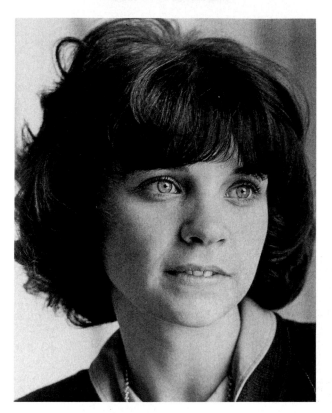

(1947 -   )

Williams has had memorable movie roles, notably as Ron Howard's cheerleader girlfriend in *American Graffiti* and as an unfaithful wife in *The Conversation*, but she is best known as Shirley Feeney on TV's *Laverne and Shirley* (1976-82). An intense rivalry prevailed between Williams and co-star Penny Marshall behind the scenes, but the two found a chemistry onscreen. "Penny and I were just terrific," Williams has recalled. "I could feel the energy at work. It was like one of those fabulous, unforgettable amusement rides."

Year	Movie	Character
1972	Travels With My Aunt	Tooley
1973	American Graffiti	Laurie
1974	The Conversation	Ann
1975	Mr. Ricco	Jamison
1979	More American Graffiti	Laurie Bolander
1980	UFOria	xxx
1989	Rude Awakening	June
1991	Bingo	Natalie Devlin

JOHN WILLIAMS

(1903 - 1983)

The suave English actor made his name as the Scotland Yard inspector in *Dial M for Murder* on Broadway in 1952 and in Alfred Hitchcock's 1954 film. Williams started acting at 13 in *Peter Pan* in London and began making American movies in 1935. After time out for World War II and the Royal Air Force, he returned to stage, screen and television. He died at 80 of an aneurism in La Jolla, CA.

Year	Movie	Character
1960	Visit to a Small Planet	Delton
1965	Dear Brigitte	Peregrine Upjohn
1966	The Last of the Secret Agents?	J. Frederick Duval
1967	Double Trouble	Gerald Waverly
1968	The Secret War of Harry Frigg	Gen. Mayhew
1976	No Deposit, No Return	Jameson
1978	Hot Lead and Cold Feet	Mansfield

TREAT WILLIAMS

(1951 -   )

Williams claims that he's often cast as lawyers, but that he'd rather play "characters on the edge, an ordinary guy in extraordinary circumstances. I like roles where people have problems to solve, where something complex is going on." A native of Rowayton, CT, Williams discovered acting as a student at Franklin and Marshall College in Pennsylvania. He began on Broadway in musicals, including the lead in *Grease*.

Year	Movie	Character
1976	The Eagle Has Landed	Capt. Harry Clark
1979	1941	Sitarski
1979	Hair	Berger
1981	Prince of the City	Daniel Ciello
1981	The Pursuit of D.B. Cooper	Meade
1984	Flashpoint	Ernie
1984	Once Upon a Time in America	Jimmy O'Donnell
1988	Dead Heat	Roger Mortis
1989	Heart of Dixie	Hoyt

FRED WILLIAMSON

(1938 -   )

Williamson has enjoyed two careers. He once played professional football, where he was known as "the Hammer" because of the rough forearm smash he used to knock down wide receivers. He left the gridiron in 1968 and became an actor, playing tough-guy roles in mostly B-movies. He has also been a producer, forming his own company known as Po' Boy Productions.

Year	Movie	Character
1970	M*A*S*H	Spearchucker
1972	Hammer	B.J.
1973	That Man Bolt	Boly
1974	Crazy Joe	Willy
1974	Three Tough Guys	Joe
1974	Three the Hard Way	Jagger
1982	Vigilante	Nick
1983	The Big Score	Hooks

NICOL WILLIAMSON

(1938 -   )

Never one to play it safe, Williamson, a native of Scotland, has been described as "intimidating, temperamental, bristling, and uninhibited." Often cast as a villain, the actor trys to live life to the fullest, spending only a minimum amount of time eating or sleeping and selecting only the most demanding roles.

Year	Movie	Character
1972	The Jerusalem File	Lang
1976	The Seven Percent Solution	Sherlock Holmes
1978	The Cheap Detective	Colonel Schissel
1981	Excalibur	Merlin
1982	I'm Dancing as Fast as I Can	Derek Bauer
1985	Return to Oz	Dr. Worley/The Nome King
1986	Black Widow	William Macauley
1990	The Exorcist III	Father Morning

CHILL WILLS

(1903 - 1978)

Wills was always a character in westerns and other outdoor films and his voice made Francis the talking mule. A Texan from Seagoville, he started in medicine shows and minstrels and moved on to nightclubs like the Trocadero in Hollywood where he got a screen test and a job in the movies. TV grabbed him for two series: *Frontier Circus* and *The Rounders*. He died at 76 of cancer at home in Encino, CA.

Year	Movie	Character
1960	The Alamo	Beekeeper
1960	Where the Boys Are	Police Captain
1963	McLintock	Drago
1963	The Cardinal	Monsignor Whittle
1963	The Wheeler Dealers	Ray Jay
1965	The Rounders	Jim Ed Love
1970	The Liberation of L.B. Jones	Mr. Ike
1973	Pat Garrett and Billy the Kid	Lemuel
1977	Mr. Billion	Col. Winkle

ELIZABETH WILSON

(1925 -   )

Familiar to movie audiences as Dustin Hoffman's mother in *The Graduate*, the comic foil in *9 to 5* and Christopher Lloyd's scheming mother in *The Addams Family*, Wilson is a veteran character actress whose career has been going strong for forty years. Often cast in eccentric parts, the actress believes that "something in me, maybe my sense of humor, my imagination or my cockeyed vision of the world, gives me the ability to play eccentrics so that their humanity can be recognized."

Year	Movie	Character
1967	The Graduate	Mrs. Braddock
1970	Jenny	Mrs. Marsh
1974	Man on a Swing	Dr. Anna Willson
1975	The Prisoner of Second Avenue	Pauline
1980	9 to 5	Roz
1981	The Incredible Shrinking Woman	Dr. Ruth Ruth
1985	Grace Quigley	Emily Watkins
1986	Where Are the Children?	Dorothy Prentiss
1987	The Believers	Kate Maslow
1991	Regarding Henry	Jessica
1991	The Addams Family	Abigail Craven

SCOTT WILSON

(1942 -   )

Wilson was a virtual unknown when he was the surprise choice in 1967 to play one of the killers' roles in a movie made from Truman Capote's famous book *In Cold Blood*. A native of Atlanta, he had hitch-hiked across the country to try an acting career in Hollywood, and had worked as an oil company clerk to support himself between acting jobs.

Year	Movie	Character
1967	In Cold Blood	Dick Hickock
1967	In the Heat of the Night	Harvey Oberst
1969	Castle Keep	Cpl. Ralph Clearboy
1969	The Gypsy Moths	Malcolm Webson
1972	The New Centurions	Gus
1973	Lolly-Madonna XXX	Thrush
1974	The Great Gatsby	George Wilson
1980	The Ninth Configuration	Captain Cutshaw
1983	The Right Stuff	Scott Crossfield
1985	The Aviator	Jerry Stiller
1986	Blue City	Perry Kerch
1987	Malone	Paul Barlow
1989	Johnny Handsome	Mikey Chalmette
1990	The Exorcist III	Dr. Temple
1991	Pure Luck	Grimes
1993	Flesh and Bone	Elliot

WILLIAM WINDOM

(1923 -   )

An ex-model friend of Windom's, when asked once what she thought of him, replied: "He's *darling*. He's absolutely unaffected. He's a boating enthusiast; he's happiest out on his catamaran. He's a good tennis player. He's very informal; he's the kind who would come to a formal dinner in loafers. He's very New England. He's absolutely wholesome. If I were painting him in abstract, I'd do him in red, white and blue." Windom has played the doctor of Cabot Cove on TV's *Murder, She Wrote* since 1984.

Year	Movie	Character
1962	To Kill a Mockingbird	Gilmer
1963	For Love or Money	Sam Travis
1964	The Americanization of Emily	Capt. Harry Spaulding
1968	The Detective	Colin MacIver
1969	The Gypsy Moths	V. John Brandon
1971	Escape from the Planet of the Apes	The President
1983	Last Plane Out	James
1984	Grandview USA	Bob
1984	Prince Jack	Ferguson
1987	Planes, Trains & Automobiles	Boss
1988	She's Having a Baby	Russ Bainbridge
1989	Street Justice	xxx
1993	Sommersby	Reverend Powell

PAUL WINFIELD

(1940 -   )

Winfield won an Academy Award nomination as best actor for his role as a black Southern sharecropper in the movie *Sounder*. He was born in the Watts district of L.A., the son of a union organizer and a construction worker. He began acting in high school and got his first break in the *Perry Mason* television series.

Year	Movie	Character
1969	The Lost Man	Orville
1972	Sounder	Nathan Lee Morgan
1973	Gordon's War	Gordon
1974	Conrack	Mad Billy
1974	Huckleberry Finn	Jim
1975	Hustle	Sgt. Louis Belgrave
1977	Damnation Alley	Keegan
1977	Twilight's Last Gleaming	Powell
1981	Carbon Copy	Bob
1982	Star Trek II: The Wrath of Khan	Terrell
1984	Mike's Murder	Phillip
1984	The Terminator	Traxler
1986	Blue City	Luther Reynolds
1987	Big Shots	Johnnie Red
1987	Death Before Dishonor	Ambassador
1988	Serpent and the Rainbow	Lucien Celine
1990	Presumed Innocent	Judge Larren Lyttle
1993	Cliffhanger	Walter Wright
1993	Dennis the Menace	Chief of Police

MARE WINNINGHAM

(1959 -   )

Discovered in a high school play by the same agent who found Richard Dreyfuss in a high school play, Winningham began acting in TV-movies immediately after graduation. She won an Emmy as a wheat farmer's daughter in 1980's *Amber Waves* and often portrays women in dire straits or handicapped in some way. She is the mother of five children and grew up in California's San Fernando Valley.

Year	Movie	Character
1980	One Trick Pony	Modeena Dandridge
1981	Threshold	Carol Severance
1985	St. Elmo's Fire	Wendy
1986	Nobody's Fool	Pat
1987	Made in Heaven	Brenda Carlucci
1987	Shy People	Candy
1989	Miracle Mile	Julie Peters
1989	Turner & Hooch	Emily Carson

MICHAEL WINSLOW

(1959 -   )

Winslow grew up on air force bases where his father, an officer, was stationed. He enrolled in the University of Colorado, but quit to try acting and hitch-hiked to California. He got his first break in a movie called *Cheech and Chong's Next Movie*, in which he hummed an imitation of a guitar. He slept on a California beach for a year and lived with pan-handlers until a career came along.

Year	Movie	Character
1984	Alphabet City	Lippy
1984	Grandview USA	Spencer
1984	Lovelines	J.D.
1984	Police Academy	Larvell
1985	Police Academy 2: Their First Assignment	Larvell Jones
1986	Police Academy 3: Back in Training	Sgt. Jones
1987	Police Academy 4: Citizens on Patrol	Jones
1987	Spaceballs	Radar Technician
1988	Police Academy 5: Assignment Miami Beach	Jones
1989	Buy & Cell	Sly
1989	Police Academy 6: City Under Siege	Jones

RAY WISE

(19?? -   )

Wise has played minor roles in several prominent film and television shows, including *Robocop* and the 1993 suspense thriller *Rising Sun*. On television, he was in two serials, *Twin Peaks*, as father Leland Plamer, who murdered his daughter, and in *The Colbys*. In the 1982 horror movie *Swamp Thing*, Wise played a scientist working on a project to make plants hardy and aggressive like animals.

Year	Movie	Character
1982	Swamp Thing	Dr. Holland
1985	The Journey of Natty Gann	Sol Gann
1987	Robocop	Leon
1992	Bob Roberts	Chet MacGregor
1992	Twin Peaks: Fire Walk With Me	Leland Palmer
1993	Rising Sun	Sen. John Morton

JOSEPH WISEMAN

(1918 -   )

A veteran actor of the stage, films and television, Wiseman started out in the New York theater world acting with the likes of Katharine Cornell, Helen Hayes and Ingrid Bergman. He was born in Montreal, but grew up in New York City's borough of Queens. Movie audiences remember him as the sinister Dr. No in the first James Bond picture. In recent years, he has performed concert readings of Yiddish and related literature in the U.S. and Canada under the auspices of B'nai B'rith.

Year	Movie	Character
1960	The Unforgiven	Abe Kelsey
1962	Dr. No	Dr. No
1968	Bye Bye Braverman	Felix Ottensteen
1968	The Counterfeit Killer	Rajeski
1968	The Night They Raided Minsky's	Louis Minsky
1971	Lawman	Lucas
1972	The Valachi Papers	Salvatore Maranzano
1974	The Apprenticeship of Duddy Kravitz	Uncle Benjy
1978	The Betsy	Jake Weinstein
1979	Buck Rogers in the 25th Century	Draco
1979	Jaguar Lives!	Ben Ashir

VICTOR WONG

(19?? -   )

Wong was born and raised in San Francisco and grew up learning tales of Chinese myths and legends from his mother. A political science major at Berkeley, he was an Emmy Award-winning TV journalist before he turned to acting. His beat was San Francisco's Chinatown, but he also covered the 1968 Democratic convention, the Zodiac Killer and Patty Hearst and the Symbionese Liberation Army. He got his theatrical start in his hometown's Asian-American Theater.

Year	Movie	Character
1986	Big Trouble in Little China	Egg Shen
1986	The Golden Child	The Old Man
1987	Prince of Darkness	Birack
1987	The Last Emperor	Chen Pao Shen
1990	Tremors	Walter Chang
1991	Mystery Date	Janitor
1992	3 Ninjas	Grandpa
1993	The Joy Luck Club	Old Chong

JOHN WOOD

(1931 -   )

Known mostly for his stage work, the British actor started out in the mid-1950s with the Old Vic, but his outspokenness there got him abruptly dismissed in 1957. In fact, he spent a good deal of his early career unemployed because he refused to compromise his artistic standards. He eventually revived his career in the late 1960s and 1970s on British television and in roles on the New York stage that included a Tony-winning performance in *Travesties* and a $5,000/week lead in *Deathtrap*.

Year	Movie	Character
1971	Nicholas and Alexandra	Col. Kobylinsky
1978	Somebody Killed Her Husband	Ernest Van Santen
1983	WarGames	Falken
1985	Ladyhawke	Bishop
1985	The Purple Rose of Cairo	Jason
1986	Jumpin' Jack Flash	Jeremy Talbot

ALFRE WOODARD

(1953 -   )

Woodard fell for acting in high school because, as she once explained: "I felt like I had been doing the breast stroke all my life and then someone introduced me to water. It all made sense." The Tulsa native graduated cum laude from Boston University where, for four years, she spent at least eight hours a day studying drama, dance, theater criticism, fencing and voice. She was Oscar-nominated for her portrayal of a backwoods housekeeper in *Cross Creek* and has won two Emmy awards.

Year	Movie	Character
1979	Health	xxx
1983	Cross Creek	Geechee
1986	Extremities	Patricia
1988	Scrooged	Grace Cooley
1989	Miss Firecracker	Popeye Jackson
1991	Grand Canyon	Jane
1992	Gun in Betty Lou's Handbag	Ann
1993	Heart and Souls	Penny Washington
1993	Rich in Love	Rhody Poole

MORGAN WOODWARD

(1926 -   )

Woodward had always wanted an operatic singing career and took his first roles in TV westerns to pay for voice coaching lessons. He was a drama student at the University of Texas and after college was with the Marge Jones Dallas Theater. He once ran a restaurant and did some radio singing, until he began appearing in such TV features as *The Life and Legend Wyatt Earp*.

Year	Movie	Character
1967	Cool Hand Luke	Boss Godfrey
1968	Firecreek	Willard
1971	The Wild Country	Ab
1973	Running Wild	xxx
1974	The Midnight Man	Clayborn
1976	A Small Town in Texas	C.J.
1977	Final Chapter—Walking Tall	The Boss
1977	Moonshine County Express	Sweetwater
1977	Which Way is Up?	Mann
1980	Battle Beyond the Stars	Cayman
1985	Girls Just Want to Have Fun	J.P. Sands

MARY WORONOV

(1946 -   )

Best known for her work in *Eating Raoul*, Woronov got her start in films in New York in Andy Warhol's *Chelsea Girls* back in the boom years of "underground films." Considered a cult star, Woronov once commented: "I'm *thrilled* to be a cult queen. Cult movie fans are good people. It isn't fair to denigrate them for having no taste or for liking weird films because they're twisted. Actually, the fans have better taste than the general audience. They like movies for very special reasons. And they're immensely loyal and understanding."

Year	Movie	Character
1976	Cannonball	Sandy
1976	Jackson County Jail	Pearl
1979	Rock 'n' Roll High School	Miss Togar
1982	Eating Raoul	Mary Bland
1984	Night of the Comet	Audrey
1986	Black Widow	Shelley
1986	Chopping Mall	Mrs. Bland
1989	Let It Ride	Quinella Hogan
1990	Dick Tracy	Welfare Person
1991	Rock 'n' Roll High School Forever	Dr. Vadar
1991	Warlock	Channel

AMY WRIGHT

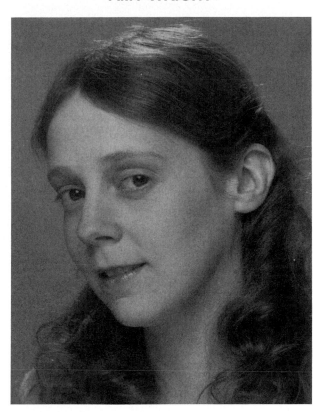

(1950 -   )

Wright, before turning to acting, was a shy girl who dreaded being called on in classes. Oddly, acting does not trouble her. "Acting is a whole different ball game," she has said. "You have your lines and your character. It's different than getting up in class and speaking extemporaneously." The Chicago-born actress majored in drama at college in Beloit, WI. She received critical acclaim for her role as William Hurt's wallflower sister in *The Accidental Tourist*.

Year	Movie	Character
1978	Girlfriends	Ceil
1979	Breaking Away	Nancy
1979	Heartland	Clara
1979	The Amityville Horror	Jackie
1979	Wise Blood	Sabbath Lilly
1980	Inside Moves	Ann
1980	Stardust Memories	Shelley
1986	Off Beat	Mary Ellen Gruenwald
1988	Crossing Delancy	Ricki
1988	The Accidental Tourist	Rose
1988	The Telephone	Honey Boxe/ Irate Neighbor
1989	Miss Firecracker	Missy Mahoney
1990	Daddy's Dyin'...Who's Got the Will?	Lurlene
1991	Deceived	Evelyn

JENNY WRIGHT

(1962 -   )

Wright has been fortunate to work consistently in Hollywood and is eager to work on the stage as well. "Being in the theater after you have done either television or film is really a turn-on," she once said. "You are able to feel a part of your craft when you are performing in front of a live audience." The actress received, in her words, a "bohemian" upbringing in New York City's SoHo art district and in a small town in upstate New York.

Year	Movie	Character
1984	The Wild Life	Eileen
1986	Out of Bounds	Dizz
1987	Valentino Returns	Sylvia Fuller
1988	The Chocolate War	Lisa
1988	Twister	Stephanie
1990	A Shock to the System	Melanie O'Connor
1992	The Lawnmower Man	Marnie Burke

KEENAN WYNN

(1916 - 1986)

For more than 50 years, the Manhattan-born Wynn was one of Hollywood's most versatile supporting actors in comedy, drama and musicals. He called television his favorite medium but put in hundreds of performances—220+ films, 250 TV shows, 100 stage productions—in all three mediums. He was a racing enthusiast who competed in airplanes, automobiles, speedboats, motorcycles and dirt bikes until a severe hearing loss curtailed his sports life. He died of cancer.

Year	Movie	Character
1960	The Crowded Sky	Nick Hyland
1961	The Absent-Minded Professor	Alonzo Hawk
1964	Bikini Beach	Harvey H. Honeywagon
1964	Dr. Strangelove or: How I Learned to Stop Worrying and Love the Bomb	Colonel "Bat" Guano
1964	Stage to Thunder Rock	Ross Sawyer
1964	The Americanization of Emily	Old Sailor
1964	The Man in the Middle	Lt. Winston
1964	The Patsy	Harry Silver
1965	Great Race	Hezekiah
1966	Around the World, Under the Sea	Hank Stahl
1966	Stagecoach	Luke Plummer

(continued on page 510)

AMANDA WYSS

SUSANNAH YORK

(19?? -   )

Wyss has played teenager roles in some scary movies aimed at kids. She had the dubious distinction of being the first teenaged victim in the 1984 classic horror picture *A Nightmare on Elm Street*. Wyss also played the fickle girlfriend who deserts her beau in *Better Off Dead*.

(1941 -   )

The British actress began her screen career when, barely out of her teens, she played with Alec Guinness and John Mills in *Tunes of Glory* (1960). York appeared in mostly ingenue roles until, hoping to break the mold, she took the controversial role of a lesbian child-woman in 1968's *The Killing of Sister George*. Nominated for a best supporting Oscar for her part in *They Shoot Horses Don't They?* (1969), she continued to work steadily in (mostly British) films into the 1980s.

Year	Movie	Character
1984	A Nightmare on Elm Street	Tina Gray
1985	Better Off Dead	Beth
1989	Powwow Highway	Rabbit Layton
1991	Son of Darkness: To Die For II	Celia

Year	Movie	Character
1962	Freud	Cecily Koertner
1965	Sands of the Kalahari	Grace
1966	A Man for All Seasons	Margaret More
1968	Duffy	Segolene
1969	Battle of Britain	Section Officer Harvey
1974	Gold	Terry Steyner
1976	Sky Riders	Ellen Bracken
1978	Superman	Lara
1978	The Silent Partner	Julie
1980	The Awakening	Jane
1980	Falling In Love Again	Sue
1980	Superman II	Lara
1983	Yellowbeard	Lady Churchill

BURT YOUNG

(1940 -   )

Young was a 1976 Oscar nominee as best supporting actor in the film *Rocky*. He had once been a prize-fighter himself, one of many odd jobs he took to earn money while he waited for acting roles to come along. He studied under Lee Strasberg in New York and made his screen debut in an underground movie called *Carnival of Blood*. Young is also a writer with several scripts to his credit.

Year	Movie	Character
1973	Cinderella Liberty	Master at Arms
1974	Chinatown	Curly
1975	The Killer Elite	Mac
1976	Harry and Walter Go to New York	Warden Durgom
1976	Rocky	Paulie
1977	The Choirboys	Scuzzi
1977	Twilight's Last Gleaming	Garvas
1978	Convoy	Pig Pen
1979	Rocky II	Paulie
1981	All the Marbles	Eddie Cisco
1982	Amityville II: The Possession	Anthony Montelli
1982	Lookin' to Get Out	Jerry Feldman
1982	Rocky III	Paulie

(continued on page 510)

GIG YOUNG

(1917 - 1978)

Young started as a used car salesman who studied acting at night and became a leading man, mostly in romantic comedies. He won an Oscar for his role in the 1969 drama *They Shoot Horses, Don't They?* and appeared in over 55 films and in TV series like *The Rogues* and *Gibbsville*. At 60, he shot and killed himself and his new bride, his fifth wife, in their New York apartment.

Year	Movie	Character
1962	Kid Galahad	Willy Grogan
1962	That Touch of Mink	Roger
1963	For Love or Money	Sonny Smith
1964	Strange Bedfellows	Richard Bramwell
1970	Lovers and Other Strangers	Hal
1974	Bring Me the Head of Alfredo Garcia	Quill
1975	The Hindenburg	Edward Douglas
1975	The Killer Elite	Laurence Weyburn
1979	Game of Death	Jim

SEAN YOUNG

(1959 -   )

Young was born in Louisville, KY, the daughter of a journalist and an NBC News employee. Planning to become a dancer she spent her last two high school years at the Interlochen Arts Academy. However, her mother's literary agent introduced her to a film agent, who promptly signed her and, in late 1980, she had her first movie role. Screen roles have included the beautiful "replicant," or robot slave, in *Blade Runner*, Bill Murray's M.P. girlfriend in *Stripes* and corporate raider Michael Douglas' ditzy wife in *Wall Street*.

Year	Movie	Character
1981	Stripes	Louise
1982	Blade Runner	Rachael
1982	Young Doctors in Love	Dr. Stephanie Brody
1984	Dune	Chani
1985	Baby...Secret of the Lost Legend	Susan Matthews-Loomis
1987	No Way Out	Susan Atwell
1987	Wall Street	Kate Gekko
1988	The Boost	Linda
1989	Cousins	Tish Kozinski
1990	Firebirds	Billie Lee Guthrie
1991	A Kiss Before Dying	Ellen Dorothy Carlsson
1992	Once Upon a Crime	Phoebe
1993	Fatal Instinct	Lola Cain

HARRIS YULIN

(1937 -   )

Yulin grew up in L.A. and got his start in acting when his father, a dentist with many film business clients, introduced him to a drama coach. He attended college at Berkeley and UCLA and made his film debut in *End of the Road* in 1970. In 1980, he stunned a Broadway audience by collapsing on stage from exhaustion at the end of the first act of a play which he had been struggling to keep from closing.

Year	Movie	Character
1971	Doc	Wyatt Earp
1974	The Midnight Man	Casey
1975	Night Moves	Marty Heller
1976	St. Ives	Oller
1980	Steel	Eddie
1983	Scarface	Bernstein
1986	Good to Go	Harrigan
1987	Fatal Beauty	Conrad Kroll
1987	The Believers	Donald Calder
1988	Another Woman	Paul
1988	Bad Dreams	Dr. Berrisford
1989	Ghostbusters II	The Judge
1990	Narrow Margin	Leo Watts

ANTHONY ZERBE

(1936 -   )

A familiar face in films and on television, Zerbe hails from California and was spurred to a theatrical career after seeing Paul Newman and Joanne Woodward in *Picnic* on Broadway. He attended Pomona College and studied for the theater at the Stella Adler Theater Studio. In 1976, Zerbe won a supporting actor Emmy for his role in *Harry O*, a few weeks after the show was cancelled.

Year	Movie	Character
1967	Cool Hand Luke	Dog Boy
1968	Will Penny	Dutchy
1970	The Liberation of L.B. Jones	Willie Joe Worth
1970	They Call Me MISTER Tibbs	Rice Weedon
1970	The Molly Maguires	Dan Dougherty
1971	The Omega Man	Matthias
1972	The Strange Vengeance of Rosalie	Fry
1973	Papillon	Leper Colony Chief
1973	The Laughing Policeman	Lt. Steiner
1974	The Parallax View	Schwartzkopf
1975	Farewell My Lovely	Brunette
1975	Rooster Cogburn	Breed
1977	The Turning Point	Rosie

(continued on page 510)

DAPHNE ZUNIGA

(1963 -   )

Zuniga grew up in Berkeley, CA, and then moved with her mother, a Unitarian minister, to Vermont after her parents' divorce. She attended, but did not graduate from, UCLA because, as she once said, "I went to college for the experience, not necessarily the credits." She spends time off-screen working for various causes such as cleaning up toxic waste and counseling high school kids against the dangers of drugs and alcohol.

Year	Movie	Character
1985	The Sure Thing	Alison Bradbury
1985	Vision Quest	Margie Epstein
1987	Spaceballs	Princess Vespa
1988	Last Rites	Angela
1989	Gross Anatomy	Laurie Rorbach
1989	Staying Together	Beverly Young
1989	The Fly II	Beth Logan

ADDITIONAL CREDITS

R.G. Armstrong (cont'd.)

1979	Fast Charlie, The Moonbeam Rider	Al
1980	Steel	Kellin
1980	Where the Buffalo Roam	Judge
1981	Raggedy Man	Rigby
1981	The Pursuit of D.B. Cooper	Dempsey
1982	The Beast Within	Doc
1983	Hammett	Lt. O'Mara
1983	Lone Wolf McQuade	Tyler
1986	Red-Headed Stranger	Scoby
1986	The Best of Times	Schutte
1987	Jocks	Beetlebom
1987	Predator	General Phillips
1988	Bulletproof	Miles Blackburn
1990	Dick Tracy	Pruneface
1993	Warlock: The Armageddon	Franks

Val Avery (cont'd.)

1976	Harry and Walter Go to New York	Chatsworth
1977	Heroes	Bus Driver
1979	The Amityville Horror	Sgt. Gionfriddo
1979	Love and Bullets	Caruso
1980	Brubaker	Wendel
1981	Choices	Coach Rizo
1981	Continental Divide	Yablonowitz
1982	Jinxed	Milt
1982	The Chosen	xxx
1983	Easy Money	Louie
1983	The Sting II	O'Malley
1984	The Pope of Greenwich Village	Nunzi
1986	Cobra	Chief Halliwell

Ned Beatty (cont'd.)

1978	Gray Lady Down	Mickey
1978	Superman	Otis
1979	1941	Ward Douglas
1979	Promises in the Dark	Bud Koenig
1979	The American Success Company	Elliot
1979	Wise Blood	Hoover Shoates
1980	Hopscotch	Myerson
1980	Superman II	Otis
1981	The Incredible Shrinking Woman	Dan Beame
1982	The Toy	Mr. Morehouse
1983	Stroker Ace	Clyde
1983	Touched	Herbie
1986	Back to School	Dean Martin
1987	The Big Easy	Jack Kellom
1987	The Trouble With Spies	Harry Lewis
1988	Midnight Crossing	Ellis
1988	Purple People Eater	Grandpa
1988	Switching Channels	Roy Ridnitz
1988	The Unholy	Lt. Stern

1989	Physical Evidence	James Nicks
1989	Time Trackers	Harry
1990	Big Bad John	xxx
1990	Chattahoochee	Dr. Harwood
1990	Repossessed	Ernest Weller
1992	Prelude to a Kiss	Dr. Boyle
1993	Rudy	Daniel Ruettiger

Wilford Brimley (cont'd.)

1984	The Natural	Pop Fisher
1984	Harry and Son	Tom
1985	Cocoon	Ben Luckett
1985	Remo Williams: The Adventure Begins	Harold Smith
1986	Jackals	Sheriff Mitchell
1987	End of the Line	Haney
1988	Cocoon: The Return	Ben Luckett
1993	Hard Target	Uncle Douvee
1993	The Firm	William Devasher

Harry Carey, Jr. (cont'd.)

1986	Crossroads	bartender
1987	The Whales of August	Joshua Brackett
1988	Cherry 2000	Snappy Tom
1988	Illegally Yours	Wally
1989	Breaking In	Shoes
1990	Bad Jim	C.J. Lee
1990	The Exorcist III	Father Kanavan
1990	Back to the Future Part III	Saloon Old Timer

John Carradine (cont'd.)

1976	The Killer Inside Me	Dr. Smith
1976	The Last Tycoon	Guide
1977	The White Buffalo	Amos Briggs
1977	The Sentinel	Halliran
1981	The Howling	Kenton
1984	The Ice Pirates	Supreme Commander
1986	Peggy Sue Got Married	Leo

Matt Clark (cont'd.)

1980	Brubaker	Purcell
1981	The Legend of the Lone Ranger	Sheriff
1981	An Eye for an Eye	Tom
1982	Honkytonk Man	Virgil
1983	Love Letters	Winter
1984	Country	Tom McMullen
1985	Tuff Turf	Stuart Hiller
1985	Return to Oz	Uncle Henry
1986	Let's Get Harry	Walt Clayton
1990	Back to the Future Part III	Bartender
1991	Class Action	Judge Symes
1992	Frozen Assets	J.F. Hughes

Dabney Coleman (cont'd.)

1980	9 to 5	Franklin Hart, Jr.
1980	How to Beat the High Co$t of Living	Heintzel
1980	Melvin and Howard	Judge Keith Hayes
1980	Nothing Personal	Tom
1981	On Golden Pond	Bill Ray
1981	Modern Problems	Mark
1982	Young Doctors in Love	Dr. Prang
1982	Tootsie	Ron
1983	WarGames	McKittrick
1984	Cloak & Dagger	Jack Flack/Hal Osborne
1984	The Muppets Take Manhattan	Producer
1985	The Man With One Red Shoe	Cooper
1987	Dragnet	Jerry Caesar
1988	Hot to Trot	Walter Sawyer
1990	Short Time	Burt Simpson
1990	Where the Heart Is	Stewart McBain
1991	Meet the Applegates	Aunt Bea
1993	Amos & Andrew	Police Chief
1993	The Beverly Hillbillies	Mr. Drysdale

Jeff Corey (cont'd.)

1978	The Wild Geese	Martin
1979	Butch and Sundance: The Early Days	Ray Bledsoe
1980	Battle Beyond the Stars	Zed
1982	The Sword and the Sorcerer	Craccus
1985	Creator	Dean Harrington
1988	Messenger of Death	Willis Beecham
1990	Bird on a Wire	Lou Baird

Beverly D'Angelo (cont'd.)

1987	Maid to Order	Stella
1988	Trading Hearts	Donna
1988	High Spirits	Sharon
1989	National Lampoon's Christmas Vacation	Ellen Griswold
1990	Pacific Heights	Anne
1990	Daddy's Dyin'...Who's Got the Will?	Evalita
1992	Man Trouble	Andy Ellerman

Royal Dano (cont'd.)

1983	Something Wicked This Way Comes	Tom Fury
1984	Teachers	Ditto
1986	Red-Headed Stranger	Larn Claver
1987	House II: The Second Story	Gramps
1988	Ghoulies 2	Uncle Ned
1988	Killer Klowns From Outer Space	Farmer Green
1990	Spaced Invaders	Wrenchmuller

Brian Dennehy (cont'd.)

1985	Twice in a Lifetime	Nick
1985	Cocoon	Walter
1986	Legal Eagles	Cavanaugh
1986	F/X	Leo McCarthy
1986	The Check is in the Mail	xxx
1987	Best Seller	Dennis Meechum
1988	Miles From Home	Frank Roberts, Sr.

1990	The Last of the Finest	Frank Daly
1990	Presumed Innocent	Raymond Horgan
1991	F/X 2	Leo McCarthy
1992	Gladiator	Horn

Charles Durning (cont'd.)

1979	The Muppet Movie	Doc Hopper
1979	When a Stranger Calls	John Clifford
1979	Starting Over	Michael "Mickey" Potter
1980	Die Laughing	Arnold
1980	The Final Countdown	Senator Chapman
1981	Sharky's Machine	Friscoe
1981	True Confessions	Jack Amsterdam
1982	The Best Little Whorehouse in Texas	Govenor
1982	Tootsie	Les
1983	Two of a Kind	Charlie
1983	To Be or Not to Be	Col. Erhardt
1984	Mass Appeal	Monsignor Burke
1985	Stick	Chucky
1985	Big Trouble	O'Mara
1985	The Man With One Red Shoe	Ross
1986	Tough Guys	Deke Yablonski
1986	Where the River Runs Black	Father O'Reilly
1986	Solarbabies	Warden
1987	Happy New Year	Charlie
1987	A Tiger's Tale	Charlie Drumm
1987	Cop	Dutch Peltz
1987	The Rosary Murders	Father Nabors
1988	Far North	Bertrum
1989	Cat Chaser	Joggs Scully
1990	Fatal Sky	Colonel Clancy
1990	Dick Tracy	Chief Brandon
1991	V.I. Warshawski	Lt. Mallory
1992	Brenda Starr	Francis I. Livright

Jack Elam (cont'd.)

1973	Pat Garrett and Billy the Kid	Alamosa Bill
1976	Pony Express Rider	Crazy
1976	Hawmps	Bad Jack Cutter
1978	The Norseman	Death Dreamer
1978	Hot Lead and Cold Feet	Rattlesnake
1978	Grayeagle	Trapper
1979	The Villain	Avery
1979	The Apple Dumpling Gang Rides Again	Big Mac
1981	The Cannonball Run	Doctor
1982	Jinxed	Otto
1983	Sacred Ground	Witcher
1984	Cannonball Run II	Doc
1990	Big Bad John	xxx
1991	Suburban Commando	Col. Dustin McHowell

Vincent Gardenia (cont'd.)

1980	Last Flight of Noah's Ark	Stoney
1982	Death Wish II	Frank Ochoa
1985	Movers and Shakers	Saul Gritz
1986	Little Shop of Horrors	Mushnik
1987	Moonstruck	Cosmo Castorini
1989	Skin Deep	Barney
1991	The Super	Big Lou Kritski

Allen Garfield (cont'd.)

1981	Continental Divide	Howard
1982	One From the Heart	Restaurant Owner
1983	Get Crazy	Max
1983	The Black Stallion Returns	Kurr
1984	Irreconcilable Differences	Phil
1984	Teachers	Rosenberg
1984	The Cotton Club	Abbadabba Berman
1986	Desert Bloom	Mr. Mosol
1987	Beverly Hills Cop II	Harold Lutz
1989	Let It Ride	Bernie Greenberg
1990	Night Visitor	Zachary Willard

Murray Hamilton (cont'd.)

1976	The Drowning Pool	Kilbourne
1978	Casey's Shadow	Tom Patterson
1978	Jaws 2	Mayor Vaughan
1979	1941	Claude
1979	The Amityville Horror	Father Ryan
1980	Brubaker	Deach
1985	Too Scared to Scream	Jack

John Heard (cont'd.)

1988	The Telephone	Telephone man
1989	The Package	Col. Glen Whitacre
1990	Awakenings	Dr. Kaufman
1990	Home Alone	Peter McCallister
1991	Deceived	John
1991	Rambling Rose	Willcox Hillyer
1991	The End of Innocence	Dean
1992	Gladiator	John Riley
1992	Home Alone 2: Lost in New York	Peter
1992	Radio Flyer	Daugherty
1993	In the Line of Fire	Professor Riger

Pat Hingle (cont'd.)

1983	Running Brave	Coach Easton
1983	Sudden Impact	Chief Jannings
1985	Brewster's Millions	Edward Roundfield
1985	The Falcon & the Snowman	Mr. Boyce
1986	Maximum Overdrive	Hendershot
1987	Baby Boom	Hughes Larrabee
1989	Batman	Commissioner Gordon
1990	The Grifters	Bobo Justus
1992	Batman Returns	Commissioner Gordon

Ben Johnson (cont'd.)

1975	Bite the Bullet	"Mister"
1975	Hustle	Marty Hollinger
1976	Breakheart Pass	Nathan Pearces
1977	The Town That Dreaded Sundown	Capt. J.D. Morales
1978	Grayeagle	Colter
1978	The Swarm	Felix
1980	Terror Train	Carne
1980	The Hunter	Sheriff Strong
1982	Tex	Cole Collins
1984	Red Dawn	Mr. Mason
1986	Let's Get Harry	Mr. Burck, Sr.

1988	Cherry 2000	Six Finger Jake
1991	My Heroes Have Always Been Cowboys	Jesse Dalton
1992	Radio Flyer	Geronimo Bill

Sally Kellerman (cont'd.)

1986	Back to School	Diane
1986	That's Life!	Holly Parrish
1987	Meatballs III	Roxy Du Jour
1987	Three for the Road	Blanche
1988	You Can't Hurry Love	Kelly Bones
1989	Limit Up	Night Club Singer
1992	Boris and Natasha	xxx
1993	Younger and Younger	ZigZag Lilian

Ed Lauter (cont'd.)

1983	The Big Score	Parks
1983	Timerider	Padre
1984	Finders Keepers	Josef
1984	Lassiter	Smoke
1985	Death Wish 3	Richard Striker
1985	Girls Just Want to Have Fun	Colonel Glenn
1985	Real Genius	CIA Man Decker
1986	3:15	Moran
1986	Raw Deal	Baker
1986	Youngblood	Murray Chadwick
1987	Revenge of the Nerds II: Nerds in Paradise	Buzz
1989	Born on the Fourth of July	Legion Commander
1989	Gleaming the Cube	Mr. Kelly
1990	My Blue Heaven	Underwood
1991	The Rocketeer	Fitch
1992	School Ties	Alan Greene

Michael Lerner (cont'd.)

1983	Strange Invaders	Willie
1985	Movers and Shakers	Arnie
1988	Eight Men Out	Arnold Rothstein
1988	Vibes	Burt Wilder
1989	Harlem Nights	Bugsy Calhoune
1990	Any Man's Death	Harvey
1990	The Closer	Doctor
1991	Barton Fink	Jack Lipnick
1992	Newsies	xxx
1993	Amos & Andrew	Phil Gillman

Geoffrey Lewis (cont'd.)

1980	Bronco Billy	John Arlington
1980	Heaven's Gate	Trapper
1982	I, the Jury	Joe
1983	Ten to Midnight	Dave Dante
1984	Night of the Comet	Carter
1988	Out of the Dark	Dennis
1989	Fletch Lives	KKK Leader
1989	Pink Cadillac	Ricky Z
1991	Double Impact	Frank Avery
1992	The Lawnmower Man	Terry McKeen
1993	The Man Without a Face	Chief Stark

Robert Loggia (cont'd.)

1987	Gaby—A True Story	Michel
1987	Hot Pursuit	Mac MacLaren
1987	Over the Top	Jason Cutler
1987	The Believers	Lt. Sean McTaggert
1988	Big	MacMillan
1989	Relentless	Bill Malloy
1989	Triumph of the Spirit	Poppa
1990	Opportunity Knocks	Milt Malkin
1991	Necessary Roughness	Coach Rig
1991	The Marrying Man	Lew Horner
1992	Gladiator	Pappy Jack
1992	Innocent Blood	Sal (the Shark) Macelli

Mako (cont'd.)

1988	Silent Assassins	Dyama
1988	Tucker: The Man and His Dream	Jimmy
1989	An Unremakable Life	Max Chin
1990	Pacific Heights	Toshio Watanabe
1990	Taking Care of Business	Sakamoto
1991	The Perfect Weapon	Kim
1993	Rising Sun	Yoshida-san
1993	Sidekicks	Mr. Lee

Kenneth Mars (cont'd.)

1984	Protocol	Lou
1985	Beer	A.J. Norbecker
1985	Fletch	Stanton Boyd
1987	Radio Days	Rabbi Baumel
1988	For Keeps	Mr. Bobrucz
1988	Illegally Yours	Hal Keeler
1989	Police Academy 6: City Under Siege	Mayor
1992	Shadows and Fog	Magician

Strother Martin (cont'd.)

1971	Hannie Caulder	Rufus
1972	Pocket Money	Garrett
1973	SSSSSSS	Dr. Stoner
1975	Hard Times	Poe
1975	Rooster Cogburn	McCoy
1976	Great Scout and Cathouse Thursday	Billy
1977	Slap Shot	Joe McGrath
1978	The End	Dr. Kling
1978	Up in Smoke	Mr. Stoner
1979	The Champ	Riley
1979	Love and Bullets	Louis Monk
1979	The Villain	Parody

Richard Masur (cont'd.)

1987	The Believers	Marty Wertheimer
1988	License to Drive	Dad
1988	Rent-a-Cop	Roger
1988	Shoot to Kill	Norman
1988	Walker	Ephraim Squier
1989	Far From Home	Duckett
1990	Flashback	Barry
1991	My Girl	Phil Sultenfus

1992	Encino Man	Mr. Morgan
1993	The Man Without a Face	Carl

Kevin McCarthy (cont'd.)

1980	Hero at Large	Calvin Donnelly
1980	Those Lips, Those Eyes	Mickey Bellinger
1981	The Howling	Fred
1983	My Tutor	Chrystal
1983	Twilight Zone—The Movie (Segment 3)	Uncle Walt
1987	Hostage	Col. Tim Shaw
1987	Innerspace	Victor Scrimshaw
1989	Fast Food	Judge Reinholte
1989	UHF	R. J. Fletcher
1991	Eve of Destruction	Old Bill Simmons
1991	Final Approach	General Geller
1992	The Distinguished Gentleman	Terry Corrigan

Kenneth McMillan (cont'd.)

1981	True Confessions	Frank Crotty
1981	Whose Life Is It Anyway?	Judge Wyler
1982	Partners	Chief Wilkens
1983	Blue Skies Again	Dirk
1984	Dune	Baron Vlaimir Harkonnen
1984	Protocol	Senator Norris
1984	Reckless	John Rourke, Sr.
1984	The Pope of Greenwich Village	Barney
1985	Cat's Eye	Cressner
1985	Runaway Train	Eddie MacDonald
1986	Armed and Dangerous	Clarence O'Connell
1987	Malone	Hawkins
1989	Three Fugitives	Dr. Horvath

Warren Oates (cont'd.)

1974	Badlands	Father
1974	Bring Me the Head of Alfredo Garcia	Bennie
1975	92 in the Shade	Nichol
1975	Race With The Devil	Frank
1976	Drum	Hammond
1978	China 9, Liberty 37	Sebanek
1978	The Brink's Job	Specs 'O'Keefe
1979	1941	Maddox
1981	Stripes	Sgt. Hulka
1982	The Border	Red
1983	Blue Thunder	Braddock
1983	Tough Enough	James

Slim Pickens (cont'd.)

1972	The Honkers	Clete
1973	Pat Garrett and Billy the Kid	Sheriff Baker
1974	Blazing Saddles	Taggart
1974	Bootleggers	Grandpa Pruitt
1975	White Line Fever	Duana Haller
1976	Hawmps	Naman Tucker
1976	Pony Express Rider	Bob
1977	Mr. Billion	Duane
1977	The White Buffalo	Abel Pinkney
1978	The Swarm	Jud
1979	1941	Hollis Wood

1979	Beyond the Poseidon Adventure	Tex
1980	Honeysuckle Rose	Garland
1980	Tom Horn	Sam Creedmore
1981	The Howling	Sam

Bert Remsen (cont'd.)

1981	Second-Hand Hearts	Voyd
1982	Lookin' to Get Out	Smitty
1982	P.K. and the Kid	Al
1983	Independence Day	Red Malone
1983	The Sting II	Kid Colors
1984	Places in the Heart	Tee Tot Hightower
1985	Code of Silence	Commander Kates
1986	Eye of the Tiger	Father Healy
1986	Tai-Pan	Tillman
1988	Remote Control	Bill Denver
1989	Miss Firecracker	Mr. Morton
1990	Daddy's Dyin'...Who's Got the Will?	Daddy
1990	Dick Tracy	Bartender
1990	Peacemaker	Doc
1991	Only the Lonely	Spats

Wallace Shawn (cont'd.)

1984	The Bostonians	Mr. Pardon
1985	Heaven Help Us	Father Abruzzi
1986	Head Office	Hoover
1987	Nice Girls Don't Explode	Ellen
1987	Radio Days	Masked Avenger
1987	The Bedroom Window	Henderson's Attorney
1987	The Princess Bride	Vizzini
1988	The Moderns	Oiseau
1989	She's Out of Control	Dr. Fishbinder
1989	We're No Angels	Translator
1992	Mom & Dad Save the World	Sibor
1992	Shadows and Fog	xxx

Tom Skerritt (cont'd.)

1986	Top Gun	Viper
1986	Wisdom	Lloyd Wisdom
1987	Maid to Order	Charles Montgomery
1987	The Big Town	Phil Carpenter
1988	Poltergeist III	Bruce Gardner
1989	Steel Magnolias	Drum Eatenton
1990	The Rookie	Eugene Ackerman
1992	A River Runs Through It	Mr. Maclean
1992	Poison Ivy	Darryl
1993	Knight Moves	Frank Sedman

Harry Dean Stanton (cont'd.)

1976	The Missouri Breaks	Calvin
1978	Straight Time	Jerry Schue
1979	Alien	Brett
1979	The Rose	Billy Ray
1979	Wise Blood	Asa Hawks
1980	Private Benjamin	Sgt. Jim Ballard
1980	The Black Marble	Philo Sinner
1980	UFOria	xxx
1981	Escape from New York	Brain
1982	One From the Heart	Moe
1982	Young Doctors in Love	Dr. Oliver Ludwig

1983	Christine	Rudolph Junkins
1984	Paris, Texas	Travis
1984	Red Dawn	Mr. Eckert
1984	Repo Man	Bud
1984	The Bear	Coach Thomas
1985	Fool for Love	Old Man
1985	One Magic Christmas	Gideon
1986	Pretty in Pink	Jack
1988	Mr. North	Henry Simmons
1988	Stars and Bars	Loomis Gage
1988	Twister	Eugene Cleveland
1989	Dream a Little Dream	Ike Baker
1990	The Fourth War	Gen. Hackworth
1990	Wild at Heart	Johnnie Farragut
1992	Man Trouble	Redmond
1992	Twin Peaks: Fire Walk With Me	Carl Rodd

Daniel Stern (cont'd.)

1988	The Milagro Beanfield War	Herbie Platt
1989	Leviathan	Sixpack
1989	Little Monsters	Glen Stevenson
1990	Coupe de Ville	Marvin Libner
1990	Home Alone	Marv
1990	My Blue Heaven	Will Stubbs
1991	City Slickers	Phil Berquist
1992	Home Alone 2: Lost in New York	Marv

J.T. Walsh (cont'd.)

1991	Defenseless	Steven Seldes
1991	True Identity	Houston
1992	A Few Good Men	Lt. Col. Markinson
1992	Hoffa	Frank Fitzsimmons
1993	Needful Things	Danforth Walsh
1993	Sniper	Chester Van Damme
1993	Morning Glory	Sheriff Reese Goodloe
1993	Red Rock West	Wayne

M. Emmet Walsh (cont'd.)

1980	Ordinary People	Swim Coach
1981	Back Roads	Arthur
1981	Reds	Speaker-Liberal Club
1982	Blade Runner	Bryant
1982	Cannery Row	Mack
1982	Fast Walking	Sgt. Sanger
1982	The Escape Artist	Fritz
1983	Silkwood	Walt Yarborough
1984	Blood Simple	Private Detective
1984	Grandview USA	Clark
1984	Missing in Action	Tuck
1984	Scandalous	Simon
1984	The Pope of Greenwich Village	Burns
1985	Fletch	Dr. Dolan
1986	Back to School	Coach Turnbull
1986	Critters	Harv
1986	The Best of Times	Charlie
1986	Wildcats	Coes
1987	Harry and the Hendersons	George Henderson, Sr.
1987	No Man's Land	Captain Haun
1987	Raising Arizona	Machine Shop earbender
1988	Clean and Sober	Richard Dirks

1988	Sunset	Chief Dibner
1988	The Milagro Beanfield War	The Govenor
1989	Red Scorpion	Dewey Ferguson
1989	The Mighty Quinn	Miller
1989	War Party	Colin Ditweiller
1990	Chattahoochee	Morris
1990	Narrow Margin	Sgt. Dominick Benti
1992	White Sands	Bert Gibson
1993	Wilder Napalm	Fire Chief

Fred Ward (cont'd.)

1989	Backtrack	Pauling
1990	Miami Blues	Sgt. Hoke Moseley
1990	Tremors	Earl Basset
1992	Bob Roberts	News Anchor
1992	The Player	Walter Stuckel
1992	Thunderheart	Jack Milton
1993	Short Cuts	Stuart Kane

Jack Warden (cont'd.)

1976	All the President's Men	Harry Rosenfeld
1977	The White Buffalo	Charlie Zane
1978	Death on the Nile	Dr. Bessner
1978	Heaven Can Wait	Max Corkle
1979	...And Justice For All	Judge Rayford
1979	Being There	President "Bobby"
1979	Beyond the Poseidon Adventure	Harold Meredith
1979	Dreamer	Harry
1979	The Champ	Jackie
1980	Used Cars	Roy & Luke Fuchs
1981	Carbon Copy	Nelson
1981	Chu Chu and the Philly Flash	Commander
1981	So Fine	Jack
1981	The Great Muppet Caper	Guest Star
1982	The Verdict	Mickey Morrissey
1984	Crackers	Garvey
1985	The Aviator	Moravia
1987	September	Lloyd
1988	The Presidio	Sgt. Major Ross Maclure
1990	Everybody Wins	Judge Harry Murdoch
1990	Problem Child	Big Ben Healy
1991	Problem Child 2	Big Ben Healy
1992	Night and the City	Al Grossman
1992	Passed Away	Jack Scanlan
1992	Toys	Zevo, Sr.
1993	Guilty as Sin	Moe

Robert Webber (cont'd.)

1978	Casey's Shadow	Mike Marsh
1978	Revenge of the Pink Panther	Douvier
1979	10	Hugh
1980	Private Benjamin	Col. Clay Thornbush
1981	S.O.B.	Ben Coogan
1982	Wrong is Right	Harvey
1985	Wild Geese II	Robert McCann
1987	Nuts	Francis MacMillan

Jack Weston (cont'd.)

1979	Cuba	Gutman
1980	Can't Stop the Music	Benny Murray
1981	The Four Seasons	Danny Zimmer

1983	High Road to China	Struts
1986	The Longshoy	Elton
1987	Dirty Dancing	Max Kellerman
1987	Ishtar	Marty Freed
1988	Short Circuit 2	Oscar Baldwin

Keenan Wynn (cont'd.)

1966	The Night of the Grizzly	Jed Curry
1967	Point Blank	Yost
1967	Run Like a Thief	Willy Gore
1967	The War Wagon	Wes Catlin
1967	Warning Shot	Sgt. Ed Musso
1967	Welcome to Hard Times	Zar
1968	Finian's Rainbow	Judge Rawkins
1969	MacKenna's Gold	Sanchez
1969	Once Upon a Time in the West	Sheriff
1971	Pretty Maids All in a Row	Pooldaski
1972	Cancel My Reservations	Sheriff Riley
1972	The Mechanic	Harry McKenna
1974	Herbie Rides Again	Alonzo Hawk
1975	Nashville	Mr. Green
1976	The Killer Inside Me	Chester
1977	Orca	Novak
1978	Laserblast	Col. Farley
1979	Sunburn	Mark
1979	The Clonus Horror	Jake
1980	Just Tell Me What You Want	Seymour Berger
1982	Best Friends	Tom Babson
1986	Black Moon Rising	Iron John

Burt Young (cont'd.)

1984	Once Upon a Time in America	Joe
1984	Over the Brooklyn Bridge	Phil
1984	The Pope of Greenwich Village	Bedbug Eddie
1985	Rocky IV	Paulie
1986	Back to School	Lou
1989	Beverly Hills Brats	Clive
1989	Wait Until Spring, Bandini	Rocco Saccone
1990	Betsy's Wedding	Georgie
1990	Rocky V	Paulie
1991	Bright Angel	Art

Anthony Zerbe (cont'd.)

1978	Who'll Stop the Rain	Antheil
1980	The First Deadly Sin	Capt. Broughton
1983	The Dead Zone	Roger Stuart
1986	Off Beat	Mr. Wareham
1986	Opposing Force	Becker
1987	Steel Dawn	Damnil
1989	Licence to Kill	Milton Krest
1989	Listen to Me	Senator McKellar
1989	See No Evil, Hear No Evil	Sutherland

INDEX

511

517

520

521

About the Author

Peter Chapman is a movie fan and a former actor. He is from Washington, D.C., has degrees from Denison University and the American Graduate School of International Management and has worked in the television and banking industries. Unable to find a book that identified movie actors, he created one himself. Peter currently resides in New York City.

ORDER FORM

Yes, I would like to order _____ copies of *The Players: Actors in Movies on Television and Videocassette*. I understand that I may return any books for a full refund   for any reason, no questions asked.

Please mail to:

NAME: _____

ADDRESS: _____

_____

CITY: _____

STATE/ZIP: _____

To order, please send check or money order for $19.95 plus S & H to:

Windsor Press
Attn: Ms. Joyce Holder
P.O. Box 82
Planetarium Station
New York, New York 10024

Sales Tax:
New York residents, please add appropriate sales tax.

Shipping:
Book Rate: $2.00 for the first book and $1.00 for each additional book
          Canada: $4.00 per book (U.S. $ only please)
(Surface shipping may take three to four weeks)

Air Mail: $4.25 per book
          Canada: $7.00 per book (U.S. $ only please)